STUDIES IN BAPTIST HISTORY AND THOUGHT
VOLUME 5

Baptist Sacramentalism

Studies in Baptist History and Thought

A full listing of all titles in this series
appears at the close of this book.

STUDIES IN BAPTIST HISTORY AND THOUGHT
VOLUME 5

Baptist Sacramentalism

Edited by

Anthony R. Cross

and

Philip E. Thompson

Foreword by James I. Packer

PATERNOSTER PRESS

Copyright © Anthony R. Cross and Philip E. Thompson
and the Contributors 2003

First published 2003 by Paternoster Press

Paternoster Press is an imprint of Authentic Media
P.O. Box 300, Carlisle, Cumbria, CA3 0QS, U.K.
and P.O. Box 1047, Waynesboro, GA 30830–2047, U.S.A

08 07 06 05 04 03 02   7 6 5 4 3 2 1

The right of Anthony R. Cross and Philip E. Thompson to be
identified as the Editors of this Work has been asserted by them
in accordance with the Copyright, Designs
and Patents Act 1988

British Library Cataloguing in Publication Data
A catalogue record for this book is available from the British Library

ISBN 1–84227–119–9

Typeset by A.R. Cross
Printed and bound in Great Britain
for Paternoster Press
by Nottingham Alpha Graphics

Series Preface

Baptists form one of the largest Christian communities in the world, and while they hold the historic faith in common with other mainstream Christian traditions, they nevertheless have important insights which they can offer to the worldwide church. Studies in Baptist History and Thought will be one means towards this end. It is an international series of academic studies which includes original monographs, revised dissertations, collections of essays and conference papers, and aims to cover any aspect of Baptist history and thought. While not all the authors are themselves Baptists, they nevertheless share an interest in relating Baptist history and thought to the other branches of the Christian church and to the wider life of the world.

The series includes studies in various aspects of Baptist history from the seventeenth century down to the present day, including biographical works, and Baptist thought is understood as covering the subject-matter of theology (including interdisciplinary studies embracing biblical studies, philosophy, sociology, practical theology, liturgy and women's studies). The diverse streams of Baptist life throughout the world are all within the scope of these volumes.

The series editors and consultants believe that the academic disciplines of history and theology are of vital importance to the spiritual vitality of the churches of the Baptist faith and order. The series sets out to discuss, examine and explore the many dimensions of their tradition and so to contribute to their on-going intellectual vigour.

A brief word of explanation is due for the series identifier on the front cover. The fountains, taken from heraldry, represent the Baptist distinctive of believer's baptism and, at the same time, the source of the water of life. There are three of them because they symbolize the Trinitarian basis of Baptist life and faith. Those who are redeemed by the Lamb, the book of Revelation reminds us, will be led to 'fountains of living waters' (Rev. 7.17).

To our wives
Jackie and Marcia
With love and thanks always

.

Contents

Contributors

John E. Colwell is Lecturer in Christian Doctrine and Ethics, Spurgeon's College, London, England.

Anthony R. Cross is an Editorial Consultant, Paternoster Press, Carlisle, England.

Stanley K. Fowler is Professor of Theology, Heritage Theological Seminary, Cambridge, Ontario, Canada.

Curtis W. Freeman is Research Professor of Theology and Director of the Baptist House of Studies, Duke Divinity School, Durham, North Carolina, USA.

Timothy George is Dean of Beeson Divinity School, Samford University, Birmingham, Alabama, USA.

Tim Grass is Associate Lecturer in Church History, Spurgeon's College, London, England.

Stanley J. Grenz is Distinguished Professor of Theology, Baylor University and Truett Seminary, Waco, Texas, USA.

Barry Harvey is Assistant Professor of Theology, Honors College, Baylor University, Waco, Texas, USA.

Michael A.G. Haykin is Professor of Church History, Heritage Theological Seminary, Cambridge, Ontario, Canada.

Brian Haymes is Minister of Bloomsbury Central Baptist Church, London, England.

Stephen R. Holmes is Lecturer in Christian Doctrine, King's College, London, England.

Elizabeth Newman is Professor of Theology and Ethics, Baptist Theological Seminary at Richmond, Virginia, USA.

Clark H. Pinnock is Professor Emeritus of Systematic Theology, McMaster Divinity College, Hamilton, Ontario, Canada.

Stanley E. Porter is President and Dean, and Professor of New Testament, McMaster Divinity College, Hamilton, Ontario, Canada.

Ian M. Randall is Lecturer in Church History and Spirituality, Spurgeon's College, London, England.

Philip E. Thompson is Assistant Professor of Systematic Theology and Christian Heritage, North American Baptist Seminary, Sioux Falls, South Dakota, USA.

Foreword

It has been well said that one's theology of the sacraments is the roof of one's theological house: holding it up, and determining both its shape and its stability, are the beliefs on which it rests—beliefs about God and the material creation; about Christ and redemption, past and future; about the Holy Spirit, faith, and salvation; about the church of God and the word of God. As Christian theology in all its forms is a circle and an organism, in which everything has integral links with everything else, so also it is a spiral and a storied building, in which what is at the top, structurally speaking, only gets there, and is only reached, via what underlies it. Different understandings of baptism and the Lord's Supper, the two sacramental ordinances that Christ told us to observe, always prove to flow from divergent views on one or more of the topics listed above.

Being known as a Reformed evangelical of Puritan–pietist type within Anglicanism, I was surprised as well as delighted to be asked to write a Foreword to the fine set of essays in this book. I had thought that, though there are Reformed Baptists a-plenty out on the right wing, Baptist thought about the church and its life was mainly along Anabaptist lines, with careful distancing from the Reformed emphasis on God's sovereignty in grace, and on local congregations as microcosmic outposts of the worldwide visible church, and on sacraments as means of grace. Anglican Article 25 declares baptism and the Lord's Supper to be

> not only badges or tokens of Christian men's profession, but rather they be certain sure witnesses, and effectual signs of grace, and God's good will towards us, by the which he doth work visibly in us, and doth not only quicken, but also strengthen and confirm our Faith in him.

And Article 27, before its anti-Anabaptist endorsement of child baptism, describes baptism as such, in terms that are carefully broad without being viciously loose, as follows:

> not only a sign of profession...but...also a sign of Regeneration or new Birth, whereby, as by an instrument, they that receive Baptism rightly are grafted into the Church; the promises of forgiveness of sin, and of our adoption to be the sons of God by the Holy Ghost, are visibly signed and sealed; Faith is confirmed, and Grace increased by virtue of prayer unto God.

('Instrument' there has raised questions, and been glossed more than one way, but there is little doubt that the term is meant to signify a legal document conveying and ratifying rights and privileges.) Then, in deliberately parallel phrasing, Article 28 says that the Lord's Supper is

> not only a sign of the love that Christians ought to have among themselves one to another; but rather is a Sacrament of our Redemption by Christ's death: insomuch that to such as rightly, worthily, and with faith, receive the same, the Bread which we break is a partaking of the Body of Christ; and likewise the Cup of Blessing is a partaking of the Blood of Christ.

Baptists, I thought, who seem to make so much of these rites as expressing faith already present and so little of them as strengthening and nourishing that faith, are on a different wavelength from the Articles, probably because of a different view of grace and of the church. But these essays have surprised me.

The above-quoted Articles, with their stress on the visible sign strengthening the faith of the heart and the blessings of union with Christ being conveyed where faith is present, resulted from modifying by biblical light inherited medieval notions. The following chapters, with their churchly focus and concern to re-anchor sacramental awareness in Baptist church life, represent a modifying of popular Baptist ideas as they have been for the best part of two centuries—and this modification, too, has been guided by biblical light. This has yielded both striking convergences with Reformation thought and much congregation-centred wisdom from which all can benefit. May this seminal collection, then, not be ignored.

J.I. Packer
Vancouver, B.C., Canada
August 2002

Acknowledgements

In bringing together a project like this there are many people who are to be thanked. First of all, the editors would like to thank all the contributors for their participation in this project. We would also like to thank the Paternoster Press for inaugurating this new series of studies: to Mark Finnie, Managing Director of Paternoster Press, and especially to Jeremy Mudditt for all his help and encouragement in ways too numerous to mention. The editors and contributors are grateful to those who have read over the papers at various stages of preparation, made helpful comments and suggestions, and who have helped us hone and develop our thoughts. We are especially grateful to Professor James I. Packer of Regent College, Vancouver, for his interest in the project and for writing the Foreword, Professor David F. Wright of the University of Edinburgh, and Pastor Nick Adams whose computer expertise and patience has assisted greatly in the preparation of the text.

We would also like to thank our families for their encouragement, patience and care during the putting together of this volume. To Marcia, Nathanael, Andrew and Matthew; and to Jackie, Laura and Katja; with love and thanks always.

Introduction:
Baptist Sacramentalism

Anthony R. Cross and Philip E. Thompson

Reading much of the theological work of Baptists will give many, Baptists and non-Baptists alike, the over-riding impression that Baptists do not hold to a sacramental understanding of anything. This, however, is to misrepresent Baptists historically and theologically, for many Baptists from the seventeenth century to the present day have held to sacramental views of baptism and the Lord's Supper, but also of the reading of scripture, prayer, the ministry and preaching. Drawing on Baptist and non-Baptist writings, this collection of essays is offered towards the furtherance of our understanding of God's operation in the lives of his people and in the world.

As children of the Enlightenment Baptists have too often unconsciously imbibed Enlightenment presuppositions.[1] Among the many that could be discussed, one in particular stands out for the subject of this collection of essays: an elevation of the spiritual over the material, in what has effectively become a modern form of Gnosticism (see the essay by Freeman). With the Enlightenment's scientific empiricism,[2] Christians in general in the West, Baptists among them, have driven a wedge between 'spirit' and 'matter'.[3] This dualism (critically explored

---

1   The influence of the Enlightenment on evangelicalism in general has been demonstrated by D.W. Bebbington, *Evangelicalism in Modern Britain: A History from the 1730s to the 1980s* (London: Unwin Hyman, 1989), pp. 50-60 and *passim*. Baptists are to be included within this.

2   C.H. Pinnock, *Flame of Love: A Theology of the Holy Spirit* (Downers Grove, Ill: InterVarsity Press, 1996), p. 128: 'The sacramental principle...has suffered from modernity, which leaves little room for the activity of God. In the modern view, what is real is what can be scientifically established. This mindset looks for physical causation and disregards divine action. It is materialistic in outlook and exalts reason while discounting revelation and tradition.'

3   The severing of spirit and matter owes much to the influence of Huldrych Zwingli (see Pinnock, *Flame of Love*, p. 125, who follows J.W. Cottrell, 'Baptism According to the Reformed Tradition', in D.W. Fletcher [ed.], *Baptism and the Remission of Sins: An Historical Perspective* [Joplin, MO: College Press, 1990], pp. 42-45). However, the Enlightenment, with its presuppositions, and rationalistic and anthropocentric view of life and religion, reinforced Zwingli's symbolic view of baptism and the Lord's Supper which has so widely influenced Baptists, particularly in their reaction against *ex opere operato* interpretations of the sacraments and, as a result, against the 'sacraments' themselves. In Britain this reaction owes a great deal to Baptist

by Pinnock in the present volume) has been critically examined recently by two prominent Baptist theologians from either side of the Atlantic. After noting that 'Moderns perceive Spirit as something ghostly, intangible, impalpable, numinous, lacking concreteness', Clark Pinnock continues: 'There is resistance to linking the Spirit to the material. Many of us shy away from physical manifestations of the divine presence and expect intangible, not real-life effects of the Spirit... Matter–spirit dualism is, however, not the Bible's view... There is a physical side of being spiritual.'[4] The physical and the spiritual, he maintains, 'are not antithetical but cooperative and synergistic... God comes to us and deals with us through material signs.'[5] Further, he writes:

> As bodily creatures, we need embodied expressions such as baptism and Eucharist to make inward grace visible and tangible... Symbols help believers apprehend the invisible things of God and serve as channels of grace. God acts in the sacraments in the context of the response of faith. They are neither magical actions nor mere symbols of human response. In the sacraments God offers grace that is effective when people receive it. The sacraments do not work automatically but derive their effectiveness from the presence of the Spirit in relation to faith.[6]

Similarly, Paul Fiddes argues that 'the sacraments are pieces of matter that God takes and uses as special places of encounter with Himself; grace transforms nature, and grace is nothing less than God's gracious coming to us and to His world... In the sacraments God's action in creation and redemption...fuses into a particular focus.'[7] He observes that Baptists

---

opposition to the ritualism and sacramentarianism of the Oxford Movement in the mid-nineteenth century, see, e.g., J.H.Y. Briggs, *The English Baptists of the Nineteenth Century* (A History of the English Baptists, 3; Didcot: Baptist Historical Society, 1994), pp. 224-27. On the influence of Zwinglianism on British Baptist eucharistic theology, see M.J. Walker, *Baptists at the Table: The Theology of the Lord's Supper amongst English Baptists in the Nineteenth Century* (Didcot: Baptist Historical Society, 1992), pp. 3-8.

   A similar pattern emerged in America in the debate between the Reformed theologians Charles Hodge of Princeton Seminary and John W. Nevin of Mercersburg (PA) Seminary. In the crucible of this disputation Hodge, a formative influence on nineteenth-century Southern Baptist theologian James P. Boyce, came to declare the Zwinglian view of the Lord's Supper the more faithful Reformed position. Cf. L.J. deBie, 'Real Presence or Real Absence? The Spoils of War in Nineteenth-Century American Eucharistic Controversy', *Pro Ecclesia* 4.4 (Fall, 1995), pp. 431-41; and T. George, 'James Petigru Boyce', in T. George and P. Basden (eds.), *Theologians of the Baptist Tradition* (Nashville, TN: Broadman and Holman, 2001), pp. 73-89.

4   Pinnock, *Flame of Love*, p. 119.

5   Pinnock, *Flame of Love*, pp. 122-23.

6   Pinnock, *Flame of Love*, p. 127.

7   P.S. Fiddes, 'Baptism and Creation', in P.S. Fiddes (ed.), *Reflections on the Water: Understanding God and the World through the Baptism of Believers* (Regent's

'have to confess that there has been a flight from the "stuff" of creation', and this is nowhere more clearly seen in the Baptist theology of baptism.[8] Later, he uses the Baptist theology of the church meeting as an example of the incongruency of this position, when he remarks on the surprise most Baptists would feel when confronted with the fact that their view of the church meeting is

> quite sacramental and is rooted in a conviction about grace in creation. They expect the Spirit of God to take something material and earthy (their own bodies, gathered together) and use it for a divine–human encounter, for a means of grace. As in the communion bread, the participants in this meeting expect to 'discern the body of Christ' (1 Cor 11:29). The initiation into the body of Christ received in baptism is continued in Lord's Supper *and* church meeting... Immersion into the death and resurrection of Christ in baptism is to be renewed in eucharistic celebration and in corporate decision making about community lifestyle and service in the world.[9]

Some Baptists may object to the use the authors of these essays make of 'sacrament', arguing that it is neither biblical nor Baptist. We simply contend that whether a word is biblical or not does not matter so long as the meaning it conveys is consonant with biblical theology. The prime example of this is the 'trinity', a term which does not occur in scripture but which is wholly scriptural and its use is defended by Baptists of all theological persuasions. Likewise, the term 'sacrament' has been employed by Baptists over the course of their four centuries of existence.

There have been many attempts to define what a sacrament is (see Grenz), but most Baptists have been happy to accept the definition of sacraments as 'means of grace'; as Pinnock puts it, 'media that transmit the grace of God to bodily creatures', adding, 'and thank God, there are many of them'.[10] This point is important because there is a widespread myth which has been promulgated by repetition and assertion, namely, that a sacramental understanding of, for example, baptism is a departure from both scripture (see Porter)[11] and is also a modern innovation with

---

Study Guides, 4; Oxford: Regent's Park College/Macon, GA: Smyth & Helwys, 1996), p. 47.

8   See the whole of Fiddes' essay, 'Baptism and Creation', pp. 47-67.

9   Fiddes, 'Baptism and Creation', pp. 63-64.

10   Pinnock, *Flame of Love*, p. 122. See also the dicussion of 'means of grace' as related to baptism, see A.R. Cross, *Baptism and the Baptists: Theology and Practice in Twentieth-Century Britain* (Studies in Baptist History and Thought, 3; Carlisle: Paternoster, 2000), pp. 103-108.

11   The scriptural basis for a sacramental reading of various New Testament passages relating to baptism, were rehearsed in the exchange between L.A. Read, 'The Ordinances', *The Fraternal* 67 (January, 1948), pp. 8-10, and G.R. Beasley-Murray, 'The Sacraments', *The Fraternal* (October, 1948), pp. 3-7. On this debate, see see Cross, *Baptism*, pp. 220-23. Further, we believe it is impossible to read Beasley-Murray's

no historic Baptist precedent. So, for example, in the controversy
surrounding the publication of the collection of essays in *Christian
Baptism* in 1959[12] (see Fowler), Ernest Kevan declared of the chapter by
Neville Clark, 'Anything less Baptist would be hard to find'.[13] Of the
volume as a whole, he stated that one of the greatest problems was 'the
ease with which some of these Baptists writers' use language of baptism's
spiritual effectiveness. He could not understand how they could reject an
ex opere operato view of baptism and yet freely use 'such verbs as
convey, effect, incorporate, and an unqualified allusion to the "efficacy"
of the rite'.[14] However, recent research has shown that from the earliest
period of their history in the seventeenth century, there have always
Baptists who have understood baptism sacramentally.[15]

Similarly, this is also true of the Lord's Supper, though in his
exposition of the Southern Baptists' *Baptist Faith and Message*, Herschel
Hobbs stated that 'Baptists believe the elements [of the Lord's Supper]
merely symbolize the body and blood of Jesus, with no saving effect in
partaking them'.[16] But yet again, not all early Baptists shared such a
symbolic view. Thomas Grantham, for instance, declared that 'Sure in
this Ordinance we have as real an offer made of the Flesh and Blood of

---

sacramentalist interpretation of baptism, *Baptism in the New Testament* (London:
Macmillan, 1962), and not be impressed by the integrity of the author in seeking to
understand New Testament baptism.

12   A. Gilmore (ed.), *Christian Baptism: A Fresh Attempt to Understand the Rite in
Terms of Scripture, History, and Theology* (London: Lutterworth, 1959).

13   E.F. Kevan, 'Christian Baptism II', *The Fraternal* 113 (July, 1959), p. 10. See
N. Clark, 'The Theology of Baptism', in Gilmore (ed.), *Christian Baptism*, pp. 306-26.
On the widespread belief that baptism is only an ordinance, see A.R. Cross, 'Dispelling
the Myth of English Baptist Baptismal Sacramentalism', *Baptist Quarterly* 38.8
(October, 2000), pp. 367-69.

14   Kevan, 'Christian Baptism II', pp. 9-10. On the issue of 'ordinance' or
'sacrament', see Cross, *Baptism*, pp. 98-102.

15   P.E. Thompson, 'A New Question in Baptist History: Seeking A Catholic Spirit
Among Early Baptists', *Pro Ecclesia* 8.1 (Winter, 1999), pp. 66-68 and 71-72, and
'Practicing the Freedom of God: Formation in Early Baptist Life', in D.M. Hammond
(ed.), *Theology and Lived Christiainity* (Annual Publication of the College Theology
Society, 45; Mystic, CT: Twenty-Third Publications, 2000), pp. 119-38; Cross,
'Dispelling the Myth', pp. 367-91; S.K. Fowler, *More Than a Symbol: The British
Baptist Recovery of Baptismal Sacramentalism* (Studies in Baptist History and Thought,
2; Carlisle: Paternoster, 2002), pp. 10-155. Fowler, p. 155, has drawn attention not
only to the ignorance of Baptist tradition of the likes of Ernest Kevan, but also to the
contributors of *Christian Baptism* who were also apparently unaware that in their seeking
to reform Baptist thought there were in fact rediscovering an early Baptist
sacramentalism.

16   H.H. Hobbs, *The Baptist Faith and Message* (Nashville, TN: Convention Press,
1971), p. 88, italics added.

Christ for us to feed upon by faith, as in any other part of the Gospel of God.'[17] Similarly, the General Baptists' *Orthodox Creed* stated that

> The supper of the Lord Jesus, was instituted...for the confirmation of the faithful believers in all the benefits of his death and resurrection, and spiritual nourishment and growth in him; sealing unto them their continuance in the covenant of grace, and to be a band and pledge of communion with him, and an obligation of obedience to Christ, both passively and actively, as also of our communion and union each with other, in the participation of this holy sacrament.[18]

Baptists have recognized other ordinances as means of grace, though examination of many seventeenth-century Baptist writings shows that while they did not use the terms 'ordinance' and 'sacrament' synonymously, they equally did not understand the ascription of 'ordinance' to baptism, for example, to preclude its sacramental nature.[19] Early Baptists believed there were a number of ordinances which were rightly located in the church's corporate worship—prayer, Bible reading, preaching and the pastoral office (see Colwell, Holmes and Haymes), as well as baptism and the Lord's Supper which were more precisely called 'sacraments' (on which see the essays by Grenz, George, Grass and Randall, Harvey, Thompson, Haykin, Newman and Freeman).[20] This does not mean, however, that they excluded the broader set of ecclesial acts from God's mediation of grace. For instance, the Particular Baptist *Somerset Confession* declares 'That the Spirit is administered by or through the word of faith preached (Gal. 3:2), which word was first declared by the Lord himself, and was confirm'd by them that heard (Heb. 2:3), which was called the gospel of God's grace (Acts 20:24)...'[21]
    What has enabled Baptists to reject sacramental efficacy in terms of the mechanical operation of various rites is their understanding of sacraments, from the human side, as expressions of faith which meet God who graciously comes to us by his Spirit. H. Wheeler Robinson (see

---

17   Thomas Grantham, *Christianismus Primitivus: or The Ancient Christian Religion* (London: n.p., 1678), II/2.vii.4.
18   *The Orthodox Creed* (1678), in W.L. Lumpkin (ed.), *Baptist Confessions of Faith* (Valley Forge, PA: Judson Press, rev. edn, 1969), p. 321.
19   E.g., *Orthodox Creed*, article XXVII, p. 317; B. Keach, *The Child's Delight: Or Instructions for Children and Youth* (London: William and Joseph Marshall, 1702), p. 38.
20   See Thompson, 'Practicing the Freedom of God', pp. 126-31. Thompson, p. 127, notes, for example of the pastoral office, that it was 'a means of God's free work for salvation through things of creation'. For Baptists, then, there is a clear link in their understanding of a sacrament as a means of grace.
21   *The Somerset Confession* (1656), article XIX, in Lumpkin (ed.), *Baptist Confessions*, p. 208.

Cross) sought to allay the fears that Baptist sacramentalism implied mechanical efficacy of various rites:

> If any reader is afraid that this may mean a sacramentalism of the lower kind, where the channel of the Spirit is thought to be the material element, rather than the evangelical truth in the hearts of believers, let it be said distinctly that we are pleading for the connection of water-baptism with the Holy Spirit exactly in the sense in which we plead for its connection with personal faith. If the New Testament teaches the latter, it assuredly teaches the former, and Baptists are really committed to both. Let us tell that the Church is the home of supernatural powers, and not merely a human society, that faith is not a mere opinion, but a personal surrender to Him through whose Spirit these powers are to be experienced, and that baptism is not simply an act of faith, but 'the sign and seal' that that faith is answered by the Holy Spirit of God. So, and only so, will He Himself have led us into all the truth concerning New Testament baptism.[22]

Sacraments, therefore, have a place in what Emil Brunner termed the divine–human encounter.[23] This is clear from the passages cited above from the *Orthodox Creed* and Thomas Grantham, both of which emphasize the need for the response of faith to the gracious movement of God: 'to feed upon by faith' and 'for the confirmation of the faithful'. This note is underscored by both R.E.O. White and George Beasley-Murray, both of whom see baptism as 'faith-baptism'. According to White, 'There is no dualism here between faith and baptism simply because for Paul baptism is always, and only, faith-baptism: given that, Paul is emphatically a sacramentalist.' Later he writes:

> Paul is a sacramentalist if it be remembered that for him the sacrament is a faith-sacrament; his thought is essentially mystical, if it be remembered that his mysticism is rooted in history, ethics, and a faith-relationship to the living Christ. Because baptism expresses such faith, it is 'actually effective in uniting a man to Christ, inititiating him into the church, ushering him into the new Age, conferring on him the Spirit, cleansing him by moral purification and divine pardon, marking his new creation in Christ, placing him within the divine family'.[24]

Beasley-Murray concurs: 'The New Testament writers...think of baptism in terms of grace and faith—always grace, always faith.'[25]

It would have been possible to arrange the essays in a number of ways and the essays themselves could fit in more than one general category,

---

22   'Are Baptists Loyal to the New Testament Baptism?', *Baptist Times and Freeman* 26 June 1914, p. 518.

23   E. Brunner, *The Divine–Human Encounter* (London: SCM Press, 1944), revised as *Truth as Encounter* (London: SCM Press, 1964).

24   R.E.O. White, *The Biblical Doctrine of Initiation* (London: Hodder & Stoughton, 1960), pp. 226 and 275-76 respectively.

25   Beasley-Murray, *Baptism*, p. 278.

but the order followed is from sacramentalism and spirituality (Pinnock and George), general studies of the sacraments (Thompson, Grass and Randall, Grenz and Harvey), baptism (Porter, Fowler and Cross), the Lord's Supper (Haykin, Freeman and Newman), ordination and ministry (Colwell and Holmes) and preaching (Haymes).

The essays in this volume continue the historic Baptist witness to God's coming to humankind by means of physical media, extending grace to faith. Just as the sacramental theology of the early Baptists was marked by diversity, so are these essays. We take this as a sign of the vitality of contemporary Baptist theology. This collection, broadly viewed, follows in this tradition of Baptist thought which sees God at work through whatever means he sovereignly chooses to work in peoples' lives and in the world. As Clark Pinnock expresses it: 'Sacraments exist because we are bodily creatures inhabiting a material world. There is in theory no limit to the number of them. Created reality is richly imbued with sacramental possibilities... [A]nything can mediate the sacred.'[26]

---

26   Pinnock, *Flame of Love*, p. 120.

CHAPTER 1

The Physical Side of Being Spiritual: God's Sacramental Presence

Clark H. Pinnock

To recognise the importance of sacraments has not been easy for me, brought up as I was in Free Church circles. But a fresh reading of gospel texts, an appreciation of Catholic, Orthodox and Protestant traditions, and forms of charismatic renewal—these have brought me to the point of seeing the value of the physical side of being spiritual. Therefore, in this essay I argue for a recovery of sacramental theology for Free Church Protestants. Not a highly technical work, it carries on a theological reflection concering the importance of sacraments.

Brought up as I was in a baptist context, I can understand why there may be resistance to recovering sacraments, but I think there are good reasons for doing so. Because as humans we are embodied and symbol-making beings, it is *a priori* likely that God's presence and self-communcation will be sacramental and involve a merging of spirit and matter. It is likely that God would give himself to us in a variety of concrete ways. Indeed I am inclined to understand the whole creation as potenially sacramental.[1]

Thinking about this topic has proved to be pleasurable because it reminds me of the gencrous self-giving of the Lord. God so loves the world that he gives and goes on giving (Jn 3.16). Just as in our own lives we give ourselves as persons to others in a variety of ways, similarly God opens up doors into the sacred for us. He reaches out to us, not only through the proclamation of the word, but in many other ways, including visible words that embody and mediate. God uses every manner of communication, every symbol and sign, to build a friendship with his creatures. This is why there are so many means of grace, so many ways of

---

1   For earlier thoughts on these themes, see C.H. Pinnock, *Flame of Love: A Theology of the Holy Spirit* (Downers Grove, Ill: InterVarsity Press, 1996), pp. 119-41.

being touched by God and be brought into closer contact. Every believer experiences a number of visible signs of invisible grace.[2]

Not All Agree

Not every baptist will share my enthusiasm. Many, perhaps most, think of our relationship to God as an immediate and unmediated move of the Spirit upon us as individuals. Besides, given the fact that faith is a deeply personal matter, this is not implausible. This too can work as an *a priori* in the other direction.

Zwingli thought so and influenced Free Church believers in this direction over time. Despite the remarkable and ancient consensus that baptism and the Lord's Supper were means of grace and works of God, he repudiated the idea. He did not believe that God was at work in these rituals to bestow benefits of the work of Christ on the faithful. By 1523, he had put aside the historic understanding and disconnected grace from sacraments. 'External things', he wrote 'avail nothing for salvation'. Such practices, he concluded, while they are given for the sake of the congregation (for example) as public testimony, have no effect upon the recipents. He separated grace from the sacraments and warned against confusing matter and spirit. In effect, he introduced a metaphysical dualism into our understanding of the ordinances and rejected fifteen hundred years of Christian thinking on the subject.[3]

Although it is difficult to do justice to the New Testament passages which associate water baptism (for example) with important spiritual benefits (like the forgiveness of sins, being united to Christ, receiving the Holy Spirit, deliverance from the powers of darkness, etc.), many baptists, especially in recent centuries, have followed Zwingli's example. They too are hesitent to acknowlege that the ordinances are means of grace and God's gifts to us.[4]

---

2   Robert W. Jenson, *Visible Words: The Interpretation and Practice of Christian Sacraments* (Philadelphia, PA: Fortress Press, 1978), and James F. White, *Sacraments as God's Self-Giving: Sacramental Practice and Faith* (Nashville, TN: Abingdon Press, 1983).

3   Consider Zwingli, 'Of Baptism', in *Zwingli and Bullinger* (ed. G.W. Bromley; Library of Christian Classics, 24; Philadelphia, PA: Westminster Press, 1953). Jack W. Cottrell, 'Baptism According to the Reformed Tradition', in David W. Fletcher (ed.), *Baptism and the Reformed Tradition* (Joplin, MO: College Press, 1990), pp. 39-81.

4   On baptism and grace, see G.R. Beasley-Murray, *Baptism in the New Testament* (London: Macmillan, 1963), pp. 263-66. Less convinced is J.D.G. Dunn, *Baptism in the Holy Spirit: A Re-examination of the New Testament Teaching on the Gift of the Spirit in relation to Pentecostalism today* (London: SCM Press, 1970), pp. 224-29. On Baptists, see Anthony R. Cross, *Baptism and the Baptists: Theology and Practice in Twentieth-*

Why is this? One factor is captured in the slogan that says: 'Abuse drives out proper use'. In this case, bad sacramentalism drives out the good. Everyone is familiar with the kind of religious formalism in which the Spirit is tied to churchly actions and in which justice is not given to our human response to grace. Grace cannot be conferred just by administering the rite, an idea which one can detect in both Catholic and Restorationist contexts. There is no automatic bestowal of grace. Baptists know for a fact that the Spirit is free to work, either with or apart from means of grace.[5]

Another factor is cultural. The sacramental principle, along with other historic beliefs, such as belief in the possibility of signs and wonders, has suffered in the modern period. Modernity leaves little room for the presence and/or the activity of God. What is 'real' is what can be scientifically established. Modernity looks only for physical causation and disregards divine action even when there is evidence of it. Modern culture is materialistic in outlook and exalts sceptical reason, discounting revelation and tradition. When influenced by this outlook, religion is powerless in both its sacramental and charismatic dimensions. It does not expect God to be present or to move in power.[6]

Modern persons also tend to perceive Spirit as intangible, impalpable, numinous, lacking in reality and concreteness. Concerning sacraments, many deny that the Spirit can be linked to such material actions. It is as though the Spirit were a 'holy ghost' which never deals with the material, never creates real effects, never manifests itself and never transforms concrete situations. We struggle here against a matter/spirit dualism. According to scriptures, the Spirit is not a ghost but the giver of life, shaper of the material creation and the power of resurrection. He implemented the coming of the Son in flesh and bone, annointed him in body, mind and spirit, brought about many concrete changes in life, and will bring about a new creation.[7]

Century Britain (Studies in Baptist History and Thought, 3; Carlisle: Paternoster, 2000), and Stanley K. Fowler, *More Than a Symbol: The British Baptist Recovery of Baptismal Sacramentalism* (Studies in Baptist History and Thought, 2; Carlisle: Paternoster, 2002).

5   Donald G. Bloesch, *The Holy Spirit: Works and Gifts* (Downers Grove, IL: InterVarsity Press, 2000), pp. 13-14, 274, 279.

6   Charles H. Kraft exposes the modern bias against belief in the supernatural in *Christianity With Power* (Ann Arbor: Servant Books, 1989). Langdon Gilkey exposes the bias against it in the area of sacraments, *Catholicism Confronts Modernity: A Protestant View* (New York: Seabury Press, 1975), chs. 1–2.

7   Brian J. Walsh and J. Richard Middleton focus on this dualism, *The Transforming Vision* (Downers Grove, IL: InterVarsity Press, 1984), Part 3. Michael Welker also counters in the biblical teaching, *God the Spirit* (Minneapolis, MN: Fortress Press, 1994).

In order to be able to take both Spirit and sacrament seriously, we need to confront the dualism in our thinking. The Enlightenment project was built on the division of reality into mind and matter, souls and bodies, the visible and the eternal. Reality has been split apart and must be healed so that we speak to people in their entirety. We must integrate the spiritual and the material and minister to the whole person. Postmodern theology must be holistic and post-dualistic.[8]

In the postmodern setting we need sacraments more than ever and should not be encouraging scepticism regarding them. The Spirit is not opposed to material media but speaks through human voices, feeds us with eucharistic bread, washes us in baptismal water and gets our feet to dance. Worship is weakened by a loss of the sacramental dimension, a loss of mystery, of liturgical beauty and of traditional practices. In repudiating sacraments we not only break with the historic churches and accelerate the influence of secularisation but impoverish ourselves.[9]

Mediations of Grace

It seems to me that the transcendent is present among us in a great variety of ways and that participation in the Spirit is often mediated not unmediated.

1. It disappoints me when I open a book on the sacraments and see reference only to familiar churchly rites. There are many more sacraments than two (the Protestant line) and many more than seven (the Catholic line). To start with I would distinguish natural and ecclesial sacraments. Our thinking is much too narrow. Beyond the church God reveals himself to everyone through created reality. Just as general revelation underlies special revelation and prefigures it, so general sacramentality underlies Christian sacramentality and heralds it. Our ordinary human experience of natural sacramentality makes faith and liturgy intelligible.

God is everywhere and in everything. As Paul said, 'In him we live and move and have our being' (Acts 17.28). God is not far from anyone and his call goes out to everyone. Encountering the created world, persons experience God's presence. Even in the myths of the world's peoples, he has made himself known. As Jonathan Edwards noted, God is at work

---

8   'Dualism', in *Sacramentum Mundi: An Encyclopedia of Theology* (6 vols; New York: Herder and Herder, 1968–70), II, pp. 112-15. C. Leonard Allen and Danny Gray Swick, *Participating in God's Life: Two Crossroads for Churches of Christ* (Orange, CA: New Leaf Books, 2001), ch. 5.

9   So Robert E. Webber, *Evangelicals on the Canterbury Trail: Why Evangelicals are attracted to the Liturgical Church* (Wilton, CN: Morehouse Barlow, 1985).

with all peoples of earth to prepare them for the gospel.[10] We all encounter God in his creatures as the heavens are telling the glory of God. The whole world is God's temple; therefore, we meditate on God's creatures—on the things that happen to us in our lives and on ordinary things.[11]

2.   Also, prior to the Christian dispensation, God revealed himself in the election of Israel and blessed her with sacramental structures. God stooped to speak in human language and fostered liturgical practices and festivals. God came to them in theophanies, in meteorological phenomena and even in human form. Israel found God especially in the events of their own history and in certain holy places. God manifests himself in the Old Testament in ways that are highly specific, tangible and formful. There is no such thing for Israel really as an unincarnate God. He encountered people in as many personal ways as possible.[12]

3.   Supremely for Christians, God makes himself present by the incarnation which I would call our primordial sacrament. In Jesus, the invisible God makes himself visible. Jesus is called God's image and exact representation of God (Col. 1. 15; Heb 1.3). Jesus said, 'He that has seen me has seen the Father' (Jn 14.9). He is our window into God and brings us into his presence. In Christ, God communicates his very self and discloses the mystery of his love. The incarnation is the paramount event of God's closeness and, therefore, the basic sacrament of our encounter with God. In Jesus, the decisive meeting takes place between God and humanity and it calls for a free response. For this reason I would say that no Christians are, strictly speaking, non-sacramental because we all embrace the most important sacrament, Jesus Christ, and observing this sacrament observe the best one. No one who confesses Christ, the primordial sacrament and loves the church, the fundamental sacrament, can fairly be called non-sacramental. Even Quakers have sacraments, in the simplicty of their meeting houses, in sitting together in a circle, in singing and praying, in waiting and in listening. The unity of

---

10   Joseph Martos, 'Sacraments in all Religions', *Doors to the Sacred: A Historical Introduction to Sacraments* (New York: Doubleday, 1981), ch. 1. Gerald R. McDermott, *Jonathan Edwards Confronts the Gods: Christian Theology, Enlightenment Religion, and Non-Christian Faiths* (New York: Oxford University Press, 2000). C.H. Pinnock, *A Wideness in God's Mercy: The Finality of Jesus Christ in a World of Religions* (Grand Rapids, MI: Zondervan, 1992).

11   Simon Chan, 'Meditation on the creature', in *Spiritual Theology: A Systematic Study of the Christian Life* (Downers Grove, IL: InterVarsity Press, 1998), pp. 180-85.

12   Terrance Fretheim, 'God in Human Form', in *The Suffering of God: An Old Testament Perspective* (Philadelphia, PA: Fortress, 1984), ch. 6.

catholic and free churches is hindered, not in principle but only in detail, as to how to understand the ordinances we all practice.[13]

4.   If Jesus is the sacrament of God, the church is a sacrament of Christ. Vatican II speaks of the church as 'sacramentum mundi' (*Dogmatic Constitution on the Church* 1.1) because she mediates God's presence and lives to bring humans into relation with God.[14] The community of the disciples, filled and guided by the Holy Spirit, continue the mission of Jesus Christ and each of her sacraments derive from Jesus, the basic sacrament. The church is a sacrament because, indwelled by the Holy Spirit, she perpetuates the presence of the risen Lord and makes it available to people. Through members of his body, Christ communicates his presence by the Spirit. The Spirit constitutes the body of Christ, making the risen presence of Christ real. The Lord lives within the community, releasing his Spirit and ever draws members to the union with God. People are almost always converted by meeting Christ in the members of his body, who become means of grace to one another. As he acted through Christ, God continues to act through these persons, their words and actions. Christ is the sacrament of God and the church is the sacrament of Christ, insofar as it represents him. Those who receive divine grace through the members of this body are brought into communion with God and sent forth to proclaim good news.

5.   As well as these two general Christian sacraments, there are many individual sacraments and many effective symbolic events. The church's life is richly sacramental and evokes God's presence in many ways. I see them everywhere. There are so many activities that mediate grace: singing and prayer, praise and thanksgiving, greeting and fellowship, teaching and instruction, loving acts and the holy kiss, footwashing. Christ is present in the church in many embodied ways. In each, the material becomes spiritual and the spiritual is conveyed through the material. To me sacraments are which ever and what ever media transmit the grace of God to us bodily creatures. By such means of grace, Christ completes his work in us as the firstfruits of a new humanity, which he wishes to offer to the Father. Sacraments are sacred signs, made up of words and actions, employing material symbols, through which God bestows life on us by the Spirit. As we open our hearts to God, we become 'the temple of the

---

13   I think that Karl Barth takes this to an extreme in naming Jesus as our only sacrament. *Church Dogmatics: The Christian Life* IV/4 (Edinburgh: T.&T. Clark, 1969).

14   Avery Dulles, 'The Church as Sacrament', in *Models of the Church* (Garden City, NY: Doubleday, 1974), ch. 4. At the end of this chapter, Dulles remarks that this notion of the church has found little by way of response from Protestant thought. Perhaps so, but it finds a positive response with me. See Timothy George's chapter in this volume.

living God, as God said: "I will live among them and move among them"' (2 Cor 6.16).[15]

6.   Many of the specifically churchly sacraments are operative in the weekly meeting. Indeed I would say that the weekly meeting, being the occasion of so many sacraments, is itself a sacrament that exceeds the sum of its parts. We are instructed to meet together for the sake of encouraging one another and building one another up (Heb. 10.25). Jesus said, 'Where two or three are gathered I am in the midst of them' (Mt. 18.20). The meeting mediates an encounter with God. In the music we are taken up into the presence of God. In the reading of the word, we listen to the Spirit. We pass along the Spirit when we lay hands on and pray for the sick. It strikes me as very odd that we only name two actions (baptism and eucharist) sacraments (if indeed we do that) when the meeting itself and half a dozen other things in it are sacraments as well. Most regretably, though, many standard church meetings are formal and repressed and the sacramentality is very weak and thin. Therefore, I would not want to see a revival of sacramentality which was not a renewal at the same time of charismaticality.

7.   Reading the scriptures in the meeting is a sacramental act—it mediates the word of God. 'God himself speaks when the holy Scriptures are read in the church' (*Constitution on the Sacred Liturgy*, par 7). For this reason, the Bible is often given ritual recognition by being carried in formally in Reformed and kissed in the Orthodox churches. As wine is the sign of the blood of Christ, these texts enable us to hear God's voice and they supply all the sacraments with their justification and content. The Bible is a channel of divine instruction being the earthen vessel in which lies the greatest treasure.[16]

8.   A ministry of grace in the community is the instruction of converts which is a kind of sacrament. Looking to the scriptures, the church provides teaching to young believers to lead them in the path of righteousness and help their faith to grow. The goal is sharing in Christ and their incorporation into the community. Jesus said, 'Baptise and make disciples' (Mt. 28.19). Receiving the Spirit in baptism is only the beginning. Disciple's must be involved in Jesus' dying and rising. Instruction points them to the way of the Spirit and gives the Spirit a means of guiding new believers in this way. More than just the passing on

---

15   For this larger sense of what sacraments are, see Hendrikus Berkhof, *Christian Faith: An Introduction to the Study of the Faith* (Grand Rapids, MI: Eerdmans, 1979), pp. 345-92. On sacraments as a means of growing into union with Christ, Georgios I. Mantzaridis, *The Deification of Man: St Gregory Palamas and the Orthodox Tradition* (Crestwood, NY: St Vladimir's Seminary Press, 1984), ch. 2.

16   On scripture as sacrament, see Donald G. Bloesch, *Holy Scripture: Revelation, Inspiration and Interpretation* (Downers Grove, Ill: InterVarsity Press, 1994), pp. 40-45.

of information, it relates salvation to the totality of life. It initiates seekers into the community and the ways of the kingdom of God.

9.   Baptism is the act in which we call upon the Spirit to initiate individuals into the fellowship of the body of Christ (1 Cor. 12.13). As Jesus being baptised in water received the Spirit, so there is the promise that he will baptise us. Born of water and Spirit, we become members of his mystical body and receive the forgiveness of sins. Jesus says (in the long ending of Mark): 'The one who believes and is baptised will be saved' (Mk 16.16). Peter called upon the people to be baptised and receive the gift of the Spirit in the context of baptism (Acts 2.38). Through the sign of water, people are baptised into Christ and put on Christ (Gal. 3.26). They receive the washing of regeneration and renewal of the Spirit (Tit. 3.5). Baptism in the New Testament is the moment when the Spirit is imparted and when people open themselves to the Spirit's gifts. Baptism is an expression of the obedience of faith and the moment when God gives the Spirit. Spirit baptism is the meaning of baptism in water and makes it a sacrament.[17] At baptism, there ought always to be an invocation of the Spirit. A nice example is this prayer in the order of baptism of the Armenian Apostolic Orthodox Church: 'We pray thee, Lord, send thy Holy Spirit into this water, and cleanse it as thou didst cleanse the Jordan by thy descent into it...prefiguring this font of baptism and of the regeneration of all men.'[18]

10.   Central to the weekly meeting is the exposition and application of the biblical message. For Free Church Protestants, the proclamation of the word is really the central sacrament. A human act, it bears witness to the good tidings of God's faithfulness. Giving more than just general truths, it aims at a specific context so that the gift of God comes in ever new and context-specific ways. The hope is that people will grow as hearers of the word of God and sense the directions in which the Spirit is leading them. Preaching looks not only to the past but seeks to anticipate the fulfilment of the gospel. With an eye to the extension of this story, preaching must exercise discernment as to what God is doing in our time. When Jesus entered Jerusalem, he wept because the people did not recognise the time of God's visitation (Lk. 19.44). On another occasion, he complained that they could predict the weather but not the present time (Lk. 12.54-56). The proclamation is sacramental when we hear the word of God as something timely and crucial.

11.   Preaching should not be a monologue. Sound teaching should be given but it must not stop there. People must engage the word and be involved. There must be dialogue. We must also be open to hear what the

---

17   Beasley-Murray, *Baptism in the New Testament*, pp. 275-79.

18   'The Armenian Rite', in E.C. Whitaker (ed.), *Documents of the Baptismal Liturgy* (London: SPCK, 2nd edn, 1979), p. 63.

Spirit is saying to the others sitting by (1 Cor. 14.30). This is not just pedogogically smart—it leads to more growth and better learning—but takes spiritual gifting seriously. The people must be involved in the hearing of the word. As many as possible must be drawn into the reflection. Sound teaching is certainly important, but promptings of the Spirit must not be muffled or else the church will become a spiritless organisation. True, we will hear some uncomfortable things when we allow for dialogue, but we may also find ourselves shaken into new life as we are moved by the Holy Spirit. What Paul says is true: 'Do not quench the Spirit—do not despise prophesying' (1 Thess. 5.19). If churches without teachers are in danger of getting off track, churches without prophets run the risk of going flat.

12.   The last supper expressed Jesus' self-surrender to God and he commanded the apostles to continue it after his death so that the charism of self-giving might be present in the church down through history. Christ promised to be present in the supper so that people might experience him when they partake of it. His charism was deposited, as it were, in the eucharist where he is present in the bread and wine as the one who surrenders himself to the Father.[19]

In the eucharist we receive Jesus in the form of bread and wine and share in his death and resurrection. Jesus 'makes himself known' in breaking of bread (Lk. 24.35). The supper is supernatural food and drink (1 Cor. 10.4). We eat the bread which came down from heaven (Jn 6.35). Therefore, we also invoke the Spirit upon the bread and wine to make them vehicles of his body and blood. The effectiveness of the sacrament is not due to any magic surrounding what happens to the elements but to the power of the Spirit in this event. There must be a coming of the Spirit upon the action and the people. Stanley Burgess cites this Ethiopic prayer of invocation at eucharist: 'We beseech thee to send thy Holy Spirit upon this oblation of the church, that in joining them together, thou mayest grant, that it be to them for holiness and for filling them with the Holy Spirit, and for strengthening of faith in truth, that they may glorify and praise thee through thy Son our saviour Jesus Christ.'[20]

By invoking the Spirit at the eucharist, we recognise that the effectiveness of the sacrament is due, not to a magical operation, but to the coming of the Spirit in response to prayer. Because it is not

---

19   Heribert Mühlen seeks to understand every sacrament as an expression of the charismatic self-surrender of Jesus, *A Charismatic Theology: Initiation in the Spirit* (New York: Burns & Oates, 1978), pp. 124-25.

20   Stanley Burgess, *The Holy Spirit: Eastern Christian Traditions* (Peabody, MA: Hendrickson, 1989), p. 167. Yves Congar, 'The part played by the Holy Spirit in the Eucharist according to the Western Tradition', in *I Believe in the Holy Spirit* (3 vols; New York: Seabury Press, 1983), III, pp. 250-74.

automatic, one must not neglect the preparation of people or their response. Grace, when it is offered, must always be received in faith and trust. A genuine response must be there. If not, the sacramental experience fails and the ritual is empty.[21]

13. Alongside the two well noticed sacraments, there are less noticed ones. Footwashing is the sacrament of servanthood and could easily have become regularised. Jesus said explicitly: 'you ought to wash one another's feet' (Jn 13.14-15).[22] The holy kiss is the sign of a family connection in Christ (1 Thess. 5.26). It has come to be known as the passing of the peace as the people greet one another. The laying on of hands is a means of transferring the Spirit. As Jesus touched the leper when he healed him (Mk 1.41). As Paul laid hands on Timothy to communicate the Spirit (1 Tim. 4.14; 2 Tim. 1.6). As Peter and John laid hands on the Samaritans that they might receive the Spirit (Acts 8.17). The physical and the spiritual are not antithetical. The Spirit is passed from one to another, from Moses to Joshua, from Elijah to Elisha. When seeking renewal, it makes sense to seek prayer and the laying on of hands. Those who have the living experience of the baptism in the Spirit often can communicate it to the seeker.[23]

14. The grace of God is conveyed sacramentally not only in churchly activities but above all in the renewal of life. The gospel is not a word only but a message in deed and with power. Jesus himself can be encountered in the poor and the hungry (Mt. 25.37-40). Grace is mediated, not only by word and symbol, but by love and concern. Because salvation touches the whole of life, we read that the early church took care of all those in need (Acts 2.44-45; 4.32). Concern for widows and orphans characterised the primitive churches. When the need arose, they appointed deacons so that the widows would not be neglected (Acts 6.1-6). The diaconate mediates grace to a suffering world.

15. Some may find it a bit of a stretch to think of offices in the church and organisational aspects as sacraments. But not much would happen if they did not arrange for things to happen. Our leaders facilitate the salvation mediating process we are talking about. Without gifted people to make things happen in an orderly way, the congregation could fall into chaos and lose direction. Therefore, we are told to respect them and expect the Lord to work through them.

---

21   On the relation of faith to sacrament, Herbert Vorgrimmler, *Sacramental Theology* (Collegeville, MN: Liturgical Press, 1992), pp. 82-86.

22   John Christopher Thomas, *Footwashing in John 13 and the Johannine Community* (Journal for the Study of the New Testament Supplement Series, 61; Sheffield: JSOT Press, 1991).

23   Beasley-Murray, 'Note on the laying on of hands', in *Baptism in the New Testament*, pp. 122-25.

Recovering a Sacramental Theology

My purpose in this essay is to create room in our baptist thinking for sacraments. More than that, I want to foster delight in an abundance of sacraments, in places and in ways that have not registered with us. The proclamation of the word does not exhaust the many different ways in which the presence of God is communicated to us. In addition to teaching, there are many visible signs and symbols of invisible grace which exist because we are embodied creatures.

In the case of sacraments, two mistakes need to be avoided. The Catholic tendency, on the one hand, is to over-emphasise the objective reality of grace in a few sacraments which are effective in and of themselves. This can suggest a quasi-magical operation which diminishes the personal encounter of humans with God. The baptist tendency, on the other hand, so stresses the importance of faith, that sacraments are more what we do than what God does. We need to recover a true objectivity in them of God acting in us.[24]

Both in creation and new creation, the material serves as a vehicle of the spiritual. Grace operates through the medium of the material and temporal. Sacraments are rooted in life as God made it. Faith tells us that a reality perceptible to our senses is more than and deeper than the surface reveals. And what a rich reality it is! There is no limit to the number of them. Life is imbued with such possibilities. The world itself reflects God's glory and practically anything can mediate the sacred, if we have eyes to see and ears to hear, since the Spirit pervades the universe. The sacramental principle operates, not only in the religious realm, but in ordinary experience too. God appears in the glory of the sunset and the towering peaks. The angel of the Lord appeared to Moses in the flame of the burning bush (Acts 7.30). Elijah listened for God to speak in the wind, the earthquake, the fire, and then the silence (1 Kgs 19.11-12). We meet God in the members of the fellowship and Jesus in the poor and the marginal. Sacraments help to foster relationship between God and ourselves when received by faith. They help us to approach the incomprehensible mystery of his love. The material signs make present God's invisible grace. Through the Lord's Supper, for example, we participate in the death and resurrection of Christ. In this action, we choose to die with Christ and live with him. We declare our intention to yield our members as instruments of righteousness unto God. We open our hands to receive bread from heaven.

---

24 Stanley J. Grenz sees a willingness in the Free Churches to change on this issue, *Theology for the Community of God* (Nashville, TN: Broadman and Holman, 1994), pp. 671-72.

Effectiveness is bound up with the Holy Spirit. Calvin writes: 'Sacraments fulfil their office only when the Spirit, that inward teacher, comes to them, by whose power alone hearts are penetrated and affections moved and our souls opened for the sacraments to enter in. If the Spirit be lacking, the sacraments can accomplish nothing more in our minds than the spendours of the sun shining upon blind eyes or a voice sounding in deaf ears'.[25]

The Second Vatican Council agrees: 'in order that the sacred liturgy may produce its full effect, it is necessary that the faithful come to it with proper dispositions, that their thoughts match their words, and that they cooperate with divine grace lest they receive it in vain (cf. 2 Cor. 6:1). Pastors of souls must therefore realize that, when the liturgy is celebrated, more is requiried than the mere observance of the laws governing valid and licit celebration. It is their duty also to ensure that the faithful take part knowingly, actively, and fruitfully.'[26]

As bodily creatures, we need embodied expressions in worship, to make the invisible visible. Our walk with God is enriched when we make use of the God-given material media. Otherwise life and worship may remain thin, abstract and notional. Symbols help believers apprehend the invisble things of God and serve as channels of grace for them. Our spirituality can become barren when it is all left brain. We need to worship with our senses through things that can be seen and heard, touched, tasted and smelled. Let us recover the sacramental in the broad sense because grace comes to us in so many different ways. Tangible experiences of grace, by drawing us in, make possible a more profound apprehension of God than can merely propositional language. Recovering the sense of the sacramental is part of the renewal the churches need.[27]

The sacramental principle has been very widely held in the churches historically. Christians have almost always seen sacraments as a means of grace. They have seen them not merely as acts of human obedience but as events where God moves. Let us not repudiate sacraments because we have misunderstood them or impoverished ourselves by over-reacting to

---

25   J. Calvin, *Institutes of the Christian Religion* (1559), 4.14.9.

26   *Constitution on the Sacred Liturgy* ch. 1 para. 11, in W.M. Abbott, SJ (ed.), *The Documents of Vatican II* (London: Geoffrey Chapman, 1966), p. 143.

27   I am concerned that we become both charismatic and sacramental as the early church was. See Kilian McDonnell and George T. Montague, *Christian Initiation and Baptism in the Holy Spirit: Evidence from the First Eight Centuries* (Collegeville, MN: Liturgical Press, 1991). Clark H. Pinnock, 'Baptists and the Latter Rain: A Contemporary Challenge and Hope for Tomorrow', in Jarold K. Zeman (ed.), *Costly Vision: The Baptist Pilgrimage in Canada* (Burlington, ON: Welch Publishing, 1988), pp. 255-72.

flawed practices. We must not repudiate embodied means of grace. Sacraments are events where God acts to transform us and where people respond. He wants to grace our lives in multiple ways and communicate his love for us.

CHAPTER 2

The Sacramentality of the Church:
An Evangelical Baptist Perspective

Timothy George

Does the church have a sacramental nature? More precisely, can we say that the church not only possesses or performs sacraments, but is itself a sacrament? This is a relatively new question on the ecumenical agenda. The key text which forms the basis of recent discussions is from the opening paragraph of the Dogmatic Constitution *Lumen Gentium,* approved 21 November 1964 at Vatican Council II:

> By her relationship with Christ, the church is a kind of sacrament or sign of intimate union with God, and of the unity of all humankind. She is also an instrument for the achievement of such union and unity.[1]

As an evangelical and a Baptist, I belong to an ecclesial tradition for whom the language of the church as sacrament is problematic, or at least not so congenial. Thus, I first need to say something about my own tradition and its location within the ecumenical space in which this conversation is taking place. Next I shall examine several specific challenges posed to evangelical Baptist ecclesiology by the concept of the church as sacrament. And, finally, I shall attempt to offer some constructive points of contact in our continuing quest to define and proclaim the mystery of that community of faith which Jesus loves, for which he gave himself up, and which he continually sustains by the power of the Spirit and the good news of the gospel.

---

1   *Lumen Gentium* 1. In Latin the text reads: 'Cum vero Ecclesia sit in Christo signum et instrumentum seu veluti sacramentum intimae totuis generis humani unitatis eiusque in Deum unionis...' Cf. W.M. Abbott, SJ (ed.), *The Documents of Vatican II* (London: Geoffrey Chapman, 1966), p. 15.

A Personal Perspective

It is important to note that I speak from the perspective of three distinct yet overlapping ecclesial and theological communities. By academic training I am a historical theologian with a special concern for Reformation theology. While appreciative of the Anabaptist vision of the church and its Free Church parallels in radical puritan, separatist and Baptist modalities, I find my theological bearings within the Reformed tradition, with a preference for Calvin over Zwingli, but with many good lessons learned from Dr Martinus of Wittenberg. In the second place, I am affiliated with the world evangelical movement through my work with the World Evangelical Fellowship, the Billy Graham Evangelistic Association, and the journal *Christianity Today*. As an international, transdenominational fellowship of some one-half billion believers around the world, evangelicalism is in its very existence an amazing ecumenical fact. However, despite its enormous success, evangelicalism as a theological movement has given meager attention to ecclesiology. What ecumenism has become for Roman Catholics and many conciliar Protestants, missions and evangelism are for evangelicalism—concerns central to our very identity and purpose. In the evangelical tradition, the words of missiologist of J.C. Hoekendijk, spoken in the early 1950s, would still be warmly received today. 'In history a keen ecclesiological interest has, almost without exception, been a sign of spiritual decadence.'[2]

In the third place, I am an ordained minister in the Southern Baptist Convention (USA), the largest Protestant denomination in North America with some 17 million members (not including infants and unbaptized children) and more than 40,000 congregations in all fifty American states as well as Canada. Unlike the American Baptist Churches with their ecumenically-friendly traditions, Southern Baptists have been notoriously suspicious of 'entangling alliances' with other denominational groups. They participate in neither the National Council of Churches nor the World Council of Churches and have recently refused to join even the National Association of Evangelicals. Strongly congregationalist in ecclesiastical polity, the Southern Baptist Convention (SBC) does not consider itself a church but rather a general missionary body through which local churches can broker their evangelistic commitments to world missions, theological education, religious publishing and the like. Organized in 1845 amidst the pre-Civil War upheaval over slavery, the SBC has been shaped historically by frontier revivalism, American pragmatism and modern individualism, and a virulent nativism with its

---

2   J.C. Hoekendijk, 'The Church and Missionary Thinking', *The International Review of Missions* 41 (1952), p. 325.

strong anti-Roman Catholic sentiments. Even though some of these forces are losing their grip on the Southern Baptist soul as denominational loyalty becomes more and more difficult to sustain, it is safe to say that the majority of Southern Baptists would find the words 'sacramental' and 'ecumenical' equally unhelpful and even deplorable.

Nonetheless, despite the strong lure of sectarianism, thus far the SBC has continued to be a participating member of the Baptist World Alliance (BWA), a loose-knit fellowship of some forty-four million Baptists around the world. Ecumenical initiatives have also been difficult for the BWA. Currently there are no ongoing official conversations with either Eastern Orthodox Christians or the Roman Catholic Church, due in some measure to indigenous Baptist resistance to such dialogues. Nonetheless, over the past thirty years, the BWA Division of Study and Research has published reports of bilateral conversations between the BWA and the World Alliance of Reformed Churches (1973), The Lutheran World Federation (1990), the Vatican Secretariat for Promoting Christian Unity (1988) and the Mennonite World Conference (1992). There is also an ongoing International Anglican–Baptist Dialogue, the first ever in the nearly five centuries of our shared history. Wearing then these multiple hats I shall try to speak from, and perhaps to, but certainly not for, the various churches and ecclesial communities to which I belong. In doing so, I shall draw on classic documents on the Reformation, Baptist confessions and statements of faith, and recent evangelical documents concerning the church and its mission in the world.

The Challenge of Sacramental Language

In his helpful survey of the reception of the language of the church as 'sacrament, sign and instrument,' Günther Gassmann traces a growing openness to use these terms to describe the place and vocation of the church and its unity in God's plan of salvation. He admits that there is no uniform understanding of what these terms mean in the various ecumenical texts in which they occur. Of the three terms, 'sacrament is the most unambiguous being used in the sense of effective mediation, representation, or anticipation'.[3] At the same time, sacrament is also the least frequently cited of these three terms. Apparently, it is less of an ecumenical stretch to describe the church as 'a persuasive sign of God's love', or as an instrument for accomplishing God's purpose in Christ, than to claim that the church is the 'sacrament of God's saving work'. At

---

3   Günther Gassmann, 'The Church as Sacrament, Sign and Instrument: The Reception of this Ecclesiological Understanding and Ecumenical Debate', *Church, Kingdom, World* (Geneva: World Council of Churches, 1986), p. 14.

times, however, 'sign' and 'sacrament' seem to be used interchangeably, as in the report of the World Conference on Mission and Evangelism in Melbourne in 1980. Here the church is defined as the body of Christ, 'the sacrament of the kingdom in every place and time', and, elsewhere in the same report, 'a sign of the kingdom of God because it is the body of Christ on earth'.[4] While Baptists and evangelicals have been largely absent in this discussion, they are likely to find 'sign' and 'instrument' more congenial terms for describing the reality and mission of the church than the more historically freighted word 'sacrament'. Here we shall explore some of the ecclesiological reservations for applying sacramental language to the church. Following this, we shall look at some possible points of contact between the evangelical tradition and more sacramental models of the church.

At the heart of Baptist and evangelical ecclesiology is a distinction which seems to play little role in recent ecumenical texts, namely, the Augustinian distinction between the church visible and invisible. Within the Baptist tradition, the classic definition of the invisible church comes from the Second London Confession, a Particular Baptist statement of faith, published in 1677, which echoes the language of the Westminster Confession:

> The Catholic or universal Church which with respect to the internal work of the Spirit, and truth of grace, may be called invisible, consists of the whole number of the elect, that have been, are, or shall be gathered into one, under Christ, the Head thereof; and is the spouse, the body, the fullness of Him, that filleth all in all.[5]

The church, then, is the body of Christ extended throughout time as well as space consisting of all persons everywhere who have been placed in vital union with Jesus Christ through the ministry of the Holy Spirit. As Georges Florovsky used to say, the church is characterized by a temporal as well as a spatial catholicity, a catholicity not reducible to, nor strictly

---

4   'Message to the Churches', in *Your Kingdom Come*, Report on the World Conference on Mission and Evangelism, Melbourne 1980 (Geneva: World Council of Churches, 1980), pp. 235-36.

5   In 1742 this same confession was published in America, with slight alterations, as the Philadelphia Confession of Faith. Cf. Timothy and Denise George (eds.), *Baptists Confessions, Covenants, and Catechisms* (Nashville, TN: Broadman and Holman, 1996), pp. 84-85. The visible/invisible church distinction is mentioned in the document, 'Towards a Common Understanding of the Church (1984–1990)', in William G. Rusch and Jeffrey Gros (eds.), *Deepening Communion: International Ecumenical Documents with Roman Catholic Participation* (Washington, DC: United States Catholic Conference, 1998), pp. 175-229, from the Reformed–Roman Catholic Dialogue where the point is to affirm the indissoluble link between the two 'sides' of the one ecclesial reality.

verifiable by, historical continuity, numerical quantity, or geographical extent.[6]

In the New Testament the church invisible and universal is depicted as a heavenly and eschatological reality, not as an earthly institution to be governed and grasped by mere mortals. The only text in the New Testament which directly refers to the church as the mother of believers is Galatians 4.26 where, in contrast to the earthly city in Judea, the church is called 'the Jerusalem that is above, the heavenly Jerusalem'. Another text of major importance which extends this idea is Hebrews 12.22-24: 'But you have come to Mount Zion, to the heavenly Jerusalem, the city of the living God. You have come to thousands upon thousands of angels of joyful assembly, to the church (*ekklesia*) of the first born, whose names are written in heaven. You have come to God, the judge of all men, to the spirits of righteous men made perfect, to Jesus the Mediator of a new covenant, and to the sprinkled blood that speaks a better word than the blood of Abel.'[7] As a reality beyond our ken, this universal church is not at our disposal and thus we can only believe it (*credo ecclesiam*)—not believe *in* it as we believe in God the Father Almighty, Jesus Christ his only Son and the Holy Spirit. Rather, when we confess that we 'believe the church', we are bearing witness to its reality. We mean to say that we believe that it exists; that we ourselves by God's grace have been placed within it, along with all others who 'bow their necks under the yoke of Jesus Christ' (Belgic Confession, art. 28); and that the gates of hell shall never prevail against it.

One objection, though perhaps not the strongest, against defining the church as a sacrament is that it seems to obscure the full celestial and eschatological reality of the church depicted in Hebrews, the book of Revelation and other apocalyptic texts. This, despite the fact that sacraments are understood as efficacious signs, that is to say, signs that point beyond themselves to a greater reality, a reality which in some sense the sacraments themselves produce or convey. But if, with the Council of Trent, we can describe a sacrament as 'the visible form of an invisible grace', then it seems to say too little about the church to call it a sacrament. Put otherwise, sacramental language about the church seems to privilege unduly *ecclesia militans* at the expense of *ecclesia triumphans*, and, for those who believe in purgatory, *ecclesia dormans* as

---

6   G. Florovsky, 'The Catholicity of the Church', in G. Florovsky, *Bible, Church, Tradition: An Eastern Orthodox View* (Belmont, MA: Nordland Publishing, 1972), pp. 39-42.

7   This passage has been called 'the most majestic panorama of the transcendent eschatological reality that is the communion of saints, the eternal fellowship of pilgrims past and present'. Markus Bockmuehl, 'The Church in Hebrews', in Markus Bockmuehl and Michael B. Thompson (eds.), *A Vision for the Church: Studies in Early Christian Ecclesiology* (Edinburgh: T. & T. Clark, 1997), p. 149.

well. While there is much about the heavenly state that we do not know, and about which it is unwise to speculate, surely the fullness of the church's communion with the triune God then and there is much more than an intensification of its pilgrim experience here and now. The eucharist is indeed a foretaste of that eschatological banquet called the marriage feast of the Lamb, and the continuity between the two is central to the meaning of *sursum corda* in the liturgy, but to quote St Paul, 'When wholeness comes, the partial will vanish...my knowledge now is partial; then it will be whole like God's knowledge of me' (1 Cor. 13.9-12 NEB). However we explain divine action in the sacraments, including the real presence of Christ in the eucharist, the Christian *sacramenta* are signs of that ultimate *mysterion* that is 'not yet' fully revealed or conveyed amidst the groanings of this present age (cf. Rom. 8.24-26).

It should be said at once that the concept of the invisible church can be (and sometimes has been) distorted into a kind of ecclesiastical docetism according to which the earthly and historical form of the church has been negated and its mission in the world reduced to a 'spiritualized' fellowship with no more gravity than a discussion group or a social club. Already in the sixteenth century, the Reformers were aware of this criticism and vigorously denied the charge that by the church they meant only a *civitas platonica*. Indeed, they sought to reconstruct a purified form of catholic Christianity, a real life and blood community of faith that would bear the 'marks of the true church' (*notae verae ecclesiae*). The *notae* do not replace the traditional Nicene attributes (*una, catholica apostolica, sancta*), but they rather call into question the unity, catholicity, apostolicity and holiness of every congregation which claims to be a church, thus subjecting it to an outward, empirical examination.[8] In this way, as Calvin says, 'the face of the church' emerges into visibility before our eyes (*Institutes* 4.1.9).

The early Baptists follow Luther and Calvin in regarding the word purely preached and the sacraments duly administered as the two irreducible marks of the visible church, although they, along with others in the Reformed tradition (cf. The Scots Confession, 1560) expanded and formalized the *notae*-concept to include discipline as an indicator of a true visible church. By thus elevating discipline as a distinguishing mark of the church, the Baptists (along with other puritans and later pietists) defined the true visible church as a covenanted company of gathered saints, separated from the world in its organization and autonomy and separating back to the world through congregational disciple those members whose lives betrayed their profession.

---

8   This concept is more fully developed in Calvin than in Luther. See Heinrich Heppe, *Reformed Dogmatics* (ed. Ernst Bizer; London: George Allen & Unwin, 1950), pp. 657-64. See also Timothy George, *Theology of the Reformers* (Nashville, TN: Broadman and Holman, 1988), pp. 172-93.

The Church Visible

Many of these themes were brought together in the response of the Baptist World Alliance to the Faith and Order document, *Baptism, Eucharist and Ministry (BEM)*. While affirming the invisible church as the whole number of the elect, inclusive of all 'spiritual, regenerate believers', that is, 'all of the redeemed of all ages', the visible church here on earth is defined in this way:

> It will thus be seen that the organized church as an institution is not for Baptists, primary but secondary, functional and instrumental. It was intended to be, and exist as, the functioning agency of the Kingdom of God on earth and of its Gospel. Ideally, it should concretely and socially embody the universal spiritual Church as the Body of Christ in each community. It is the declarative agency of that power that has no direct saving authority or power. It proclaims salvation and offers it to man in the name of the Redeemer; it does not definitely administer or withhold salvation. It has no vicarious mediatorial function, but is committed to the proclamation of the complete, exclusive priesthood and sacrifice of Jesus Christ as the Lamb of God that taketh away the sin of the world. Baptists thus find no place in, and no place for any hierarchy and no saving value in any sacrament.[9]

In this understanding of ecclesiology, there are several factors that mitigate against applying sacramental language to the visible church.

1. *The Church as Herald.* In speaking of the 'declarative agency' of the church whose primary function is to 'proclaim salvation...in the name of the Redeemer,' the BWA response to *BEM* identifies Baptists as those for whom the 'word' is primary and the 'sacrament' secondary. On this view, the church is essentially a herald of the lordship of Jesus Christ. Its essence is essentially proleptic: its message does not terminate upon itself but rather anticipates and to some extent precipitates (cf. Mt. 24.14) the coming reign of God. As Avery Dulles has shown, this view finds a parallel in Roman Catholic theology in Hans Küng who stresses the kerygmatic role of the church: 'It is the reign of God which the Church hopes for, bears witness to, proclaims. It is not the bringer or the bearer of the reign of God which is to come and is at the same time

---

9   William R. Estep, 'A Response to *Baptism, Eucharist, and Ministry: Faith and Order Paper no. 111*', in William H. Brackney and Ruby J. Burke (eds.), *Faith, Life, and Witness: The Papers of the Study and Research Division of the Baptist World Alliance, 1986–1990* (Birmingham, AL: Samford University Press, 1990), p. 3. The words quoted here are actually those of Baptist missiologist W.O. Carver. See Carver's essay, 'The Baptist Conception of the Church', printed under the title 'Denominational Statements 6. Baptist Churches', in R. Newton Flew (ed.), *The Nature of the Church* (New York: Harper and Brothers Publishers, 1951), p. 289. I take this statement and the paper in which it was quoted as fairly representative of Baptist views, although it was not endorsed officially by the Baptist World Alliance.

already present, but its voice, its announcer, its *herald*. God alone can bring his reign; the Church is devoted entirely to its service.'[10]

This is not to say, of course, that the event of proclamation is devoid of sacramental power. Quite the contrary. In declaring that 'the preaching of the Word of God is the Word of God,' the Second Helvetic Confession (1566) exalted the *ex opere operato* character of Christian proclamation. As the Lord says through the prophet Isaiah, it is my word that goes forth from my mouth: It will not return to me empty' (Isa. 55.11). Or, in the language of St Paul, the preaching of the gospel has an irrevocable effect: it conveys either the sweet fragrance of salvation or the noxious odor of perdition (2 Cor. 2.14-16). The dominical sacraments of baptism and the Lord's Supper also have a heraldic function in the economy of salvation. They are 'the visible words of God' proclaiming in visual, tactile and olfactory ways what the preacher has declared audibly in the exposition of holy scripture.

One of the questions posed here is this: can the kerygmatic and sacramental understandings of the church reinforce and support, rather than cancel out, one another? The most helpful effort in this direction thus far has come from the second phase of the Reformed–Roman Catholic Dialogue in the document, 'Towards a Common Understanding of the Church (1984–1990)'. Here the two conceptions of the church as '*creatura verbi*' and 'sacrament of grace,' are seen as possibly 'expressing the same instrumental reality under different aspects, as complimentary to each other or as two sides of the same coin'. At the same time, it is noted that these two conceptions provide a basis of creative tension between Roman Catholic and Reformed communities, a tension that comes to the fore on issues of ecclesial continuity and ministerial order.

2.   *The Primacy of Jesus Christ.* In describing the non-sacramental character of the visible church, the BWA statement declares that the church in its terrestrial form 'has no vicarious mediatorial function, but is committed to the proclamation of the complete, exclusive priesthood and sacrifice of Jesus Christ as the Lamb of God that taketh away the sin of the world'.[11] No ecclesial community in Christendom would deny that this latter statement is also true of its ministry and witness. However, to describe the church as sacramental seems to many Baptists and evangelicals to qualify the primacy of Christ in a way that compromises his essential lordship over the church both visible and invisible. We see this, for example, in the famous encyclical of Pope Pius XII, *Mystici corporis* (1943), in which the church is referred to *quasi altera Christi*

---

10   Hans Küng, *The Church* (New York: Sheed and Ward, 1968), p. 96. See also Avery Dulles, *Models of the Church* (New York: Doubleday, 1974), pp. 76-88.

11   Estep, 'A Response to Baptism, Eucharist, and Ministry', p. 3.

persona ('as if it were another person of Christ').[12] True enough, in some expressions of popular evangelical piety, the church is seen as the direct continuation of the incarnation in an almost crass way. As one popular ditty has it, 'Jesus has no hands but our hands to do his work today, no feet but ours to help folks on their way'. Quite apart from the pelagian and deistic overtones of such a statement, evangelicals at their best recoil from directly identifying Christ and the church lest the latter be made into an object of faith alongside of its Lord. Paul Tillich, among others, saw the temptation to put the historical church in the place of God as a step toward unwitting idolatry.[13] In the New Testament the metaphor of the body of Christ describes the relationship of believers to one another (in 1 Corinthians) and to Christ (in Ephesians and Colossians, where the body is distinguished from Christ, its head), but not to the environing world. In other words, 'the body image looks inwards and upwards but not outwards'.[14] This is not to project some monstrous discotomizing of head and body, but rather to insist on a proper distinguishing of the two.

3. *The Sovereignty of the Holy Spirit.* In describing the visible church as 'not primary but secondary, functional and instrumental', the BWA statement reflects the conviction, rooted in the Augustinian and Calvinist traditions, that the church and its sacraments never become eminent subjects of causality, that God the Holy Spirit remains sovereign even over the means he has chosen to draw men and women unto himself. Christ neither shares his glory nor gives his lordship to anyone else, not even to the church. The wind of the Spirit blows wherever it pleases (cf. Jn 3.8). This means that the church is the body of Christ, created and continually renewed by the awakening power of the Holy Spirit. It is the Holy Spirit who imparts faith to the believer and thus makes effective the *opus operatum* of the sacraments. The sacraments are thus seals of assurance and may not be dispensed with without spiritual detriment. But while *we* are bound to the sacraments, God is not. By no

---

12   Quoted from Paul Schrotenboer (ed.), *Roman Catholicism: A Contemporary Evangelical Perspective* (Grand Rapids, MI: Baker Book House, 1988), p. 21. However, the following statement in *Lumen Gentium* 8 does not equate, but only compares the church and the incarnation: 'For this reason the church is compared, not without significance, to the mystery of the incarnate Word. As the assumed nature, inseparably united to him, serves the divine Word as a living organ of salvation, so, in a somewhat similar way, does the social structure of the Church serve the spirit of Christ who vivifies it, in the building up of his body (cf. Eph. 4:15).'

13   Paul Tillich, *Systematic Theology* (Chicago: University of Chicago Press, 1963) III, pp. 162-82.

14   P.T. O'Brien, 'The Church as a Heavenly and Eschatological Entity', in D.A. Carson (ed.), *The Church in the Bible and the World: An International Study* (Grand Rapids, MI: Baker Book House, 1993), pp. 113-14.

means should we disparage the external means of grace God has given to the church in its earthly pilgrimage, but neither should we be surprised when by his Spirit God works in ways that go beyond our understanding but a touch less—*etiam extra ecclesiam*!

In thus shying away from sacramental language about the church, often preferring the word 'ordinances' instead of 'sacraments' when referring to the Lord's Supper and baptism, the Baptist and evangelical traditions have made a conscious protest against a kind of sacramental imperialism that seems to endow the sacraments with an importance such that without them salvation is not possible, a view undergirded by an exaggerated ecclesiology that treats the church as though it were itself divine. At least, statements such as 'the church contains Christ' and 'the sacraments make the church' seem to call into question the sovereign freedom of the Spirit no less than the lordship of Christ.

4.   *The Provisionality of the Visible Church.* Within the Baptist tradition, and especially within the Southern Baptist Convention, there are some who teach that there is an inviolate continuity of true visible churches, an unbroken ecclesial succession, extending back across the centuries to Jesus, John the Baptist, or 'the First Baptist Church of Jerusalem,' as the primitive Christian community described in Acts is anachronistically called. According to this view, no other true churches have ever existed except those that have received valid 'orders' and authentic 'sacraments' through this palpable, pipeline succession. Often enough, 'the trail of blood', as this view of church succession is sometimes called after a popular tract of the early twentieth century, leads through various dissenting and frequently quite heretical groups such as the Montanists, the Donatists, the Cathari, the Petrobrusiani, etc.. While no credible Baptist historian supports this thesis, it is still widely held in some quarters. Most Baptist theologians, however, reject this view as not only historically incredulous but also theologically unnecessary. While Jesus promised that the gates of hades would not prevail against his church, no where does scripture guarantee the permanence or perpetuity of any local congregation. In fact, in speaking to the churches of Asia Minor in Revelation 2 and 3, the risen Christ calls on them to repent lest their lampstands be removed (Rev. 2.5).

Evangelicals do not define the apostolicity of the church in terms of a literal, linear succession of duly ordained bishops, but point rather to the inscripturated witness of the apostles and the succession of apostolic proclamation. This is why failure to be faithful to the gospel is not a minor offense to be lightly passed over, but rather a life-threatening disorder to be constantly on guard against. Still, God has never left himself without a witness, even though it be the witness of a small remnant, sometimes persecuted, perhaps unseen and unknown to the chroniclers of church history (cf. Luther's *ecclesia latens*). In this sense, the Blessed Virgin Mary can indeed be *mater ecclesiae* for Baptists and evangelicals no less than for Orthodox and Roman Catholic Christians: Mary received the word of annunciation in faith ('She would not have conceived had she not believed,' said Luther) and she was at the center of those faithful few who stood vigil under the cross while others scurried for safety.

5.   *Protests against Impersonalism.* For Baptists and evangelicals, to say that the sacraments are constitutive of the church is to misunderstand our common sharing in holy things (*communio in sanctis*). The Pentecostal discussion partners in the Pentecostal–Roman Catholic Dialogue speak for all evangelicals when they declare that 'the central element of worship is the preaching of the Word. As persons respond to the proclamation of the Word, the Spirit gives them new birth, which is a presacramental experience, thereby making them Christians and in this sense creating the church.'[15] Baptists, of course, carry this principle even further delaying baptism until there is some evidence of conversion, with the result that this sacrament is really a testimony to a faith already openly professed. Baptists and other evangelicals are leery of defining the church as sacramental, in part because this appears to make the church and its sacraments automatic dispensers of salvation, thus undercutting the necessity of a personal appropriation of grace in the experience of the 'new birth'. Gerald Bray has posed four questions which evangelicals bring to the ecumenical conversation concerning their understanding of conversion: 'Why is the evangelical experience of salvation so important to those who have had it that they are often ready to discount other forms of Christianity as inauthentic? Can the evangelical experience not be found in other Christian traditions, expressed in a different way? And if it can, why do evangelicals stand apart from the rest of the church? On the other hand, if it can not, what claim do evangelicals have to be authentically Christian, especially in a way that implies that exclusion of others?'[16] These are questions that bear further investigation, but the Evangelical–Roman Catholic Dialogue on Mission (ERCDOM), a series of meetings which took place over a period of seven years (1977–1984), represents the most sustained engagement with these issues thus far.

---

15   'Final Report of the Pentecostal–Roman Catholic Dialogue', in Rusch and JGros (eds.), *Deepening Communion*, p. 416.

16   Gerald Bray, 'Evangelicals, Salvation, and Church History', in Thomas P. Rausch (ed.), *Catholics and Evangelicals: Do They Share a Common Future?* (New York: Paulist Press, 2000), p. 79.

Ecumenical Implications

From what has been said thus far, it is clear that most Baptists and evangelicals hold serious reservations about the ecumenical usefulness of describing the church itself as a sacrament. The reasons for this include, among others, the following points:

1.   As a term of ecumenical consensus, 'the church as sacrament' is of recent vintage, lacking sufficient biblical and patristic warrant. One well-known text from Cyprian is sometimes cited to the contrary: 'The Church is the indissoluble sacrament of unity'.[17] But these words which come from a letter of Cyprian dealing with the Novatian controversy are not without ambiguity and certainly cannot serve as a *Stichwort* for contemporary ecclesiology. Other concepts for the church such as 'the people of God', 'the Body of Christ' and 'the temple of the Holy Spirit' do not suffer from this disadvantage being firmly rooted in both scripture and tradition.

2.   Quite apart from ecclesial traditions which find sacramental language problematic, there are different, and perhaps contradictory, understandings of what a sacrament is not only, among, but also within, distinct communities of faith.

3.   Despite protests against ecclesiastical triumphalism and organizationalism, to define the church as sacrament serves in an ironic way to demystify it, that is, to make it less, rather than more, of a mystery. Historically, this has sometimes reinforced a sacramental will-to-power and resulted in an ecclesiology of glory, a temptation admittedly faced by all denominations and church traditions, not merely the so-called sacramental ones.

4.   Finally, to define the church as sacrament obscures the sole sufficiency and sovereignty of Jesus Christ who remains supremely free and does not surrender his royal prerogative even to the community that bears his name, nor to the signs and seals with which he blesses, nourishes and sanctifies his body. Christ, not the church, is both the *sacramentum* and the *res sacramenti*, both the sign and the reality signified: Christ alone is the *Ursakrament*.

Without surrendering these fundamental convictions, is it possible for Baptists and evangelicals to learn from and even appropriate the sacramental imagery of the church? In exploring such ecumenical challenges and opportunities, it is well to remember that we have come a long way since the time of Emil Brunner who remarked in his controversy over the church with Otto Karrer, 'It always remains

---

17   Cyprian, 'Treatise I. On the Unity of the Church', in A. Roberts and J. Donaldson (eds.), *The Ante-Nicene Fathers: Translations of the Fathers down to A.D. 325* (rev. A.C. Coxe; Grand Rapids, MI: Eerdmans, 1995), V, p. 422.

improbable that a genuine Catholic will ever allow himself to be persuaded by a genuine Protestant'.[18] Baptists and evangelicals still have far to go before we can talk meaningfully about a reconciliation of memories with our ecumenical partners, but we can applaud this statement from the Reformed–Roman Catholic dialogue: 'Shared memories, even if painful may in time become a basis for new mutual bonding and a growing sense of shared identity.'[19]

Cardinal Joseph Ratzinger offers a possible way forward in our present discussion in his description of the origin of the word *sacramentum* as a designation for the church in Vatican Council II. Ratzinger points out that the language of the church as sacrament, originally introduced to the council fathers from a draft composed by German theologians, was significantly altered by the Belgian theologian Gérard Philips.

> The German theologians state plainly and without more ads that the church is the sacrament of the union of men among themselves and with God. The Belgian text is more cautious in its approach. It begins by defining *sacramentum* as 'a sign and an instrument' but even then introduces the word itself with circumspection and a qualifying *veluti* ('as it were'), thus characterizing the usage as figurative by comparison with the usual use of the term and explaining it at the outset.[20]

The Latin *veluti* is frequently used to introduce a hypothetical comparative clause; it means 'as if', 'as though', 'just as', 'like as'. In rejecting the straightforward equation of church and sacrament in favor of the more considered, qualified expression *veluti sacramentum*, the council fathers showed great wisdom in recognizing the fundamentally analogous nature of this designation. The church *is* the people of God, the church *is* the body of Christ, but the church is 'like a sacrament', or 'a sort of sacrament'. If Ratzinger's explanation of this textual history is correct, then perhaps concerns raised by Baptists, evangelicals and other Protestants can be addressed in ways that benefit our common ecumenical quest. In conclusion, I suggest four possible avenues of further investigation along this line.

1.   Without actually defining the church as the continuation of the Incarnation, evangelicals can appreciate and affirm the incarnational character of Christ's presence and ministry in the work and witness of his people on earth. The language of the church 'embodying' the gospel points helpfully in this direction, as seen in this statement from the *Manila Manifesto* (1989), a document produced by a gathering of

18   Emil Brunner, *The Christian Doctrine of the Church, Faith and the Consummation* (Philadelphia: Westminster Press, 1960), p. 60.

19   'Towards a Common Understanding of the Church', pp. 224-25.

20   J. Ratzinger, *Principles of Catholic Theology* (San Francisco: Ignatius Press, 1987), pp. 44-45.

evangelicals committed to 'calling the whole church to take the whole gospel to the whole world':

> The church is intended by God to be a sign of His kingdom, that is, an indication of what human community looks like when it comes under His rule of righteousness and peace. As with individuals, so with churches, the Gospel has to be embodied if it is to be communicated effectively. It is through our love for one another that the invisible God reveals Himself today, especially when our fellowship is expressed in small groups, and when it transcends the barriers of race, rank, sex and age which divides other communities.[21]

2.   One of the most important pre-conciliar theologians who emphasized the sacramentality of the church was Henri de Lubac. For him the designation of the church as a sacrament stood in opposition to a kind of sacramental individualism that in essence reduced the Christian faith to a modern mystery religion.[22] Regrettably, many Baptists and evangelicals interpret their own conversion as a supreme act of individualism, a private response detached, if not divorced, from the corporate community of faith. Without diminishing the call for personal repentance and faith, evangelicals need to develop an authentic churchly spirituality drawn from the riches from the whole Christian tradition. And we might well begin this journey by recognizing the sacrament-*like* character of our own historic confessions, covenants and catechisms.[23]

3.   In the 1984 Apostolic Exhortation, *Reconciliatio et Paenitentia*, Pope John Paul II delineated three ways in which the church can be spoken of as sacrament: first, as a reconciled community which witnesses to the work of Christ in the world; second, as the custodian and interpreter of holy scripture, calling the entire world to the good news of reconciliation in Christ; and, finally, by reason of the seven sacraments each of which in its own way 'makes the church' and serve as means of 'conversion to God'. For reasons already stated, Baptist evangelicals have great difficulty accepting the third explanation given by the holy

---

21   John Stott (ed.), *Making Christ Known: Historic Mission Documents from the Lausanne Movement, 1974–1989* (Grand Rapids, MI: Eerdmans, 1996), pp. 241-42.

22   Ratzinger describes de Lubac's concern in this way: 'The concept of a Christianity concerned only with *my* soul in which I seek only *my* justification before God, *my* saving grace, *my* entrance into heaven, is for de Lubac that caricature of Christianity, that, in the nineteenth and twentieth centuries, made possible the rise of Atheism.' Ratzinger, *Principles*, p. 49. See also Henri de Lubac, *Catholicism: A Study of Dogma in Relation to the Corporate Destiny of Mankind* (trans. Lancelot C. Sheppard; London: Burns, Oates & Washbourne, 1950).

23   See Timothy George, 'An Evangelical Reflection on Scripture and Tradition', *Pro Ecclesia* 9 (2000), pp. 184-207.

father.[24] However, the first and second interpretations of sacramentality are surely consonant with Baptist and evangelical understandings of the church's mission and witness. Committed as they are to the sufficiency of holy scripture and the Reformation principle of *sola scriptura*, evangelicals do not accept the infallible teaching authority of any ecclesial jurisdiction. They do regard the Bible itself *veluti sacramentum* and believe that the scriptures are to be read and interpreted in the context of a covenanted community of faith. Indeed, Baptist evangelicals would likely respond more warmly to ecumenical initiatives and projects centered on the common study of holy scripture than to theological investigations of the nature of the church.

4. One aspect of regarding the church 'like a sacrament' points to its character as a community that necessarily points beyond itself. Put otherwise, the church *veluti sacramentum* may serve, when and where God so wills it and permits it by his grace, as a sign that conveys that which it signifies (e.g. the 'real presence of Christ in the eucharist'), but the church is always a sign that does not rest in itself; it is always on the way to something else. Here on earth, the church is always *ecclesia in via*. This means that the church always exists in a state of becoming, buffeted by struggles, under the sign of the cross. As Luther says in *The Large Catechism*, the church on earth is 'God's little holy flock...it is called together in one faith, one mind and understanding. It possesses a variety of gifts, yet it is united in love without sect or schism...until the last day the Holy Spirit remains with the holy community or Christian people.'[25]

---

24   An extract from this text is printed in J. Neuner and J. Dupuis (eds.), *The Christian Faith* (New York: Alba House, 1996), pp. 316-17.

25   Theodore Tappert (ed.), *The Book of Concord* (Philadelphia: Fortress, 1981), p. 417.

CHAPTER 3

Sacraments and Religious Liberty: From Critical Practice to Rejected Infringement[1]

Philip E. Thompson

A cliché of Baptist self-understanding is that Baptists have been champions of religious liberty from their beginnings. 'We (Baptists) did not stumble upon the doctrine', J.D. Freeman declared before the Baptist World Alliance in 1905: 'It inheres in the very essence of our belief.'[2] This is certainly true. Clichés would not achieve the status of cliché were they not at a basic level true. Yet clichés may also obscure when they are accepted uncritically and handed on without examination. This particular cliché, I believe, obscures something vital: the fact of radical changes in Baptist discourse concerning the very religious liberty that lies at the heart of their heritage. Nowhere is this more evident than in their

---

1   This essay was developed from material first presented in P.E. Thompson, 'Religious Liberty, Sacraments, God Image, and the State in Two Periods in Baptist Life and Thought' (paper presented to the Forty-Sixth Annual Convention of the College Theology Society, Philadelphia, PA, 4 June 2000). I wish to thank Mr Aaron Kilbourn, my teaching assistant at North American Baptist Seminary, for his assistance in conducting research that enabled me to further the work I began in that presentation.

2   J.D. Freeman, 'The Place of Baptists in the Christian Church', in W. Shurden (ed.) *The Life of Baptists in the Life of the World: 80 Years of the Baptist World Alliance* (Nashville, TN: Broadman Press, 1985), p. 20.

A short list of other representative texts may include E.Y. Mullins, 'The Baptist Conception of Religious Liberty', in Shurden (ed.), *Life of Baptists*, pp. 57-64; H.H. Hobbs, *The Baptist Faith and Message* (Nashville, TN: Convention Press, 1971), p. 143; B. Hays and J. Steely, *The Baptist Way of Life* (Macon, GA: Mercer University Press, 1981), p. 187; Norman Cavender, 'Freedom for the Church in a Free State', in A. Neeley (ed.), *Being Baptist Means Freedom* (Charlotte, NC: Southern Baptist Alliance, 1988), p. 83; W. Shurden, *The Baptist Identity: Four Fragile Freedoms* (Macon, GA: Smyth & Helwys, 1993), pp. 54-55; and G.C. Cothen and J.M. Dunn, *Soul Freedom: Baptist Battle Cry* (Macon, GA: Smyth & Helwys, 2000), pp. 27-48, 61-67, 83-87, 123-129, *et passim*. See the overview study by John Coffey, 'From Helwys to Leland: Baptists and Religious Toleration in England and America, 1612–1791', in D.W. Bebbington (ed.), *The Gospel in the World: International Baptist Studies* (Studies in Baptist History and Thought, 1; Carlisle: Paternoster, 2002), pp. 13-37.

discussion of the sacraments. In this essay I shall demonstrate how a sacramentalism born of the early Baptists' theological genius informed the parameters within which they spoke of religious liberty, and how in the North American context since the American Revolution this genius has been compromised in the very name of religious liberty.

Contours of Contemporary Baptist Views of Religious Liberty

Before turning to early Baptist sacramentalism, allow me to set forth a broadly inclusive sketch of contemporary Baptist understanding of religious liberty. Many Baptists reject the even the possibility of a historic sacramentalism in their heritage. They do so because they tend to retroject their own sensitivities and sensibilities onto their forebears.[3] We will keep the contemporary position in mind as we look back, asking whether such an agreement was in fact the case.

Many contemporary Baptists, following a convention some two centuries old, speak against the union of church and state and sacraments in one breath. Both fall under critique driven by concerns for religious (or 'soul') liberty and freedom of conscience. A large segment of Baptist scholars in America frequently correlates both strictures with the idea of 'soul competency', defined by E.Y. Mullins as the historic significance of the Baptists.[4] Soul competency basically posits a human right of direct dealing with God predicated upon human capacity to receive direct

---

3   A.R. Cross, for example, noted in a 1999 colloquium at Regent's Park College, Oxford, that the juxtaposition of 'Baptist' and 'sacramentalism' is unthinkable to many Baptists. The dominant belief is that Baptists early and late have been either non-sacramentalist or anti-sacramentalist. 'Dispelling the Myth of English Baptist Baptismal Sacramentalism', *Baptist Quarterly* 38.8 (October, 2000), pp. 367-91. See also Stanley K. Fowler's contribution to the present volume as another example of this. This may be something to which Baptists in America are particularly prone. B.A. Shain, *The Myth of American Individualism: The Protestant Origins of American Political Thought* (Princeton, NJ: Princeton University Press, 1994), p. xvii, notes that Americans are a 'people without a past' largely because Americans constantly recreate their past. E.Y. Mullins, 'Baptist Life in the World's Life', in Shurden (ed.), *Life of Baptists*, pp. 75-76, provides a Baptist example of this tendency: 'Now the Baptist type (of Christianity) is now and has been since the Anabaptist days of pre-Reformation times, different from any of the [other] types'. Mullins lists among these other the 'sacramental type'. Baptists, he notes, 'have no citadel of sacramental grace to defend'. Among Baptists' more 'evangelical' wing, cf. F.L. Anderson, 'Historic Baptist Principles', in *Baptist Fundamentals* (Philadelphia, PA: Judson Press, 1920), p. 17; and S.J. Grenz, *The Baptist Congregation: A Guide to Baptist Belief and Practice* (Valley Forge, PA: Judson, Press, 1985), p. 87, make similar statements.

4   E.Y. Mullins, *The Axioms of Religion: A New Interpretation of the Baptist Faith* (Phiadelphia, PA: Judson Press, 1908), pp. 45-58.

address from God. Mullins formulated the idea in connection with the cliché with which I began this discussion. He located the idea within a discussion of religious liberty in which he noted that 'There is no evidence that Baptists came to their view of soul freedom and separation of Church and State gradually.'[5] Thus Mullins made the competency of the human soul the foundation of what Baptists have 'ever' believed concerning religious liberty. Religious liberty, according to this interpretation, has always entailed Baptists' rejection of *any* external interference in the religious quest of the individual soul.

Mullins presented soul competency as a comprehensive truth, uniting and concentrating certain 'great streams of tendency in modern times'.[6] Among these streams he included 'the Anglo-Saxon principle of individualism which has been so potent a political force in modern times', and 'the Reformation principle, justification by faith'.[7] The trajectory of these assertions is clear. Yet there was more to the Baptist logic as Mullins delineated it. 'Baptists...have changed all these tendencies and modified them by elevating them to nobler forms and made them more fruitful.'[8] According to Mullins, Baptists had erected upon the 'platform of human rights in religion' a structure that recovered nothing less than 'New Testament Christianity' by their rejection of, among other things, church–state union *and a sacramental understanding of baptism and Lord's Supper.*[9] I will return to this line of thought presently. Let us first consider whether this presentation of 'historic Baptist identity' is in fact faithful to the early Baptists' own witness.

Baptist Beginnings: A Sacramentalism Both Careful and Critical

As persecuted Dissenters, the earliest Baptists quite naturally rejected the union of church and state and called for religious liberty. There is evidence in their writings that might lead to the conclusion that they were anti-sacramentalists as well. For example, the *Second London Confession* of 1677 very often follows verbatim its model, *The Westminster Confession*. Yet in articles XXVIII-XXX of the Baptist confession, sacramental terminology is replaced with the term 'ordinance', more

---

5   Mullins, *Axioms*, p. 47.
6   Mullins, *Axioms*, p. 57.
7   Mullins, *Axioms*, pp. 60-63.
8   Mullins, *Axioms*, p. 57.
9   Mullins, *Axioms, passim*; and Mullins, 'Baptist Conception', pp. 57-64. He also rejected sacerdotalism, civil or ecclesiastical imposition of creeds, and polity other than congregational.

familiar to Baptists.[10] Indeed, with the exception of the 1678 *Orthodox Creed*, all major confessions of the Baptists' first century of existence either employed the term 'ordinance', or simply called the rites by name and thus avoided the issue of terminology.

We also find strident criticism of sacramental practices from the pens of seventeenth-century Baptists. Of these rites John Bunyan exclaimed, 'But shall they be my God? or shall I have of them so foul and impious a Thought, To think that from the Curse they can me save?'[11] Elsewhere Bunyan cautioned that, notwithstanding the dominical institution of baptism, '[i]t is possible to commit idolatry with God's own appointments'.[12] In good Calvinist fashion, Benjamin Keach asked whether baptism was capable of bringing persons into God's election; or whether lack of it could cast them out.[13] Very early in the Baptist movement, Thomas Helwys questioned the Reformed insistence that baptism was a sacramental seal; though he took matters rather too literally. Water, he argued, cannot seal since it makes no physical impression.[14] Rejection of transubstantiation and the sacrifice of the Mass was commonplace in Baptists' confessions.[15]

It might seem from these examples that those who portray early Baptists as the anti-sacramentalists their contemporary namesakes are have solid grounds upon which to build their case. These statements do not, however, exhaust early Baptist sentiment. The earliest Baptists did indeed call baptism and the Lord's Supper 'ordinances'. Yet 'ordinance' was a broadly inclusive term that encompassed as well preaching, corporate and private prayer, works of mercy, and personal reading of scripture. Within this broad category, baptism and the Supper had special eminence. 'What are those Gospel Ordinances called Sacraments, which do confirm us in this Faith?', asked Keach's

---

10   *Second London Confession*(1677), in W.L. Lumpkin (ed.), *Baptist Confessions of Faith* (Valley Forge, PA: Judson Press, rev. edn, 1969), pp. 290-93. Cf. J.H. Leith (ed.) *Creeds of the Churches* (Louisville, KY: John Knox Press, 3rd edn, 1982), pp. 223-27.

11   J. Bunyan, 'A Book for Boys and Girls', in Graham Midgley (ed.), *The Miscellaneous Works of John Bunyan* (11 vols; Oxford: Clarendon Press, 1980–85), IV, p. 212.

12   J. Bunyan, *A Confession of My Faith and A Reason of My Practice—or—With Who, And Who Not, I Can Hold Church Fellowship*, in George Offor (ed.), *The Works of John Bunyan* (2 vols; Glasgow: Blackie & Son, 1853), p. 604.

13   B. Keach, *A Counter-Antidote* (London: H. Bernard, 1694), p. 32.

14   T. Helwys, *A Short Declaration of the Mistery of Iniquity* (London: Thomas Helwys, 1611), pp. 175-76.

15   *Second London Confession* and the *Orthodox Creed* (1679), in Lumpkin (ed.), *Baptist Confessions*, pp. 291-93 and 321-22 respectively.

catechetical work, *The Child's Delight*.[16] There is ample evidence that
early Baptists regarded the sacraments as means of grace appointed by
God to strengthen and increase faith unto salvation.[17] 'And as [Israel]
had the manna to nourish them in the wilderness to Canaan', confessed
the Midlands General Baptists, 'so have we the sacraments, to nourish us
in the church, and in our wilderness condition'.[18] Even Bunyan, who
cautioned against idolatry with God's appointments, said of baptism and
the Table, 'Here's such as helpeth Man's Salvation.'[19]

This careful nuance of sacramental thought displays the same dynamic
that drove the Baptists' critical stance vis-à-vis the state. I am not aware of
extensive scholarly attention devoted to this aspect of early Baptist
witness. To enable our analysis, I will draw upon elements of Peter
Berger's sociological theory of religion.

Sacraments as Legitimating and Delegitimating Rites

Berger's discussion of legitimation and alienation enables us to
appreciate a crucial aspect of the dynamics of early Baptists'
sacramentalism. Society, according to Berger, is an enterprise of human
world building. It is human meaning externalized in human activity. The
great 'societal hypostases' such as 'the economy' and 'the state' are
reducible to the human activity that is their underlying substance. There
is thus an inherent precariousness to socially constructed worlds. To
support these, in Berger's terminology, 'swaying edifices', society often
manifests coercive power. Ultimately, society's final coerciveness lies not
in 'machineries of social control', the legislative and judicial systems,

---

16   B. Keach, *The Child's Delight: Or Instructions for Children and Youth* (London:
William and Joseph Marshall, 1702), p. 38. Cf. B. Keach's *The Baptist Catechism*
(Grand Rapids, MI: Baker Book House, 1952 [1683]), pp. 39-40.

17   This understanding was present even in confessions that did not employ
explicit sacramental terminology. Cf. the *Second London Confession*, p. 268, 'The
Grace of *Faith*, whereby the Elect are enabled to believe to the saving of their souls, is
the work of the *Spirit of Christ*; in their hearts; and is ordinarily wrought by the Ministry
of the Word; by which also, and by the administration of *Baptisme*, and the *Lords Supper*,
Prayer and other *Means* appointed of *God*, it is increased and strengthened', emphasis
original.

18   *Orthodox Creed*, pp. 311-12.

19   J. Bunyan, *A Discourse on the Building, Nature, Excellency and Government of
the House of God*, in Midgley (ed.), *Miscellaneous Works*, VI p. 276. For a more
developed presentation of this reading of early Baptist thought, cf. P.E. Thompson, 'A
New Question in Baptist History: Seeking a Catholic Spirit Among Early Baptists', *Pro
Ecclesia* 8.1 (Winter, 1999), pp. 51-72.

'but in (society's) power to constitute and impose itself as a reality' beyond human construction.[20]

This comes about through processes of legitimation, which Berger defines as the impartation of 'socially objectivated "knowledge" that serves to explain and justify the social order', implying a symmetry between objective and subjective definitions of reality.[21] When this symmetry becomes thoroughly internalized, the fact of society's human construction is lost. Berger calls this condition 'alienation'.[22]

Religion, according to Berger, has been the most effective and widely used means of legitimation throughout human history. It is also, therefore, the great underwriter of alienation. Religion serves to legitimate the power arrangements of the social order through bestowal of 'an ultimately valid ontological status', and then alienate the arrangements by 'locating them within a sacred cosmic frame of reference'.[23] Examination of the ecclesio–political context within which Baptists arose provides us with concrete examples of these processes.

In 1628, Charles I began 'The King's Declaration'

> Being by God's ordinance...Defender of the Faith and Supreme Governor of the Church within these our dominions, we hold it most agreeable to this our kingly office and our own religious zeal to conserve and maintain the Church committed to our charge in unity of true religion and the bond of peace; and not to suffer unnecessary disputations, altercations or questions to be raised which may nourish factionalism both in the Church and commonwealth.[24]

He warned further that 'Any disputes should be shut up in God's promises, as they be generally set forth to us in the Holy Scriptures and the general meanings of the Articles of the Church of England according to them.'[25]

While this declaration primarily addressed factions within the Church of England rather than those who had already embarked along the path of separation, the legitimating function is evident. Following the Interregnum (1649–59) it was even more urgent that the state and state church be legitimated. Already England had suffered the social and political convulsions of the Saints' Regime. Berger notes, 'To go against the order of society is always to risk plunging into anomy. To go against

---

20   P. Berger, *The Sacred Canopy: Elements of a Sociological Theory of Religion* (New York: Doubleday, 1967), pp. 3-12 and 29.

21   Berger, *Canopy*, pp. 29-32. Berger notes further that '[a]ll legitimation serve to maintain reality—reality, that is, as defined in a particular human collectivity'.

22   Berger, *Canopy*, p. 85.

23   Berger, *Canopy*, pp. 32-34.

24   'The King's Declaration, 1628', in G. Bray (ed.), *Documents of the English Reformation* (Minneapolis, MN: Fortress Press, 1994), p. 481.

25   'The King's Declaration, 1628', p. 481.

the order of society as religiously legitimated...is to make a compact with the primeval forces of darkness.'[26] Just this strategy was employed in the Restoration of the Monarchy. The 1662 'Act of Uniformity' of Charles II hearkened to the Elizabethan 'Act of Uniformity', remembering that it was 'very comfortable to all good people desirous to live in Christian conversation and most profitable to the estate of this realm'.[27] Indeed, on said realm, 'the mercy, favour and blessing of Almighty God is in no wise so readily and plentifully poured as by common prayers, [and] due use of the sacraments'.[28] Dissenters, against whom penalties were levied for refusal to conform, were defined as 'following their own sensuality, and living without knowledge and due fear of God'.[29]

The 'Act of Uniformity' served to justify employment of 'machineries of social control' against Baptists and other Dissenters. The 'Act of Indulgence' brought some measure of relief in 1672, but the next year brought the 'Test Act'. According to Gerald Bray, this act represented High Church Anglicanism in which the English state was the political manifestation of the Christian people of England. Thus anyone not a member in good standing in the state church was barred from full privileges of citizenship. Dissenters on the right and left were

> Disabled from thenceforth to sue or use any action, bill, plaint, or information in course of law, or to prosecute any suit in any court of equity, or to be guardian of any child, or executor or administrator of any person, or capable of any legacy or deed of gift, or to bear any office in this realm of England...[30]

Not only official acts and legally binding documents serve to legitimate the meanings and arrangements of societies and their institutions. Berger notes that ritual acts share this function.[31] While Berger acknowledges the place of ritual, he attends more to formal explanations, the *'legoumena'* rather than the *'dromena'*. We cannot allow ritual to be minimized, however. Paul Connerton has observed that rites are not merely expressive; simply visual representations of ideas. Ritual performances are essentially legitimating performances that form persons as dwellers of a given social world.[32] Thus 'common prayers and the due use of the sacraments' and the unifying theology of the *Thirty-Nine Articles* were both critical in preservation of the social world of

---

26   Berger, *Canopy*, p. 39.

27   'The Act of Uniformity, 1662', in Bray (ed.), *Documents*, pp. 547-48.

28   'The Act of Uniformity, 1662', p. 548.

29   'The Acts of Uniformity, 1662', p. 548; cf. pp. 550-59.

30   'The Test Act, 1673', in Bray (ed.), *Documents*, p. 566.

31   Berger, *Canopy*, p. 40.

32   P. Connerton, *How Societies Remember* (Cambridge: Cambridge University Press, 1989), pp. 35-45.

seventeenth-century England. Ritual and explanation, sacrament and theology, were alike vital components in Baptist critique of and resistance to the state and its church.

The theology and practices of seventeenth-century Baptists revealed a guiding conviction that God must be free to exercise divine prerogative in salvation. Their critique of and resistance to the state church were rooted in this theological intuition. The early Baptists, General and Particular, were consistent in holding steadfastly to the absolute ontological unlikeness between God and humanity, the epistemological corollaries of this unlikeness, and the full implications of both. In this, the Baptists reveal the most consistent development of the Reformed tradition's impulse against idolatry.[33]

With the exception of the *Second London Confession*, all major Baptist confessions of their first century began by declaring this ontological gap.[34] The hymnody and catechesis of the Baptist forebears echoes this witness. When they began to sing, early Baptists sang of 'God whom we cannot see; He dwells in light inaccessible, Which can't approachéd be.'[35] Thomas Grantham prefaced his *St. Paul's Catechism* with the assertion that the sum of revelation may be comprehended in two particulars: first, 'there is but one true and living God'; and second, that it is unlawful to form any shape, image, or representation of God, not even 'so much as in our minds or imaginations'.[36] Why this is so important finds explanation in a catechetical piece by Keach. God is 'increated Spirit' who is 'of and from himselfe', and so 'Inconceivable in his Being'. Human beings, on the other hand, are '[c]reated finite spirits'. Human spirits, no less created from nothing than physical bodies, are no more like the divine being than human bodies.[37] These affirmations concerning God and corresponding denials with regard to humanity are crucial to the subject of religious liberty.

---

33   I can give only the barest sketch of this here. For fuller treatment, cf. P.E. Thompson, 'People of the Free God: The Passion of Seventeenth Century Baptists', *American Baptist Quarterly* 15.3 (September, 1996), pp. 223-41.

34   Cf., e.g., the Particular Baptist *London Confession* (1644), in Lumpkin (ed.), *Baptist Confessions*, p. 156, which declares 'That God as he is in himselfe, cannot be comprehended by any but himselfe, dwelling in that inaccessible light, that no eye can attaine unto, whom never man saw, nor can see', and p. 225, where the General Baptist *Standard Confession (1660)* confesses God to be 'unwordable in all his attributes'.

35   B. Keach, *Spiritual Melody* (London: n.p., 1691), p. 49. Since hymn singing was itself long a controverted practice, it seems likely that extra care would be taken to keep the sung theology well within generally accepted parameters.

36   T. Grantham, *St. Paul's Catechism* (London: n.p., 1687), pp. 4-6.

37   B. Keach, *Instructions for Children* (London: n.p., n.d.), p. 19. Cf. J. Bunyan, *Instructions for the Ignorant Being a Salve To Cure That Great Want of Knowledge...*, in Offor (ed.) *Works of John Bunyan*, II, p. 676.

This ontological distance provided Baptists with great critical leverage vis-à-vis the state, its church and its claims. Their conviction was firm that God's prerogatives could not be usurped, yet precisely this was what happened in the rites, prescriptions and theology of the state church. We need to be clear that the early Baptists believed the state church to be an affront not against individual conscience, but against God. Thomas Helwys criticized the Church of England's prescription of prayers and rites of repentance because then people 'must pray and repent as you by your power appoint them'. This work by Helwys is identified by Baptist historians as quite possibly the earliest English plea for universal religious liberty.[38] The basis of this plea becomes clear only as we continue with Helwys' invective. 'Have you the power', he continued, 'also to appoint the Lord to accept these praiers and repentances? Or do you not care whether the Lord accept them or no, so that you be submitted to?'[39] '[A]ll the power on Earth cannot make one Institute or Divine ceremony in Religion', declared Grantham.[40] The reason, again, was 'because (as we conceive) God's Authority is then usurped by Man'.[41] Helwys argued further that the desire of the state was not merely the usurpation of the power of God, but the glory that was due God alone.[42] In other words, the sin of the state church was not in the first place violation of the rights of conscience, but idolatry.[43]

Berger would have us remember that religion not only legitimates the social order and alienates it, it may also serve to de-alienate and de-legitimate it. Religious legitimation depicts institutions, the 'societal hypostases', as existing *sub specie aeternitatis* thus bestowing upon precarious human constructions the illusion of being part of the divine order as they are. Yet precisely by viewing these hypostases *sub specie aeternitatis*, they may also be radically relativized. '[T]he confrontation of the social order with the...transcendent God may also relativize this order to such an extent that one may validly speak of de-alienation—in the sense that before the face of God, the institutions are revealed as

38   H.L. McBeth, *The Baptist Heritage: Four Centuries of Baptist Witness* (Nashville, TN: Broadman Press, 1987), p. 103.

39   Helwys, *Mistery*, p. 19.

40   T. Grantham, *The Loyal Baptist or An Apology for Baptized Believers* (London: Tho. Grantham, 1684), p. 8.

41   Grantham, *Loyal Baptist*, p. 10.

42   Helwys, *Mistery*, pp. 23 and 44.

43   Helwys, *Mistery*, pp. 18-19, likened the rites of the state church to the golden calves set up by Jeroboam (1 Kgs 12.25-33). J. Smyth, *Principles and Inferences Concerning the Visible Church*, in W.T. Whitley (ed.), *The Works of John Smyth, Fellow of Christ's College 1594-98* (2 vols; Cambridge: Cambridge University Press, 1915), I, p. 253, said that to worship according to Anglican rites was 'to joyne to Idols, or to worship God in or by Idols'.

nothing but human works'.[44] This is precisely what the early Baptists' insistence upon the ontological gap between God and humanity and the corresponding freedom of God from all things human did.

The Baptists of seventeenth century England believed that the society in which they lived had itself become a false god because it was built upon idolatry. Early in the century, John Smyth had observed, 'the Idolatryes of Antichrist are not heathenish & paganish, but of another nature, viz. not false gods, but means invented by men to worship the true God by'.[45] This logic endured throughout the century. A subtle, yet striking example of this is the way in which the *Orthodox Creed*, written between the 'Test Act' (1673) and the 'Act of Toleration' (1689), actually appropriated the language of the *Thirty-Nine Articles* at key points, couching the Anglican affirmations in such a way as to critique them powerfully. The *Articles'* Preface stated their purpose 'for the avoiding of diversities of opinions, and for the stablishing of consent touching true religion'.[46] The First Article then declares that 'There is but one living and true God, everlasting, without body, parts or passions'.[47] God is 'without body, parts, or passions', and yet we have seen how God was to be identified through, and so in some sense with, the state church, its rites and articles. The Midlands Baptists thus began their confession

> We verily believe, that *there is but one*, only *living and true God*; whose subsistence is in and of himself; a most pure, spiritual, or invisible substance; who hath absolute, independent, unchangeable, and infinite being; *without* matter or form, *body, parts or passions*. For I am the Lord, I change not; God is a spirit. Now unto the king eternal, immortal, invisible, the only wise God, be honour and glory, for ever and ever, Amen. Ye heard a Voice, but saw no similitude.[48]

The embedding of the Anglican terminology within the absolute rejection of any earthly representation of God was not, I believe, coincidental, but reveals a strongly critical stance.

The logic of contemporary Baptists, were it truly that of the earliest Baptists as well, would dictate that the forebears reject sacraments altogether in response to the sacraments of the idolatrous state church. As we have seen, however, they did not reject sacraments. Indeed, the sacraments, baptism in particular, were of special importance to the early Baptists' critical stance. This was so because the full logic of the Baptists'

---

44   Berger, *Canopy*, pp. 96-99.

45   J. Smyth, *Parallels: Censures: Observations*, in Whitley (ed.), *Works of John Smyth*, II, p. 344.

46   *The Thirty-Nine Articles*, in Bray (ed.), *Documents*, p. 285.

47   *Thirty-Nine Articles*, p. 285.

48   *Orthodox Creed*, p. 298, italics mine.

theology of God's freedom required a principle of mediation. The only
living and true God was free to work in and through the things of earth as
God ordained. Certainly, the Baptists strove to maintain a careful balance
at this point, but they did not reject the sacramental idea. The locus of
this second aspect of God's freedom, that to mediate grace unto salvation,
was the church and sacraments.

While considerable attention in our own time is given to the
political/ethical dimensions of the eucharist, the early Baptists emphasized
baptism. Baptism was the sacrament that set the boundary that situated
and gave proper significance to all human bodies: individual, communal
or political.[49] It relativized all other political expressions by locating the
true politics within the church. We might say, adapting William
Cavanaugh's phrase, our Baptists practiced 'baptismal anarchism'.[50] We
see this relocation of politics from state to church in the *London
Confession* (1644). Here the early Particular Baptists confessed that

> Christ hath here on earth a spirituall Kingdome, which is the Church, which he hath
> purchased and redeemed unto himself, as a peculiar inheritance: which Church, as it
> is visible to us, is a company of visible Saints, called & separated from the world,
> by the word and Spirit of God, to the visible profession of the faith of the Gospel,
> being baptized into that faith, and joyned to the Lord, and each other, by mutuall
> agreement, in the practical injoyment of the Ordinances, commanded by Christ
> their head and King.[51]

The church for the early Baptists was the earthly arena in which the reign
of Christ was embodied, and as such was the interruption and
delegitimization of the idolatrous politics of the state. There was no
equivocation concerning where true government lay. It was in the politics
of the risen and ascended Lord.

> Touching his Kingdome, Christ being risen from the dead, ascended into heaven,
> sat on the right hand of God the Father, having all power in heaven and earth, given
> to him, he doth spiritually govern his Church, exercising his power over all Angels
> and Men, good and bad, to the preservation and salvation of the elect, to the
> overruling and destruction of his enemies...communicating and applying the
> benefits, vertue, and fruit of his Prophesie and Priesthood to his elect...to their
> justification and adoption as Sonnes, regeneration, sanctification, preservation
> and strengthening in all their conflicts against Satan, the World, the Flesh, and the
> temptations of them...notwithstanding through our own unbeliefe, and the
> temptations of Satan, the sensible sight of this light and love be clouded and

---

49   Cf. G. Ward, 'Bodies: The Displaced Body of Jesus Christ', in J. Milbank, C.
Pickstock and G. Ward (eds.), *Radical Orthodoxy* (London: Routledge, 1999), p. 176.
50   W. Cavanaugh, 'The City: Beyond Secular Parodies', in Milbank, Pickstock and
Ward (eds), *Radical Orthodoxy*, pp. 194-98.
51   *London Confession* (1644), p. 165.

overwhelmed for the time. And on the contrary, ruling in the world over his enemies, Satan, and all the vessels of wrath, limiting, using, restraining them by his mighty power, as seems good in his divine wisdome & justice to the execution of his determinate counsel...to be kept through their own deserts in darknesse and sensuality unto judgment.[52]

Grantham similarly indicted the state church of sin against God by bringing persons 'by the lump into the Name of Christian Churches' and using state power to suppress the true church, so overlaying the politics of Christ with its own.

Let us give Precedency to Christ's Church which doth live this day in Jayls, in holes and dens of Thieves...the Minster laid great claim Unto [Christ's] Churches Interest and Name; And yet, by her most earnest procuration, Some men she did surprise by captivation, And lock't them up within [prison] gates, because they would not cease to keep [Christ's] Antient Laws.[53]

Salvation for these early Baptists, was available by the freedom of God in the church, but only as the church practiced the politics of Christ. Again at this crucial juncture, the Midlands General Baptists appropriated the Anglican terminology to make their own critical case. The twentieth Anglican *Article* states:

The visible Church of Christ is a congregation of faithful men in which the pure Word of God is preached and the sacraments be duly administered, according to Christ's ordinance...[54]

By way of contrast, the Baptists utilized the language of the congregation, but related this to the practices and politics of the Body of Christ.

[We] believe the *visible church of Christ* on earth, is made up of several distinct *congregations*, which make up that one catholick church, or mystical body of Christ. And the marks by which she is known to be the true spouse of Christ, are these, viz., Where *the word of God* is rightly *preached*, and *the sacraments* truly *administered, according to Christ's* institution...; to which church and not elsewhere, all persons that seek for eternal life, should gladly join themselves...[55]

---

52   *London Confession* (1644), pp. 161-62. Cf. *The Faith and Practice of Thirty Congregations* (1651), p. 183; *The Somerset (Particular Baptist) Confession* (1656), pp. 207-208; *The Standard Confession* (1660), pp. 231-35; *Second London Confession*, pp. 279-80; *Orthodox Creed*, pp. 331-32, all in Lumpkin (ed.), *Baptist Confessions*.

53   T. Grantham, *The Prisoner Against the Prelate...* (n.p.: n.d., c.1662), pp. 23-27, 76-77.

54   *The Forty-Two Articles, 1553*, in Bray (ed.), *Documents*, p. 296.

55   *Orthodox Creed*, pp. 318-19, emphasis mine.

Persons were not to seek salvation in a church in which God's prerogatives had been idolatrously usurped.

We must hasten to note that the Baptists realized that the sacraments had to be not mere symbols, but truly sacraments that mediate the free grace of the unimageable God. For this salvation to be really the case, Christ had to be really and externally present. Why was this? Christ had to take form in the politics of the community of faith, or else the Baptists' claim lost its sure foundation. Robert Jenson has appropriately observed that a disembodied personal presence cannot bless, but only curse. The presence of Christ, Jenson argues, is sacramentally embodied among the community in order that this presence not simply pass into subjectivity, whether individual or collective. For the presence of Christ to become subjectivized would make participation in it a variety of 'work', and so another sort of usurpation of God's prerogatives. Jenson quotes Luther on baptism, 'faith here hangs on the water'.[56] This is, perhaps surprisingly, not far from the early Baptists' views, certainly not as far as the contemporary position might lead one to surmise.

Early Baptists believed that Christ was present in baptism by the power of the Holy Spirit, and so was salvifically active in the rite. According to Grantham, 'it is Christ who is held forth in baptism, which saveth'.[57] Helwys argued that in Christ, the water of baptism and the Holy Spirit are bound together inseparably.[58] As the sacrament of Christ's presence, baptism was also the sacrament of initiation into Christ's body the church. In this sense, Grantham affirmed the propriety of calling baptism the 'sacrament of regeneration'. There are two moments in regeneration, he explained, mortification and vivification. '[T]hat first is called burial with Christ, and second a rising with Christ' to new life not only with Christ, but in Christ, that is, in the church.[59] The Particular Baptist *Somerset Confession* described baptism as 'planting' people in the church, while the General Baptist *Faith and Practice of Thirty Congregations* equated the time of baptism with the time at which one becomes a member of the visible church.[60] The *Orthodox Creed* defined baptism as 'a sign of our entrance into the covenant of grace, and

---

56   R. Jenson, 'The Church and the Sacraments', in C. Gunton (ed.), *The Cambridge Companion to Christian Doctrine* (Cambridge: Cambridge University Press, 1997), pp. 211-13.

57   Grantham, *St. Paul's' Catechism*, pp. 35-36.

58   Helwys, *Mistery*, pp. 137-39.

59   T. Grantham, *Loyal Baptist*, p. 12. This work, despite the title, appears to be two conjoined works with separate pagination. This reference comes from the second work. Cf. T. Grantham, *Christianismus Primitivus: or The Ancient Christian Religion* (London: n.p., 1678), II/2.i.3, II/2.ii.3, II/2.ii.4; and Grantham, *St. Paul's Catechism*, p. 36.

60   *Somerset Confession*, p. 209; and *Thirty Congregations*, p. 182.

ingrafting into Christ, and into the body of Christ, which is his church; and of remission of sin in the blood of Christ, and of our fellowship with Christ in his death and resurrection'.[61]

The theological dispute over baptism among Particular Baptists is also enlightening in this regard. At issue was the necessity of baptism to church communion. John Bunyan argued that it was not. William Kiffin and Thomas Paul contended that it was.[62] It was in the context of this debate that Bunyan warned against making idols of God's appointments. Kiffin's rejoinder was that to discard what God has freely chosen for the work of salvation was a worse idolatry still, for it elevated human judgment over God's commands. As Jenson would put it, Bunyan's position reduced Christ's presence to mere subjectivity.[63] According to Kiffin, the one who cared not for 'Christ sacramental' cared not for 'Christ God', for in the former the latter draws near.[64] Christ had to be truly present in true sacramental practice, otherwise Baptist criticism of the state church's idolatrous practices would flounder on the shoals of a worse idolatry still, thus leveling the difference between the state and gathered churches.

Alteration and Loss in Post-Revolutionary America

Language concerning religious liberty has come to have a different grounding among Baptists in America since the American Revolution. Rather than approaching religious liberty from concern for the freedom of God, Baptists in America have largely adopted an anthropocentric calculus.[65] This has led to profound losses in Baptist thought and life, ironically in the name of preserving a hallmark Baptist belief. Fearing most encroachment upon human freedom, Baptists have, in their anthropocentric version of religious liberty, rejected the sacraments that

---

61   *Orthodox Creed*, p. 317. Cf. the similar, though not as elaborate, language in the 1677 *Second London Confession*, pp. 290-91.

62   Cf. J. Bunyan, *A Confession of My Faith and A Reason of My Practice:* ..., in Offor (ed.) *Works*, II, pp. 593-616; W. Kiffin, *A Sober Discourse on the Right to Church Communion* (London: George Larkin, 1681); and T. Paul, *Some Serious Reflections on that Part of Mr. Bunyan's Confession of Faith...* (London: n.p., 1673).

63   Indeed, Bunyan's case rested on a claim that faith is the spiritual antitype of circumcision, and so is the initiating 'rite' for Christians.

64   Kiffin, *Sober Discourse*, pp. 42-43.

65   The limitations of this paper do not allow careful tracing of this shift in American Baptist thought from the late eighteenth century into twentieth. For a more thorough discussion, see P.E. Thompson, 'Re-envisioning Baptist Identity: Historical, Theological, and Liturgical Analysis', *Perspectives in Religious Studies* 27.3 (Fall, 2000), pp. 287-302.

earlier served a critical function vis-à-vis the state, and fallen prey to what they fear the least. Unsuspectingly legitimating the liberal democratic state in the name of religious liberty, they have effected a union of sorts between the earthly and heavenly cities.

Cavanaugh interprets the modern state as the source of a soteriology alternative to that of the church. He contends that modern Christians have tended to succumb to the power of state soteriology, and often on Christian grounds.[66] Baptists in America, beginning significantly with John Leland (1754–1841), have fallen prey to precisely this, embracing a soteriology of a Jeffersonian cast.[67]

Cavanaugh claims that it was John Locke who eliminated the church body as a rival to the state body by redefining religion as a purely internal matter, an affair of the soul.[68] So removed, religion could then be interpreted in terms quite amenable to the goals of liberal democracy. Displaying what William McLoughlin has described as 'Calvinist-glossed Lockeanism', Leland located sovereign right not in God, but in the human conscience, and so defined religion as a matter between God and individuals, with the latter having the right of first refusal.[69] '[B]y liberty

---

66   Cavanaugh, 'The City', pp. 182 and 190.

67   R. McNeal, 'The Priesthood of All Believers', in P.A. Basden (ed.), *Has Our Theology Changed: Southern Baptist Thought Since 1845* (Nashville, TN: Broadman & Holman, 1994), p. 210, who notes that Baptists of the late eighteenth century, continuing into the nineteenth, merged experiential religion and Jeffersonian republicanism in a manner that allowed them to see liberal democracy as an authentic expression of early Christianity. Cf. J. Leland, 'Short Sayings', in L.F. Greene (ed.) *The Writings of John Leland* (New York: Arno Press and New York Times, 1969 [1845]), p. 579, in which Leland refers to Thomas Jefferson as 'the patriarch of liberty'. In 'A Blow at the Root: Being a Fashionable Fast-Day Sermon', in Greene (ed.), *Writings*, p. 255, Leland waxes eloquent that '[E]xertion of the American genius has brought forth the <u>Man of the People</u>, the defender of the rights of man and the rights of conscience, to fill the chair of state; who, in his inaugural speech, cries out, "America, be free, be happy, guard your own rights, and leave them not to the disposition of officers." Pardon me...if I am over-warm... The beneficent influence of my hero was too generally felt (when I lived in Virginia) to leave me stoic... Now the greatest orbit in America is occupied by the brightest orb.' Emphasis original.

That this was evident even in the twentieth century is clear from the 1923 comment by Mullins to the Baptist World Alliance meeting in Stockholm, 'Baptist Conception', p. 58, 'Jefferson had the spiritual vision to see that liberty is the fountainhead of civilization and that religious liberty is the mother of all other forms of liberty.'

68   Cavanaugh, 'The City', p. 190.

69   W.G. McLoughlin, *New England Dissent 1630–1833: The Baptists and the Separation of Church and State* (2 vols; Cambridge, MA: Harvard University Press, 1971), II, pp.751-752. Cf. N. Hatch, *The Democratization of American Christianity* (New Haven, CT: Yale University Press, 1989), pp. 97-100, who notes that as early as 1790 Leland began sounding the clarion call that 'conscience should be free from human

of conscience', wrote Leland, 'I mean, the inalienable right that each individual has of worshipping his God according to the dictates of his own conscience'.[70]

As this perspective developed, Baptists came to see the state and church in univocal terms; quite ironically to join the church and state in two ways. First, either could encroach upon the sovereign conscience; the state by legislation in 'matters of religion' (Leland and those who followed in his train would say 'matters of conscience'), and the church by creeds and sacraments.[71] Given the guarantee of institutional separation of church and state, however, Baptists seemed to believe that the more present danger was that presented by the church. Thus when Mullins declared that priestly and sacramental mediation in salvation was a violation of religious liberty, he was standing in a wide and long-flowing stream.[72]

We may find evidence of this in a peculiar myth that has operated in many Baptists' interpretation of ecclesiastical history, that of the church's fall into corruption. Certainly, the idea of a 'fall of the church' is not in itself peculiar to Baptists, but is an idea shared widely by evangelical Protestants.[73] Baptists in America since the late eighteenth century, though, have pressed the idea into their own peculiar polemical and apologetic service. Leland noted, displaying inadequate historical awareness, that grasping for position and pre-eminence within the church led to a situation in which '[t]he mystery of iniquity began to work, and anti-Christs arose, before the close of the apostolic age', in which bishops grasped after illicit power in the churches, imposing their own precepts in place of the 'essentials of Bible religion [which] are articles that lie between God and individuals'.[74] In the chapter of *The Axioms of Religion* in which he discusses religious liberty and defines soul competency, Mullins wrote of a struggle for supremacy between church and state that

---

control', and that Leland's passion was to protect the 'empire of conscience'. Together these worked to create his legacy of 'an exaggerated opposition to official Christianity'. McLoughlin, *New England Dissent*, pp. 928-29, notes tellingly that this was not innate to Baptists generally. Indeed, Leland's views were quite scandalous and widely deplored in many Baptist circles.

70   Leland, 'Short Sayings', p. 579. Cf. Shain, *Myth*, p. 141.

71   Hatch, *Democratization*, p. 97, quotes Leland as referring to creeds as 'this Virgin Mary between the souls of men and the Scriptures'. Such should not be surprising from one who, as McLoughlin, *New England Dissent*, p. 931, reminds us regarded all religious conviction as mere 'opinion'. Cf. Hatch, 'Sacred Cause', p. 153, and A. Hovey, *Religion and the State* (Boston, MA: Estes and Lauriat, 1874), pp. 21-25.

72   Mullins, 'Baptist Conception', p. 59.

73   Cf. D.H. Williams, *Retrieving the Tradition and Renewing Evangelicalism: A Primer for Suspicious Protestants* (Grand Rapids, MI: Eerdmans, 1999), pp. 101-31.

74   Leland, 'Short Sayings', pp. 579 and 581.

was resolved when '[i]n Gregory the spirit of the Roman Church became incarnated and conquered'.[75] The tragedy of the union of church and state appears to have been that the church, fallen from the purity of its early 'proto-Jeffersonian' ideals, co-opted the state. Gaines Dobbins cast the scenario thus: 'The Bishop of Rome gained ascendancy in the Patriarchate... At first he claimed powers that paralleled those of the Emperor, but with the decline of the Empire he boldly asserted his claim to spiritual and political supremacy, including progressively the nations of the Western world.'[76] The imposition upon conscience by which Baptist interpreters have characterized the Church of Rome found a vehicle in the civil realm. Mullins believed that the corruption of church and state stemmed from two yoked violators of conscience: imperialism and scaramentalism.[77] Why is the tragedy so construed?

The upshot of this interpretation has been the emergence of the liberal democratic state as the true guarantor of religious liberty and the rights of individual conscience, a second joining of church and state in principle and spirit if not in fact. Just prior to addressing the infiltration of the church by 'anti-Christs', Leland noted that it was the design of government to defend persons and rights, so that all may live together peacefully in the same domain.[78] It is the great end of human government, asserted Hovey, to protect individuals in the exercise of their natural rights. As such, the civil government 'may be called to protect the lives of the people against the violence of religious fanaticism'.[79] We might hope that Hovey intended to censure religion-inspired mob violence. Yet, he was not careful so to limit his stricture. Human government, he continued, is bound to conserve 'the liberties of the people against *all persons or influences* that would destroy them; and therefore, if any religious sect were known to deprive members of their personal freedom, it would be the duty of the state to restore them'.[80] Would this apply to a 'sect' that held sacramental and creedal convictions? We see the secular soteriology operating here in full force.

So blind have Baptists been to this alteration in their basic orientation, they have believed themselves in the vanguard of a great advance in Christian faith and earthly government. '[T]he intelligent Baptist', Mullins asserted, 'can yield to none in his patriotism, for his religious

---

75   Mullins, *Axioms*, pp. 47-48.
76   G.S. Dobbins, *Baptist Churches in Action* (Nashville, TN: Sunday School Board of the Southern Baptist Convention, 1929), p. 30.
77   Mullins, *Axioms*, p. 100.
78   Leland, 'Short Sayings', p. 579. This overcoming of conflict, which may be religious in nature, is precisely the focus of the secular soteriology of the modern state as Cavanaugh develops the idea.
79   Hovey, *Religion and the State*, pp. 33 and 40.
80   Hovey, *Religion and the State*, pp. 57-58.

ideals are the bed-rock of the political fabric'.[81] The remedy for
'tyranny' in any form became for Baptists a union of 'civil and religious
republicanism', a peculiar union of church and state. Yet this allowed *the
latter* to function as bearer of meaning in history.[82] We see this rather
plainly in Dobbins, who celebrated the frustrations of 'the ambitions of
shrewd ecclesiastics' by the grand sweep of political change that
culminated in democracy. 'As governments change, so eventually will the
polity of the churches; and as certainly as the democratic movement
succeeds, so certainly will the churches of the future govern
themselves.'[83]

Thus for Mullins, the final outworking of soul competency is seen in
the state at least as much as in the church, and perhaps to a greater
degree. He concluded his treatment of soul competency with these
remarkable assertions:

> Properly understood the doctrine of the soul's competency in religion is the
> summary of our progressive life and civilization. The religious principle is always
> the dominant force which gives its leading characteristics to any civilization. The
> competency of man in religion is the competency of man everywhere. Every
> significant movement of our day is one form or another of that high purpose of man
> to make his way back to God...[84]

If this is indeed the case, then the church has become superfluous, merely
a religious expression of tendencies present in the politics of the earthly
city; and one that is perhaps more fraught with danger of tyranny over
conscience than the state. Again, Mullins continued:

---

81   Mullins, *Axioms*, p. 275. Cf. Mullins, 'Baptist Conception', p. 63, in which
he described loyalty to the state as a duty of religious liberty.

82   N.O. Hatch, *The Sacred Cause of Liberty: Republican Thought and the
Millennium in Revolutionary New England* (New Haven, CT: Yale University Press,
1977), pp. 145-48 and 170-71, has indicated that this recasting of soteriology is rooted
in and enabled by a striking alteration in eschatological views, views that were
admittedly not limited to Baptists. Hatch notes that American ministers of the late
eighteenth century sought a way to assign the new American republic a major role in the
scheme of providential history. They accomplished this through bringing the republican
values of civil and religious liberty to the heart of redemptive history. This in turn led to
a reordering of allegiance from the church to the secular *polis*. The state became the
bearer of providential history, and 'a "republican eschatology" emerged'. This continued,
he notes, p. 144, into prominent mid-nineteenth century Baptist leaders such as Francis
Wayland. The phrase quoted above Hatch took from a sermon by Baptist preacher Daniel
Lee, p. 155.

83   Dobbins, *Baptist Churches*, pp. 32-35. He proceeded, p. 39, to list as an aspect
of the pure democracy of Baptist churches the symbolic understanding of the ordinances.

84   Mullins, *Axioms*, pp. 65-66.

[P]olitics and government and the social institutions assume man's moral competency, his capacity for moral progress under God in a well-ordered society. Society is the bold assertion that under God's leadership eternal right will be attained in the human sphere. If you let the gold and the pearl stand for the highest moral values; if you let the walls of jasper and the twelve foundations stand for the reign of moral law; if you let the sunless yet resplendent heavens above stand for the light and glory of truth in its triumph in the human soul; and if you let the hallelujahs of the tearless and shadowless and triumphant multitude in white stand for a purified social order, then you have the unmatched glory and beauty of the New Jerusalem which the prophet saw descending from heaven to earth, the fitting symbol of what is going on in the world all about us—man under God achieving for himself an ideal social order. The absence of the temple from the perfected city means that all life will become a temple, all its manifestations an act of worship. The absence of the sun means that all light and all truth are now ours through the indwelling God.[85]

The 'mother principle' of contemporary Baptist Christianity has become a legitimator of liberal democracy. He confidently exclaimed that we are approaching 'the Baptist age of the world'.[86] The sad truth of this may well be that he believed this because Baptists in America, bereft of the external mediation of the sacraments, had taken as their own the world's soteriology in the name of religious liberty.

85   Mullins, *Axioms*, pp. 66-67.
86   Mullins, *Axioms*, p. 275.

CHAPTER 4

C.H. Spurgeon on the Sacraments

Tim Grass and Ian Randall

Preaching at the Metropolitan Tabernacle, London, in 1874, C.H. Spurgeon (1834–92), the most famous preacher of the Victorian age, spoke to his huge congregation of the way the 'ordinances', as he normally called them, of baptism and the Lord's Supper had become 'nests in which the foul bird of superstition has laid her eggs'. He expressed his joy, however, that despite the tendency among some people to think of the power of water, bread and wine in a superstitious way, it was possible 'through these material symbols, to get nearer to him whose body was material...whose blood was real blood'.[1] Although Spurgeon was reluctant to use the word 'sacrament', in his thinking the ordinances of baptism and the Lord's Supper were not empty symbols. Indeed he was happy to employ the common definition of a sacrament—'an outward and visible sign of an inward and spiritual grace'—to explain what he meant by ordinance.[2] For Spurgeon the ordinances were associated with God's gracious activity.

In this study slightly more attention will be given to Spurgeon's approach to baptism than to his view of communion. Spurgeon's views of the Lord's Supper received perceptive treatment in Michael Walker's *Baptists at the Table*,[3] whereas his approach to baptism has not been analysed in the same way. Spurgeon himself commented on numerous occasions about both ordinances, and in 1877, at a communion service at the Metropolitan Tabernacle, made a significant comparison. The Lord's table, he said 'is the bond of Christian union'. He continued: 'I am afraid it will be many long years before we shall get all believers to agree concerning baptism. I hope right views of that ordinance are spreading,

---

1   'The Double Forget-me-not', *Metropolitan Tabernacle Pulpit* (*MTP*) (London: Passmore & Alabaster, 1856–1917), Vol. 54, Sermon No. 3099, 1 Cor. 11.24, delivered 5 July 1874, p. 315.

2   'The Greatest Exhibition of the Age', *MTP*, Vol. 39, S. No. 2307, 1 Cor. 11. 26, delivered 5 May 1889, p. 222.

3   M.J. Walker, *Baptists at the Table: The Theology of the Lord's Supper amongst English Baptists in the Nineteenth Century* (Didcot: Baptist Historical Society, 1992), ch. 5.

but it does not seem to me to be a point where all Christians are likely yet to unite; but concerning our Lord's death all who really are his people are agreed.'[4] Evangelical disputes over baptism were something Spurgeon accepted. Indeed he provoked disagreement through his attempts to set out a clear view of baptism. In his approach to the Lord's Supper, by contrast, his deeply-held belief was that this ordinance offered an experience that could be shared by all Christian believers, not only Baptists. Yet, as we will see, it was his concern as a Baptist to be true to scripture that governed Spurgeon's thinking about both baptism and the Lord's Supper.

Spurgeon's Experience of Baptism

Spurgeon was not a 'cradle Baptist', having been baptised as an infant among the Independents, his father and grandfather being Independent pastors. In 1889 he recalled his schooldays in a sermon, asserting with pardonable exaggeration that 'it is due to the Church of England Catechism that I am a Baptist.'[5] An Anglican clergyman inadvertently challenged him to take seriously the idea of believer's baptism. Shortly before his conversion, Spurgeon spent a year at school in Maidstone, Kent, and a local clergyman used to instruct the pupils in the Prayer Book Catechism. The clergyman explained the catechism's teaching that repentance and faith were necessary for baptism, and that these were promised by the sponsors. Said Spurgeon:

> Proceeding with the Catechism, he suddenly turned to me and said—
> Spurgeon, you were never properly baptized.
> S.—Oh, yes, sir, I was; my grandfather baptized me in the little parlour, and he is a minister, so I know he did it right!
> C.—Ah, but you had neither faith nor repentance, and therefore ought not to have received baptism!
> S.—Why, sir, that has nothing to do with it! All infants ought to be baptized.
> C.—How do you know that? Does not the Prayer Book say that faith and repentance are necessary before baptism?[6]

The clergyman gave him a week to examine the scriptures and prove that this was so and then explained that this was why the Church required sponsors who promised repentance and faith on behalf of the child.

---

4   'The Object of the Lord's Supper', *MTP*, Vol. 51, S. No. 2942, 1 Cor. 11.26, delivered 2 September 1877, p. 317.

5   Iain H. Murray (ed.), *C.H. Spurgeon: The Early Years 1834–1859* (London: Banner of Truth, 1962), p. 45.

6   Murray (ed.), *The Early Years*, p. 34.

Studying the New Testament, Spurgeon concluded that repentance and faith were indeed prerequisites for baptism, but that these could not be promised by others on behalf of an infant. His sprinkling as an infant was, therefore, not baptism, and he resolved to be baptised as soon as he should be converted.[7] Elsewhere he stated that he learned enough Greek to conclude that *baptizein* did not refer to the sprinkling of infants, and concluded that baptism as a believer by immersion was the right way.[8] It would appear that he came to his convictions independently of any consciousness of Baptist influence, for he asserted that he knew of nobody who held such views, nor that Baptists even existed.[9] He averred that he had never witnessed a baptism by immersion before the service at which he was baptised.[10]

On 3 May 1850 Spurgeon was baptised as a believer in the River Lark at Isleham, on the border of Cambridgeshire and Suffolk. In his own words, 'I was privileged to follow my Lord, and to be buried with Him in baptism.' The rite was a '[s]weet emblem of my death to all the world' in which he dedicated himself to live for Christ alone.[11] In Spurgeon's accounts of his baptism as a believer the main features of his baptismal theology appear. Firstly, he viewed the baptism of believers by immersion as a clear command in scripture, which fittingly symbolised the believer's death to the world, burial with Christ and resurrection to a new way of life. Secondly, baptism was not purely a matter of the individual believer's obedience to Christ; it was a church ordinance. The church administered it and by it the new believer publicly identified with the people of God. Thirdly, though a convinced Baptist who was ready to defend his views, he tended to distance himself from what he regarded as sectarian Baptist thinking, seeking to remain in fellowship with paedobaptist evangelicals wherever possible. There is thus a tension in his thinking about baptism between his firm adherence to Baptist principles and his belief that differing views on baptism were not in themselves grounds for a breach of fellowship.

Spurgeon's sacramental thinking was shaped decisively by his experience, particularly his upbringing in the Puritan tradition as an Independent. In the case of the Lord's Supper, as we will see, this was a constructive factor, but in the case of baptism he reacted against what he came to regard as the unscriptural superstition associated with infant baptism. This reaction made him wary of any idea that spiritual power was imparted at the point of baptism. By way of example, there were no

---

7   Murray (ed.), *Early Years*, pp. 35, 38.
8   Murray (ed.), *Early Years*, pp. 145-46.
9   'God's Pupil, God's Preacher: An Autobiography', *MTP*, Vol. 39, S. No. 2318, Ps. 71.17, pp. 354-55; Murray (ed.), *Early Years*, p. 38.
10   Murray (ed.), *Early Years*, p. 149.
11   Murray (ed.), *Early Years*, p. 131 (Diary, 3 May 1850).

hymns praying for the descent of the Spirit in connection with baptism in
Our Own Hymn Book (1866) which Spurgeon compiled—a contrast with
the book which had previously been used at the Tabernacle, John
Rippon's *Selection*.[12] Since Baptists were writing and using such hymns,
it is likely that they were deliberately excluded by Spurgeon. It was more
or less inevitable that in his ministry, given the forthright person he was,
Spurgeon would feel it necessary to express this aspect of his views on
baptism in a way that would cause controversy.

The Baptism of Believers

Despite his forthright approach, Spurgeon asserted that he rarely
mentioned the subject of baptism in his weekly preaching because his
people learned about it without his help as the Holy Spirit applied the
teaching of the scriptures to their hearts.[13] Although this was an
exaggeration, it was certainly not his usual habit to emphasis baptism in
his preaching at the Tabernacle. However, there is enough material in his
sermons and elsewhere to build up a clear picture of his views concerning
baptism and the relationship between the gospel, baptism and church.

For Spurgeon, baptism was a matter of personal conscience. Even
before his conversion he came to the conclusion that an individual must
be personally convinced that Christ commanded believers to be baptised.
He believed that it was his responsibility to judge for himself what
scripture taught, rather than blindly following the practice of his father
and grandfather. Whatever his family thought, he considered that he must
follow the dictates of conscience and be baptised as a believer.[14] In fact,
his family indicated their willingness for him to follow his convictions
and his baptism as a believer was no barrier to some of the members of
his family (who remained Independents) preaching for him in London in
later years.

The fact that baptism was a matter of conscience did not stop Spurgeon
from arguing that it was also a matter of obedience. Since, he stated,
'God gives the command, it is mine to enforce it.' As far as he was
concerned, believer's baptism was taught in scripture and Baptists were
distinguished by their acknowledgement of scripture as supremely
authoritative.[15] He felt that baptism was part of the gospel and could not
be omitted without risking loss of divine blessing. Failure to preach

---

12   J. Rippon, *Selection of Hymns from the best authors, intended as an appendix to Dr. Watts's Psalms and Hymns* (1787).

13   'Who should be Baptized?', *MTP*, Vol. 47, S. No. 2737, Acts 8.37, delivered Summer 1859, p. 349.

14   Murray (ed.), *Early Years*, pp. 145-47.

15   Murray (ed.), *Early Years*, p. 152.

baptism was a mistake, just as preaching baptismal regeneration was an error.[16] Spurgeon was baptised, he tells us, because he 'believed it to be an ordinance of Christ, very specially joined by Him with faith in his name'.[17] In a sermon on Mark 16.16 entitled 'Baptism essential to Obedience', he made the point that baptism was to follow faith; although it was unique in being placed alongside faith, there was nothing saving in the rite itself, because it was the outward expression of inward trust. Such confession was essential, for without it there would be no visible church, no body of people acknowledging Christ before men. Those who refused to confess Christ openly could not be acknowledged by him.[18] As Spurgeon put it elsewhere, 'The promise of salvation is not made to a faith which is never avowed.'[19]

While baptism did not save, Spurgeon rejected the idea that it was therefore non-essential: the requirement to be baptised served as a test of obedience, essential simply because Christ commanded it. It was vital for Christian obedience, if not for salvation.[20] Spurgeon looked askance at the profession of anyone who refused to be baptised: 'though baptism is not saving, yet, if men would be saved, they must not be disobedient'.[21] He asked why Christ would have instituted visible ordinances if Christians were at liberty to accept or reject them; rejection implied that Christ was not being regarded as Master.[22] Those who loved Christ would keep his commands, including the requirement to be baptised.[23] Christ both commanded and exemplified baptism;[24] thus baptism was not only a matter of obedience but also of imitation.

In Spurgeon's thinking, baptism was primarily the believer's action, not God's, although God blessed those who obeyed Christ in this way. Baptism by immersion symbolized death to the world, burial with Christ, and resurrection to new life.[25] He argued that Christ was not sprinkled but immersed when baptised in the Jordan and when he answered John's protestations by saying 'thus it becometh us to fulfil all righteousness'

16   'The Good Ananias: A Lesson for Believers', *MTP*, Vol. 31, S. No. 1838, Acts 9.10, delivered 26 April 1885, p. 251

17   Murray (ed.), *Early Years*, p. 151.

18   'Baptism essential to Obedience', *MTP*, Vol. 39, S. No. 2339, Mk 16.16, delivered 13 October 1889, pp. 601-609.

19   'Belief, Baptism, Blessing', *MTP*, Vol. 38, S. No. 2275, Acts 16.33-34, delivered 9 February 1890, p. 462.

20   'Baptism essential to Obedience', pp. 607-608.

21   Murray (ed.), *Early Years*, p. 147.

22   'Belief, Baptism, Blessing', p. 463.

23   'Love's Law and Life', *MTP*, Vol. 32, S. No. 1932, Jn 14.15, delivered 30 June 1886, p. 658.

24   Murray (ed.), *Early Years*, p. 150.

25   Murray (ed.), *Early Years*, p. 150.

(Mt. 3.15), he was referring to all believers. Immersion was therefore for all who believed.[26] As with circumcision, the spiritual meaning was more important than the outward rite, but the rite was not to be omitted on that account. Those who had been buried and raised with Christ should not despise the sign which set this forth.[27] In *Our Own Hymn Book*, the baptismal hymns focus mostly on the symbolism of baptism and on the example of Christ's baptism. This was the example to follow.

How did this emphasis on human response fit with the Calvinistic belief in God's saving initiative and his covenant of grace? By contrast with Puritan covenant theologians, Spurgeon emphasised the discontinuity between the Old Testament people of God and the church, though he also made clear his belief that grace could not be hereditary in either dispensation. The antitype of circumcision was inward renewal, not baptism. Indeed, the baptism of infants, Spurgeon concluded, was a violation of infants' rights, because it forced religious profession upon them without their awareness or consent. Spurgeon was responsible for the publication in 1890 of a modernised edition of *A Body of Divinity* by the Puritan writer Thomas Watson. In the reprint, he added an appendix on baptism to counter Watson's paedobaptist views.[28] The meaning of the word 'baptise', he insisted, was 'immerse'. In response to the argument that children of believing parents were included in the covenant of grace, Spurgeon asserted that

> God graciously entered into covenant with all Abraham's descendants for his sake, and instituted a sign to be fixed on every male, is no evidence that God has entered into covenant with the natural children of every believer, and with each child for the parent's sake, and that the baptism of male and female *infants* of believers is the appointed sign of this covenant.[29]

The true church was a believers' church.

Baptism and the Church

This leads to the consideration of baptism and the church. In keeping with his Puritan sympathies, but unlike many Baptists of his day, Spurgeon regarded baptism as a church ordinance. Here Spurgeon went beyond the *1689 Confession*, which he had reprinted in 1855. This spoke only of the significance of baptism for the individual's relationship with

---

26   'Consecration to God—Illustrated by Abraham's circumcision', *MTP*, Vol. 14, S. No. 845, Gen. 17.1-2, delivered 13 December 1868, p. 695.
27   'Consecration to God—Illustrated by Abraham's circumcision', p. 694.
28   Reprinted as *Spurgeon on Baptism* (Worthing: H.E. Walter, 1966).
29   *Spurgeon on Baptism*, p.23.

God as a sign of fellowship with Christ in his death, burial and resurrection, of grafting into Christ, of remission of sins, and of his commitment to walk in newness of life. For Spurgeon, 'Baptism is the mark of distinction between the Church and the world', because 'it sets forth the death of the baptized person to the world' and his resurrection to a new life. It should be the point at which believers begin their visible connection with the church. It was a crucial point in the believer's progress, 'the crossing of the Rubicon'. Small wonder, then, that he felt his timidity had been washed away at his baptism: 'Baptism', he stated, 'also loosed my tongue, and from that day it has never been quiet.'[30]

Spurgeon believed that the New Testament order was for baptism to precede admission to the church.[31] As a new convert he had been invited to take the Lord's Supper but refused to do so until he had been baptised; he allowed that those who had not seen the necessity of believer's baptism might do so, but he felt himself to be in a different category because he knew that baptism was 'Christ's appointed way of professing Him'.[32] His diary indicated that he was admitted to church fellowship with the Independents at Newmarket on 4 April, but did not take the Lord's Supper until 5 May, two days after his baptism.[33] His practice at his London churches, New Park Street and the Metropolitan Tabernacle, developed from these convictions. For Spurgeon, open membership and closed communion were both erroneous and injurious.[34] He believed that opening up membership in Baptist churches to those baptised as infants was 'eating out the very vitals of the denomination'. But the church did not control the Lord's Table; thus, while membership at the Tabernacle was restricted to those baptised as believers, members of recognised churches of Christ, even if they were paedobaptist, had a right to participate.[35] This was in accordance with the Trust Deeds.[36] The paedobaptists were presumably visitors from other churches rather than regular attenders at the Tabernacle. The latter would have been well aware that believer's baptism was a prerequisite for church membership.

30   See Murray (ed.), *Early Years*, pp. 147-50.

31   Murray (ed.), *Early Years*, p. 145.

32   Murrray (ed.), *Early Years*, p. 115 (Spurgeon to his father, 6 April 1850).

33   Murray (ed.), *Early Years*, p. 125.

34   On these see T. George, 'Controversy and Communion: The Limits of Baptist Fellowship from Bunyan to Spurgeon', in D. Bebbington (ed.), *The Gospel in the World: International Baptist Studies* (Studies in Baptist History and Thought, 1; Carlisle: Paternoster, 2002), pp. 55-58.

35   Report of a church meeting at the Metropolitan Tabernacle, *MTP*, Vol. 7, 8 April 1861, p. 260.

36   A.C. Underwood, *A History of the English Baptists* (London: Kingsgate Press, 1947), p. 205.

Although Spurgeon always hoped that differences regarding baptism would not divide believers—he wrote to his father in 1850, 'We are all one in Christ Jesus; forms and ceremonies, I trust, will not make us divided.'[37]—he was nonetheless convinced that baptism should be at the heart of the life of the local church. At the opening of the Metropolitan Tabernacle, Spurgeon indicated that the baptistery would usually be left uncovered since the church was not ashamed to confess its Baptist beliefs.[38] Similarly, he thought baptising in a river a valuable public affirmation of faith: 'Baptism in the open river is so Scriptural, and, withal, such a public testimony, that I hope our friends will never abandon it... We are most numerous where the ordinance is most known.' There were echoes here of his own baptism. 'Next to the Word of God', Spurgeon suggested, a baptising service was 'the best argument for baptism'.[39]

Baptismal Regeneration

We have seen that Spurgeon preferred to describe baptism as an ordinance rather than a sacrament. Behind this lay his belief in the personal nature of true Christian religion as a saving relationship with God. He was thus opposed to anything which smacked of superstition or 'doing it right', since the gospel was threatened as people put their trust in ceremonies instead of in Christ. In his mind, even Nonconformists were not immune to this tendency. He recalled a couple of incidents from his Independent upbringing:

> I remember seeing a baby sprinkled within less than an hour of its death, and I seem to hear even now the comfort which a certain good man gave to the bereaved parents—'What a mercy the child was baptized! What a consolation it must be!' This was in an Independent family, and the words were spoken by an Independent minister.

> I knew an instance of an aged minister, of the same persuasion, who sprinkled a little boy, although the father was averse to it. The child was running about in the hall of the minister's house, and his mother was looking on. He was caught up, and the pious man exclaimed, 'Come along, Mrs. S---, the poor child shall not live like a heathen any longer.' So the conjuration was performed, and the little boy was put

37   Murray (ed.), *Early Years*, p. 116 (Spurgeon to his father, 6 April 1850).
38   Iain H. Murray (ed.), *C.H. Spurgeon: The Full Harvest 1860–1892* (London: Banner of Truth, 1973), p. 37.
39   Spurgeon to Mr Soper, 13 May 1885, in Iain H. Murray (ed.), *Letters of Charles Haddon Spurgeon* (Edinburgh: Banner of Truth, 1992), p. 156.

into the Paedo-Baptist covenant. He was not only suffered to come, but forced to come, and, doubtless, went on his way rejoicing to think it was over.[40]

Such rituals contrasted, Spurgeon believed, with the intelligent and voluntary believing response called forth by the gospel.

Early in his London ministry, Spurgeon expressed his opposition to the doctrine of baptismal regeneration as set out in the baptismal service of the *Book of Common Prayer*. He argued that it was contrary to common sense, was contradicted by the evidence in the lives of many who had received infant baptism, and was a delusive substitute for the new birth.[41] Infant baptism was not saving, Spurgeon contended, but was 'a human and carnal invention, an addition to the Word of God, and therefore wicked and injurious'. It was rendered, he continued 'something worse than superstition by being accompanied with falsehood', the falsehood being the proclamation that those baptised were made children of God and heirs of the kingdom of heaven.[42] In 1859, Spurgeon criticised as inconsistent those who asserted the necessity of repentance and faith before baptism (as did the catechism of the Church of England) and then baptised infants using a service containing such declarations.[43]

The definitive expression of his views, however, came in a sermon on 'Baptismal Regeneration' preached by Spurgeon at the Tabernacle on 5 June 1864.[44] Spurgeon explained that he felt a burden to testify in this sermon to what he believed to be the truth, whatever the cost. The great error with which preachers of the gospel in England had to contend was that of baptismal regeneration. The only Protestant church in the nation teaching this was the Church of England, whose Prayer Book explicitly avowed it. Quoting the same Anglican catechism which had spoken to him in his youth, Spurgeon asserted that the Church of England plainly taught that through baptism infants were made members of Christ, children of God and heirs of the kingdom of heaven. The baptismal service included thanksgiving that those baptised had thus been made regenerate. This was the plain meaning of these formularies and it was impossible to explain them otherwise. He asserted that he was focusing on the issue of baptismal regeneration, not that of infant baptism.

---

40   Murray (ed.), *Early Years*, 45.

41   'The Victory of Faith', *New Park Street Pulpit*, Vol. 1, 1 Jn 5.4, delivered 18 March 1855, p. 105.

42   'Infant Salvation', *MTP*, Vol. 7, S. No. 411, 2 Kgs 4.26, 29 September 1861, p. 506.

43   'Who should be Baptized?', p. 352.

44   'Baptismal Regeneration', *MTP*, Vol. 10, S. No. 573, Mk 16.15-16, pp. 313-28.

Aware that some might point to the presence within the Church of England of many evangelical clergy who did not accept this doctrine, Spurgeon's response was trenchant: 'I rejoice in their enlightenment, but I question, gravely question their morality.'[45] He virtually accused them of perjury, assenting on oath to the Church's teaching and then denying it, taking money from the Church and yet preaching against its doctrines. His fear was that outsiders would see the cavalier attitude of such evangelical clergy and conclude that in fact doctrine mattered little so long as a person lived a charitable life. He made clear his respect for those who honestly believed and preached baptismal regeneration, stating: 'I hate their doctrine, but I love their honesty';[46] with such people it was possible to engage in open disagreement, each side knowing where they stood.

Spurgeon offered three arguments against the theology of the Prayer Book service. Firstly, apart from faith, baptism saved nobody. Salvation by mechanical performance of a rite was out of keeping with the spiritual religion inaugurated by Christ; it belonged to the era of types and shadows. He could see no connection between the application of water to the body and the regeneration of the soul. Secondly, it was all too clear that the vast majority of those baptised as infants were unregenerate. Baptism, whether of infants or professing believers, regenerated nobody. Thirdly (and here it does appear that he was opposing infant baptism and not only baptismal regeneration, in spite of his earlier avowal), he challenged the legitimacy of making promises on behalf of an unconscious infant. Godly parents promised what their conscience must condemn, and ungodly parents promised what they could not perform—in neither case would their promises be acceptable to God. The reason he spoke out was because the error of baptismal regeneration led many to believe that they were already born again. Preachers might tell their hearers that they needed to be born again, but this message was drowned out by the false assurance given by the baptismal service.

There were many responses—often quite vehement in nature—to what Spurgeon said. Spurgeon returned to his theme on 24 July 1864 in a sermon on Mark 10.13-16 entitled 'Children brought to Christ, and Not to the Font'.[47] He chose this passage as his text because it was quoted by several of those responding to his attack on baptismal regeneration. He was distinctly unimpressed by the arguments of his opponents. Most, he felt, had missed the whole point of his first sermon: 'The whole question is, Do you believe that baptism regenerates? If so—prove that your belief is Scriptural! Do you believe that baptism does not regenerate? Then

45   'Baptismal Regeneration', p. 316.
46   'Baptismal Regeneration', p. 317.
47   'Children brought to Christ, and Not to the Font', *MTP*, Vol. 10, S. No. 581, Mk. 10. 13-16, delivered 24 July 1864, pp. 413-24.

justify your swearing that it does.'[48] He observed that the passage had nothing to do with baptism, for the children were not being brought to be baptised. Most of the sermon consisted of encouragement to those who sought, by whatever means, to present the gospel to sinners and condemnation of any who hindered seekers from coming to Christ. Even very young children, he asserted, could be regenerated; his critics were wrong to allege that he denied this. What he denied was that regeneration could come through 'their godparents telling lies at a font'.[49]

Spurgeon took up the theme once more on 25 September 1864, in a sermon on Ezekiel 11.15. The sermon, entitled '"Thus saith the Lord:" or, The Book of Common Prayer Weighed in the Balances of the Sanctuary',[50] enforced the theme of the necessity of scriptural warrant for everything which should be taught or done in the church. Responding to attacks on his criticisms of the Prayer Book, he denied the existence of any such warrant for the use of proxies in baptism, religion being a personal matter. Again, he denied that infant baptism could regenerate, rejecting the explanations of the term put forward by his respondents in favour of what he saw as the plain meaning of scripture; whatever the meaning of the term, it was nowhere stated that baptism regenerated an individual. What is interesting is that this sermon includes far stronger criticism of the rites, as well as the canons, of the Church of England, yet it did not provoke the response that followed his first sermon on baptismal regeneration.

Baptism and Evangelical Unity

Why, then, did Spurgeon's sermon of 5 June 1864 provoke such controversy? In part it was because of the deliberately confrontational approach Spurgeon adopted. Spurgeon expected that his sermon would provoke opposition and that American sales of his sermons would be affected; this had happened when he preached a sermon against slavery.[51] In fact, the sermon on baptismal regeneration proved to be the best-selling sermon he ever produced, by the end of the year 350,000 had been printed, and by 1900 the figure was half a million.[52] The sermon

---

48   'Children brought to Christ, and Not to the Font', p. 413.

49   'Children brought to Christ, and Not to the Font', p. 422.

50   '"Thus saith the Lord:" or, The Book of Common Prayer Weighed in the Balances of the Sanctuary', *MTP*, Vol. 10, S. No. 591, Ezek. 11.15, delivered 25 September 1864, pp. 533-48.

51   Murray (ed.), *Full Harvest*, p. 55; G. Holden Pike, *The Life and Work of Charles Haddon Spurgeon* (6 vols; London: Cassell, n.d.) III, p. 95.

52   Lewis A. Drummond, *Spurgeon: Prince of Preachers* (Grand Rapids, MI: Kregel Publications, 1992), p. 490.

provoked a vast response: Spurgeon collected 135 sermons and pamphlets, which he had bound into three large volumes.[53] He entered the fray because he believed the gospel to be at stake and he was not afraid of controversy. Indeed perhaps he wished to stir it up. Many years later he recalled how another Baptist had said to him: "'You have got into hot water." I replied, "No; I do not feel the water to be hot. The truth is far otherwise. I am cool enough; I am only the stoker, and other folks are in the hot water, which I am doing my best to make so hot that they will be glad to get out of it.'"[54]

Patricia Kruppa has suggested that Spurgeon aimed to expose the 'compromise' between evangelical Anglicans and those Anglicans associated with the Oxford Movement (the Tractarians), in which each interpreted the Prayer Book according to their own conscience and the issue of baptismal regeneration was not discussed.[55] She also suggests that there was a political dimension to this, in that the sermon marked the beginning of Spurgeon's career as a 'political dissenter'.[56] It is true that infant baptism, along with the doctrine of baptismal regeneration, was regarded by many Baptists as the cornerstone of 'state-churchism', as Hugh Stowell Brown declared at one of the services marking the opening of the Metropolitan Tabernacle,[57] but for Spurgeon the theological and pastoral issues were much more fundamental than the political ones. Iain Murray suggests that Spurgeon's sermon is evidence of a new attitude on his part, occasioned by the increase of 'popery'.[58] However, most of the elements of Spurgeon's polemic against baptismal regeneration were present in earlier utterances and had not alienated his paedobaptist supporters: the exception was his attack on the integrity of the clergy.

Spurgeon was not the first Baptist to suggest that Anglican clergy belied their principles by their practice: Charles Stovel had done so in 1842.[59] However, Spurgeon's sermon was bound to create far more of a stir than Stovel had done for two reasons. Firstly, Spurgeon was probably the most prominent evangelical leader in England during the 1860s and his following included many Anglican clergy and laity. Secondly, in tackling this subject in such a forthright manner, Spurgeon was touching some very raw Anglican nerves. Many responses came from evangelical

---

53   Murray (ed.), *Full Harvest*, p. 56.

54   *An All-Round Ministry* (London: Passmore & Alabaster, 1900), p. 403.

55   P.S. Kruppa, *Charles Haddon Spurgeon—A Preacher's Progress* (New York & London, Garland Publishing, 1982), p. 258.

56   Kruppa, *Spurgeon*, p. 279.

57   'Christian Baptism', *MTP*, Vol. 7, Col. 2.12, delivered 9 April 1861, p. 272.

58   Iain H. Murray, *The Forgotten Spurgeon* (London: Banner of Truth, 1973), p. 127.

59   J.H.Y. Briggs, *The English Baptists of the Nineteenth Century* (A History of the English Baptists, 3; Didcot: Baptist Historical Society, 1994), p. 46.

Churchmen who objected to his allegations of equivocation and dishonesty and his refusal to distinguish between the teaching of the Prayer Book and that of the Tractarians.[60] It has been suggested that some evangelical Anglicans believed that Spurgeon had failed to take into account their belief in covenant theology. The child, for evangelical Anglicans, was being brought to baptism by believing parents and could be regarded as a recipient of the covenant promises.[61] However, Spurgeon would undoubtedly have been sensitive to this issue in view of his own background. What mattered (as he pointed out in a baptismal sermon in 1859) was an individual's covenant standing, not that of their parents, because religion was a personal matter.[62]

His sermon was widely regarded as undermining co-operation between evangelicals of different denominations, of which a notable example was the Evangelical Alliance. The former Anglican clergyman Baptist W. Noel, who had become a Baptist in 1848, accused Spurgeon of violating the Alliance's fourth resolution, which laid down that members should avoid 'all rash and groundless insinuations, personal imputations, or irritating allusions'.[63] The secretary of the Alliance, James Davis, wrote privately to Spurgeon, calling on him to retract or resign. Spurgeon, under the mistaken impression that Davis was writing in his official capacity, resigned.[64] He issued two letters defending his conduct.[65] His view was that he had not broken the Evangelical Alliance resolution. He had waited until all hope of reform was gone, he had proved rather than merely 'imputed' his charge, and he had avoided being 'irritating' by not listing all the sins of the Establishment. 'I have not violated the union of believers', he insisted, 'but those have done so who, knowing the truth and loving it, nevertheless lend their name, their countenance, and their subscription to a lie'.[66] Spurgeon withdrew from the Alliance because some within it were aggrieved at his statements. However, a few years later he rejoined, reaffirming his belief in evangelical unity despite differences over baptism.

---

60   Murray, *Forgotten Spurgeon*, p. 129.

61   Murray, *Forgotten Spurgeon*, p. 130.

62   'Who should be Baptized?', p. 354.

63   Pike, *Charles Haddon Spurgeon*, III, p. 97.

64   Murray, *Full Harvest*, p. 57.

65   *Two Letters from C.H. Spurgeon; one to the Evangelical Alliance, signifying his withdrawal from that association; and another to the Christian public, proving that his accusations against the Evangelical clergy are neither novel nor singular* (London: Passmore & Alabaster, [1864]).

66   *Two Letters*, p. 3.

Spurgeon's Theology of the Lord's Supper

Whereas Spurgeon had difficulty in reconciling his theology of baptism with his desire for evangelical unity, when it came to the Lord's Supper his theology was decidedly 'ecumenical'. A volume of Spurgeon's communion addresses, *Till He Come*, has a preface which notes that a number of the addresses were delivered to 'the little companies of Christians,—of different denominations, and of various nationalities,—who gathered around the communion table in Mr. Spurgeon's sitting room at Mentone'.[67] These services, which took place when Spurgeon was away from London in the south of France, often for the purpose of recuperation, give an insight into Spurgeon's vision of the supper as a uniting sacrament. In an address at Mentone entitled 'The Well-beloved', he stated: 'In this room we have an example of how closely we are united in Christ. Some of you are more at home in this assembly, taken out of all churches, than you are in the churches to which you nominally belong. Our union in one body as Episcopalians, Baptists, Presbyterians or Independents, is not the thing which our Lord prayed for: but our union in Himself. That union we do at this moment enjoy; and therefore do we eat of one bread, and drink of one Spirit, at His feet who is to each one of us, and so to all of us, ALTOGETHER LOVELY.'[68] This ecumenical spirit was expressed especially at Mentone. But preaching at the Metropolitan Tabernacle in 1877, Spurgeon affirmed: 'We are all one in Christ Jesus; we do not come to this table as Baptists, or Episcopalians, or Methodists, or Presbyterians; we come here simply as those who form one body in Christ.'[69]

Communion addresses by Spurgeon in which he referred to Christians of the past also indicate his wide sympathies. Christian literature, he told one gathering at Mentone, 'contains no words more precious than those which have been spoken at the time of communion'. Spurgeon spoke of these times as 'sacramental occasions'. Sermons by the seventeenth-century Scottish Presbyterian, Samuel Rutherford, said Spurgeon, 'have a sacred unction on them'. At the same time, Spurgeon commended the poems of the Anglican George Herbert, suggesting that most of them were inspired by 'the sight of Christ in this ordinance'. He also appreciated 'the canticles of holy Bernard' (of Clairvaux), describing how they 'flame with devotion'.[70] Preaching at the Metropolitan Tabernacle in 1861, Spurgeon described past communion services in 'the

---

67   '*Till He Come': Communion Meditations and Addresses by C.H. Spurgeon* (London: Passmore & Alabaster, 1894), Preface.
68   'The Well-beloved', *Till He Come*, p. 113.
69   'The Object of the Lord's Supper', p. 317.
70   'The Well-beloved's Vineyard', *Till He Come*, p. 149.

darkness of the catacombs of Rome, where only a tiny taper afforded light', and in the present time in 'the far-off isles of the sea'. I may say, he declared in dramatic style, 'O sacred Eucharist, thou hast the dew of thy youth'.[71] When arguing in 1876 for frequent communion, Spurgeon adduced Augustine and other early church Fathers.[72] A year later he spoke in romantic vein about 'the simple breaking of bread and the pouring out of wine' being observed by persecuted believers of the past, 'in the mountains of Bohemia, in the Vaudois valleys, in the wild glens of Scotland', and then talked of 'these brighter days' in which thousands gathered openly. His point was that communion was a mark that there had always been and would always be a church of Christ.[73] For Spurgeon the Lord's Supper was an ordinance that connected the church through the centuries and across denominational divides.

On the other hand, Spurgeon considered that some beliefs about communion were wholly unacceptable. 'The Romish church', he commented tersely in one of his Mentone addresses, 'says much more about the *real* presence; meaning thereby, the corporeal presence of the Lord Jesus'. Spurgeon's reply was: 'Nay, you believe in knowing Christ after the flesh, and in that sense the only real presence is in heaven; but we firmly believe in the real presence of Christ which is spiritual and yet certain.'[74] It is significant that Spurgeon based his opposition to Catholic eucharistic theology not only on the Bible but also on reason. 'Because we are rational', he maintained, 'and because we are spiritual, both our reason and our spiritual nature revolt against anything so atrocious as to believe that the body of Christ—the absolute flesh and blood—can be eaten and drank, or that if it could be done it ought to be done, or that it could confer any spiritual benefit upon those who could perform so cannibal and revolting an act.' In the same sermon he affirmed his belief 'in the real presence, but not in the corporeal presence'.[75] Michael Walker rightly points out that Spurgeon's concept of Christ's body being in heaven but his spiritual presence being known in the bread and wine is in line with the teaching of Calvin.[76] However, Spurgeon's theology owed much to his idea of what made sense and to what resonated with his own experience. It was because of these factors that he could make statements about the Lord's table: 'We believe', he said, 'that Jesus Christ spiritually

---

71   'The Lord's Supper', *MTP*, Vol. 50, S. No. 2872, 1 Cor. 11.26, delivered in the autumn of 1861, p. 101.

72   'Fencing the Table', *MTP*, Vol. 50, S. No. 2865, 1 Cor. 11.28, delivered 2 January 1876, p. 14.

73   'The Object of the Lord's Supper', p. 320.

74   'Mysterious Visits', *Till he Come*, p. 17.

75   'The Witness of the Lord's Supper', *MTP*, Vol. 59, S. No. 3338, 1 Cor. 11.26, undated, p. 38.

76   Walker, *Baptists at the Table*, p. 174.

comes to us and refreshes us, and in that sense we eat his flesh and drink his blood.'[77] This was what Spurgeon had experienced.

We have seen that in the case of baptism the high church revival in the Church of England, with its stress on the efficacy of baptism, provoked a strong reaction in Spurgeon. With the Lord's Supper, by contrast, Anglo–Catholic advocacy of the central place of the eucharist did not provoke Spurgeon to engage in controversy. He condemned in sermons in 1874 and 1877 rituals such as the adoration of the sacrament, with people bowing down, as he crudely put it, 'to worship Jack-in-the box'. These forms were to be found in 'the Romish church' and also in 'another church, nearer to home, that is a twin sister to it, and is getting very like it'[78]—a clear reference to the Church of England. At the same time, however, as opposing high church practices, Spurgeon encouraged his hearers to use the Lord's Supper as a time to 'renew your vows of affection and devotion'. He ended his 1877 sermon in mystical vein, with an appeal: 'Come and put your finger into the print of the nails, and thrust your hand into his pierced side.'[79] In a famous passage reflecting his belief in an encounter with Christ, Spurgeon said: 'At this table Jesus feeds us with His body and His blood. His corporeal presence we have not, but his real spiritual presence we perceive. We are like the disciples when none of them durst ask Him, "Who art Thou?" knowing that it was the Lord. He is come. He looketh forth at these windows,—I mean this bread and wine; showing Himself through the lattices of this instructive and endearing ordinance.'[80]

At the heart of Spurgeon's theology of the Lord's Supper was the conviction that Christ was present among his people as they took bread and wine. This was expressed in the communion hymn which Spurgeon wrote in 1866:

> Amidst us our Beloved stands,
> And bids us view His pierced hands,
> Points to His wounded feet and side,
> Blest emblems of the Crucified.

Speaking to the small group at Mentone, on the subject 'I will give you rest', Spurgeon employed the same imagery: 'By faith, I see our Lord standing in our midst, and I hear Him say, with voice of sweetest music, first to all of us together, and then to each one individually, "I will give you rest." May the Holy Spirit bring to each of us the fulness of the rest

---

77   'The Witness of the Lord's Supper', p. 38.
78   'The Object of the Lord's Supper', p. 314.
79   'The Object of the Lord's Supper', p. 322.
80   'Over the Mountains', *Till He Come*, p. 69.

and peace of God!'[81] For Spurgeon this awareness of the presence of the crucified and risen Jesus was associated with the gathering together of groups of believers, whether large or small. In a sermon in 1866, 'The Lord's Supper, Simple but Sublime!', Spurgeon spoke about the impossibility of celebrating the ordinance alone. 'I must have you with me', he said, 'I cannot do without you.' The group celebrating, however, might be only five or six. Spurgeon referred to communion services in which he had participated—held in hotel rooms as he stayed in Venice, Milan or Paris—as occasions in which those present saw, in symbol, Christ crucified.[82] The same expectation marked the communion services at the Metropolitan Tabernacle. In 1883 Spurgeon thought that he could hear the footfall of Christ, and opened his eyes after the prayer before the communion sermon 'almost expecting to see the Master here'.[83] This encapsulates Spurgeon's view of the real presence.

The Lord's Supper in Practice

For Spurgeon, the celebration of the Lord's Supper should always be simple. He referred to the 'sacred institution, the Lord's supper', as being, like believers' baptism, 'simplicity itself'.[84] This emphasis was consistent with his opposition to high church practice. He dismissed what happened in 'very ritualistic' churches as a 'little game played by the priest with his napkin held out under the chin of the communicant and telling him to open his mouth, and popping the wafer in'. Spurgeon's view was that this was not a proper observance of the Lord's Supper, since the command at the institution of the Lord's Supper was: 'Take, eat.'[85] He saw the meal as a very simple matter of eating and drinking, with the minimum of ritual, since he always associated ritual with superstition. This was one reason why Spurgeon was opposed to any posture other than sitting at the Lord's table. He argued that since Jesus had instituted an 'ordinary meal' as the way to remember him, to kneel to receive the bread and wine was inappropriate. He believed that the normal Baptist practice of sitting, 'as we would at our own table', expressed resting in Christ and feeding on him.[86] Spurgeon also attempted to argue that being seated corresponded to the way in which the disciples reclined with Jesus, 'as the

81   'I will Give you Rest', *Till He Come*, p. 197.
82   'The Lord's Supper, Simple but Sublime!', *MTP*, Vol. 55, S. No. 3151, 1 Cor. 11.25-26, delivered 1866, pp. 316-18.
83   'What the Lord's Supper sees and says', *MTP*, Vol. 39, S. No. 2595, 1 Cor. 11.26, delivered 1 July 1883, p. 530.
84   'Christ and His table companions', *Till He Come*, p. 266
85   'The Greatest Exhibition of the Age', p. 222.
86   'The Object of the Lord's Supper', p. 316.

Orientals still do, at their ease, so much at their ease that the head of John was on the breast of Jesus'.[87] It takes a certain leap of the imagination to move from the picture of this reclining group around Jesus to people on hard pews in a Nonconformist chapel, but Spurgeon believed that the connection was a credible one.

A second important principle for Spurgeon was that the Lord's Supper should be celebrated frequently. In line with what Spurgeon considered 'apostolic precedents', at the Metropolitan Tabernacle the custom was to have a communion service each Sunday evening. On the first Sunday evening of the month the downstairs area and the larger part of the first gallery were filled with communicants. Many hundreds of non-communicant 'spectators' also remained on these occasions, filling the building. This communion service was referred to as the 'great communion'. On the other Sunday evenings the Lord's Supper was observed at the close of the evening service. It seems that a significant number of worshippers did not remain for this service, but Spurgeon himself made clear that he encouraged participation in the Lord's Supper every Sunday, if possible.[88] He told the Tabernacle congregation in 1883: 'I have been in the habit of coming to the Lord's table every first day of the week now for many years... Has it lost its freshness? Oh, dear, no!'[89] Six years later he made a similar, deeply personal statement: 'I love to come every Lord's day to the Communion table; I should be very sorry to come only once a month, or, as some do, only once a year. I could not afford to come as seldom as that. I need to be reminded, forcibly reminded, of my dear Lord and Master very often. We do so soon forget, and our unloving hearts so soon grow cold.'[90] Spurgeon's practice was based not only on theology but was also indebted to his own spiritual experience.

Although Spurgeon believed in simple, frequent communion services, he insisted that they should also be solemn occasions. This is well illustrated by a communion sermon that he preached in 1857. On that occasion he said that he saw it as his duty to ensure, as far as he could, that 'unworthy persons are not received at the Lord's table'. By 'unworthy' Spurgeon meant primarily those who had no personal faith. He made this clear by warning, 'solemnly and earnestly', those who were 'about to draw nigh unto this table', that if they had no faith in Christ, then 'they do stop before they, with sacrilegious hands, touch the elements of this sacred supper.' Christians were also exhorted by

---

87   'The Greatest Exhibition of the Age', pp. 223-24.

88   C.H. Spurgeon, *Autobiography; compiled from his diary, letters, and records by his wife and his private secretary* (4 vols; London: Passmore & Alabaster, 1899), IV, p. 72.

89   'What the Lord's Supper sees and says', p. 537.

90   'The Greatest Exhibition of the Age', p. 220.

Spurgeon in this sermon to prepare themselves for the Lord's table, by 'contemplation and meditation'. Yet Spurgeon also emphasised that he did not want to 'bar the table' but rather to welcome, as he put it, 'all ye who love the Lord Jesus'.[91] Sermons preached by Spurgeon on preparation for the Lord's Supper show that he was aware that people could come complacently to the Lord's table, relying on their church membership, while on the other hand some sensitive people could be held back from communicating by rigorous 'fencing' of the table. He urged the first group not to feel that it was 'any certificate of genuine discipleship to have been seen by the elders, or to have had the pastor satisfied of your conversion'. People should, he said, examine themselves. [92]

Yet Spurgeon did not want the solemnity of the occasion of communion to be oppressive. He was concerned for ordinary people who found it difficult to cope with a forbidding religious atmosphere. 'Ye sons of toil', he once said, 'ye can come here [to the table] with your garments still covered with the dust of your labour.' In a sermon in 1881, 'Examination before communion', preached on the text 1 Corinthians 11.28, he referred to churches which emphasised 'fencing the tables' as defending the table against the approach of improper characters. He regarded this a proper thing to do, but was concerned that some ministers had so guarded the table in the way they spoke about the communion that very few had dared to come to it. Those who did come, Spurgeon added, had 'often been persons who had more conceit than grace'. He commented that it would appear from the exhortations of these ministers, as if Paul must have said, 'Let a man examine himself, but never let him eat of this bread, nor drink of this cup. Let him so examine himself that he shall come to the conclusion that he has no right to sit at the table of the Lord, and therefore shall go his way feeling that he is utterly unworthy of that high privilege.' Rather, Spurgeon argued, the text about self-examination in 1 Corinthians 11 taught that it was the duty of those who had examined themselves to go on to eat the bread and drink the cup. [93]

Ultimately, as Spurgeon saw it, a note of joy needed to be struck at the Lord's Supper. This belief flowed from his understanding of the real presence of Christ. Preaching at New Park Street Chapel in 1855, Spurgeon made this appeal: 'Behold the whole mystery of the sacred Eucharist. It is bread and wine which are lively emblems of the body and

91 'Preparation necessary for the Communion', *MTP*, Vol. 45, S. No. 2647, 1 Cor. 11. 28, delivered Autumn 1857, pp. 530-36.

92 'Preparation for the Lord's Supper', *MTP*, Vol. 60, S. No. 3391, 1 Cor. 11.28, undated, p. 50

93 'Examination before communion', *MTP*, Vol. 46, S. No. 2699, 1 Cor. 11.28, delivered 2 October 1881, p. 518.

blood of Christ. The power to excite remembrance consists in the appeal
thus made to the senses. Here the eye, the hand, the mouth find joyful
work. He spoke of how the senses 'which are usually clogs to the soul,
become wings to lift the mind in contemplation'.[94] Joy was readily
expressed in the hymns sung during the communion service. Among the
fifteen hymns that were included in the section on the Lord's Supper in
Spurgeon's hymnbook were hymns with opening lines such as:

> We'll praise our risen Lord,
> While at His feast we sit...

> (Joseph Stennett, 1709)

and

> How happy are Thy servants, Lord,
> Who thus remember Thee!

> (Charles Wesley, 1745)

Commenting on the use of hymns at communion, Spurgeon imagined
Christ saying: 'Here, at the table, I am your Singing-master, and set you
lessons in music, in which My dying voice shall lead you'. He urged that
those coming to the Lord's table ought not to come to it as to a funeral.
He recommended solemn hymns, but not dirges. 'Let us sing softly', he
said, 'but nonetheless joyfully. These are no burial feasts; those are not
funeral cakes which lie upon this table, and yonder fair white linen cloth
is no winding sheet.' Regarding the hymns to be chosen for communion,
he had this to say: 'My music must be sweet and soft when I sing of Him.
But, oh! it must also be *strong*; there must be a full swell in my praise.'[95]
This service, for Spurgeon, was one of thanksgiving, a eucharist.

Conclusion

C.H. Spurgeon gave considerable attention to baptism and the Lord's
Supper. His own experience was vital in shaping his thinking. Spurgeon's
baptism as a believer expressed his convictions about the personal nature
of faith and he continued throughout his ministry to advocate believer's
baptism as a necessary step for the Christian who wished to be obedient to

---

94   'The remembrance of Christ', New Park Street Chapel, evening 7 January 1855,
1 Cor. 11.24, Vol. 1 (1855), p. 15.
95   'The Memorable Hymn', *Till He Come*, pp. 217-18, 225.

Christ. The view he developed of the Lord's Supper as a weekly necessity also sprang from his experience. But he was deeply committed to a faith which was not only subjective but which had its foundation in God's revelation. His acute anxiety about religious rites that he could not find in scripture led him to take a strong stand against the Church of England's teaching about infant baptism, a stand which strained evangelical unity. He was also concerned about the way in which the Oxford Movement stressed ritualistic practices in eucharistic worship. In both these instances he saw the gospel as a simple message of grace being compromised. A third shaping factor was his Puritan upbringing. Spurgeon shared with others within the Calvinistic Christian tradition a belief that believers were to come to the Lord's table and to feed spiritually on Christ. Both in baptism and the Lord's Supper, for Spurgeon, Christ was presented. Many Baptists would have agreed with the first part of a sermon that Spurgeon preached in 1889 when he spoke of the Lord's Supper as a memorial. But Spurgeon went on to say that the Lord's Supper 'is more than a memorial, it is a fellowship, a communion. Those who eat of this bread, spiritually understanding what they do, those who drink of this cup, entering into the real meaning of that reception of the wine, do therein receive Christ spiritually into their hearts.'[96] Finally, as a Baptist Spurgeon was determined to follow the example of the early church as found in the New Testament. This meant, as he expressed it in one of his sermons, that baptism was 'essential to obedience'. It also meant that weekly observance of the Lord's Supper was the model to follow. 'I have', said Spurgeon, 'never omitted it except I have been too ill to move'.[97] The sacraments were central to the spirituality of C.H. Spurgeon.

---

96   'The Greatest Exhibition of the Age', pp. 217-18.
97   'What the Lord's Supper sees and says', p. 537.

CHAPTER 5

Baptism and the Lord's Supper as Community Acts: Toward a Sacramental Understanding of the Ordinances

Stanley J. Grenz

Baptists take their name from one of the two sacred rites that they—like Protestants in general—practice as 'visible signs of the saving truth of the gospel', to cite the description offered by Augustus Hopkins Strong.[1] Despite the unity of namesake that they enjoy, Baptists are not of one mind regarding the meaning of the sacred practices that they share with other Christian churches. Dale Moody noted already in 1967 that Faith and Order discussions had revealed a division among Baptist theologians into those who see baptism (and, by extension, the Lord's supper) as solely human acts and those who add that the church's rites are also acts in which God is active.[2] This theological division extends even to terminology. Baptists who champion the idea that the church's rites are simply the divinely-given means whereby believers initially affirm and subsequently reaffirm their faith typically prefer to speak of these two practices as 'ordinances'. Baptists who see God at work in the rites of the church, in contrast, tend to be more willing to invoke the older language of 'sacrament'.

The goal of this essay is to draw implications from contemporary communitarian theory for this intra-Baptist fray. To this end, I begin by reviewing the historical developments that gave rise to the reticence to retain the use of the term 'sacrament'. I then suggest a manner in which viewing the church as a community opens the way for articulating a theology of the church's rites that recasts their sacramental value in a way that also honors their status as ordinances. Finally, I draw the essay to a close by looking specifically at baptism and the Lord's supper through communitarian lenses.

---

1   Augustus Hopkins Strong, *Systematic Theology* (3 vols; Philadelphia: Griffith and Rowland, 1909), III, p. 930.

2   Dale Moody, *Baptism: Foundation for Christian Unity* (Philadelphia: Westminster, 1967), p. 242.

Baptists and Terminology: Sacraments versus Ordinances

Baptists, especially in the USA, have stood at the vanguard in upholding the idea that baptism and the Lord's supper are ordinances and not sacraments. So entrenched has this idea become in some circles that the language of ordinance is taken for granted. Hence, in a 1934 expose on the New Hampshire Confession, published by what was then known as the Sunday School Board of the Southern Baptist Convention under the title *What Baptists Believe*, O.C.S. Wallace declared forthrightly, 'There are two ordinances belonging to a church of Christ...baptism and the Lord's Supper'.[3] Later in that decade, the typical Baptist claim regarding the appropriateness of the designation 'ordinance' and the objectionable character of the term 'sacrament' was even more forcefully declared in the opening paragraph of W.T. Conner's chapter on the topic in his influential work, *Christian Doctrine*. The highly regarded Southern Baptist theologian declared,

> Christ has instituted two ceremonial ordinances and committed them to his people for perpetual observance—baptism and the Lord's Supper. These two ceremonies are pictorial representations of the fundamental facts of the gospel and of our salvation through the gospel. Over against this view is the view of the Roman Catholic Church that these two ordinances, with five others, are 'sacraments' that convey grace to the participant.[4]

As these remarks suggest, the preference for 'ordinance' and the rejection of 'sacrament' are closely tied to a dispute with Rome regarding the efficacy of the rites of the church, a controversy that goes back to the Reformation, but whose roots lie in a terminological discussion dating to the patristic era.

The Question of Terminology in Theological History

Initially, the terms theologians chose to denote the sacred practices were a function of the linguistic context in which the church tradition they represented developed. Hence, Greek-speaking theologians deployed the term *mysterion*,[5] citing as their basis certain New Testament texts such as

---

3   O.C.S. Wallace, *What Baptists Believe* (Nashville: Sunday School Board of the Southern Baptist Convention, 1934), p. 93.

4   W.T. Conner, *Christian Doctrine* (Nashville: Broadman, 1937), p. 273.

5   John Chrysostom, for example, referred to the eucharist (Lord's supper) as a 'mystery'. *Homilies on 1 Corinthians*, 7.1, as cited in Timothy Ware, *The Orthodox Church* (New York: Penguin, 1983), p. 281. 'Mystery' remains the normal designation for the sacraments in the Orthodox Church. See Anthony M. Coniaris, *Introducing the*

Paul's description of his work as the administration of the divine *mysterion* (Eph. 3.2-3).[6] Theologians in the West, in contrast, appropriated a secular concept, *sacramentum*, to designate the rites of the church. This Latin term carried as its primary meaning the oath of fidelity and obedience to the commander sworn by a Roman soldier when he enlisted in the army.[7]

In the patristic era, the idea of a sacrament as an oath of fidelity came to be overshadowed by other meanings. Augustine, to cite one influential voice in this development, differentiated between the rite itself and the grace the Spirit imparts, a differentiation that led to the widely-held understanding of sacraments as outward or visible signs of an inward or invisible grace.[8] The Augustinian conception raised a question that has exercised Western theologians since the fifth century, namely, the vexing issue regarding the relationship between the outward sign and the inward reality.

By the Middle Ages theologians had concluded that an integral connection exists between the two dimensions of the great sacramental mystery. On the basis of the resultant sacramental theology, the medieval church developed an elaborate ecclesiastical system around the sacred rites. This system was held aloft by two important pillars, sacramentalism and sacerdotalism,[9] that when taken together produced what William Adams Brown has called 'sacramentarianism'.[10] Medieval church life centered on participation in the sacred rites (sacramentalism), which were viewed as means of grace, insofar as they convey or dynamically effect what they signify.[11] More specifically, a sacrament was said to be a cause of grace, insofar as it was God's chosen means of dispensing grace, understood as a supernatural power God infuses into the soul. This infused grace was believed to work without regard to the spiritual

---

Orthodox Church (Minneapolis: Light and Life Publishing, 1982), pp. 126-27. Hence, baptism may be called the 'mystery of water'. Alexander Schmemann, *Of Water and the Spirit* (n.p.: St Vladimir's Seminary Press, 1974), p. 40.

6   Heron notes, however, that in such texts *mysterion* does not refer to sacred rites, but to the hidden things of God disclosed in Christ. Alasdair I.C. Heron, *Table and Tradition: Toward an Ecumenical Understanding of the Eucharist* (Philadelphia: Westminster, 1983), p. 55.

7   Heron, *Table and Tradition*, p. 69.

8   Augustine, *Epistles* 98.2, as cited in J.N.D. Kelly, *Early Christian Doctrines* (San Francisco: Harper and Row, 5th edn, 1978), pp. 422-23.

9   For a discussion of this system, see Heron, *Table and Tradition*, pp. 89-91.

10   William Adams Brown, *Christian Theology in Outline* (New York: Charles Scribner's Sons, 1906), p. 404.

11   For this judgement regarding the sacramental theology of Aquinas, see Regis A. Duffy, 'Sacraments in General', in Francis Schuessler Fiorenza and John P. Galvin (eds.), *Systematic Theology: Roman Catholic Perspectives* (2 vols; Minneapolis: Fortress, 1991), II, p. 196.

condition of either the participant or the administrator of the sacrament. So long as the recipient did not resist the working of God in the sacraments, these acts—when properly administered—infused grace by their very operation (*ex opere operato*).

Because the church taught that the working of the sacraments rested on their being dispensed by a duly consecrated officiator, the sacramental system focused on the ordained clergy, who were thought to have the prerogative to administer these rites. Medieval theologians theorized that through ordination God endowed each priest with the power to transform mundane, physical elements—i.e., water, and bread and wine—into means of grace, a view known as 'sacerdotalism'. The priest's action, therefore, occasions a true sacrament, an act through which God infuses grace into the communicants. In this way, sacerdotalism entailed the elevation of clergy as chosen instruments of God who function as channels of divine grace.

Baptists and the Language Question

Medieval sacramentarianism came under attack in the Reformation. Although Martin Luther agreed with the medieval church that the sacred rites infuse spiritual vitality into the participant, he rejected the claim that they did so *ex opere operato*. Luther declared that a valid sacrament required more than the power of the priest. It demanded the faith of the participant. In the eyes of many Protestants, however, Luther had not gone far enough. They feared that the great reformer had not shut the door to what they perceived to be the magical outlook toward the church's rites indicative of Roman Catholic sacramental theology. Some Protestants concluded that the necessary break with Rome could not be effected without terminological surgery. In their estimation, 'sacrament' had become so tied to medieval sacramentarianism that the word was unsalvageable. The alternative designation that took root in English soil was 'ordinance'. Although the term may have appeared as early as the writings of Menno Simons,[12] the English Calvinist Baptists provided an important impetus for its subsequent acceptance by means of their use of 'ordinance' to designate baptism and the Lord's supper in several of

---

12   Simons speaks about the ordained character of the initiatory rite in his treatise on baptism (1539). Menno Simons, 'Christian Baptism', in J.C. Wenger (ed.), *The Complete Writings of Menno Simons* (trans. Leonard Verduin; Scottdale, PA: Herald, 1956), p. 238.

their early doctrinal statements, including the London confessions of 1644[13] and 1677.[14]

The appeal of 'ordinance' to Baptists in English-speaking circles is due in part to its derivation from the verb 'to ordain' and hence to its ability to convey the idea that baptism and the Lord's supper are to be practiced because Christ himself ordained—or commanded—their observance.[15] This appeal is evident, for example, in Emery Bancroft's definition of 'ordinance'. On the basis of its derivation from the Latin *ordo* and *ordinare* ('to establish' or 'to command'), Bancroft declares that the word 'comes to mean something established, commanded, enforced by proper authority' and consequently that the two church rites are 'symbolic acts which Christians are commanded [by the Lord] to observe'.[16]

Viewing baptism and the Lord's supper in this manner readily leads to the parallel idea that participation in these rites signifies the believer's obedience to Christ and hence that baptism and the Lord's supper are 'acts of obedience' (*Gehorsamakte*), to cite the designation advocated by Markus Barth.[17] Believers participate in the ordinances out of a desire to be obedient to the one who ordained that his followers perpetuate these acts. This perspective was suggested as early as the 1651 confession of faith of the General Baptists, in which baptism was cited as an 'Action of obedience'.[18]

If baptism and the Lord's supper are acts of obedience, participation in them is not only a symbol of the believer's personal obedience to Christ; it serves as an expression of personal faith as well. Baptists generally argue that such faith precedes baptism. Hence, from their survey of the biblical texts, Gordon Lewis and Bruce Demarest conclude, '*faith* rather than baptism is the means of being saved', an observation that leads them to the seemingly obvious implication: 'Baptism outwardly expresses a

13   'The Confession of Faith, of those Churches which are commonly (though falsely) called Anabaptists', article 39, in W.J. McGlothlin (ed.), *Baptist Confessions of Faith* (Philadelphia: American Baptist Publication Society, 1911), p. 185.

14   'Confession of Faith Put forth by the Elders and Brethren of many congregations of Christians', ch. 28, in McGlothlin (ed.), *Baptist Confessions of Faith*, p. 269.

15   See, for example, Strong, *Systematic Theology*, III, p. 930.

16   Emery H. Bancroft, *Christian Theology: Systematic and Biblical* (Grand Rapids, MI: Zondervan, rev. edn, 1961), p. 274.

17   See, especially, Markus Barth, *Die Taufe: Ein Sakrament? Ein exegetischer Beitrag zum Gespräch über die kirchliche Taufe* (Zollikon–Zurich: Evangelischer Verlag, 1951).

18   'The Faith and Practise of Thirty Congregations, Gathered according to the Primitive Pattern', 49, in McGlothlin (ed.), *Baptist Confessions of Faith*, p. 103.

person's inner faith.'[19] Dallas Roark offers a fuller explication of the typical Baptist idea. After pointing out that rather than occasioning grace, faith responds to it, Roark applies the principle to baptism and the Lord's supper: 'These rites do not strengthen grace in the heart of man; they speak of faith and commitment on man's part.'[20] Appealing to Calvin's suggestion that baptism is an occasion in which 'we publicly assert our faith'[21] and citing the words of Emil Brunner, Roark then concludes that 'baptism is the visible means of expressing what has already happened "invisibly through the word and faith"',[22] Later, he offers a similar perspective on the other major church rite: 'The Lord's Supper does not transmit any mysterious spiritual power. The Lord's Supper does not bring Christ any closer to the believer than he was before. The believer may feel existentially, but not geographically, nearer to God. The Lord's Supper thus regarded is a memorial, convenantal (sic), and prophetic symbol... Because the living Saviour indwells the believing (sic), the Lord's Supper does not increase any quantitative grace content in his life.'[23]

Baptists routinely link the inner faith that they see given public expression in the ordinances to a prior conversion experience. E.Y. Mullins, to cite one interesting example, claims that this is the perspective of the New Testament itself. In referring to the baptismal texts, he asserts, 'Baptism was the outward sign of an inward change which had already taken place in the believer.'[24] Strong goes so far as to suggest that understanding the ordinances as symbolizing a prior divine work in the human heart (which he denotes 'union with Christ') is the touchstone dividing Protestants from Roman Catholic sacramental theology: 'In contrast with this characteristically Protestant view, the Romanist regards the ordinances as actually conferring grace and producing holiness. Instead of being the external manifestation of a preceding union with Christ, they are the physical means of constituting and maintaining this union.'[25]

Viewing the rites of the church as ordinances rather than sacraments leads many Baptists, finally, to understand baptism and the Lord's supper as thoroughly human, rather than divine, acts. Instead of acts in which

---

19   Gordon R. Lewis and Bruce A. Demarest, *Integrative Theology* (3 vols; Grand Rapids, MI: Zondervan, 1987-94), III, p. 285.

20   Dallas M. Roark, *The Christian Faith* (Nashville: Broadman, 1969), p. 289.

21   Roark, *Christian Faith*, citing John Calvin, *Institutes of the Christian Religion* (Grand Rapids, MI: Eerdmans, 1957), II, p. 520.

22   Roark, *Christian Faith*, p. 291.

23   Roark, *Christian Faith*, p. 302.

24   Edgar Young Mullins, *The Christian Faith in Its Doctrinal Expression* (Philadelphia: Roger Williams Press, 1917), p. 384.

25   Strong, *Systematic Theology*, III, p. 930.

God imparts grace to the communicant, baptism and the Lord's supper are seen as occasions for participants to bear testimony to the spiritual truths symbolized in these rites. In their commitment to uphold in this manner the language of 'ordinances', Baptists routinely claim that they are the true heirs to Luther's insistence on the necessity of faith to the working of a sacrament.

Baptists and the Term 'Sacrament'

The early Baptists were surely correct in reacting against the overemphasis on the sacraments and the magical understanding of their workings that they saw in medieval sacramental theology. Yet not all participants in the movement sensed the need to reject the term 'sacrament' to accomplish this goal.[26] For example, the seventeenth-century General Baptists were quite willing to retain the older descriptor, while using the word 'ordinance' as well. Hence, the Orthodox Creed of 1678, declared, 'Those two sacraments, viz. Baptism, and the Lord's-supper, are ordinances of positive, sovereign, and holy institution, appointed by the Lord Jesus Christ, the only lawgiver, to be continued in his church, to the end of the world.'[27] This approach has continued into the present among some British Baptists, as is evident in Bruce Milne's handbook of theology, *Know the Truth*, which treats baptism and the Lord's supper under the heading 'The Sacraments' while also referring to the church rites as 'ordinances'.[28] Even some Baptists who are quite outspoken in their preference of the designation 'ordinance' will also call the rites 'sacraments' if the term is understood properly. Hence, the 'fine print' of Strong's treatment of the ordinances reads, 'as the

---

26   That there have always been a significant number of Baptists from the seventeenth century onwards who have held to a 'sacramental' understanding of baptism, see Philip E. Thompson, 'A New Question in Baptist History: Seeking a Catholic Spirit Among Early Baptists', *Pro Ecclesia* 8.1 (Winter, 1999), pp. 66-69 and 71-72, and 'Practicing the Freedom of God: Formation in Early Baptist Life', in David M. Hammond (ed.), *Theology and Lived Christianity* (Annual Publication of the College Theological Society, 45; Mystic, CT: Twenty-Third Publications, 2000), pp. 119-38; Anthony R. Cross, *Baptism and the Baptists: Theology and Practice in Twentieth-Century Britain* (Studies in Baptist History and Thought, 3; Carlisle: Paternoster, 2000), pp. 6-17, and 'Dispelling the Myth of English Baptist Baptismal Sacramentalism', *Baptist Quarterly* 38.8 (October, 2000), pp. 367-91; Stanley K. Fowler, *More Than a Symbol: The British Baptist Recovery of Baptismal Sacramentalism* (Studies in Baptist History and Thought, 2; Carlisle: Paternoster, 2002), pp. 10-155.

27   'An Orthodox Creed', Article 27, in McGlothlin (ed.), *Baptist Confessions of Faith*, p. 144.

28   Bruce Milne, *Know the Truth: A Handbook of Christian Belief* (Leicester, England: InterVarsity Press, 2nd edn, 1998), pp. 284-93.

sacramentum was the oath taken by the Roman soldier to obey his commander even unto death, so Baptism and the Lord's Supper are sacraments, in the sense of vows of allegiance to Christ our Master'.[29] As this terminological fluidity suggests, the crucial issue dividing Baptists is not so much the propriety of the terms 'sacrament' and 'ordinance', but the character of the rites themselves.

Viewed from this perspective, we must admit that the preference for the designation 'ordinance' has not been without ill effects in both theology and church practice. Beginning in the Age of Reason in which the Baptist movement initially flourished, many Baptists moved sharply in the direction of reducing baptism and the Lord's supper to being 'merely' ordinances, i.e., acts whose chief purposes are to demonstrate personal obedience to Christ and to bear public witness to an already completed inward working of God, and hence acts that have no direct connection to divine grace. One debilitating by-product of such reductionism has been a marked devaluing of both baptism and the Lord's supper in certain Baptist circles, a tendency that is most pronounced in widespread attitudes toward baptism. Today many Baptists, who share a denominational name derived from the initiatory rite of the church, view this act as having no real importance beyond serving as a personal statement of faith that fulfills one of several requirements for entrance into the local congregation. R.E.O. White offers a sobering appraisal of this situation: 'The view that our baptism is essentially an elaborate and slightly meritorious expression of our own enlightened opinion, an announcement to the congregation and to God that we have decided that the gospel is true, is a gross betrayal of all that the New Testament says about baptism.'[30]

Although a large number of Baptists today, at least in the USA, continue to eschew the language of 'sacrament', recent decades have witnessed a growing interest among some to recapture a depth of meaning in the church's rites, that they sense their forebears had discarded in a more 'rationalistic' era,[31] without undermining the important critique of sacramentarianism offered by their tradition.[32] In

---

29   Strong, *Systematic Theology*, III, p. 930. For a similar perspective, see James William McClendon, Jr., *Systematic Theology* (3 vols; Nashville: Abingdon, 1986–2000), II, p. 388.

30   R.E.O. White, *The Biblical Doctrine of Initiation* (London: Hodder and Stoughton, 1960), p. 295.

31   A.C. Underwood 'Views of Modern Churches (g) Baptists (2)', in Roderic Dunkerley (ed.), *The Ministry and the Sacraments* (London: SCM, 1937), p. 223-29.

32   For a recent example, see Christopher Ellis, 'Baptism and the Sacramental Freedom of God', in Paul S. Fiddes (ed.), *Reflections on the Water: Understanding God and the World through the Baptism of Believers* (Regent's Study Guides, 4; Macon, GA: Smyth and Helwys, 1996), pp. 23-45.

keeping with G.R. Beasley-Murray's judgment that 'the idea that baptism is a purely symbolic act must be pronounced not alone unsatisfactory but out of harmony with the New Testament itself',[33] theologians such as R.E.O. White have called for the reintroduction into Baptist life of the kind of 'dynamic sacramentalism' they see present in the initiation rite practiced by the early church.[34] According to White's characterization, 'Primitive Christian baptism was a rite of spiritual enduement, eschatologically effective, conferring remission, performed on divine authority and in the assurance that God as well as man was at work in each administration.'[35]

Attempts to resurrect a fuller sacramental understanding of the ordinances together with a reintroduction of the term 'sacrament' have not won universal applause. Critics aver that the day has not yet dawned when the term 'sacrament' can be rehabilitated without engendering misunderstanding. For this reason, Lewis and Demarest suggest that baptism (and, by extension, the Lord's supper) be deemed 'an ordained sign with sacred significance'.[36] Is there a way to move beyond the current impasse in content, if not in terminology as well?

Baptists and the Believing Fellowship: The Church as Community

The intra-Baptist debate regarding the proper designation and meaning of the church's rites pits theologians who see baptism and the Lord's supper as human acts against those who give place to a divine acting as well. Despite the apparently wide chasm separating them, the voices in the debate often reveal that they share a common standpoint. The question as to whether these rites are acts of the believer or occasions of God's acting in the believer can all-too-readily belie an underlying individualistic outlook. If this is the case, then the way forward might well be to consider the manner in which church rites are in fact that—rites of the *church*. Doing so requires a cursory look at contemporary understandings as to how communities function, as well as the role of rituals in community life.[37]

---

33   George R. Beasley-Murray, *Baptism in the New Testament* (Grand Rapids, MI: Eerdmans, 1962), p. 263.

34   For detailed studies of British Baptists, see A.R. Cross, *Baptism and the Baptists: Theology and Practice in Twentieth-Century Britain* (Studies in Baptist History and Thought, 3; Carlisle: Paternoster, 2000); and Fowler, *More Than a Symbol*.

35   White, *Biblical Doctrine of Initiation*, p. 305.

36   Lewis and Demarest, *Integrative Theology*, III, p. 287.

37   For a fuller treatment of contemporary communitarian thought, see Stanley J. Grenz and John R. Franke, *Beyond Foundationalism: Shaping Theology in a Postmodern Context* (Louisville, KY: Westminster John Knox, 2001), pp. 204-23.

Like many terms that are 'in vogue' today, *community* defies any single, agreed-upon definition. Nevertheless, contemporary descriptions generally suggest that a community consists of persons who are conscious that they share a similar frame of reference. Hence, members of a particular community tend to have a similar outlook toward life, view the world in a similar manner, and construct the symbolic world they inhabit using similar linguistic and symbolic building materials, even if they are not of one mind as to the meaning of their shared world-constructing symbols. In addition, operative in all communities is a group focus that readily evokes among the members a sense of a shared identity, a common task and a group solidarity.[38] This group focus likewise includes a shared commitment to participating in an ongoing discussion as to what constitutes the identity of the group, as well as a shared goal of determining and attempting to create what the members hold to be a good community.[39]

Balancing the group orientation of a community is its 'person focus'. Insofar as members draw their personal identity from their participation in it, the group becomes a crucial factor in forming the identity of its members. Hence, Michael Sandel declares the members of a society 'conceive their identity—the subject and not just the object of their feelings and aspirations—as defined to some extent by the community of which they are a part. For them, community describes not just what they *have* as fellow citizens but also what they *are*, not a relationship they choose (as in a voluntary association) but an attachment they discover, not merely an attribute but a constituent of their identity.'[40]

Perhaps the pioneer in articulating the idea that personal identity is socially produced was George Herbert Mead (1863–1931). According to Mead, meaning is interpersonal or relational, the mind is not only individual but also a social phenomenon,[41] and hence the self—the maturing personality or one's personal identity—is socially produced;[42] it emerges as a product of the process of social interaction.

Certain contemporary thinkers have blended the insights of Mead (and others) with narrative theory. Alasdair MacIntyre, to cite one influential

---

38   Derek L. Phillips, *Looking Backward: A Critical Appraisal of Communitarian Thought* (Princeton, NJ: Princeton University Press, 1993), p. 17.

39   Robert N. Bellah, 'Community Properly Understood: A Defense of "Democratic Communitarianism"', in Amitai Etzioni (ed.), *The Essential Communitarian Reader* (Lanham, MD: Rowman and Littlefield, 1998), p. 16.

40   Michael J. Sandel, *Liberalism and the Limits of Justice* (Cambridge: Cambridge University Press, 2nd edn, 1998), p. 150.

41   George Herbert Mead, *Mind, Self and Society* (ed. Charles W. Morris; Chicago: University of Chicago Press, 1962 [1934]), pp. 118-25, 134.

42   For Mead's argument, see *Mind, Self and Society*, pp. 144-64.

example, argues that humans are story-tellers.[43] Personal identity, he theorizes, develops through the telling of a personal narrative, in accordance with which one's life 'makes sense'.[44] These personal stories, MacIntyre adds, are tied up with the larger group story, in that we enter human society 'with one or more imputed characters—roles into which we have been drafted'.[45] George Stroup provides a fuller treatment of this dynamic.[46] He postulates that identity emerges as a person, through the exercise of memory, selects certain events from the past and uses them as a basis for interpreting the significance of the whole of the person's life on the basis of an 'interpretive scheme' that provides the 'plot' through which the entire personal chronicle makes sense. This interpretive framework arises from one's social context, i.e., from the community in which the person participates.[47] Sociologists designate the particular community from which a person derives the fundamental sense of identity his or her 'reference group'[48] or 'community of reference'.

The role of a community of reference in identity formation is predicated upon its ability to link the present to both the past and the future. An early voice in bringing to light this crucial aspect was Josiah Royce (1855–1916),[49] who described a vibrant community as functioning both as a 'community of memory' and as a 'community of hope'.[50] According to Royce, a community of memory emerges, in that each member 'accepts as part of his own individual life and self the same

---

43   Alasdair MacIntyre, *After Virtue: A Study in Moral Theory* (Notre Dame, IN: University of Notre Dame Press, 2nd edn, 1984), p. 216.

44   On this point, see also, Robert N. Bellah, *et al.*, *Habits of the Heart: Individualism and Commitment in American Life* (Perennial Library edition; New York: Harper and Row, 1986), p. 81.

45   MacIntyre, *After Virtue*, p. 216.

46   George W. Stroup, *The Promise of Narrative Theology* (Atlanta: John Knox, 1981), pp. 101-98.

47   Here Stroup is in substantial agreement with social constructionist sociologists, such as Peter Berger. See, for example, Peter L. Berger, *The Sacred Canopy: Elements of a Sociological Theory of Religion* (Anchor Books edn; Garden City, NY: Doubleday, 1969), p. 20.

48   Peter L. Berger, *Invitation to Sociology: A Humanistic Perspective* (Anchor Books edn; Garden City, NY: Doubleday, 1963), p. 118.

49   For a recent summary of the importance of Royce, see Frank M. Oppenheim, 'A Roycean Response to the Challenge of Individualism', in Donald L. Gelpi (ed.), *Beyond Individualism: Toward a Retrieval of Moral Discourse in America* (Notre Dame: University of Notre Dame Press, 1989), pp. 87-119.

50   For a short overview, see 'Josiah Royce', in William L. Reese (ed.), *Dictionary of Philosophy and Religion* (Atlantic Highlands, NJ: Humanities Press, 1980), pp. 498-99.

past events that each of his follow-members accepts'.[51] The group functions as a 'community of hope', in turn, as 'each of its members accepts, as part of his own individual life and self, the same expected *future* events that each of his fellows accepts'.[52]

Building upon Royce's insight, contemporary communitarians delimit the role of a community in connecting the present with both past and future so as to constitute not only the 'self' of its members[53] but also the group as a whole. To this end, they explain that a community is constituted by a communal narrative that begins in the past and extends into the future. This 'constitutive narrative' commences with the primal event(s) that called the community into being and then moves through the crucial milestones that mark its subsequent trajectory, including accounts of shared suffering and even of past evils,[54] as well as the stories of persons who have embodied or exemplified the communal ideals. More important than merely retelling past occurrences, reciting the narrative retrieves the constitutive past for the sake of personal and communal life in the present. This act places the contemporary community within the primal events that constituted their forebears as this particular community. By retrieving the past, such a recital reconstitutes the community in the present as the contemporary embodiment of a communal tradition that spans the years.

Rather than ending in the past·or even the present, the constitutive narrative extends into the future. By reciting this aspect of its narrative, a community turns the gaze of its members toward the future, anticipating the continuation and further development of the community. In this manner, the group senses that it is moving toward an ideal that lies yet before it in the 'eschatological' fullness, when the purpose and goals—the *telos*—of the community will be perfectly actualized. This expectation of a glorious future serves as an ongoing admonition to its members to embody the communal vision in the present, so as to be in the here-and-now the anticipatory manifestation of the complete reality that will one day characterize the community.

As it is recited in the present, the community's constitutive narrative provides a transcendent vantage point for life in the here-and-now. It bestows a qualitative meaning upon life, upon time and space, and upon present community members. It provides the overarching theme through which members of the community can view their lives, together with the

51   Josiah Royce, *The Problem of Christianity* (2 vols; New York: Macmillan, 1913), II, p. 50.

52   Royce, *Problem of Christianity*, II, p. 51.

53   For the author's book-length treatment of the social constitution of the 'self', see Stanley J. Grenz, *The Social God and the Relational Self: A Trinitarian Theology of the Imago Dei* (Louisville, KY: Westminster John Knox, 2001).

54   Bellah, *et al.*, *Habits of the Heart*, pp. 152-55.

present, as integral parts of a temporal stream that transcends every particular 'now'. Likewise, the constitutive narrative supplies a context of meaning that allows community members to connect their personal aspirations with those of a larger whole, and it facilitates them in seeing their efforts as contributions to that whole.

The telling of the constitutive narrative is accentuated through certain sacred practices, that anthropologists call 'rites of intensification'. Stephen Grunlan and Marvin Mayers note that such rituals 'bring the community together, increase group solidarity, and reinforce commitment to the beliefs of the group'.[55] Moreover, these 'practices of commitment', to cite the designation coined by the Robert Bellah group, define the community way of life as well as the patterns of loyalty and obligation that keep the community alive.[56] Through their participation in these acts, the members of a community gain a heightened sense of communal belonging—what Robert Nisbet describes as 'a fusion of feeling and thought, of tradition and commitment, of membership and volition'.[57]

The sociological perspective outlined above provides a helpful vantage point from which to understand the church as community. It suggests that the church may be viewed as a particular people imbued with a particular 'constitutive narrative' that spans the ages from the primordial past to the eschatological future. As the church retells this constitutive narrative, it functions as a community of memory and hope, for it links the present with the entire stream of God's action that commences 'in the beginning' (Gen. 1.1) and spans the ages climaxing in 'a new heaven and a new earth' (Rev. 21.1). This narrative provides the interpretive framework—the narrative plot—through which the members of Christ's community find meaning in their personal and communal stories, as through their connection with this people, believers discover the link between their personal lives and a transcendent story—the narrative of the work of the biblical God in history.

As a consequence of this shared narrative, believers sense a special solidarity with each other. Within the context of the church, this solidarity works its way out in the practical dimensions of fellowship, support and nurture that its members discover in relationship with each other as a communal people. In this manner, as James McClendon succinctly states, the church becomes a community 'understood not as privileged access to

55   Stephen A. Grunlan and Marvin K. Mayers, *Cultural Anthropology: A Christian Perspective* (Grand Rapids, MI: Zondervan, 2nd edn, 1988), p. 222.
56   Bellah, *et al.*, *Habits of the Heart*, pp. 152-54.
57   Robert A. Nisbet, *The Sociological Tradition* (New York: Basic Books, 1966), p. 48.

God or to sacred status, but as sharing together in a storied life of obedient service to and with Christ'.[58]

Baptists and Church Rites: Baptism and the Lord's Supper as Communal Acts

Many Baptists, especially in the USA, maintain the primacy of the term 'ordinance' as providing the conceptual basis for understanding the character of the church's rites. This perspective is not misguided. Designating baptism and the Lord's supper as 'ordinances' facilitates the church in keeping clearly in view the crucial connection between the sacred acts and both Christ's command and our obedient response. This term stands as a reminder that baptism and the Lord's supper stand as a divinely-given means for Christ's disciples to declare their loyalty to Jesus as Lord. Yet the designation 'ordinance' raises the question, *Why* did Jesus ordain these acts? John Calvin offered what might well be the best answer, and one that has gained acceptance by many Christian traditions:[59] 'they have been instituted by the Lord to the end that they may serve to establish and increase faith'.[60] This question, however, triggers a second: *How* does participation in these acts strengthen us? Responding to this question brings the designation *sacrament* into view.

The primary original meaning of the term suggests that baptism and the Lord's supper are sacraments in that they constitute occasions for believers to confess their faith and thereby affirm their fidelity to Jesus Christ as Lord. Pursued on the basis of this connection, the central task of a theology of the church's rites becomes that of delineating the manner in which God is present and active in acts through which human faith comes to symbolic confession. To this end, baptism and the Lord's supper may be viewed as enacted pictures or symbols of God's grace given in Christ. As Augustine and the Reformers declared, the church's rites are visual sermons, the word of God symbolically proclaimed.[61] Through our participation we not only declare the truth of the gospel; we also bear testimony to our reception of the grace symbolized. Hence, through these rites, we 'act out' our faith, and baptism and the Lord's supper become what we might call 'acts of commitment', enactments of our appropriation of God's action in Christ. Yet such enactments are also

---

58   McClendon, *Systematic Theology*, I, p. 28.

59   Exceptions include the Salvation Army and the Quakers, who do not practice the traditional acts of commitment.

60   John Calvin, *Institutes of the Christian Religion*, 1559 edition, 4.14.9 (Library of Christian Classics, 21; ed. John T. McNeill; trans. Ford Lewis Battles; Philadelphia: Westminster, 1960), p. 1284.

61   Calvin, *Institutes*, 4.14.4 (p. 1279).

sacramental, for as we affirm our faith in this vivid symbolic manner, the Holy Spirit facilitates our participation in the reality the rites symbolize. In short, as a growing ecumenical consensus suggests, the church's rites are divine–human events. God is graciously present in baptism and the Lord's supper, and God's personal presence calls for 'free personal response', to cite the words of Daniel Migliore.[62] And the Roman Catholic theologian Regis Duffy might even find echo among Baptists when he describes a sacrament as 'a presence-filled event in which God gratuitously enables us to welcome the message of salvation, to enter more deeply into the paschal mystery, and to receive gratefully that transforming and healing power that gathers us as the community of God's Son so as to announce the reign of God in the power of the Spirit'.[63]

In articulating this perspective, however, we are not yet at our goal of setting forth an explicitly communitarian understanding of the church's rites. To this end, we must view the ordinances through the lens of the church's role in the process of forming the identity of its members. That is, we must understand the 'acts of commitment' as 'community acts' or 'rites of belonging'. Coming to see baptism and the Lord's supper as community acts provides the vantage point for gaining a renewed sense of the connection of the divine and the human in the church's rites, and hence for understanding the manner in which the ordinances are sacramental. The two ordinances carry sacramental significance in that they are identity-conveying and identity-forming events. The identity announced and confirmed in the church's rites does not arise *sui generis*, however, but comes as a gift that God graciously bestows upon the participants both individually and corporately. At the same time, the rites are personal events, acts that believers freely do, both as individuals and as a group. And finally, no person acts unilaterally in either baptism or the Lord's supper; instead, these acts remain always rites of the church.

The Church's Rites as Community Acts

Paul and other New Testament writers declare that to be a Christian means fundamentally to be united with Christ. This union entails not only mental assent to a set of doctrines, but more importantly the embodiment in one's beliefs, attitudes and actions the meanings and values that characterized Jesus' own life. In this process, the Christian community is crucial, for it transmits from generation to generation the salvation story

---

62   Daniel L. Migliore, *Faith Seeking Understanding: An Introduction to Christian Theology* (Grand Rapids, MI: Eerdmans, 1991), p. 213.

63   Duffy, 'Sacraments in General', p. 185.

and thereby mediates to its members the framework for the formation of personal identity and values. Central to this identity-shaping task is the recital of the church's constituting narrative. As it declares anew the biblical salvation story, which moves from creation to new creation with Christ as its focal point, the church functions as a community of memory and hope, linking the present to the past and the future.

Within this process, the church's rites play a crucial role. These acts are an indispensable means whereby the group is placed ritually into the narrative that constitutes them as a community. To this end, baptism and the Lord's supper serve as symbols of the relationship of believers to God and to one another. These acts symbolize, vividly portray and ritually enact the participation of the community as a whole in the divine story and the participation of its members in the believing community. In this manner, these rites become community acts.

The ability of baptism and the Lord's supper to function as community acts is closely bound up with their essential connection to the central events of the biblical narrative, namely, the life, passion and resurrection of Jesus, together with the sending of the Spirit. The church's rites recount in a dramatic, symbolic manner the Christian declaration that 'in Christ God was reconciling the world to himself' (2 Cor. 5.19 NRSV). They portray the gospel story that Jesus died to bring forgiveness and rose from the dead to bring new life. Consequently, they are vivid 'memorials', for they call to mind the events that form the heart of the gospel. Yet the memorial character of the rites does not exhaust their meaning. Participation in baptism and the Lord's supper facilitates symbolic participation in the saving events to which they point and which form the narrative basis for the identity of believers as those who are united with Christ. The church's rites, therefore, transport the contemporary community into the past. Participants in these acts enact the gospel declaration that they died with Christ. Thereby, the Holy Spirit confirms in them their identity as new persons in Christ. By perpetuating these rites, therefore, the church functions as a community of memory.

The church's rites lift our gaze from the past to the future. They speak not only of God's past salvation, but also of the glorious eschatological future that one day will come as God's gift, for the crucified and risen Lord will return in glory. Because of their connection with the church's eschatological hope, the rites of the church are a powerful means whereby the community sustains its constitutive vision. These acts declare symbolically that the fullness of community, the perfect fellowship toward which the church now strives and which marks its true identity, together with the fullness of the personal identity of its members, lies yet in the future. The connection between rite and reality is stronger than mere announcement, however. In baptism and the Lord's supper, the community symbolically anticipates the grand eschatological event to which these rites point. Thereby the community celebrates in the midst of the brokenness of the present the glorious future fullness, and it proleptically participates in the eschatological reality.

In short, the celebration of the ordinances facilitates the symbolic retelling of the old, old story of God's action in Jesus, an action that includes not only the past but extends to the eschatological future. As we tell the story in this vivid, pictorial manner, we are transported into both the past and the future. We symbolically experience both Christ's death and his resurrection, which constitutes our identity as those who are in Christ. As we are en-storied in this manner—as we are caught up into both God's past action in Christ and the vision of God's future—we find purpose and meaning for our own lives, for we gain a sense of the connectedness of all history, and we come to see our present within the flow of God's story. Through the church's rites, the Spirit confirms in us that we are en route toward the fullness of God's intention for us, thereby mediating to us a sense of our ultimate identity and the empowerment needed for godly living in the here and now.

Baptism and the Lord's Supper as Acts of Belonging[64]

The rites of the church take their meaning from the gospel, for baptism and the Lord's supper are dramatic community enactments of its constitutive narrative, the biblical story of salvation. More specifically, these acts memorialize the events of Jesus' passion and resurrection, and bear witness to the experience of union with Christ shared by the entire community. The idea of a shared union with Christ embodied in the church's rites suggests that as community acts baptism and the Lord's supper function as acts of belonging, albeit each in a distinctive manner.

Baptism marks the initiation of a person into the Christian community, for it serves as the divinely-given means of giving symbolic expression to the joining of a person's own story with the narrative of Jesus and hence with the story of the discipleship group. The church rightly sees in baptism the symbol of the new birth and the new identity that members enjoy, in that this rite symbolically effects a change of context, the transference from 'the power of darkness' into the kingdom of God's Son, to cite the language of Colossians (Col. 1.13). Viewed from this perspective, in baptism a person symbolically and publically recounts his or her personal narrative in accordance with the gospel story, and as a consequence receives a new identity in keeping with that story, with its

---

64   For a longer, albeit less developed, treatment of some of these themes, see Stanley J. Grenz, *Theology for the Community of God* (Grand Rapids, MI: Eerdmans, 2000 [1994]), pp. 511-41.

declaration that 'everything old has passed away...everything has become new' (2 Cor. 5.17).

To this end, baptism is an act of the church. It entails the incorporation of the baptismal candidate into the life of the community. Such incorporation functions on the level of participation in congregational life, of course. But lying behind the practical dimension is the deeper dimenson of incorporation into the narrative community, the community whose constitutive narrative has now become the identity-forming narrative of the baptismal candidate. In baptism, the story of the participant comes to be linked with the story of God's past action in Jesus, as recited by the narrating community. Baptism thereby symbolically bestows upon the participant a new identity based on the past event of Jesus' death, for the baptismal candidate is being initiated into the company of those who have died with Christ (Rom. 6.3). At the same time, the new identity symbolically conferred through baptism has its basis in the future. Just as Jesus' story did not end on Resurrection Sunday but remains incomplete until his future *parousia* as the reigning Lord, so the believer's story does not end with the new birth but anticipates a future participation in the eternal community. For this reason, baptism points beyond initiation into the Christian life to the goal of God's saving activity, namely, the eschatological transformation of all believers within the context of the establishment of the new creation.

The goal toward which baptism points and which it anticipates is already being accomplished by the renewing work of the indwelling Holy Spirit, whose presence is the pledge of the eschatological fullness of salvation (2 Cor. 1.22; 5.5; Eph. 1.14) and whose reception is likewise symbolically experienced in baptism. Consequently, baptism symbolically anticipates the eschatological fullness of life for the sake of living to the glory of God in the present. Furthermore, it remains in every aspect a community act, for it does not confer identity on the initiate in isolation, but speaks about a communal identity shared by those who together are in Christ and consequently are the fellowship of the baptized.

Whereas baptism is the grand declaration of belonging, the Lord's supper stands as the repeated reaffirmation of that belonging. The Lord's supper marks the reprise of the great refrain, 'You/I/we belong', that in baptism the identity-conferring God, the identifying community and the identity-acknowledging candidate sang together.[65]

As the designation 'Lord's supper' suggests, the celebration entails a symbolic participation in the past. The pageantry of the meal involves a reenactment of the Last Supper, when Jesus instituted the rite and

---

65   For a somewhat similar attempt to understand baptism as a 'triply enacted sign', see McClendon, *Systematic Theology*, II, p. 390.

explained its significance. Participants in the Lord's supper, therefore, symbolically enter into the Jesus story, as they sit with him in the upper room, as it were, recalling his teaching about the pathway to life and, of course, his death as the provision for their salvation. Moreover, the Lord's supper serves as a symbolic participation in Christ himself (1 Cor. 10.16). The acts of eating and drinking form appropriate symbols of this participation, for they metaphorically represent the character of faith as the ongoing reception of God's gracious provision in Christ. Participants are symbolically declaring that just as the act of ingesting bread and wine is the means of drawing vitality from food and drink so also faith entails the continuous appropriation of Christ—i.e., ongoing union with Christ—for spiritual vitality. Therefore, by transporting contemporary participants into the biblical narrative, the Spirit not only rekindles their devotion and commitment to the Lord, but also constitutes them as, while strengthening them to be, Christ's community in the present.

Because the Lord's supper occurs in the context of Jesus' promise of a future 'drinking anew' in the kingdom, it directs attention to the future as well as the past. Participants in the church's rite remember Jesus' sacrificial death in accordance with its promissory significance. By means of this link to the future fulfillment of Jesus' promise, the past event of Christ's death constitutes the identity of the community that has gathered around the Lord's table as those who belong to him. Furthermore, the rite draws participants into the future, where they meet the risen Jesus who has gone before them into God's eschatological kingdom through his resurrection, which, according to his promise, they will one day share.

The future that Jesus promises and toward which the Lord's supper is oriented is characterized by fellowship—i.e., 'belongingness'. In the upper room, Jesus directed his disciples toward the time when they would enjoy the fullness of communion. Nevertheless, participation in the church's rite does not anticipate eschatological fellowship merely as a hope for the distant future. Rather, it entails a proleptic experience of the future reality that gives meaning to and confers identity upon the community in the present. As the community gathers at the table, their Lord—through the Holy Spirit—is present among them and communes with them. Moreover, his presence—by the Spirit—constitutes the gathered community anew as the fellowship of those who together are in Christ. In this manner, sharing in the one loaf at the Lord's supper becomes the great communal act of belonging, the great symbol of the fellowship with Christ and each other shared by the participants who belong to each other as the one body of Christ (1 Cor. 10.17). For this reason, the presence of Christ through the Holy Spirit transforms the observance of the Lord's supper from merely a solemn memorial of a crucified Savior into a joyous celebration of the risen and returning Lord who is even now present among his people.

To conclude: as symbols of his story which is now our story, baptism and the Lord's supper form significant rites within the community of faith. Through these two acts we enact our faith, in that as we symbolically reenact the story of salvation. We memorialize the events of Jesus' passion and resurrection, we bear testimony to the experience of union with Christ that we share as the one community of faith, and we lift our sights to the grand future awaiting us as participants together in the covenant community of God. When baptism and the Lord's supper truly function in this manner as church rites—that is, when they truly become community acts of belonging—these ordinances are well able to carry the sacramental significance intended by the Lord of the church who ordained that they be perpetuated among those who belong to him, until the glorious day when the eternal community to which they point is present in its fullness.

CHAPTER 6

Re-Membering the Body:
Baptism, Eucharist and the Politics of
Disestablishment

Barry Harvey

The old habits of establishmentarianism, it would seem, have proven to be far more difficult for Baptists to break than anyone ever imagined. Our earliest forebears regarded the builders of earthly kingdoms with a wary eye because they invariably laid stake to an authority that belonged to Christ alone. Our mothers and fathers also knew that the rule of Christ claimed the whole of their lives, which meant that the church was, as Philip Thompson has put it, 'the earthly arena in which the reign of Christ was embodied, and as such was an interruption and delegitimization of the false politics of the state'.[1] They knew that once baptism incorporated them into this body politic their day-to-day lives were not merely surveyed, categorized, inventoried and supplemented as needed by religious discourse, but were radically transfigured in a way that touched on every aspect of their existence. And they knew that this transfiguration of life frequently put them into conflict with those who actively sought to usurp the place and power of God.

Somewhere along the line, however, the offspring and heirs of John Bunyan and Muriel Lester, Anne Hutchinson and Roger Williams made their peace with the earthly city. As toleration was gradually extended to them in England, accompanied by an increase in wealth and social standing, and with the institutionalization of religious liberty in the New World, Baptist churches (together with other Christian communities) increasingly settled for the care of 'souls', ceding virtually all claims to

---

1   P.E. Thompson, 'Religious Liberty, Sacraments, God Image, and the State in Two Periods in Baptist Life and Thought' (unpublished paper presented to the Forty-Sixth Annual Convention of the College Theological Society, Philadelphia, PA, 4 June 2000), p. 15. This paper is revised and expanded in the present volume. See P.E. Thompson, 'Sacraments and Religious Liberty: From Critical Practice to Rejected Infringement'.

the bodies of their members to the civil authorities.[2] And with the privatization of 'religion' in the modern world even this limited jurisdiction was stripped from their purview. The offer and acceptance of forgiveness was no longer a communal practice that binds and looses on earth and in heaven (Mt. 18.18), but 'an individual transaction between God and a particular person, largely devoid of its eschatological context and with virtually no consequences for either Christian community or social and political life'.[3] Abdication from the public realm effectively made the church incidental to salvation, reducing it to a *collegium pietatis*, a social club for the cultivation of a privatized spirituality.[4]

Baptist churches in Europe and North America have for the most part accepted the accommodations arranged for them by the modern world, arrangements that perpetuate the oligarchic dominion of the powers that be. I shall contend, however, that the God of Israel summons the church to a way of life and language that stands in marked contrast to the practices of establishment. This life and language, however, is only evidenced by a people who have been gathered together by the Spirit, principally through the sacramental celebrations of baptism and eucharist. These signs and seals of God's rule do not function within a private 'religious' world, for the drama they re-enact and the body they re-member narrate the story of all creation and history. The content, logic and trajectory of the baptism and eucharist, writes Rodney Clapp, propel us out of the boundaries set for them by the powers of the present age, and 'push us toward [their] reconnection with the Christian discipline of our social and physical bodies'.[5]

If disestablishment is not just to be a nostalgic slogan, but a practical condition for becoming 'a people who find in Christ their center, in the

2   Mark Bell documents how Baptists moved gradually toward cultural establishment during the Interregnum, particularly among the leadership in London who 'pushed radicalism to the perimeters, both geographically and theologically'. He notes moreover that 'during the seventeenth century, a number of the leading Baptists eager for accommodation with society had gained considerable wealth. This increase in wealth was frequently accompanied by a change in social position, which gave many Baptists a greater incentive to accommodate with society.' M.R. Bell, *Apocalypse How? Baptist Movements During the English Revolution* (Macon, GA: Mercer University Press, 2000), pp. 129–30.

3   L.G. Jones, *Embodying Forgiveness: A Theological Analysis* (Grand Rapids, MI: Eerdmans, 1995), p. 38. Cf. O. Tjørhom, 'The Church as the Place of Salvation: On the Interrelation between Justification and Ecclesiology', *Pro Ecclesia* 9.3 (Summer, 2000), pp. 285–96.

4   See D. Bonhoeffer, *Dietrich Bonhoeffer Works*: 5. *Life Together and Prayerbook of the Bible* (Minneapolis, MN: Fortress, 1996), p. 45.

5   R. Clapp, 'At the Intersection of Eucharist and Capital', in *Border Crossings: Christian Trespasses on Popular Culture and Public Affairs* (Grand Rapids, MI: Brazos, 2000), p. 99.

Spirit their communion, in God's reign their rule of life',[6] then Baptists must learn to recognize and refuse the updated forms of political, social and economic accommodation fashioned for them by the rulers and authorities of the present age. To do this they must be receptive to the work of the Spirit which, because it consists 'not in talk but in power' (1 Cor. 4.20), takes concrete form in and through the sacramental signs that shape the disciplinary sinews of the church's common life and language. In what follows, then, I shall attempt to tease out some of what is entailed in the liturgical re-membering of the body of Christ by first sketching the outlines of the 'original disestablishment' accomplished by Jesus and the early church. I shall then detail briefly how the disciplinary activities of the modern world work to re-establish Christian life and language by dismembering the sacramental sinews of the Christian body in both its communal and its personal aspects. In the final section I shall attempt to indicate how baptism and eucharist effectively re-member Christ's earthly-historical body in ways that allow its members to recognize the current structures of accommodation and to cultivate the alternative patterns that provide for the world a sign and foretaste of that 'perfectly ordered and perfectly harmonious fellowship in the enjoyment of God, and of one another in God'.[7]

Original Disestablishment

Though it is now commonplace to speak of Christianity as a 'worldview', one would be hard pressed to find such a description in scripture or the early church fathers. Instead the sense and significance of Christian convictions were part of a communal discipline embodied in the public life of the church. This is not to say by any stretch of the imagination that beliefs and doctrines were somehow incidental to the common life of this body politic. 'Thanks be to God', writes the apostle Paul, 'that you, having once been slaves of sin, have become obedient from the heart to the form of teaching to which you were entrusted, and that you, having been set free from sin, have become slaves of righteousness' (Rom. 6.17–18). But these teachings are like threads in the complex weave of a garment. If they are removed from that piece of cloth they lose all pattern and texture.[8] As N.T. Wright puts it, ecclesial convictions are 'a

---

    6   J.W. McClendon, Jr., *Systematic Theology: 2. Doctrine* (Nashville, TN: Abingdon, 1994), p. 21.
    7   Augustine, *The City of God Against the Pagans*, 19.17 (ed. R.W. Dyson; New York: Cambridge University Press, 1998), p. 947.
    8   See B. Harvey, 'Doctrinally Speaking: James McClendon on the Nature of Doctrine', *Perspectives in Religious Studies* 27.1 (Spring, 2000), pp. 39–60.

shorthand way of articulating the points of pressure, tension and conflict between different actual communities'.[9]

The community of Jesus' followers articulated these differences by referring to itself from the outset as an *ekklesia*, a term drawn from the political vocabulary of Greek antiquity designating the civic assembly of those holding rights of citizenship within the *polis*. When the church adopted this term for their community rather than that of the ancient guilds and civic clubs, it was claiming the status of a public assembly of the whole community. The ethos of this particular political association, however, was neither that of the Greek *polis* nor the Roman *imperium*. The designation of God's people as *ekklesia* originates in the Old Testament, and more specifically in the gathering of the Hebrews at Mt Sinai following their deliverance from Egypt. The day when Israel gathered at the mountain of God to enter into covenant with God is called the day of the assembly (*yom haqqahal*, in the LXX, *hemera tes ekklesias*, Dt. 9.10). When the fledgling Christian community in Jerusalem took for itself the designation of the foundational assembly at Sinai that constituted Israel as a people, it strongly suggests 'that it understood itself as the eschatological fulfillment of that gathering at Sinai'.[10]

The conduct and convictions of this body politic so questioned the established social and political categories of its time that the resulting reorganization of human life and language became a never-ending task. In the words of Rowan Williams, this people had the temerity to claim 'that all "meaning", every assertion about the significance of life and reality, must be judged by reference to a brief succession of contingent events in Palestine'. The sense and direction of all created life could therefore only be truthfully discerned in relation to the events that swirled around one seemingly insignificant Jewish man. This unlikely figure was an itinerant rabbi who spent his days pursuing a way of life which, though it was the way of peace, moved inexorably toward confrontation and violence. His life was tragically cut short by a peculiar alliance between the mightiest and most efficient empire the world has ever known, and those whom this empire had selected to administer the affairs of the Jewish people. And yet his mysterious triumph over death, together with what he accomplished during his lifetime, so radically called into question the dominant categories and relations that the restructuring of language and life continues to this day.[11]

---

9   N.T. Wright, *The Climax of the Covenant* (Minneapolis, MN: Fortress Press, 1992), p. 122.

10   G. Lohfink, *Does God Need The Church? Toward a Theology of the People of God* (trans. Linda M. Maloney; Collegeville, MN: Liturgical Press, 1999) p. 219.

11   R. Williams, *The Wound of Knowledge* (Boston, MA: Cowley, 2nd edn, 1990), p. 1.

In and through these events, the church proclaimed, the world witnessed the beginning of the long-awaited reign of God, and with it the making of a new covenant that brought with it the first fruits of a new humanity. In Jesus and his followers the messianic age became a present reality, not in some kind of private religious experience or moral ideal, but in terms of the day-to-day concerns and celebrations of life. Over against the forces and powers that governed the course and content of life in the ancient world, Jesus and the church extended the offer of an alternative pattern of life, a distinctive set of habits and relations, and a different story in terms of which to make sense of the order of things.

So disruptive was the drawing near of God's rule to the established course of events it took Jesus' followers centuries to develop adequate ways of saying what needed to be said about the sense and direction of his life, death and resurrection. In particular, new uses had to be put to the word 'God'. Without jeopardizing the mystery and simplicity of God, they determined that the only way to do justice to all that Jesus did and suffered was to speak of him as the incarnate Word of God. In the words of Ignatius of Antioch, Christ 'is the mouth...by which the Father has truly spoken', or as Rowan Williams unpacks it, 'he is himself "what the Father says"'.[12] In the person of Jesus, God assumed the day-to-day realities of human existence in order to reweave its tattered fabric, so that we might in turn share in the life-giving activity of God. Without effacing the difference between the speaker and the word spoken, the church confessed that it was *God* who appeared in the particular events and circumstances of this man's life and work to gather together what had been dispersed by humankind's disobedience.

The church's confession that God's address and agency took flesh in a particular person who lived at a certain time and place, who said and did and suffered certain things, did not cancel or set aside the particularity of Jesus' own history. On the contrary, so crucial were the events of his life, the only appropriate form in which the truth about him could be told was that of a story. But as pivotal as his personal story is, it is not sufficient to confess that the Son entered fully into time and history, and in so doing perfectly fulfilled the will of the Father. As Hans Urs von Balthasar observes, 'In that light his life is still only one existence among others; and if it is no more it can only be, even in its highest perfection, a (perhaps unattainable) moral example for others living before and after him.'[13] And so when Jesus' disciples struggled with what to make of the idea of God they concluded that they could not stop with the confession of Jesus as God's address, for to do so would reduce his story 'to the

12   Ignatius of Antioch, *Epistle to the Romans* 8; Williams, *Wound of Knowledge*, p. 19.
13   H.U. von Balthasar, *A Theology of History* (New York: Sheed and Ward, 1963), p. 79.

status of an *anecdote*: a tale without enduring or universal significance'.[14]

The story of this one man's life, as remarkable as it was, thus remains by itself extrinsically related to the warp and woof of our own lives. What does *this* life we now live have to do with *that* life of faithfulness to God, *that* death willingly accepted, and *that* triumph over death? If we are to grasp the significance of Jesus for those of us who live in a different time and place, who say and do and endure things in different circumstances that are also marked by their own particularity and contingency, we must know how to narrate our own lives as a continuation of that same story. This will happen only as the universal efficacy that the gospel attributes to Christ's concrete historical existence is performatively extended to, and displayed in, every time and place so that it becomes the immediate norm of every human being's singular existence.

It is the work of the Spirit to repeat differently (and therefore precisely) the polyphony of life[15] that has been revealed in Christ, and in both the New Testament and the early church fathers that work is mediated in large part by baptism and eucharist to gathered communities throughout the globe. This sacramental labor is ongoing, a never-ending endeavor, because times and circumstances change. New characters, social settings and historical events are constantly being incorporated within the ebb and flow of time around its center. The meaning of this process is therefore never fixed, but continues to unfold in the style of a historical drama that is never over and done with.[16] The unity of this drama's story line resides not in the sameness of its performance, but in timely transpositions of the rhythms and progressions of human acting and relating decisively enacted by the life and passion of Jesus.

The depth and breadth of the triune God's reign, then, is encountered in both the utterance of the Word *and* the breathing forth of the Holy Spirit. It is in the power of the Spirit that the sovereign address of God in Christ Jesus becomes for all humankind a word of redemption, the sign that life and not death is the goal of creation. The movement of God's Spirit in the world, however, is inseparable from the history of God's people, the story of Israel and the church. This people universalizes in the

14   N. Lash, *Easter in Ordinary: Reflections on Human Experience and the Knowledge of God* (Charlottesville, VA: University Press of Virginia, 1988), p. 282.

15   See D. Bonhoeffer, *Letters and Papers from Prison* (trans. R.H. Fuller, J. Bowden, *et al.*, New York: Macmillan, enlarged edn, 1971), p. 303.

16   E.g., the ways that Christ's body gathers in those of African descent in the United States will differ in certain respects from the ways it interacts with other persons and groups. The dissonance involved in the struggle of African American Christians finds no more poignant expression than in the poem by Harlem Renaissance poet Countee Cullen, 'The Black Christ'. C. Cullen, *The Black Christ and Other Poems* (New York: Harper & Brothers, 1929), pp. 67–110.

power of the Spirit the concrete singularity of this one Jewish man, for 'the personal in Christ can only confront the personal in the individual Christian in union with what appears to be impersonal, the church and the sacraments'.[17] The gift of the Spirit, though it cannot be contained by any created thing, creates and sustains a people who display before the world a different kind of existence in which relations misshapen by death and sin are transfigured into patterns of life and wholeness. The restructuring of life and language according to the pattern of Jesus' life and death gathers together persons from every tribe and language, people and nation, and re-members them into the body politic of Christ, the *corpus verum* or earthly-historical form of the crucified and risen Christ.

'Religion' as the Politics of Re-Establishment

The *raison d'être* of the church, writes Alexander Schmemann, is 'not to exist "in itself" but to be the "sacrament", the *epiphany*, of the new creation'. The action of the sacraments establishes the performative links between the day-to-day life of this people and its hope in the resurrection and the world to come. With these powerful signs God fashions from the resources of this time and place an alternative idiom for creaturely existence over against the sinews of the world's body politic. Time and again baptism and eucharist introduce this new social dimension into the world and are therefore not just the *means* but also the *media* of grace. It is precisely in and through these practices 'that the Church is *informed* of her cosmical and eschatological vocation, *receives* the power to fulfill it and thus truly *becomes* "what she is": the sacrament, in Christ, of the new creation; the sacrament, in Christ, of the Kingdom'.[18]

With the conversion of Constantine in the fourth century, however, the church faced a new situation for which it was largely unprepared and its sacramental mission was ultimately co-opted by the earthly city. The same empire that had regularly ridiculed (and from time to time persecuted) the members of Christ's body was now expressing interest in their story of salvation and its criteria of true universality, even to the point of inviting the church to order the imperial household. Oliver O'Donovan, in a sterling apology for the idea of Christendom, rightly notes that this idea was at the outset a response to the Gentile mission of the church, 'constituted not by the church's seizing alien power, but by alien power's become attentive to the church'. In other words, the Christendom idea initially presupposed the eschatology of the early

17   Von Balthasar, *Theology of History*, p. 81.
18   A. Schmemann, *Church, World, Mission: Reflections on Orthodoxy in the West* (Crestwood, NY: St Vladimir's Seminary Press, 1979), pp. 136–37, emphasis Schmemann's.

church, with its missional *vis-à-vis* of church and secular rule as distinct structures belonging to two distinct societies or cities: 'Until the end of the patristic period this *vis-à-vis* is constantly in evidence, and the meaning of the Christian empire as a *capitulation* to the throne of Christ is not forgotten.'[19]

Not surprisingly, the church responded to its new situation 'by accepting this invitation to render a "holy service" for the world'.[20] Christian jubilation over the Constantinian and Theodosian establishment of a Christian empire was, as O'Donovan and R.A. Markus point out, a continuation of the church's missional confidence in the triumph of God over the rulers and idols of this age.[21] The church thus set out to exorcise the world of its demonic powers, to liberate the empire from the thraldom of the 'prince of the air', in short, to make 'this world "new" before God by the power of the Holy Spirit'. The church of early Christendom sought to serve the world while remaining true to its identity as the sacrament of the kingdom, 'God's eschatological vehicle of passage for this world through time into the world to come'. Unfortunately it failed in the attempt, and in spite of its best intentions the blame rests largely with the church, because in the end it 'endeavored to be not what it is but what it is not'.[22]

It must be noted, however, that though the institutions of Christendom never achieved what its proponents set out to accomplish—to liberate the present world from the dominion of death and darkness, and make it new before God by the power of the Holy Spirit—neither did they completely abandon the narrative understanding of history embodied in the life and ministry of Jesus and in the early church. As John Yoder observes, the 'higher level of morality asked of the clergy, the international character of the hierarchy, the visibility of the hierarchy in opposition to the princes, the gradual moral education of barbarians into monogamy and legality, foreign missions, apocalypticism and mysticism—all of these

---

19 O. O'Donovan, *The Desire of the Nations: Rediscovering the Roots of Political Theology* (Cambridge: Cambridge University Press, 1996), pp. 195–96.

20 V. Guroian, *Incarnate Love: Essays in Orthodox Ethics* (Notre Dame, IN: University of Notre Dame Press, 1987), p. 122.

21 O'Donovan, *Desire of the Nations*, pp. 193–99; R.A. Markus, *Saeculum: History and Society in the Theology of St Augustine* (Cambridge: Cambridge University Press, 1970), p. 31. O'Donovan, *Desire of the Nations*, p. 198, also notes that prior to the time of Constantine Christian apologists identified the rise of the Roman empire as a sign of the rout of demons, the plurality of nations previous to it being an aspect of polytheism.

22 Guroian, *Incarnate Love*, p. 122. According to Bell, *Apocalypse How?*, pp. 23–31, similar sorts of impulses characterized early Baptist eschatology.

preserved an awareness, however distorted and polluted, of the strangeness of God's people in a rebellious world'.[23]

Beginning in the late fifteenth and early sixteenth centuries, however, the eschatological framework of early Christianity was largely jettisoned, along with the ecclesial practices and relationships that sought (albeit imperfectly) to bind life between ascension and *parousia* to its beginning and end in the mystery of God's providential design. In place of the biblical story about the collision between two ages, the leading figures of the Renaissance and the Enlightenment imagined not a time, but a space over which human beings were sovereign. Human beings were thus dissociated from the constraints of local communities, and for many from what was considered to be a dubious and altogether extraneous idea called 'God'. The idea of the secular came to refer to this carefully demarcated sphere of action that supposedly contained and ordered (both practically and theoretically) all finite entities and events in isolation from any relationship to the infinite.

Another postulate of modernity that did not exist previously, the idea of 'religion', was invented alongside the working hypothesis of a secular domain. Prior to the fifteenth century no one used this term to speak either about a universal impulse embedded in human consciousness, or about beliefs held privately by individuals with no direct bearing on their public lives. When *religio* does occur in medieval writings (which is rare) it usually refers to monastic life, and on occasion to an acquired virtue which—in concert with other virtues—directs the faithful to know and love God. Either way the term presupposed a context of ecclesial practices embodied in the communal life of the church.

Beginning with the Renaissance, however, these convictions were gradually separated from these practices and converted into systems of beliefs embraced voluntarily by individuals about what is ultimately true and important in their lives. Christian identity and church authority were thus relegated to this separate sphere of private life, converted into abstract systems of beliefs embraced voluntarily by individuals about what is ultimately true and important to them. More importantly, the conversion of church-based convictions into 'worldviews' allowed them to exist and operate apart from loyalty to the key political innovation of the period, namely, the nation-state. In short, the community that had for centuries embodied Christian convictions was systematically dismembered.[24]

---

23   J.H. Yoder, *The Royal Priesthood: Essays Ecclesiological and Ecumenical* (ed. M.G. Cartwright; Grand Rapids, MI: Eerdmans, 1994), p. 58.

24   See W.T. Cavanaugh, '"A Fire Strong Enough to Consume the House": The Wars of Religion and the Rise of the State', *Modern Theology* 11.4 (October, 1995), pp. 397–420.

Changes in sacramental practice and theory in the late medieval context helped to prepare the way for the privatizing work of 'religion'. The intimate connection emphasized in the patristic era between the sacramental body (*corpus mysticum*) and the ecclesial body (*corpus verum*) was obscured by a dramatic reversal that took place between the meaning of sacrament and of sacrifice. In the early church the liturgical emphasis was on the active participation of the church—the true body of Christ performing his will—in his sacrificial offering. The nature of the sacrament depended upon the sacrifice. As William Cavanaugh describes it:

> The Eucharist enacts the presence not simply of what Christ did in the past, but also and especially the future fulfillment of Christ's work through the Spirit. The past and present receive their significance and continuity from the future, when Christ's salvific will is manifested in full in a new heaven and a new earth. In Eucharistic time the past is not simply an historical object, a given quantity to be parsed by the community; nor is the future Kingdom something simply to be awaited patiently as we muddle through history. In the Eucharist, past and future simultaneously converge, and the whole Christ, the eschatological church of all times and places, is present.[25]

Beginning in the late twelfth century, however, the meaning of sacrifice was made dependent on the sacerdotal consecration of the bread and wine, with the actions performed by the cleric coming to have the dominant (and sometimes the sole) role in the proceedings. Since the words of consecration in some sense turn the bread and wine into the body and blood of Christ, what the church does in the eucharist must be what Christ did with his body and blood, namely, offer them in sacrifice.[26] As the corporate and social emphasis of the eucharist diminished in the later Middle Ages, it eventually became a focal point for the subjective devotional life of the individual in the isolation of her or his own thoughts and affections.

---

25 W. Cavanaugh, *Torture and Eucharist: Theology, Politics, and the Body of Christ* (Malden, MA: Blackwell, 1998), p. 234. It is important to note here that the extension of 'sacrifice' to speak of both the passion of Jesus and our participation in what he offered to God is metaphorical, since strictly defined neither can properly be called a sacrifice. The technical term for this particular work of metaphor is catachresis, which as McClendon, *Doctrine*, p. 107, observes is the deliberate use of a word drawn from one sphere of activity to denote something in another sphere that would otherwise elude expression.

26 D.G. Dix, *The Shape of the Liturgy* (with additional notes by P.V. Marshall; New York: Seabury, 1982), pp. 245–46. The original, metaphorical sense of sacrifice in reference to Jesus' passion is thereby abandoned, and replaced with a univocal understanding of the term.

Joseph Powers goes so far as to suggest that the dominant eucharistic understanding of that time was not 'Take and Eat' and 'Take and Drink', but 'Gaze on the Host and find your salvation in the gazing.'[27] Once the move away from active participation in the sacrificial offering of Christ to God was established, the foundations for the privatizing impulse of 'religion' were securely laid. Dom Gregory Dix puts the problem succinctly: 'The part of the individual layman...had long ago been reduced from "doing" to "seeing" and "hearing". Now it is retreating within himself to "thinking" and "feeling." He is even beginning to think that over-much "seeing" (ceremonial) and "hearing" (music) are detrimental to proper "thinking" and "feeling".'[28] According to this conception, nothing inessential should be allowed to intrude upon an individual's private encounter with the divine, a proscription that could conceivably extend to the sacrament elements themselves.

These shifts in eucharistic practice did not occur in a vacuum, but were part of a series of changes within the church that helped pave the way first for the modern nation-state and then the postmodern republic of commerce and consumption. Among crucial changes that took place were the centralization of clerical administration, elevation of the priestly role in the institution of the sacrament, and a rationalization of ecclesiastical power in terms of formal right and contract that reached its apex in the eleventh century during the papacy of Gregory VII, when the church hierarchy extracted from the right of property as set forth in Roman and feudal law the theory of 'the absolute and universal jurisdiction of the supreme authority, and developed it into the doctrine of the *plenitudo potestatis* of the Pope'.[29]

The dismembering of Christian identity by means of 'religion' during the modern era further eviscerated the public and bodily character of biblical and patristic Christianity. As faith was restricted to 'the inner man', the bonds the church fostered between those who saw themselves as members of one body were gradually effaced. Sequestering religion in the private sphere reserved the public realm exclusively for the coercive rule of both state and market, and helped to provide an effective mode of social discipline to those in control of these political entities to claim absolute sovereignty over the bodies of their subjects. With Christian identity safely confined to the realm of individual values, the work of the church was increasingly devoted to nurturing the 'soul'. Thusly defined this work not only posed little threat to the state, it could more easily be conscripted as a mode of social discipline in support of its aims and

---

27   J.M. Powers, *Eucharistic Theology* (New York: Herder and Herder, 1967), p. 31.
28   Dix, *Shape of the Liturgy*, p. 599.
29   J.N. Figgis, *Studies of Political Thought from Gerson to Grotius, 1414–1625* (Cambridge: Cambridge University Press, 1956), p. 4.

policies. The political challenge the church potentially posed to the state was effectively eliminated.

As Thompson points out, Baptists in the seventeenth century understood, at least intuitively, this form of political captivity. Their theology and practices, and in particular their critique of and resistance to the Church of England, were rooted in their conviction that God's salvific work could not be constrained by any human institution. Idolatry, not violation of liberty of conscience, was the principal sin of the crown's attempt to usurp divine authority over the church. The attention they gave to what constitutes the faithful practice of baptism reflects this concern. They rightly saw baptism as the sacrament that conferred the proper significance to all bodies—communal as well as individual—thus relativizing all other political expressions by locating true politics within the church.[30]

The initial trajectory plotted by the first generation of Baptists was not, however, generally sustained by later generations, particularly in North America and Europe. They began to embrace the division of spheres implemented under the auspices of 'religion', which they interpreted as the liberation of Christian faith from all political entanglements. One of the most prominent names in this unrecognized retrenchment in the eighteenth and nineteenth centuries was that of John Leland of Virginia (1754–1841). As Curtis Freeman has shown, Leland adopted Lockean and Madisonian language with its theories of natural rights and voluntary associations to justify and display the historic Baptist convictions of liberty of conscience and the disestablishment of the church from the state. Liberty of conscience was for Leland 'the inalienable right that each individual has, of worshipping his God according to the dictates of his conscience, without being prohibited, directed, or controlled therein by human law, either in time, place, or manner'.[31]

What Leland and his supporters did not understand is that no world is free of political discipline of some sort. Their position unwittingly contributed to the double dismemberment of Christianity—the separation of the disciple from the body politic of the church and of their faith from their own physical bodies.[32] They did not realize that the church was thereby re-established socially and politically, in a new form to be sure, but one that nonetheless fit perfectly into the world they thought they were challenging. The institutional disestablishment of 'religion' they sought took place under the auspices of a social arrangement that sanctioned a moral identity of the church with the state and its

---

30   Thompson, 'Religious Liberty, Sacraments, God Image', p. 11.

31   J. Leland, 'A Blow at the Root', in L.F. Greene (ed.), *The Writings of John Leland* (New York: Arno, 1969 [1845]), p. 239, cited by C.W. Freeman, 'Can Baptist Theology Be Revisioned?' *Perspectives in Religious Studies* 24.3 (Fall, 1997), p. 281.

32   Clapp, 'At the Intersection of Eucharist and Capital', p. 97.

commercial republic.[33] Persons were now cast as 'autonomous individuals', and thus required to render to 'Caesar' (the political consortium of managerial government and the global market) their unconditional loyalty. This new Caesar in his sovereign benevolence then permitted, or rather *guaranteed* these newly minted individuals the right to 'religious beliefs', which are perfectly free as long as they are perfectly private ('in the closet' of one's mind or heart, so to speak). As a result, Baptist groups now find themselves in the ironic position of refusing out of principle to force their religion on anyone, but sense nothing amiss in supporting the mandatory establishment (by any and all means available, including force of arms) of liberal democratic capitalism.

The social institutions of the state and market continue unabated to reconfigure what it means to be human beings, divesting the world of the 'old, old stories', and reinvesting its human capital in global networks of production and consumption. Practically speaking these networks congeal in a curious mixture of permissiveness and supervision, as people do exactly what these institutions want them to do, all the while reassuring them that this is what it means to be free. As a result, says Wendell Berry, 'we have been reduced almost to a state...in which people and all other creatures and things may be considered purely as economic "units", or integers of production, and in which a human being may be dealt with..."merely as a covetous machine".'[34] Effectively sundered from meaningful points of reference beyond our present self-defined wants and desires, men and women are little more than the sequence of economic roles they perform. Day-to-day life is little more than a series of consumer choices to make and a series of jobs from which to be made redundant.

The workings of the market determine, not particular acts, but the range of possible acts available to us as individuals, the 'rational' patterns that govern our day-to-day lives, in public *and* in private. Within the logic of the earthly city's commercial republic, then, the 'question of what you permanently are, or what permanently is, and is permanently valuable, does not arise'.[35] There is little possibility of this question ever arising, for our age lacks the sort of imagination that would allow it even to pose such a question in an authoritative way. The control that this form of rationality exercises over us is therefore anonymous and indirect, but precisely for this reason all the more sweeping. It determines where we

---

33   See N.O. Hatch, *The Democratization of American Christianity* (New Haven, CT: Yale University Press, 1989).

34   W. Berry, 'Economy and Pleasure', in *What Are People For?* (New York: North Point, 1990), p. 130.

35   N. Boyle, *Who Are We Now? Christian Humanism and the Global Market from Hegel to Heaney* (Notre Dame, IN: University of Notre Dame Press, 1998), pp. 78–79.

will live (and when we will move), what kind of clothes we will wear (proper 'business' attire and uniforms with the company logo), and what sorts of food we may eat (no sack lunches at the desk, please). As Clapp observes, if a church were to impose this sort of discipline on its members it would quickly be denounced as 'authoritarian' if not worse.[36]

The degree to which the discipline of the market determines the shape and direction of our lives may be grasped in the way it decides how much time we may devote to matters 'outside work'. Because people's labor and thus time is very expensive, it becomes necessary both to ration the use of it and to account for it in intimate detail. Like expensive computer time, people's time must either be used to the full or switched off when it is no longer needed, that is, they must be flexible or laid off. According to Boyle, human beings are therefore 'dismembered', stripped of any residual identity and reduced to a series of functions that are exercised solely in accordance with the demands of the market:

> They must not be tied to a place, but prepared to move to follow employment. They must not be tied by time, but prepared to work all hours and days of the week, especially Sundays. It follows that they must not be tied to any particular group of people or community: that they have families, even, is of no social significance since it is of no significance to the market, except as distracting from their flexibility. Above all they must expect to retrain, to work to satisfy quite different needs several times in their working life.[37]

Moreover, by ruling out of bounds from the outset any substantive understanding of the human good in favor of consumer freedom, the market excludes 'an entire way of life postulated upon nonconsumerist conceptions of human fulfillment, and so to favor a particular vision of the human good'. It thus tacitly dictates that 'choice is itself the highest good'.[38] This is the shadow side that the market seeks to conceal from us, adds Boyle, its functioning as a highly efficient mode of social discipline.[39] Virtually everything else is optional with respect to the undifferentiated individuality of the market, where every thing and every body is packaged as a product to be consumed (including having children and friends), and the value of every product is determined by its 'market share', that is, its ability to satisfy consumers.

---

36   Clapp, 'At the Intersection of Eucharist and Capital', p. 100.

37   Boyle, *Who Are We Now?*, p. 28.

38   R. Beiner, *What's the Matter with Liberalism?* (Berkeley, CA: University of California Press, 1992), p. 8.

39   Boyle, *Who Are We Now?*, p. 154.

Recovering the Politics of Disestablishment

In virtually every corner of the globe men, women and children are being carefully scripted as 'individuals', that is, as interchangeable integers of consumption and production, making choices from a wide range of options which are controlled by institutions they cannot see, and managed by people they never meet face-to-face. Effectively sundered from meaningful points of reference beyond their self-defined wants and desires, their identity as persons consists of little more than a series of consumer choices to make and a sequence of jobs from which they will be laid off.

When one is immersed in these patterns, however, it is extremely difficult to recognize the ways that state and market rules their lives. Something more than simply being in a position to see and hear what is going on around is needed if we are to penetrate the language and logic of the earthly city. It requires the acquisition of new habits of life and language, new ways of assessing the world in which we live our lives—in other words, a different faith, a different hope and a different love—to recognize and then to understand what we once took for granted. Put another way, it requires a setting in which human beings have the opportunity to acquire and nurture 'the many skills and virtues that transpose simple seeing into discernment and mere existing into holy habitation.

Such habits are not maintained by mere symbols that somehow affix themselves to what occurs primarily to individuals in their solitude and prior to their engagement with others, that is, to inner states of heightened awareness or emotional intensity. They are cultivated instead in the company of friends through their shared participation in the disciplinary activities of social practices and institutions.[40] Through their participation in these disciplines they learn how to identify, reidentify, classify, call and respond to all the things and persons we encounter in the world. In short, through these activities Jesus' followers learn to name and thereby to deal with the world as *world*, that is, as fallen and yet still cherished by its creator. The celebrations of baptism and eucharist find their occasion and significance, not in the validation of our private 'experiences', but in the reconfiguring of language and life which God's utterance of the Word in history and breathing forth of the Spirit upon the church set into motion.

Put somewhat differently, the ability to name the significance of the activities and institutions that shape the events going on around us, like reading the marks in a text, is inseparable from communal practices that

---

40   See T. Asad, *Genealogies of Religion: Discipline and Reasons of Power in Christianity and Islam* (Baltimore, MD: Johns Hopkins University Press, 1993), p. 35.

mediate the 'transaction of signs with other selves'.[41] Practices of this sort do not fall from the sky, but are constituted by actual communities over time, and therefore are irreducibly social and political. The ecclesial practices that re-member the body of Christ propel human beings beyond the boundaries within which the twin authorities of state and market seek to confine them by binding them together in a new political association that has a center but no boundaries. Hence Paul can write to the Galatians that, 'As many of you as were baptized into Christ have clothed yourselves with Christ. There is no longer Jew or Greek, there is no longer slave or free, there is no longer male and female; for all of you are one in Christ Jesus' (Gal. 3.27-28).[42] In similar fashion he regards the sharing of bread and wine as causally constitutive of Christ's body: 'Because there is one bread, we who are many are one body, for we all partake of one bread' (1 Cor. 10.17).

Participation in the sacraments does not, however, render these transactions immediately transparent. On the contrary, says Rowan Williams, Jesus is God's revelation in a decisive sense 'not because he makes things plainer...but because he makes things darker'.[43] The identity and conduct of Jesus' followers are 'at least as much a matter of promise, of prospect, and of the task that is laid upon us, as they are a matter of past achievement or present reality'.[44] As a consequence, the impetus of baptism and eucharist is for each member of Christ's body to make 'his or her own that engagement with the questioning at the heart of faith which is so evident in the classical documents of Christian belief'.[45] The questioning engendered by these signs and seals has little to do with fashionable notions about the relative nature of all human endeavors, nor does it encourage romantic sentiments about the self-made individual who, while half-believing, withholds assent from all commitments in order to preserve some sort of moral and intellectual autonomy. 'The question involved here', Williams insists,

is not our interrogation of the data, but its interrogation of us. It is the *strangeness* of the ground of belief that must constantly be allowed to challenge the fixed assumptions of religiosity; it is a *given*, whose question to each succeeding age is fundamentally one and the same. And the greatness of the great Christian saints lies

---

41   W. Percy, *Lost in the Cosmos: The Last Self-Help Book* (New York: Farrar, Straus & Giroux, 1983), pp. 105 and 87.

42   This passage is often cited in defense of liberal egalitarianism, but more accurately describes the constitution of a new household, where one's identity is conferred by a gift of the Spirit and not by the conventions of a fallen world.

43   R. Williams, *On Christian Theology* (Malden, MA: Blackwell, 2000), p. 134.

44   Lash, *Easter in Ordinary*, p. 268.

45   Williams, *Wound of Knowledge*, p. 1.

in their readiness to be questioned, judged, stripped naked and left speechless by that which lies at the center of their faith.[46]

The purpose of this process of sacramental interpellation—of learning how to become a question to oneself—is not to condemn, but is located in the triune mission of gathering all things in heaven and on earth together in Christ (Eph. 1.10). In our own context it serves first to exegete the idea of the autonomous individual as a tragic character within the dramatic work of fiction that is the world as ordered by the power of the state and the principality of the market. It then resituates the self within the reign of Israel's God that establishes the goal toward which all things tend and sets the limits for the exercise of power by all worldly authorities. In and through the commonwealth of the body politic of Christ everything in the created order, all life, is 'now, at once, immediately confronted with a claim that is non-negotiable in the sense that in the end God will irrefutably be—God'.[47]

Baptism is the sign and seal of a person's induction into a new *polis*, marking the passage from death to life and the transfer of rulership and change of allegiance from the powers of this world to the reign of God. Paul's discussion of dying and rising with Christ in baptism (Rom 6.3-4) should therefore not be read as a 'symbol' or an 'inner experience' of an individual, but as the moment of transition from the old society into a new form of life in the company of the crucified.[48] Immersion in the baptismal waters divests us of all previous definitions of identity based on class, ethnic or national origin, gender and family ties. It quite literally strips off the old human being with its practices and clothes the one baptized with Christ's new humanity, 'which is being renewed in knowledge according to the image of its creator, and where there is no longer Greek and Jew, circumcised and uncircumcised, barbarian and Scythian, slave and free; but Christ is all and in all' (Col. 3.10). In this new humanity the one baptized is not only joined individually to the Head who is Christ, but to one another as members of one body.

Gathered by baptism 'from every tribe and language and people and nation' (Rev. 5.9), the eucharist then forms men and women time and again into one sacrificial body, recasting them as characters in a new drama 'that purports to be about a comprehensive truth affecting one's identity and future'. Immersion in the baptismal waters thus admits new members of Christ's body to the eucharistic feast, where around the table in the presence of the risen Lord they are given new roles to improvise and unfamiliar points on which to stand and speak, drawing them 'into a share in the vulnerability of God, into a new kind of life and a new

---

46   Williams, *Wound of Knowledge*, p. 1.
47   McClendon, *Doctrine*, p. 66.
48   Lohfink, *Does God Need the Church?*, p. 210.

identity'. There are, of course, no guarantees about what will happen in these engagements. With some, as with the figure of the rich ruler (Lk. 18.18-25), the inability to grasp their identity as a cherished creature of God 'becomes visible and utterable in the form of complicity in rejecting Jesus'. With others, as with the Zacchaeus (Lk. 19.1-10), the 'readiness to come to judgment and to recognize the possibility of truth and meaning becomes visible and utterable in the form of discipleship, abiding in the community created by God's love'.[49]

The love that creates this community should not, however, be confused with cheap sentiment. The re-membering of Christ's body in the world takes place according to the pattern attested to in both the baptismal imagery of the New Testament and the institution narratives for the Lord's Supper. The words spoken from above at Jesus' own baptism, 'This is my Son, the Beloved, with whom I am well pleased' (Mt. 3.17; cf. Mk 1.11, Lk. 3.22), are drawn in part from the first of the suffering servant songs in Isaiah (Is. 42.1), thus directing the attention of the reader at the beginning of Jesus' ministry toward its end at the cross. As he travels the path that takes him to that end at Calvary Jesus tells the sons of Zebedee that only those who are able to be baptized with the baptism that he is baptized with are worthy of sitting at his right and left hands (Mk 10.35-40; cf. Mt. 20.20-28, Lk. 22.24-27). In his Epistle to the Romans Paul reminds his readers that 'all of us who have been baptized into Christ Jesus were baptized into his death...so that, just as Christ was raised from the dead by the glory of the father, so we too might walk in newness of life' (Rom. 6.3-4).

In like fashion the proceedings of the Lord's Table 'always and necessarily [operate] between the two poles of Maundy Thursday and Easter Sunday, between Gethsemane and Emmaus, between the Upper Room before the crucifixion and the Upper Room to which the risen Jesus comes'. Our participation in the life and mission of God thus takes concrete form in the interval of Holy Week made historical by the eucharistic feast. This gathering of the Spirit signifies the restoration of a fellowship broken time and again by human infidelity, including our own. The communal practice of discernment, forgiveness and reconciliation is thus presupposed by this meal. In this meal, 'the wounded body and the shed blood are inescapably present'.[50]

The performance of the sacraments thus exposes all that the world stipulates as true, good, right and proper to a new and unexpected light. Nothing remains as it once had been, for 'in Christ there is a new

49   R.D. Williams, 'Postmodern Theology and the Judgment of the World', in F.B. Burnham (ed.), *Postmodern Theology: Christian Faith in a Pluralist World* (San Francisco, CA: Harper & Row, 1989), pp. 96–97, 108.

50   R. Williams, *Resurrection: Interpreting the Easter Gospel* (New York: Pilgrim, 1984), p. 40.

creation: everything old has passed away; see, everything has become new!' (2 Cor. 5.17). But the drawing near of the age to come does not occur in a social vacuum, for the life, passion and resurrection of Jesus have as their primary consequence and goal the formation of a new race of human beings on earth to be governed by 'the politics of the Lamb'.[51] This community of the coming messianic age announces to the world in both word and deed that the end toward which history is moving is not determined by those whom this age calls powerful, but by the one who gathers together all things in heaven and on earth in the crucified Messiah of Israel.

Because the whole of existence is claimed and transfigured by this drama, its participants must attend to those practices that 'constitute the corporeality of the people: its flesh, sexuality, commerce, and all those concerns that motivate the majority of any people'.[52] These matters are not restricted to the private sphere of 'religion', but have to do with the cares and concerns that make up the business of everyday life: building houses, tending gardens, buying and selling, marrying and giving in marriage, and raising children (cf. Jer. 29.5-6). As the church engages in these public activities, its mission is not simply to survive in what can at times be a hostile environment.[53] The primary task of the church is instead to glorify God in the world (Jn 17.20-26), which takes place in the performative interaction between the liturgy of baptism and eucharist and the 'liturgy' of mission.

The connection between the two forms of the liturgy is exemplified in relationship of the eucharist to the practice of hospitality. Before bread is brought to Christ's table, it is a product of a fallen creation, a world in rebellion, dominated by fear, greed, hunger and division. But when it is blessed, it becomes a sign of God's new creation, where perfect love casts out fear, generosity reaches out to the stranger in the gate and reconciliation heals the world's divisions. This shared meal prefigures the hope of the messianic age, when—as Mary's song magnifying the Lord puts it—the rich will give up what we now call their capital, and the poor will be well-fed (Lk. 1.53). The sharing of bread around the Lord's Table thus summons Christians to reclaim in different modes the common life and purse of the first disciples, whom Jesus formed into a new household that relativized the claims of their 'biological' or 'ethnic'

51   McClendon, *Doctrine*, p. 98. Lohfink, *Does God Need the Church?*, pp. 51–60, contends that gathering a people of God to serve as a contrast society is one of the characteristic signs of Israel that extends even to its beginnings, when it was originally composed from quite different ethnic groups.

52   M. Wyschogrod, *The Body of Faith: God in the People Israel* (San Francisco, CA: Harper & Row, 1983), p. 24.

53   For a community to render any kind of useful service to the world it must survive with its identity intact. From this standpoint survival and service are not antitheses.

families on their material resources. They continued their pattern of eating together following the ascension, considering it 'the right way both to remember his death and his resurrection appearances and to affirm their hope of his return'.[54]

The universal significance of Messiah Jesus is thus made particular by the work of the Spirit, who calls the church into being and into communion as a community of differences.[55] The twin errors of collectivism and individualism are thus ruled out from the start, for in this fellowship neither the whole nor the members are simply functions of the other. On the contrary, baptism and eucharist establish a new mode of social relations that, unlike the so-called egalitarianism prescribed by liberal democracies, does not treat us as faceless integers of production and consumption. With their incorporation into the body of Christ through water, wine and word persons receive what the New Testament calls a spiritual gift—the distinctive singularity of personal existence in the body politic of Christ. Differences are therefore not embraced for their own sake, to be consumed as yet one more commodity, but so that all might share in one calling—to be for the sake of the world sign, foretaste and herald of the destiny of all things in God's new creation.

The social idiom of the sacraments embodies the end (which is both *telos* and *eschaton*) of all true sacrifice in the atoning death of the righteous one by incorporating the bodies of Jesus' followers into the messianic suffering of God. In the words of Augustine, 'the whole of the redeemed City—that is to say, the congregation and fellowship of the saints—is offered to God as a universal sacrifice for us through the great High Priest Who offered even Himself for us in the form of a servant, so that we might be the body of so great a Head'.[56] As the dwelling place of God in this age, the members of Christ's commonwealth offer up their own bodies to become the living door posts and lintels on which the Spirit places the blood of the Paschal Lamb of God who takes away the sins of the world. Incarnation and atonement, reconciliation and the sharing of burdens, are thereby communicated, not as abstract facts but as a concrete mode of being, that is, as 'a new kind of efficacious sacrifice of praise, self-sharing and probable attendant suffering which unites us with [Christ] in the heavenly city, and at the same time totally obliterates...all the contours of inside and outside which constitute human power'.[57]

---

54   J.H. Yoder, *For the Nations: Essays Evangelical and Public* (Grand Rapids, MI: Eerdmans, 1997), p. 44.

55   See J.J. Buckley, 'A Field of Living Fire: Karl Barth on the Spirit and the Church', *Modern Theology* 10.1 (January, 1994), p. 91.

56   Augustine, *City of God*, 10.6 (p. 400).

57   J. Milbank, 'The Name of Jesus', in *The Word Made Strange: Theology, Language, Culture* (Cambridge, MA: Blackwell, 1997), p. 151.

Baptists and the Future of Disestablishment

If Baptists are to come to terms with the momentous changes that have occurred over the last three hundred and fifty years they must set aside the deception that our identity as persons is defined exclusively by what goes on 'inside' us, that is, by our 'experiences' and our choices. This definition tacitly secures the mechanisms of state and market from 'restrictive practices' such as the church that impede the otherwise free flow of the market and of government directions.[58] Human identity is truthfully shaped through social networks, 'sedimented from histories of significant relationships'.[59] It is to these social processes that the discipline of the Christian body—personal and social—must attend if it is to offer an alternative mode of life, and that discipline can only be orchestrated by the sorts of sacramental practices cultivated from the beginning by the disciples of Jesus.

As the means *and* media by which human beings are gathered into the messianic sacrifice, the eschatological rhythms and progressions of baptism and eucharist transpose the confrontation between the present world and the age to come inaugurated by Jesus' life and ministry into ever new contexts. The unfolding of history in convergence upon and divergence from the reality of God taking flesh in the world is *tangibly* manifested through the habits and relations of Christ's true body to the rulers and powers who claim an authority that properly belongs to God. The sacramental practices and institutions that bound the members of the early church together in a new style of public life continue to serve as a definitive sign to the world that this new creation has dawned. The church thus takes up, participates in, is transformed by, and offers to the world the idiom of the new creation—the peaceable relationships, the reconciling patterns of conduct, *and* the tribulations—introduced into the midst of the old by Christ. Without the sacramental (that is, bodily) participation of the church in what God has accomplished (and continues to accomplish) in Christ, the universal meaning of the event of God's own self-expression taking flesh and dwelling among us (Jn 1.14), is missed.

58   Boyle, *Who Are We Now?*, p. 29.
59   A.I. McFadyen, *The Call to Personhood: A Christian Theory of the Individual in Social Relationships* (New York: Cambridge University Press, 1990), p. 72.

CHAPTER 7

Baptism in Acts:
The Sacramental Dimension

Stanley E. Porter

Episodes involving baptism occur roughly nine times in the book of Acts (Acts 2.37-42; 8.12-17; 8.26-39; 9.10-19 [cf. 22.16]; 10.44-48; 16.14-15; 16.25-34; 18.8; 19.1-7). These passages have been written upon many times and in many different commentaries, monographs and journal articles and chapters. I do not intend to pick up all of the issues raised, but to focus upon the issue of sacramentalism and these passages. There is much more that could be said about the book of Acts in relation to baptism, conversion, initiation into Christianity, faith, forgiveness, repentance, the laying on of hands, the Holy Spirit, the gifts of the Spirit, and the like. What I wish to address here is the role that a sacramental view of baptism might play in relation to these baptism passages.

James Dunn is clear in his view of the role of baptism in these episodes:

[W]hile recognizing that one cannot say 'faith' without also saying 'water-baptism', we must recognize that of the two it is the former which is the significant element. Baptism gives expression to faith, but without faith baptism is meaningless, an empty symbol. It is false to say that water-baptism conveys, confers or effects forgiveness of sins. It may symbolize cleansing, but it is the faith and repentance which receives the forgiveness, and the Holy Spirit who conveys, confers and effects it. Luke never mentions water-baptism by itself as the condition of or means to receiving forgiveness; he mentions it only in connection with some other attitude (repentance—Luke 3.3; Acts 2.38) or act (calling on his name—Acts 22.16). But whereas water-baptism is never spoken of as the sole prerequisite to receiving forgiveness, Luke on a number of occasions speaks of repentance or faith as the sole prerequisite... In other words, water-baptism is neither the sole preliminary nor in itself an essential preliminary to receiving forgiveness... Moreover,...in Luke where repentance is joined to water-baptism it is the former alone which is really decisive for forgiveness... The essential characteristic of the Christian and that which matters on the human side is in the last analysis faith and not water-baptism. The sacrament 'acts on' faith, but only faith 'acts on' God. Schweizer is therefore correct when he states: 'For Luke baptism is simply a natural episode in what he regards as much more important, namely conversion'.[1]

There is no doubt that much of what Dunn says is true. There certainly are passages in Acts where repentance or faith is spoken of apart from or as the sole prerequisite of forgiveness.[2] It is also true that water-baptism is often mentioned in connection with some other attitude or act, such as repentance or calling on the name of Jesus Christ. Dunn may likewise be correct that, in a hierarchy of attitudes and actions surrounding conversion-initiation, others may be theologically more important than water-baptism.[3] There may be other things on which Dunn is correct as well. However, it is also questionable whether the above statements warrant the anti-sacramentalist view that Dunn explicitly advocates.

There are a number of reasons for doubting this, in particular with reference to baptism in the book of Acts. One of the reasons is that Dunn has in fact mis-stated some of the facts regarding these passages in Acts. Two in particular—Acts 8.26-39 and Acts 19.1-7—are more difficult to fit within the straightjacket that he has created, as will be seen below. I will take the occasion to examine briefly each of the passages in Acts to see if insights can be gained that indicate conclusions other than those of Dunn. A further consideration is that Dunn seems to be thinking disjunctively regarding the notion of sacramentalism. At the outset of his work he defines a 'sacrament' in terms of Reformed theology as consisting of the 'outward and sensible sign' and 'an inward and spiritual grace thereby signified'.[4] It appears to me that he is intent upon

---

1   J.D.G. Dunn, *Baptism in the Holy Spirit: A Re-examination of the New Testament Teaching on the Gift of the Spirit in Relation to Pentecostalism Today* (Philadelphia: Westminster Press, 1970), pp. 97-98; citing E. Schweizer, 'πνεῦμα, πνευματικός', in G. Kittel and G. Friedrich (eds.), *Theologisches Wörterbuch zum Neuen Testament* (9 vols; Stuttgart: W. Kohlhammer Verlag, 1933–73), VI, p. 411. Cf. W.F. Flemington, *The New Testament Doctrine of Baptism* (London: SPCK, 1957), p. 49, who links hearing the word and believing with baptism, with baptism as symbolizing the gospel.

2   Among other passages, Dunn, *Baptism in the Holy Spirit*, p. 97, cites Acts 3.19; 5.31; 10.43; 13.38; 26.18.

3   Dunn's views on the separation of Spirit- and water-baptism are critically examined by A.R. Cross, 'Spirit- and Water-Baptism in 1 Corinthians 12.13', in S.E. Porter and A.R. Cross (eds.), *Dimensions of Baptism: Biblical and Theological Studies* (*Journal for the Study of the New Testament*, Supplement Series, 234; Sheffield: Sheffield Academic Press, forthcoming 2002).

4   Dunn, *Baptism in the Holy Spirit*, p. 6, citing *The Westminster Larger Catechism*, p. 163, further supported by H.J. Wotherspoon and J.M. Kirkpatrick, *A Manual of Church Doctrine According to the Church of Scotland* (rev. T.F. Torrance and R.S. Wright; 1965 [1920]), pp. 17-19, and, of course that great and oft-cited source of theological insight, the *Oxford English Dictionary*.

creating a systematic theology regarding the Holy Spirit, into which he wishes to fit all of the passages of the New Testament. A further problem is that Dunn rejects (and probably rightly so) the well-defined Reformation definition of sacramentalism. A more nuanced form of sacramentalism might well be compatible with the actions found in Acts, however. R.E.O. White, recognizing the difficulty of defining a word such as 'sacramental', which has been subject to such theological debate, believes that there is a 'rudimentary and germinal sacramentalism' in Jewish proselyte baptism, in which he defines sacramentalism as the 'undoubted truth' that in baptism 'something was expected to be achieved: it was no empty performance, no merely traditional ceremony. The difficulty lies in defining the relation of the results achieved to the means used, and the heart of the difficulty would appear to be the stress on "material means"'. In the last analysis it is the person doing what God wills that is the sacramental fact: 'in this, so to speak, "dynamic sacramentalist" sense it is true to say that every act done in obedience to the received will of God is sacramental, and will achieve its end in divine blessing.'[5]

In the rest of this paper, I would like to examine briefly the nine passages, to see if there is a sense of dynamic sacramentalism present in those passages where baptism is discussed, whatever other elements there may be as well.

Acts 2.37-42

In this passage of Pentecost, there is a clear linkage of repentance, baptism in the name of Jesus Christ for the forgiveness of sins, and reception of the gift of the Holy Spirit.[6] When the people were pierced to the heart when they had heard Peter speak, Peter told them to repent and be baptized and they would receive the gift of the Holy Spirit. Dunn is correct that here is an instance where repentance and baptism are linked.[7] There seems to be more to the episode than that, however. Repentance and baptism are linked, to be sure, but baptism is also clearly linked with

---

5   R.E.O. White, *The Biblical Doctrine of Initiation* (London: Hodder & Stoughton, 1960), pp. 71, 72. He is not cited on this point by Dunn.

6   Many scholars have seen these four items, or ones like them, as forming a complex of often associated ideas. See, for example, S. New, 'The Name, Baptism, and the Laying on of Hands', in F.J. Foakes Jackson and K. Lake (eds.), *The Beginnings of Christianity*. I. *The Acts of the Apostles* (5 vols; London: Macmillan, 1920–33), V, pp. 121-40, esp. p. 134, where she singles out belief, baptism, remission of sins, laying on of hands and reception of the Spirit. Dunn, *Baptism in the Holy Spirit*, pp. 4, 98, delimits water baptism, the Holy Spirit and faith.

7   Dunn, *Baptism in the Holy Spirit*, p. 97.

the name of Jesus Christ and the forgiveness of sins. The Greek reads: βαπτισθήτω ἕκαστος ὑμῶν ἐπὶ τῷ ὀνόματι Ἰησοῦ Χριστοῦ εἰς ἄφεσιν τῶν ἁμαρτιῶν ὑμῶν.[8] There are at least two issues of debate in this passage. One is the significance of the use of the preposition in the phrase 'upon the name of Jesus Christ', and the other is the meaning of the preposition in 'for forgiveness of your sins'. Many scholars, but excluding Dunn, seem to think that there is no clear difference between the use of the prepositions ἐπί, εἰς and ἐν with the name of Jesus.[9] Although there is certainly some semantic overlap between the prepositions, I am not convinced that the phrases are completely synonymous. Nevertheless, it seems as if the words—coming in response to the words of Matthew 28.19—indicate full enrolment as a disciple of Jesus Christ.[10] Further, there is a difference of opinion over whether 'for the forgiveness of sins' means that baptism leads to forgiveness of sins (the preposition having its directional sense) or that forgiveness of sins is the grounds or basis of baptism.[11] The former is more likely.[12] In any event, the important fact to notice is that baptism in the name of Jesus and forgiveness of sins are inextricably linked in this passage. Some have thought that reference to baptism was an editorial addition by the author of Acts, since the apostles received the Holy Spirit without baptism, whereas this passage makes it clear that receiving the Holy Spirit is conditional upon repentance and baptism.[13] I am doubtful regarding the editorial addition, but agree that the repentance and baptism are linked and, in this passage, become the precondition for receipt of the Spirit. It is only when repentance and baptism occur—whether the baptism is the result of forgiveness or the

---

8   Cf. Mk 1.4 and Lk. 3.3, discussed in S.E. Porter, 'Mark 1.4, Baptism and Translation', in S.E. Porter and A.R. Cross (eds.), *Baptism, the New Testament and the Church: Historical and Contemporary Studies in Honour of R.E.O. White* (*Journal for the Study of the New Testament*, Supplement Series, 171; Sheffield: Sheffield Academic Press, 1999), pp. 81-98.

9   E.g. New, 'Name, Baptism', pp. 123-24, and J.B. Polhill, *Acts* (New American Commentary, 26; Nashville, TN: Broadman Press, 1992), p. 117 n. 132; cf. Dunn, *Baptism in the Holy Spirit*, pp. 96-97, but without substantial argumentation.

10   See G.R. Beasley-Murray, *Baptism in the New Testament* (Grand Rapids, MI: Eerdmans, 1962), p. 102, followed by Dunn, *Baptism in the Holy Spirit*, p. 97; cf. New, 'Name, Baptism', p. 124.

11   Polhill, *Acts*, p. 117.

12   See C.K. Barrett, *A Critical and Exegetical Commentary on the Acts of the Apostles* (International Critical Commentary; 2 vols; Edinburgh: T. & T. Clark, 1994–98), I, p. 154.

13   Foakes Jackson and Lake (eds.), *Beginnings of Christianity*, I, pp. 339-40.

condition for it—that one can expect the Holy Spirit to come.[14] As New says:

> It is possible that the reference to baptism is editorial...but if so it is all the more important as illustrating Luke's own opinion. We are clearly confronted with an evolution of thought in which eschatological salvation, baptism 'in the name,' and the gift of the Spirit are concerned. The final step, which makes baptism effect a sacramental change of nature as in Catholic Christianity, is not taken, but it is imminent. Similarly, it is not actually stated that baptism confers the Spirit, but a close connexion between the two is implied and baptism is at least a prerequisite.[15]

This seems to fit well the definition of a proto-sacramentalism alluded to by White.

Acts 8.12-17

In this episode in Samaria, there is a linkage of belief and baptism.[16] The first time baptism is stated without modification (v. 12) but the second time as 'into (εἰς) the name of the Lord Jesus' (v. 16). The major critical issue for this passage seems to be the separation between belief and baptism at the instigation of the preaching of Philip and the reception of the Holy Spirit when Peter and John arrive. Dunn goes to lengths to defend the view that there was something deficient in the belief of the Samarians as a result of Philip's preaching before the reception of the Spirit,[17] but his arguments have failed to convince everyone.[18] In any case, whether one believes there was something deficient or not, the

---

14   On the semantics of the future tense-form in Greek, see S.E. Porter, *Verbal Aspect in the Greek of the New Testament, with Reference to Tense and Mood* (Studies in Biblical Greek, 1; New York: Lang, 1989), pp. 403-39, esp. pp. 409-16.

15   New, 'Name, Baptism', p. 134.

16   I will not deal with the Simon part of the episode.

17   Dunn, *Baptism in the Holy Spirit*, pp. 63-68.

18   E.g. Polhill, *Acts*, p. 217; B. Witherington, *The Acts of the Apostles: A Socio-Rhetorical Commentary* (Grand Rapids, MI: Eerdmans, 1998), pp. 285-86; E.A. Russell, 'They Believed Philip Preaching (Acts 8, 12)', *Irish Biblical Studies* 1 (1979), pp. 169-76 (but cf. J.D.G. Dunn, 'They Believed Philip Preaching: A Reply', *Irish Biblical Studies* 1 [1979], pp. 177-83). I find some of Dunn's arguments particularly difficult to imagine a first-century reader grasping. I especially question his interpretation, *Baptism in the Holy Spirit*, p. 65, of the verb πιστεύω in v. 12 (see also below). This verse may contain a dative absolute ('when they believed, while Philip was preaching concerning the good news..., both men and women were being baptized...'), since the use of the verb πιστεύω in the parallel construction in v. 13 is used absolutely. Dunn admits that the use here in v. 12 is unique for Acts.

linkage in the passage is clear. Belief and baptism go together in v. 12.
When this baptism is restated in v. 16 it is linked to baptism into the name
of the Lord Jesus, which seems to me to indicate that the baptism of v. 12
is seen to be the baptism of full enrolment into Christian discipleship.
Further, in the restatement in v. 16 belief is not mentioned, its apparently
having been subsumed under the notion of baptism into the name. In this
case, baptism into the name of Jesus Christ comes to stand for the act of
faith and the act of baptism, regardless of how one thinks that this relates
to the coming of the Holy Spirit. In that sense, baptism is a sacramental
act.

Acts 8.26-39

In the episode of the conversion of the Ethiopian eunuch, he reads in
Isaiah 53 and turns to Philip and asks of whom the prophet is speaking.
Philip, Luke says, preached Jesus to the eunuch. Then the eunuch sees
water and asks what prevents him from being baptized.[19] Philip then
baptizes him, and is then taken away. Dunn states that 'Luke never
mentions water-baptism by itself as the condition of or means to
receiving forgiveness'.[20] He also says that faith and baptism are normally
closely linked, and cites Acts 8.37-38 (D).[21] However, as Dunn has
clearly recognized, Acts 8.26-39 does not have any explicit reference to
faith, repentance, forgiveness or any of the other acts often linked with
baptism in conversion-initiation. The verse that Dunn cites as linking
faith and baptism, Acts 8.37, is in fact not included in most of the earliest
Greek manuscripts (nor in D, apparently), but is in a sixth-century
manuscript, E, and attested by Irenaeus (late second century).[22] In other
words, unless we are led to believe that this was simply a vacant act

---

19   There has been much discussion of this phrasing ('What prevents me from being
baptized?') as an early baptismal formula. See O. Cullmann, *Baptism in the New
Testament* (Studies in Biblical Theology, 1; trans. J.K.S. Reid; London: SCM Press,
1950), pp. 71-80, who originated the hypothesis.
20   Dunn, *Baptism in the Holy Spirit*, p. 97.
21   Dunn, *Baptism in the Holy Spirit*, p. 96.
22   See B.M. Metzger, *A Textual Commentary on the Greek New Testament* (New
York: American Bible Society, 1994), p. 315, who notes that there is no apparent reason
why early scribes would have omitted this verse if it were authentic to the earlier text, and
it contains non-Lukan phrasing. He speculates that it may have been an early baptismal
formula written in a margin of a manuscript of Acts that was later inserted into the text,
since without it the eunuch is not recorded as making a profession of his faith. The verse
reads, with some variations: 'And Philip said to him, "If you believe with the whole of
your heart, it is permitted". And he answered and said, "I believe Jesus Christ to be the
son of God".'

without substance, the baptism here is meant to represent the act of belief and repentance on the part of the eunuch, and in that sense has sacramental qualities.

Acts 9.10-19 (cf. 22.16)

I am including here both Paul's conversion as recorded in Acts 9 and his recapitulation in ch. 22. Dunn is at pains to insist that Paul's conversion took place over the course of three days, beginning with the vision on the Damascus road and ending with his receiving of the Holy Spirit when Ananias lays hands on him.[23] There are of course two sides to this debate.[24] However, more important in Acts 9 is the linkage of laying on of hands, the filling of the Holy Spirit, healing (regaining his sight) and being baptized. The laying on of hands seems to be an act of imparting a blessing to someone.[25] In this case, it conveys the blessing of healing and the Holy Spirit, and is not directly linked to baptism. In Acts 22.16 the linkage is between baptism, the washing away of sins and calling on his name. It is worth noting that the filling of the Holy Spirit is not mentioned in the later accounts in either Acts 22 or 26, nor is Paul's baptism mentioned in Acts 26.[26] Even so, scholars are widely divided on what can be known about Paul's being filled with the Holy Spirit from this passage. As Swete says, 'In the case of Saul...it is not clear whether the gift of the Spirit preceded, accompanied, or followed baptism; nor is it necessary to distinguish the stages of an illumination which was practically a single act'.[27] That seems to be the important point in regard to Paul's baptism. Rather than it being a merely symbolic act, it appears to have been inextricably intertwined with the events surrounding Paul's

23   Dunn, *Baptism in the Holy Spirit*, pp. 73-78. Not all of his arguments are equally strong. One of Dunn's major arguments is that 'Lord' may simply mean the equivalent of 'Sir' when it is used by Paul in this account (e.g. Acts 9.5; 22.8, 10; 26.15). What he does not note is that this 'Lord' addresses Ananias in Acts 9.10, 11, 15, who also responds with 'Lord' (vv. 10, 13) and informs Paul that the 'Lord' had spoken to him (v. 17). See also S.E. Porter, *The Paul of Acts: Essays in Literary Criticism, Rhetoric, and Theology* (Wissenschaftliche Untersuchungen zum Neuen Testament, 115; Tübingen: Mohr Siebeck, 1999 [repr. *Paul in Acts* (Library of Pauline Studies; Peabody, MA: Hendrickson, 2001)]), pp. 70-73.

24   R.P. Menzies, *The Development of Early Christian Pneumatology with Special Reference to Luke-Acts* (*Journal for the Study of the New Testament*, Supplement Series, 54; Sheffield: JSOT Press, 1991), pp. 260-63.

25   Beasley-Murray, *Baptism*, p. 123.

26   On differences in the three accounts of Paul's conversion, see Barrett, *Acts*, I, pp. 439-40.

27   H.B. Swete, *The Holy Spirit in the New Testament: A Study of Primitive Christian Teaching* (London: Macmillan, 2nd edn, 1910), p. 96.

conversion (whether that was one or three days in length) and linked at
least in his own mind with the washing away of his sins and his calling on
the name of Jesus. The phrasing in Acts 22.16 is worth noting. Two
imperative forms are used, βάπτισαι and ἀπόλουσαι.[28] The first is
preceded by a dependent participle, ἀναστὰς, and the second followed by
another, ἐπικαλεσάμενος. Although it is tempting to see the first
dependent upon the first main verb and the second on the second, which
is perhaps technically correct, there is a sense in which the first participle
introduces the subsequent actions as linked together, in which the baptism
and the washing away of sins go together, perhaps the latter by the
former.[29] The second participle then summarizes what the two actions of
baptism and washing represent—the public confession and
acknowledgement of the cleansing faith in the Lord. These actions are
linked together grammatically and conceptually.[30] The result is that
baptism is an integral part, and has sacramental features, of the
conversion experience.

Acts 10.44-48

In this episode with Cornelius, there is a close linkage of the coming of
the Holy Spirit, and then baptism 'in (ἐν) the name of Jesus Christ'. As
Polhill notes, however, there is the implication of belief and forgiveness
of sins,[31] since these are Peter's closing words in Acts 10.43 before the
Holy Spirit came upon those listening. But this is just an implication. The
two events that are specified are the coming of the Holy Spirit, and
manifestations that accompany this, and Peter's impassioned response
that these people cannot be refused the water for being baptized. They
are then baptized in the name of Jesus Christ, signifying full
incorporation into the believing community. This is the closing episode
of the event.

---

28   The verb βάπτισαι is in the middle voice. Some have seen this in terms of self-
baptism, but this is based upon a misunderstanding of the Greek voice system. See S.E.
Porter, 'Did Paul Baptize Himself? A Problem of the Greek Voice System', in Porter and
Cross (eds.), *Dimensions of Baptism*.
29   Beasley-Murray, *Baptism*, p. 102; Barrett, *Acts*, II, p. 1043; J.A. Fitzmyer, *The
Acts of the Apostles* (Anchor Bible, 31; New York: Doubleday, 1997), p. 707.
30   See Porter, *Verbal Aspect*, pp. 377-88, on the placement of the participle and
what this conveys in terms of concomitant action.
31   Polhill, *Acts*, p. 264.

Acts 16.14-15

The account of Lydia is indirect in a number of ways. The author says that the Lord opened her heart to respond to the things spoken by Paul, evidently implying belief and repentance even though these are not explicitly stated, and that when she and her household had been baptized, she invited Paul and his companions to stay with her, seeing their staying as a way of determining whether she had been faithful to the Lord (note the use of the conditional statement). One might think of baptism as wholly symbolic in significance, but it is then odd that the only act associated with conversion-initiation is the singular rite of baptism.[32]

Acts 16.25-34

In the episode of the Philippian jailer's conversion, once the jailer was assured that Paul and Silas were there, the jailer asked what he must do to be saved (v. 30). Paul and Silas responded that he must believe in the Lord Jesus and he could expect to be saved (v. 31).[33] They then spoke the word of the Lord to the jailer and his household. Later that night, he and his household were baptized (v. 33). The jailer's initial question is probably not concerning his personal salvation, since Paul and Silas had not escaped, but was concerning his spiritual salvation.[34] This is the way Paul and Silas answer. Here the act of baptism is not as closely linked to belief and salvation, except as the only ritual associated with conversion-initiation.

Acts 18.8

Crispus, the leader of the synagogue, believed in the Lord, and many of the Corinthians also believed and were baptized. Here there is a clear link between belief and baptism in the case of the many Corinthians who heard what Paul was preaching, and it can probably be assumed that Crispus was among those. Dunn makes the odd comment that the use of πιστεύω in 18.8, among others, 'should also probably be given the sense of accepting the disclosures about rather than commitment to'.[35] He probably does not mean the first use in the verse, since that is linked with

---

32   As Dunn, *Baptism in the Holy Spirit*, p. 59, admits.

33   On the semantics of the future tense-form, see Porter, *Verbal Aspect*, pp. 409-16.

34   Polhill, *Acts*, p. 355; Barrett, *Acts*, II, pp. 796-97.

35   Dunn, *Baptism in the Holy Spirit*, p. 65.

the dative of 'Lord', which he notes as a possible exception. Instead, he appears to mean that in the instance where the belief is followed by baptism it is simply 'intellectual assent'. What the evidence for this position might be is hard to tell, and in fact it is counter-intuitive to the context, since there is nothing further to indicate a lack of genuine belief. In any case, belief and baptism seem to go hand in hand here.

<h2 style="text-align:center">Acts 19.1-7</h2>

The Ephesian episode is certainly one of the most complex in exegesis of the book of Acts. The major problems revolve around whether the Ephesians were genuine believers when Paul visited them, and if they were, why they had not received the Holy Spirit, but only the baptism of John. I have elsewhere surveyed in detail the six views that seem to pertain to this passage today.[36] I will briefly summarize them here. One argues that there are different sources behind Acts 19.2 and 3, which has led to the confusion.[37] Another is that it is a holy spirit, not the Holy Spirit, that is being referred to in v. 2.[38] A third explanation is that those in Ephesus were disciples of John the Baptist, who was viewed messianically by some in the early church, and that the author of Acts wishes to subordinate these disciples into one legitimate church.[39] A fourth solution is that the account in Acts 19 is written from Paul's perspective as he first observed the situation (they were believers), only to find out that since they had not received the Holy Spirit they were not and required baptism.[40] A fifth perspective is that the Ephesians are not disciples or believers, even though the term 'disciple' is used (but without the article, which Dunn claims is a special usage), but that Paul's question reveals his suspicion regarding their status, rather than affirming it.[41] Lastly, a sixth perspective is that the Ephesians were believers, as Paul's question implies, but that they had not received the Holy Spirit but only

36   See Porter, *Paul of Acts*, pp. 80-86.
37   J.C. O'Neill, 'The Connection between Baptism and the Gift of the Spirit in Acts', *Journal for the Study of the New Testament* 63 (1996), pp. 96-102.
38   R. Strelan, *Paul, Artemis, and the Jews in Ephesus* (Beihefte zur Zeitschrift für die neutestamentliche Wissenschaft, 80; Berlin: de Gruyter, 1996), pp. 230-45.
39   E. Käsemann, 'The Disciples of John the Baptist at Ephesus', in his *Essays on New Testament Themes* (trans. W.J. Montague; London: SCM Press, 1964), pp. 136-48, a position followed by a number of others.
40   I.H. Marshall, *The Acts of the Apostles* (Tyndale New Testament Commentary; Grand Rapids, MI: Eerdmans, 1980), pp. 305-308, following K. Haacker, 'Einige Fälle von "Erlebter Rede" im Neuen Testament', *Novum Testamentum* 12 (1970), pp. 70-77.
41   Dunn, *Baptism in the Holy Spirit*, pp. 83-89, followed by a number of others.

the baptism of John.[42] Whereas there is no set of arguments with overwhelming force, it appears that the last position has the most strength. It appears that those in Ephesus were believers, but that they had been baptized into John's baptism, but had not received the Holy Spirit or baptism into the Lord Jesus.

In many ways, this passage is a very strong one for establishing the sacramental value of baptism as presented in the book of Acts. There are two sets of events depicted here. The first is the historical account of when the Ephesian believers believed and were baptized into John's baptism. Whether or not this was genuine belief, the two events are linked. The second set of events occurs when Paul visits Ephesus. Here it appears that their initial belief is sufficient, with Paul clarifying that John had baptized a certain way (his baptism of repentance), and had told people to believe in Jesus (v. 4), but their baptism is not. After hearing Paul's recapitulation they were baptized 'into (εἰς) the name of the Lord Jesus' (v. 5), apparently evidencing their acknowledgement of entry into the Christian community already attested by their belief. Then Paul lays hands upon them and the Holy Spirit comes and they speak in tongues and prophecy. This is the only passage where Paul lays his hands on someone and the only instance where the laying on of hands follows baptism directly.[43] The two important acts in this passage are baptism into the name of Jesus and the receipt of the Holy Spirit. It appears that baptism in this instance, since it is 'repeated', indicates more than a symbolic value, but one that sacramentally mirrors the receipt of the Holy Spirit.

Conclusion

This brief survey has attempted to examine a number of passages in Acts that figure prominently in the discussion of conversion-initiation. They are not the only passages in this discussion. Their significance, however, is increased when it is realized that they speak to the issue of the sacramental value of baptism in the early church. Dunn is no doubt correct that the kind of Reformed view of sacraments that he refers to is not endorsed by the various episodes of baptism in the book of Acts. However, this kind of an argument sets up a straw man for knocking down. One can acknowledge that Dunn is correct without denying that there is a proto-sacramental character to the occasions of baptism in Acts that indicate that the early Christians depicted seemed to acknowledge

---

42   Menzies, *Development of Early Christian Pneumatology*, pp. 268-77.

43   Polhill, *Acts*, p. 400.

that God was in some way working through these rites to indicate their incorporation into the early Christian community.

CHAPTER 8

Is 'Baptist Sacramentalism' an Oxymoron?: Reactions in Britain to *Christian Baptism* (1959)

Stanley K. Fowler

Christian Baptism (1959)

In the summer of 1955 four Baptist ministers in London began meeting to discuss baptism, aware that the topic was near the top of the ecumenical agenda but also that Baptists had contributed very little to the discussion. They solicited the involvement of other Baptists, and ultimately ten scholars, both pastors and theological educators, formed a working group in which the individuals researched specific parts of the question and submitted their conclusions for evaluation by the group. The results were published in 1959, edited by Alec Gilmore (b. 1928), under the title of *Christian Baptism: A Fresh Attempt to Understand the Rite in terms of Scripture, History, and Theology*. Ernest A. Payne, who was then the General Secretary of the Baptist Union, wrote an introductory chapter describing 'Baptism in Recent Discussion' to set the historical context, but he was not a member of the working group and did not commit himself to the positions of the group.[1] The book proved to be a watershed in the twentieth-century reformulation of baptismal doctrine among British Baptists,[2] providing for public scrutiny the relatively

---

1   E.A. Payne, 'Baptism in Recent Discussion', in A. Gilmore (ed.), *Christian Baptism: A Fresh Attempt to Understand the Rite in terms of Scripture, History, and Theology* (London: Lutterworth Press, 1959), pp. 15-24.

2   For a thorough history of this process, see Anthony R. Cross, *Baptism and the Baptists: Theology and Practice in Twentieth-Century Britain* (Studies in Baptist History and Thought, 3; Carlisle: Paternoster, 2000), or for a brief summary, see the same author's article, 'Baptists and Baptism–A British Perspective', *Baptist History and Heritage* 35.1 (Winter, 2000), pp. 104-121. For a narrowly focused account of the shift from a symbolic to a sacramental perspective, see Stanley K. Fowler, *More Than a Symbol: The British Baptist Recovery of Baptismal Sacramentalism* (Studies in Baptist History and Thought, 2; Carlisle: Paternoster, 2002), pp. 89-155. This chapter is a revised version of pp. 113-33 of that book.

advanced sacramentalism of a group of younger Baptist leaders and thus provoking public criticism from those who lamented this new departure. What follows is a summary of the sacramental contribution of the book and the criticisms directed toward it. This particular episode in British Baptist life illustrates the fact that Baptists, in spite of their name, are not really unified by a common and coherent baptismal theology—a fact that comes as a great surprise to many Baptists.

Stephen Winward launched the book with a discussion of 'Scripture, Tradition, and Baptism'. This chapter did not deal explicitly with the sacramental question, but it did argue for a view of the Bible and tradition which was significantly different from the typical Baptist approach. He rejected a simple biblicism which functions on the assumption that the Bible is a level collection of fully adequate insights and proof-texts, and argued that apostolic practice is normative only when it reflects what is essential to the gospel.[3] He accepted the idea that apostolic tradition has been perpetuated not only through the New Testament writings, but also through successive generations of the church (although this latter transmission always stands under the judgment of the uniquely valuable apostolic deposit in the scriptures).[4] This allows for the possible adoption of theological constructs which are legitimate developments of apostolic teaching, although not explicitly present in the New Testament, but this has more relevance for issues of the subject and mode of baptism than for the sacramental question. A high view of baptismal efficacy can in fact be argued on the basis of a primitive biblicism—the long-standing Baptist reduction of baptism to a mere symbol of a completed conversion requires the assertion that key New Testament texts do not mean what they *seem* to mean when they speak, for example, of being 'baptized into Christ' (e.g. Rom. 6.3 and Gal. 3.27).

Alec Gilmore analyzed the Jewish antecedents to baptism. Exploring the relation of baptism to circumcision, which has always been at the heart of the debate, he suggested a kind of confirmatory significance for baptism:

> Under the new covenant, union with Christ did away with the need for circumcision, and created the need for something to bring home to a man his union with Christ

---

3   Stephen F. Winward, 'Scripture, Tradition, and Baptism', in Gilmore (ed.), *Christian Baptism*, p. 51. Winward (1911–86) was minister of Highams Park Baptist Church, Walthamstow, London, and the one contributor who had also been a member of the group that produced a similar book in the 1940s, Robert C. Walton, *The Gathered Community* (London: Carey Press, 1946).

4   Winward, 'Scripture, Tradition, and Baptism', p. 49.

and the realization that he was possessed by Christ's spirit. It was this need which was filled by baptism.[5]

Here the point of 'bring home' seems to be that baptism mediates the conscious experience of entrance into the sphere of redemption; in other words, he interpreted baptism along the lines of a 'seal' that has no efficacy in itself but does by virtue of its connection to a recognized authority or benefactor, having an efficacy at the level of assurance.

At the heart of the book is the exegesis of the New Testament evidence, and R.E O. White treated both 'The Baptism of Jesus' and 'Baptism in the Synoptic Gospels'.[6] White provided a balanced and carefully nuanced interpretation of baptism as an event embodying both a human act of obedience to the gospel and a divine act of grace conveying the benefits of the gospel. He posited a strong connection of this sacramental sense to the baptism of Jesus, in that the bestowal of the Spirit at the baptism of Jesus indicated that the focus of the rite was shifting from an act of obedience to a divine empowering of obedience. Although the baptism of Jesus is unique in some ways, he argued (like H. Wheeler Robinson[7] before him) that there is 'ample suggestion and warrant for a new and vastly enriched conception of what baptism could mean also for those who followed in His steps'.[8]

White expanded the significance of the baptism of Jesus along at least five lines. '[I]t lends to the practice his personal authority'. Secondly, 'it lends a note of positive enrichment, rather than of negative renunciation, to baptism'. Thirdly, it provides as a motive for baptism emulation of Jesus' 'personal dedication and obedience', in that this is the meaning of a baptism of 'repentance' for the one sinless human. Fourthly, it connects the rite to personal assurance of being a child of God, that is, it has 'filial overtones'. Finally, it links baptism to the reception of the Spirit, the promise of the Hebrew prophets for the last days, and thus 'baptism becomes the sacrament for the transmission of the Spirit'.[9] The last two points of this reorientation of baptism indicate something of its

---

5   Alec Gilmore, 'Jewish Antecedents,' in Gilmore (ed.), *Christian Baptism*, p. 65. Gilmore was a minister in Northampton.

6   White wrote a great deal on baptism, the best known being *The Biblical Doctrine of Initiation* (London: Hodder & Stoughton, 1960) and *Invitation to Baptism: A Manual for Inquirers* (London: Carey Kingsgate Press, 1962). White (b. 1914) was a minister in Birkenhead.

7   See Fowler, *More Than a Symbol*, pp. 89-97. See also Anthony R. Cross, 'The Pneumatological Key to H. Wheeler Robinson's Baptismal Sacramentalism', in the present volume.

8   R.E.O. White, 'The Baptism of Jesus', in Gilmore (ed.), *Christian Baptism*, p. 93.

9   White, 'The Baptism of Jesus', pp. 96-97.

sacramental significance for those who 'follow the Lord' in baptism. In some sense the Spirit is conveyed to the baptizand in the event, and the presence of the Spirit is an experiential reality which gives assurance that the individual is indeed accepted by grace as a child of God (not a Son of God in the same sense as Jesus, but in a related sense).

White argued that Jesus provided two kinds of warnings which relate to baptism: one against the temptation to disparage baptism as a mere ceremony that is an optional extra; and the other against the attempt to make baptism absolutely necessary for salvation. In his words:

> Unquestionably Jesus opposed any reliance upon the performance of religious acts as efficacious in themselves apart from the state of the heart which they express...
>
> Nowhere does Jesus suggest that religion can consist in wholly inward states of soul that seek and find no expression in appropriate acts of devotion and commitment, such as baptism might provide.[10]

S.I. Buse treated 'Baptism in the Acts of the Apostles' and 'Baptism in Other New Testament Writings'. In his treatment of Acts he was very hesitant to dogmatize and he posited a very moderate kind of sacramentalism. He was only prepared to say that baptism *may* have been the normal rite of initiation into the primitive church, but 'it can hardly be described as either universal or necessary for salvation'.[11] He attempted to steer a middle course between Oscar Cullmann, who considered the baptizand as a passive person, and Markus Barth, who considered baptism to be a purely human act.[12] Buse denied that the human activity in baptism is the whole essence of the event, thus parting company with a sizable part of Baptist tradition. The two sides of baptism are seen in the fact that the individual chooses to be baptized, but baptism is done by an administrator (not by self-baptism). Therefore, 'Only when the two sides of baptism, the human and the divine, are seen together is Luke's picture viewed whole.'[13]

Central to the treatment of Acts is the issue of the relation between baptism and the gift of the Spirit. Buse recognized that there is no

---

10   R.E.O. White, 'Baptism in the Synoptic Gospels', in Gilmore (ed.), *Christian Baptism*, pp. 110-11.

11   S.I. Buse, 'Baptism in the Acts of the Apostles', in Gilmore (ed.), *Christian Baptism*, p. 116. Buse (1913–71) was Lecturer in New Testament Studies, University College of North Wales.

12   O. Cullmann, *Baptism in the New Testament* (Studies in Biblical Theology, 1; London: SCM Press, 1950), e.g., p. 32; and M. Barth, *Die Taufe: Ein Sakrament? Ein exegetischer Beitrag zum Gespräch über die kirchliche Taufe* (Zollikon–Zurich: Evangelischer Verlag, 1951), pp. 135-36. See Buse, 'Baptism in the Acts of the Apostles', pp. 125-27.

13   Buse, 'Baptism in the Acts of the Apostles', p. 127.

standard description of this in Acts, and the challenge is to identify the norm (if there is one) and the exceptions. He summarized his modest conclusions thus:

(i) There is no indication that Spirit-baptism at any stage superseded water-baptism,

(ii) to assert that baptism and the gift of the Spirit always go together in Acts is to go beyond the evidence,

(iii) in part of Acts there is a close connection between the gift of the Spirit and the laying-on of hands, but there are signs that this was a development later than the primitive Jerusalem church.[14]

In the end, he saw too much diversity of experience represented in Acts to draw any firm conclusions about the exact relation between baptism and the benefits signified by it.

Buse found more explicit indications of the efficacy of baptism in other New Testament texts. For example, he asserted concerning 1 Peter 3.21:

Once more we have an approximation to the kind of teaching we find in the Pauline letters: the Christian dies with Christ in the waters of baptism, and in that experience he finds salvation.[15]

Concerning the Epistle to the Hebrews he argued:

In 10:22 the tense of the participles, 'sprinkled' and 'washed', justifies us in regarding them as references to baptism. Christian initiation is pictured as succeeding where the older Levitical rites failed: it gives the cleansing essential for men's approach to God... *The writer of the Epistle to the Hebrews thus regards baptism as the point in Christian experience where the results of the death of Christ are made effective by entry into that close fellowship with God which is represented as the Holy of Holies.*[16]

This inference from the combination of washing imagery and an aorist participle to a baptismal reference is quite common[17] but questionable. In particular, the grammatical significance of the aorist tense is not sufficiently precise to justify the inference that these participles must refer to one specific event.

---

14   Buse, 'Baptism in the Acts of the Apostles', p. 122.

15   S.I. Buse, 'Baptism in Other New Testament Writings', in Gilmore (ed.), *Christian Baptism*, p. 179, italics his.

16   Buse, 'Baptism in Other New Testament Writings', p. 183, italics his.

17   For other examples, see G.R. Beasley-Murray, *Baptism in the New Testament* (Grand Rapids: Eerdmans, 1962), pp. 163 and 173.

Given the dominance of Paul in the formulation of Christian theology, George Beasley-Murray's 'Baptism in the Epistles of Paul' was in many ways the most crucial part of the book. He began his chapter with Romans 10.9-10, which does not explicitly refer to baptism but has been interpreted as an allusion to confession of faith in Jesus in baptism. Even though the text is not explicitly baptismal, it does clearly show that Paul can treat some outward human action (verbal confession that Jesus is Lord) that goes beyond faith as instrumental in the reception of salvation, thus demonstrating that great care must be taken in drawing inferences from his *sola fide* teaching. As Beasley-Murray argued that

> Since faith in Jesus as the risen Lord brings justification, and confession of His name deliverance from this world and the life of the age to come (verse 10), the baptismal act in which both are expressed is the supreme moment in the believer's experience of salvation. The enigma of the relation of the Pauline teaching on salvation by faith and his high estimate of the value of baptism come most nearly to solution in this verse. For Paul the inner and outer acts of the decision of faith and its expression in baptism form one indissoluble event.[18]

He then proceeded to accumulate the evidence of Paul's explicit statements about baptism, the consistent tendency of which is to see it as the event in which sinners are salvifically united to Christ by faith. For example, on Galatians 3.27, he wrote:

> The union was realized in baptism. It is evident that baptism *into* Christ results in being *in* Christ, which is a *putting on* Christ... Baptism brings unity with Christ and His church. *And in that order of precedence* .[19]

He recognized that there is a social dimension to being in Christ, but he vigorously argued that union with Christ is the logical foundation of union with his body. It is, he asserted, Christ who redeems, not the church.[20] In this logical order he was countering the order defended in earlier books by both Robert Walton and Neville Clark,[21] although without naming them.

Romans 6.3-4 and Colossians 2.12 both express Paul's conviction that what happened for our benefit objectively in the death and resurrection

18   G.R. Beasley-Murray, 'Baptism in the Epistles of Paul', in Gilmore (ed.), *Christian Baptism*, pp. 129-30. Beasley-Murray (1916–2000) served as Principal of Spurgeon's College, 1958–73, and Professor of New Testament at the Southern Baptist Theological Seminary, Louisville, Kentucky, 1973–80.
19   Beasley-Murray, 'Baptism in the Epistles of Paul', p. 138, italics his.
20   Beasley-Murray, 'Baptism in the Epistles of Paul', p. 139.
21   Walton, *Gathered Community*, p. 30; Neville Clark, *An Approach to the Theology of the Sacraments* (Studies in Biblical Theology, 17; London: SCM Press, 1956), p. 33.

of Christ also happens in us subjectively at conversion, which is to say at baptism. Romans 6 is the more frequently quoted text, but Colossians 2 brings certain elements of Romans 6 to clearer expression, in particular the experience of resurrection with Christ *in the baptismal event* and the fact that what happens in baptism does so 'through faith'.[22]

Titus 3.5 has been interpreted in various ways by Baptists, some accepting the 'washing' terminology as an allusion to baptism,[23] while others have argued that it is a reference to spiritual cleansing and not to baptism.[24] The underlying theological concern of the latter group has been to avoid traditional concepts of baptismal regeneration. Beasley-Murray said:

> Its central conception is that in baptism the corresponding event occurs in the life of the individual as happened to the church at Pentecost: the Spirit is 'poured out' through the risen Christ—an idea in direct line with the earliest interpretation of baptism, Acts 2:33, 38. Certainly the saying implies a realistic rather than symbolic understanding of baptism, but that applies to most of the Pauline utterances on baptism.[25]

Beasley-Murray described the effect of the gospel in an individual life, according to Paul, as a 'radical influence' when it is received in faith, but the 'decisive expression' of faith is baptism.[26] To say that baptism is 'decisive' in salvation is to say that whatever may be true invisibly of the relation of the individual to God (and only God knows this), baptism is the means by which faith is translated from attitude into action, and thus the means by which salvation becomes visible and an assured personal reality. Baptism is, for Paul, an effective sign precisely because it is tied to faith. To assert that baptism saves apart from faith is to sever baptismal doctrine from Paul's teaching, but to assert that baptism saves by virtue of being the vehicle of faith is to take seriously what Paul says about both faith and baptism.

D.R. Griffiths examined baptism in the Fourth Gospel and 1 John. He recognized that there is great diversity in scholarly opinion about the extent to which sacramentalism is taught by, or even congruous with, the Johannine literature, and he concluded that the only safe path is to treat every text on its own, rather than assuming a comprehensive sacramental

---

22   Beasley-Murray, 'Baptism in the Epistles of Paul', pp. 136, 140.

23   For example, Benjamin Keach, *Gold Refin'd; or Baptism in its Primitive Purity* (London: Nathaniel Crouch, 1689), p. 83; Baptist W. Noel, *Essay on Christian Baptism* (New York: Harper & Brothers, 1850), p. 113.

24   E.g., John Gill, *An Exposition of the New Testament* (3 vols; Philadelphia: William W. Woodward, 1811 [1746–48]), III, p. 365.

25   Beasley-Murray, 'Baptism in the Epistles of Paul', pp. 143-44.

26   Beasley-Murray, 'Baptism in the Epistles of Paul', p. 148.

grid.[27] He was prepared to admit the presence of allusions to baptism in
various texts about water: probably in John 13.1-11 and 19.31-37, and
possibly in 1 John 5.5-8.[28] However, the important text in John is the
reference to a birth 'of water and Spirit' in John 3.5. Many Baptists (and
others) have argued that this does not refer to baptism at all, but instead is
a figurative reference to something else, perhaps the spiritual cleansing
wrought by the Spirit.[29] But Griffiths considered it impossible to imagine
an early Christian writer using 'water' in this way without thinking of
baptism, concluding that it is both a positive statement about the
significance of Christian baptism and 'an underlying polemical allusion
to John's baptism'.[30] He concluded:

> The positive teaching of 3:5 is thus, very briefly, that entrance into the kingdom
> of God is impossible except by means of the rebirth in baptism which is both a
> water-baptism and a bestowal of the Spirit; the very form of the construction
> suggests their indissoluble connection.[31]

This concept of spiritual rebirth (or birth from above) is the Johannine
parallel to the Pauline concept of spiritual death and resurrection, and in
both cases it is connected to baptism. Why does John not speak explicitly
of baptism here? Griffiths followed C.H. Dodd on this point, concluding
that John's audience included pagans whom he wanted to bring to
Christian faith, and this kind of allusive language conveys an appropriate
kind of sacramentalism without misleading his readers in magical or
superstitious directions with which they would be familiar.[32] As will be
noted below, his relatively modest sacramental interpretation of John 3.5
was severely criticized by some fellow Baptists as a capitulation to
magical ideas of baptismal regeneration.

Turning to the historical development of baptismal doctrine and
practice, A.W. Argyle surveyed 'Baptism in the Early Christian
Centuries'. He chronicled what he interpreted as the descent of the early
church into superstitious views of baptismal efficacy which depart from
the New Testament, and traced the rise of infant baptism as a corollary of

27   D.R. Griffiths, 'Baptism in the Fourth Gospel and the First Epistle of John', in
Gilmore (ed.), *Christian Baptism*, pp. 150-51. Griffiths (1915–90) was Lecturer in
Biblical Studies, University College, Cardiff.
28   Griffiths, 'Fourth Gospel and the First Epistle of John', pp. 162, 164 and 167.
29   E.g., Gill, *Exposition*, I, p. 793; John Howard Hinton, 'The Ultimatum; or
"What saith the Scripture?"', in J.H. Hinton, *The Theological Works of the Rev. John
Howard Hinton, M.A.* (6 vols; London: Houlston & Wright, 1864–65), V, p. 469.
30   Griffiths, 'Fourth Gospel and the First Epistle of John', p. 156.
31   Griffiths, 'Fourth Gospel and the First Epistle of John', p. 158, italics his.
32   Griffiths, 'Fourth Gospel and the First Epistle of John', pp. 156-57. Cf. C.H.
Dodd, *The Interpretation of the Fourth Gospel* (Cambridge: Cambridge University Press,
1970), pp. 309-10.

this shift. He vigorously denied 'the superstitious notion that water-baptism itself was regenerative'.[33] For many Baptists this is equivalent to denying the sacramental character of baptism, but that was not his point. His comment was that, 'The growth of infant baptism inevitably obscured the New Testament significance of baptism as a sacrament of penitence and faith in which the Holy Spirit is received.'[34] Therefore, he was defending the idea that baptism is sacramental and specifically that it mediates the gift of the Spirit, which gift is in fact at the heart of the benefits of the new covenant. What he was attacking was the idea that baptism *per se* regenerates apart from faith in the baptizand. In this regard he was like many earlier Baptists who, when they denied baptismal regeneration, were not rejecting the idea that God conveys spiritual benefits (indeed, the Spirit himself) through baptism, only the idea that the act of baptism conveys such benefits to infants or others who have not believed the gospel.[35]

Morris West wrote on 'The Anabaptists and the Rise of the Baptist Movement'.[36] There was little in this chapter that related to the sacramental issue: the material was focused on the rise of the 'believers' church' among the Anabaptists and ultimately the origin of Baptists through the application of the same ecclesiology among English Separatists in the first decade of the seventeenth century. The major burden of the chapter was to show the link between believer's baptism and the concept of the church as a company of confessing believers voluntarily associated with one another. Unfortunately, West did not seek to interpret in any detail the baptismal language of early Baptists like John Smyth, who spoke of baptism as a 'sacrament' and a 'visible word' offering Christ to believing recipients.[37]

D. Mervyn Himbury's survey of 'Baptismal Controversies, 1640–1900' focused on Baptist debates about the subjects and mode of baptism, and the relation of baptism to communion. The only significant reference to the sacramental question occurres in his suggestion that near

---

33   A.W. Argyle, 'Baptism in the Early Christian Centuries', Gilmore (ed.), *Christian Baptism*, p. 217. Argyle (1910–81) was a Tutor at Regent's Park College, Oxford.

34   Argyle, 'Baptism in the Early Christian Centuries', p. 205.

35   E.g., see Charles Stovel, *The Baptismal Regeneration Controversy Considered* (London: Houlston & Stoneman, and Dyer, 1843), pp. 18 and 113. For an analysis of Stovel's nuanced treatment of baptismal regeneration, see Fowler, *More Than a Symbol*, pp. 65-72.

36   W.M.S. West, 'The Anabaptists and the Rise of the Baptist Movement', in Gilmore (ed.), *Christian Baptism*, pp. 223-72. West (1922–99) was a Tutor at Regent's Park College, Oxford, 1953–59, then later Principal of Bristol Baptist College, 1971–87.

37   See Fowler, *More Than a Symbol*, pp. 12-14.

the end of the period surveyed, the latter part of the nineteenth century, some Baptists articulated a more sacramental view of baptism in the sense that 'God really acts; by it the believer enters the church and receives new power by the gift of the Spirit'.[38] This assertion is a bit mystifying, because he offered no examples of this supposed trend, and it is generally recognized that Baptist thought at that time was largely in revolt against sacramentalism, due in large measure to a reaction against Tractarianism. He indicated that he was following J.R.C. Perkin on this point, but Perkin suggested that this Baptist sacramentalism was relatively insignificant numerically and was in no way indicative of a trend.[39] Earlier Baptists had sometimes posited an empowering work of the Spirit through baptism, often as a kind of second, post-conversion, crisis,[40] but this is not true of later Baptist thought. This chapter accurately focused on the baptismal debates that consumed the energy of Baptists, but for that very reason it did little to advance the understanding of Baptist sacramentalism.

The final chapter, 'The Theology of Baptism,' was authored by Neville Clark and was generally considered to be the most controversial chapter. This chapter covered much of the same ground as his 1956 book, *An Approach to the Theology of the Sacraments*, but perhaps in a more aggressive tone. There is no doubt about his affirmation of the sacramental nature of baptism. For example:

> Grounded in the atoning work of Christ, which it applies and extends, its theology must always be an inference from Christology transposed into its true eschatological key... Baptism, in this normative period, implies, embodies and effects forgiveness of sin, initiation into the church and the gift of the Holy Spirit.[41]

Again he wrote:

38   D.M. Himbury, 'Baptismal Controversies, 1640-1900', in Gilmore (ed.), *Christian Baptism*, p. 274. Himbury (b. 1922) and was Principal of The Baptist College of Victoria, Melbourne, 1959–86.

39   J.R.C. Perkin, 'Baptism in Nonconformist Theology, 1820–1920, with Special Reference to the Baptists' (DPhil Thesis, University of Oxford, 1955), p. 10.

40   Both the *Somerset Confession* (1656) and the *Standard Confession* (1660) posit the idea of a post-conversion gift of the Spirit conditioned partly on baptism; for the full text of the confessions, see William L. Lumpkin (ed.), *Baptist Confessions of Faith* (Valley Forge, PA: Judson Press, rev. edn, 1969), pp. 203-16, 224-35. See also the commentary on Acts 2.38 in Gill, *Exposition*, II, p. 167.

41   Neville Clark, 'The Theology of Baptism', in Gilmore (ed.), *Christian Baptism*, p. 308. At the time Clark (1926–2002) was a Baptist Minister in Rochester, moving to Amersham Free Church in 1959, and later became Principal of the South Wales Baptist College, 1985–91.

Baptism effects initiation into the life of the blessed Trinity and all the blessings of the new 'age', and so embodies the wholeness of redemption. It is 'into Christ', into the crucified, risen and ascended Lord, into the whole drama of His redemption achievement.[42]

In fact, he was emphatic in his assertion that the divine action in baptism is the fundamental aspect of the event:

Baptism is a sacrament of the Gospel, not of our experience of it; of God's faithfulness, not of our faithful response to Him; and any theological formulation which lends itself so readily to an interpretation of the rite primarily in terms of a public confession of faith must at once be suspect.[43]

The most significant advance beyond his earlier treatment of the sacraments was his development of the analogy between the Christ-event and the baptism-into-Christ-event. The basic point was that 'Since baptism initiates into the fulness of redemption, into the crucified and glorified humanity of the Lord, the pattern of the Christ event must be interpretively decisive'.[44] If baptism into Christ means a share in the vicarious work of Christ (cf. Rom. 6), then the pattern of divine and human action in the work of Christ is presumed to be operative in the event of baptism into that work. One implication is that the governing action in baptism is the divine work:

The priority is always with God, for the incarnation is rightly to be understood not in terms of Adoptionist Christology but of the *assumptio carnis*; and this principle remains regulative for the theology of baptism.[45]

However, just as the divine and human in Christ are distinguishable but not separable, this governing nature of the divine action in baptism does not imply the irrelevance of human response and thus paedobaptism.

What is, however, demanded of us is a reading of baptism in terms of the redemptive work of the God-man which fits uneasily with the Paedo-Baptist position. Salvation is not to be effected outside of, apart from, over the head of man. To deny this would be to deny both the principle of incarnation and the pattern of the life and death of the incarnate Son. But just as the baptism unto death of the Lord is constituted by the conjunction of divine action and human response, so the baptism into His death of His followers demands for its reality their ratification of His response, in obedience to the word proclaimed to them.[46]

---

42   Clark, 'Theology of Baptism', p. 309.
43   Clark, 'Theology of Baptism', p. 316.
44   Clark, 'Theology of Baptism', p. 311.
45   Clark, 'Theology of Baptism', p. 311.
46   Clark, 'Theology of Baptism', pp. 313-14.

In spite of this critique of paedobaptism, Clark argued emphatically against the rebaptism as believers of those who were baptized in infancy. He was not simply saying that rebaptism should not be demanded as a condition of church membership—he was asserting that any such rebaptism is 'a blow at the heart of the Christian faith'.[47] His argument here is rooted in the once-for-allness of redemption which is reflected in baptism, the proleptic nature of every baptism (infant or believer), and the assumption that to reject the validity of infant baptism is to deny the validity of paedobaptist churches.[48] It should come as no surprise to note that this argument was widely rejected by his fellow Baptists. Many other Baptists who would defend the principle of 'open membership' would at the same time allow for (and perhaps encourage) rebaptism of those whose conscience called for it, which is a reminder that 'open membership' is more a practical policy than a theology of baptism.

Reviews of *Christian Baptism* show that Clark's chapter rated the highest praise of all the chapters from paedobaptist critics[49] and the strongest protest from Baptists.[50] His own explanation of this was that he was writing with non-Baptists in mind and thus using conceptual categories that were much more intelligible in the ecumenical discussion of 'biblical theology' than in typical Baptist circles.[51] While this may make sense at one level, concern to bring fellow Baptists along with him ought to have had some impact on the shape of his argument. It may be that his choice of rhetorical style was simply an unfortunate tactical error which diluted the potential impact of his argument among Baptists, but it may also be true, as H.H. Rowley noted, that Clark was just more acute as a thinker than he was lucid as a writer.[52]

Criticisms of the Book by Baptists

Within a very short time after the publication of *Christian Baptism* it was under attack as an unbiblical and unbaptistic capitulation to alien theologies. For several months there was a sustained flow of critical letters

---

47   Clark, 'Theology of Baptism', p. 326.

48   Clark, 'Theology of Baptism', p. 326.

49   See, e.g., John Heron, '*Christian Baptism.* Edited by A. Gilmore', *Scottish Journal of Theology* 13 (March, 1960), pp. 102-103.

50   For a mild criticism see Norman H. Maring, '*Christian Baptism.* A. Gilmore, ed.', *Foundations* 3.1 (January, 1960), p. 91; for a strong criticism see Ernest F. Kevan, 'Christian Baptism II', *The Fraternal* 113 (July, 1959), pp. 10-12.

51   Neville Clark, 'Christian Baptism Under Fire', *The Fraternal* 114 (October, 1959), pp. 17-18.

52   H.H. Rowley, '*Christian Baptism*', *Expository Times* 70.10 (July, 1959), p. 302.

to the *Baptist Times*, the denomination's weekly newspaper published in London, and ultimately a critical article in that publication by J.D. Hughey (1914–84) of the International Baptist Theological Seminary in Rüschlikon, Switzerland. There was also a strongly critical review of the book by Ernest Kevan (1903–65, Principal of London Bible College) in *The Fraternal*, the journal of the Baptist Ministers' Fellowship. George Beasley-Murray wrote two articles in the *Baptist Times* clarifying and defending the general perspective of the book, but the critical letters continued. Robert Child also contributed an article in the *Baptist Times* defending a moderate sacramentalism which posits some kind of divine action in baptism, although he was reluctant to define it very precisely.[53] The following material is an explanation of five lines of criticism which continually recurred in the letters and articles, followed by a summary of the response by Beasley-Murray.

First, *that the sacramental view denies the 'faith alone' character of salvation so clearly taught in the New Testament.* Hughey, along with many others, emphasized the Pauline texts which affirm the reality of justification by faith apart from works (Paul's letters to the Romans and Galatians and Eph. 2.8).[54] Others pointed to Acts 16 and Paul's answer to the Philippian jailor's question which promised salvation through faith with no reference to baptism.[55] Still others pointed to Acts 10 and the salvation of Cornelius and his household, when the Spirit was bestowed on them as they received the gospel with a believing attitude prior to any outward response.[56] One letter pointed out that if one assumes that faith is a condition of baptism (as do all Baptists, even the authors of the book in question), then there is posited some interval (short or long) between faith and baptism, so that if salvation comes to all who believe, then it must come prior to baptism.[57] One referred to Neville Clark's chapter and his three tenses of redemption (cross/resurrection, baptism, parousia) and noted that conversion is omitted.[58] This was by far the most common criticism of the book, which is understandable in view of the Baptist commitment to the Reformation principle of *sola fide*.

Second, *that the book teaches baptismal regeneration in a way that is equivalent to traditional Catholic doctrine, thus viewing baptism as a*

---

53   R.L. Child, 'What Happens in Baptism?', *Baptist Times* 4 February 1960, pp. 8 and 10. Child (1891–1971), was Principal-Emeritus of Regent's Park College, Oxford.

54   J.D. Hughey, Jr., 'The New Trend in Baptism', *Baptist Times* 18 February 1960, p. 7.

55   S.F. Carter, 'Christian Baptism', *Baptist Times* 28 January 1960, p. 6.

56   L.S. Jaeger, 'Sacramentalism among Baptists', *Baptist Times* 24 September 1959, p. 6.

57   L.J. Stones, 'Sacramentalism Among Baptists', *Baptist Times* 10 September 1959, p. 6.

58   Robert Clarke, 'Christian Baptism', *Baptist Times* 8 October 1959, p. 6.

kind of magical ceremony. In particular, this criticism was directed at the treatment of John 3.5 by D.R. Griffiths (see above). One writer asserted that this was clearly an affirmation of baptismal regeneration,[59] and another writer concurred with this judgment, adding that it was an example of an *ex opere operato* view and as such it constituted 'heresy'.[60] Griffiths wrote one letter to the *Baptist Times* admitting that his words, if read superficially, might be taken in that sense, but emphasized that his assertion of the role of the Spirit in baptism safeguarded his interpretation from 'the materialistic and the magical', and so 'most readers would agree that this is hardly the way in which a writer arguing in favour of baptismal regeneration would put things'.[61] Others phrased the criticism more generally, noting that the book betrayed an unbiblical focus on ceremony which was seriously at variance with the spiritual/moral tone of New Testament teaching.[62] Hughey took issue with Neville Clark's statement that baptism not only 'implies' and 'embodies' the benefits of salvation, but also 'effects' them. He was prepared to admit a close relation between the sign and the benefits signified, 'but not one of cause and effect'.[63] Thus he concluded that Clark's language was at best misleading and unfortunate, and probably fallacious.

Third, *that the writers of the book misinterpret key scripture texts which are capable of non-sacramental readings.* One text that looms large in any attempt to understand the role of baptism in primitive Christian preaching is Acts 2.38, which on the surface seems to clearly view baptism as a means to both forgiveness of sins and the gift of the Holy Spirit. However, Hughey and others utilized the noted Southern Baptist and Greek scholar, A.T. Robertson, to argue that the preposition εἰς in that passage should be translated 'because of' or 'on the basis of', thus reversing the logical/temporal order of baptism and forgiveness.[64] Robertson admitted that 'for' in the sense of aim or purpose would be a possible rendering of εἰς, but argued that in a few places it means 'because of' (Mt. 10.41 and 12.41), and the analogy of faith calls for that meaning in Acts 2.38. Hughey quoted Robertson as follows:

> One will decide the use here according as he believes that baptism is essential to the remission of sins or not. My view is decidedly against the idea that Peter, Paul, or

---

59   Clarke, 'Christian Baptism', *Baptist Times* 8 October 1959, p. 6.
60   S.B. John, 'Christian Baptism', *Baptist Times* 25 February 1960, p. 6.
61   D.R. Griffiths, 'Christian Baptism', *Baptist Times* 10 December 1959, p. 6.
62   S.B. John, 'Sacramentalism among Baptists', *Baptist Times* 8 October 1959, p. 6.
63   Hughey, 'New Trend', p. 7.
64   Hughey, 'New Trend', p. 7; Robert Clarke, 'Christian Baptism', *Baptist Times* 7 January 1960, p. 6.

any one in the *New Testament* taught baptism as essential to the remission of sins or the means of securing such remission. So I understand Peter to be urging baptism on each of them who had already turned (repented) and for it to be done in the name of Jesus Christ on the basis of the forgiveness of sins which they had already received.[65]

What tends to go unnoticed by those who suggest this re-translation is that even if it be accepted, the words of Peter still suggest that the gift of the Spirit is dependent on both repentance and baptism, and the 'problem' of sacramental language remains.

The apparent teaching of baptismal regeneration in John 3.5 is often dealt with by an exegesis which denies that 'water' in this text refers to baptism. One writer argued, following Calvin and some others, that the καί in the statement is epexegetical, giving the sense 'of water, that is, of the Spirit'.[66] Another writer suggested that 'water' denotes natural birth, making the statement a declaration of the need for those who have been born physically to be born again spiritually.[67]

Romans 6.1-4 is a classic text which has always been central to any discussion of the baptismal theology of Paul and it has played a crucial role from the beginning in the Baptist defence of immersion as the appropriate mode of baptism. However, at least one critic alleged that the text is actually a reference to Spirit-baptism, not to water-baptism at all, claiming to follow the lead of 'many Spirit-filled expositors of the Word'.[68] As Beasley-Murray noted, the application of this approach to Paul's Epistles as a whole might well leave us with virtually no Pauline references to water-baptism at all. It should also be noted that if this reading of Romans 6 (and presumably the parallel in Col. 2.12) is accurate, then the idea of baptism as a symbol of death and resurrection appears to be unfounded.

Kevan took the authors to task for seeing a baptismal reference in various texts which do not refer to it explicitly but do use images like 'water' or 'washing'. Included in this list would be texts like 1 Corinthians 6.11, Ephesians 5.26 and Titus 3.5, which, he argued, 'no one would ever have dreamed of interpreting sacramentally unless the dilemma of Paedo-Baptists had brought them into the discussion'.[69] He concluded that 'it is astonishing, therefore, to find that the authors are

---

65   Hughey, 'New Trend', p. 7, citing A.T. Robertson, *Word Pictures in the New Testament* (6 vols; Nashville, TN: Broadman Press, 1930), II, pp. 35-36. Robertson (1863–1934) was a Professor of Greek and New Testament at the Southern Baptist Theological Seminary , Louisville, Kentucky.

66   Clarke, 'Christian Baptism', *Baptist Times* 7 January 1960, p. 6.

67   John, 'Christian Baptism', *Baptist Times* 25 February 1960, p. 6.

68   Clarke, 'Christian Baptism', *Baptist Times* 7 January 1960, p. 6.

69   Kevan, 'Christian Baptism II', p. 9.

willing to concede a reference to Baptism in these passages'.[70] It is difficult to understand his connecting the sacramental use of these texts to the issue of paedobaptism—each of the texts looks more like a description of sacramental action in the case of adult converts, especially in 1 Corinthians and Titus, where in both cases the previously pagan lifestyle of the readers is assumed. Even if none of these texts is an allusion to baptism, it is still not difficult to understand why allusions to washing with water might be read that way.

Fourth, *that the authors' sacramental view of baptism excludes the unbaptized from salvation and the church.* This particular criticism was rooted in an alleged inference from the basic principle of Baptist sacramentalism. One writer phrased it as a 'defective definition of the Church as including only baptized believers and not the whole body of believing people'.[71] Another argued that if baptism 'results in being in Christ' (to quote from *Christian Baptism*), 'then it follows that all the fine Christians who are unbaptized are still *out of Christ*'.[72] These unbaptized Christians would include Quakers, members of the Salvation Army, and (from a Baptist viewpoint) those baptized in infancy. Hughey emphasized that experience, not to mention scripture, makes it undeniably clear that saving grace is experienced by huge numbers of persons who have not been baptized as believers.[73] The critics recognized that the Baptist sacramentalists did not draw this inference about the unbaptized, but they argued that this simply represented an incoherence in their theology.

Fifth, *that the teaching of the book is contrary to historic Baptist theology, so that whatever else may be said about it, it does not deserve the label 'Baptist'.* None of the critics who made this point were saying that Baptist tradition is infallible, only that the label is not sufficiently elastic to include this kind of baptismal theology. One writer pointed out that he became a Baptist because he was assured that Baptists think of baptism as a symbol rather than a sacrament.[74] Another writer argued that the view was ostensibly rooted in ecumenical concerns, but it would in fact cause division within the Baptist family where no division presently existed.[75] Hughey suggested that the debate was actually a repetition of that between the Baptists and Disciples of Christ in North America over a century earlier, thus equating the 'new view' with the Disciples' view.[76]

---

70   Kevan, 'Christian Baptism II', p. 9.

71   Stones, 'Sacramentalism among Baptists', *Baptist Times* 10 September 1959, p. 6.

72   Clarke, 'Christian Baptism', *Baptist Times* 7 January 1960, p. 6; also John, 'Christian Baptism', *Baptist Times* 14 January 1960, p. 6.

73   Hughey, 'New Trend', p. 7.

74   Stones, 'Sacramentalism among Baptists', 10 September 1959, p. 6.

75   John, 'Sacramentalism among Baptists', 8 October 1959, p. 6.

76   Hughey, 'New Trend', p. 7.

Kevan was perhaps the most forceful critic on this point, especially in his response to Clark's chapter on the theology of baptism:

> It was an editorial blunder of the highest kind to assign this important chapter to a man who, apart from his pastoral inexperience, is an individualist in his views and does not realise how completely out of step he is with his fellow Baptists. Anything less Baptist written by an avowedly Baptist minister it will be hard to find. It is difficult indeed to recognise a Baptist in this chapter, for the magic wand of ecumenicity has been laid on his thinking... The historical sense of every Baptist will rise up within him and say, 'John Smythe I know, and Thomas Helwys I know, but who are you?'[77]

The 'Preface' to *Christian Baptism* indicated that one purpose of the book was to clarify for the broader Christian world what Baptists think about baptismal issues,[78] but according to Kevan, 'No Paedo-Baptist enquirer could gather from this chapter even the remotest idea of what is normally in the mind of the Baptist minister and the believer at the time of Baptism.'[79] Kevan's words were probably accurate as a description of most Baptist thinking about baptism in his day—the book in question was probably more idiosyncratic than representative.[80] However, recent research indicates that the kind of Baptist thinking represented by Kevan differs significantly from the first century of Baptist thought which was often sacramental.[81] It is unfortunately possible to dogmatize about alleged Baptist distinctives while being relatively ignorant of the actual history of Baptist thought.

As an illustration of early Baptist thought, consider the example of Benjamin Keach, who had a long and influential ministry among Particular Baptists. In a book published in 1689, he attempted to interpret baptism 'in its primitive purity', and in so doing provided modest but clear evidence for a sacramental understanding of baptism. First of all, he referred to 'the special ends of this holy Sacrament',[82] showing that this leading signatory of the Second London Confession did not assume that baptism was an 'ordinance' (the language of most confessions) *as opposed to* a 'sacrament'. Second, he referred to baptism as 'the Baptism of Repentance for the Remission of Sins' (with reference to Acts 2.38)

---

77   Kevan, 'Christian Baptism II', pp. 10-11.

78   A. Gilmore, 'Preface', in Gilmore (ed.), *Christian Baptism*, p. 7.

79   Kevan, 'Christian Baptism II', p. 11.

80   This is candidly admitted by Beasley-Murray, *Baptism*, p. vi, who refers to his thinking as 'a' Baptist view with the emphasis on the indefinite article.

81   Fowler, *More Than a Symbol*, pp. 10-32; Philip E. Thompson, 'A New Question in Baptist History: Seeking A Catholic Spirit Among Early Baptists', *Pro Ecclesia* 8.1 (Winter, 1999), pp. 66-68; and Anthony R. Cross, 'Dispelling the Myth of English Baptist Baptismal Sacramentalism', *Baptist Quarterly* 38.8 (October, 2000), pp. 367-91.

82   Keach, *Gold Refin'd*, p. 78.

and 'the Washing of Regeneration' (with reference to Titus 3.5), without any apparent nervousness about the language.[83] Third, he indicated that baptism looks forward to salvation as its goal:

> Consider the great Promises made to those who are obedient to it, amongst other things, Lo, I am with you always, even to the end of the World. And again, He that believeth, and is baptized, shall be saved. If a Prince shall offer a Rebel his Life in doing two things, would he neglect one of them, and say this I will do, but the other is a trivial thing, I'll not do that? Surely no, he would not run the hazard of his Life so foolishly... And then in Acts 2.38. Repent, and be baptized every one of you for Remission of Sin, and ye shall receive the Gift of the Holy Spirit: See what great Promises are made to Believers in Baptism.[84]

Fourth, and most clearly, Keach quoted approvingly from Stephen Charnock (1628–80), a Puritan pastor who spoke 'excellently' in Keach's opinion on the connection between baptism and regeneration:

> Outward Water cannot convey inward Life. How can Water, an external thing, work upon the Soul in a physical manner? Neither can it be proved, that ever the Spirit of God is ty'd by any Promise, to apply himself to the Soul in a gracious Operation, when Water is applyed to the Body... Baptism is a means of conveying this Grace, when the Spirit is pleased to operate with it; but it doth not work as a physical Cause upon the Soul as a Purge doth upon the Humours of the Body: for 'tis the Sacrament of Regeneration, as the Lord's Supper is of Nourishment... Faith only is the Principle of spiritual Life, and the Principle which draws Nourishment from the Means of God's Appointments.[85]

The specific point at issue in this quotation is the practice of baptizing infants who cannot confess faith, so that Keach's primary concern was to argue that baptism does not accomplish regeneration in any mechanical way and is thus of no value in the case of purely passive infants. However, he argued this point, with Charnock's help, by asserting that the true way in which baptism works is as an instrument of the Spirit who sovereignly employs it in the regeneration of conscious believers. That is, although baptism has no inherent power, it is by the work of the Holy Spirit an effective sign, instrumentally conveying what it signifies. It is a sign, but not merely a sign.

Among other things, the interchange between the contributors of *Christian Baptism* and their critics about what can properly be called 'Baptist' theology illustrates the distressing and ongoing Baptist tendency to ignore the work of previous Baptists as if there were no Baptist tradition at all. Thus John Gill wrote about baptism as if his

---

83   Keach, *Gold Refin'd*, pp. 82-83.
84   Keach, *Gold Refin'd*, p. 173.
85   Keach, *Gold Refin'd*, pp. 128-29.

influential predecessor, Benjamin Keach, never existed; Robert Walton wrote about baptism as one example of a broader sacramental principle with references to various Catholic and Anglican scholars, but never referred to Wheeler Robinson, even though Robinson did not retire from academic duties until after Walton's study group began their discussions; and the authors of *Christian Baptism* almost never included Baptist sources in their footnotes, except in historical chapters devoted to Baptist debates, and even there they failed to note precursors of their own viewpoint.

G.R. Beasley-Murray's Response

At the end of 1959, following a series of very critical letters about *Christian Baptism*, G.R. Beasley-Murray wrote an article in the *Baptist Times* to respond to the major criticisms. He began by dealing with the charge of teaching baptismal regeneration, noting that the phrase is 'a slogan with an unpleasant odour about it', inasmuch as it tends to mean (among Baptists, at least) 'automatic production of spiritual and moral ends by going through external motions according to prescription'.[86] He vigorously denied that he and his colleagues meant anything like this in their interpretation of baptism, but he did assert that baptism is a significant means of grace as 'the climax of God's dealing with the penitent seeker and of the convert's return to God'.[87]

This high view of baptism was defended by showing that it is the natural way to read the actual baptismal texts of the New Testament. The baptismal commission in Matthew 28.19, by its use of εἰς τὸ ὄνομα, conceives of baptism as the event in which the baptizand hands themself over to and is appropriated by the Triune God. The 'plain import' of Peter's statement in Acts 2.38 is that repentance and baptism are answered by God's bestowal of forgiveness and the Holy Spirit. Paul's account of his own baptism in Acts 22.16 does not mean that there is morally cleansing power in the water of baptism, 'but it does mean that Paul and the Lord are going to have dealings on that occasion with the stated result'.[88] Texts like Romans 6.1-4, Colossians 2.12 and Galatians 3.26-27 indicate that saving union with Christ, which includes a spiritual death and resurrection, is mediated through baptism. Peter's statement that 'baptism now saves you' (1 Pet. 3.21) indicates that through the commitment expressed in baptism God saves penitent sinners. The point of this list of texts is to show that the common Baptist idea of baptism as a

---

86   G.R. Beasley-Murray, 'Baptism Controversy—"The Spirit Is There"', *Baptist Times* 10 December 1959, p. 8.
87   Beasley-Murray, 'Baptism Controversy', p. 8.
88   Beasley-Murray, 'Baptism Controversy', p. 8.

mere symbol pointing backward to a completed conversion has to be read into the actual baptismal references of the New Testament.

He then emphasized that the point of the book was to articulate baptism in the 'Church of the Apostles', while recognizing that it may be impossible to replicate it thoroughly today. When viewed in the light of that kind of baptismal experience and theology, current Baptist practice and theology are judged to represent a reduced and impoverished baptism. As he put it:

> This teaching relates to *baptism in the apostolic Church*, not to baptism in the average modern Baptist church. Where baptism is sundered from conversion on the one hand, and from entry into the Church on the other, this language cannot be applied to it; such a baptism is a reduced baptism... My concern, along with my colleagues, is to put before Baptists the picture of ideal baptism, as it is portrayed in the apostolic writings, in the hope that we may strive to recover it or get somewhere near it. To insist on keeping our impoverished version of baptism would be a tragedy among a people who pride themselves on being the people of the New Testament.[89]

The authors of the book acknowledged that God's grace touches many persons today in patterns that do not correspond to the patterns assumed in the apostolic writings, but this is just to say that God is not bound to sacraments.

He concluded the article by noting that the Baptist tradition needs to be seriously examined before anyone makes sweeping statements as to who are the faithful heirs of that tradition, if in fact there is a consistent tradition. Unfortunately, he did not take the time to uncover the evidence of this tradition which would have supported his case.

After several more critical letters to the *Baptist Times* in response to this article, Beasley-Murray penned a second article to provide further clarification. His first, and most crucial, point was to argue that in the New Testament baptism is normatively an integral part of conversion, the climax of entrance into the Christian life. If that be the case, then the idea of being baptized in order to enjoy the benefits of Christ ought not seem strange to Baptists, because to be baptized for salvation is essentially another way to describe being converted for salvation. He wrote:

> We are not contending that God justifies by faith but gives the Spirit and unites to Christ by baptism, as though baptism was a 'work' alongside faith. That would be a perversion of the Gospel. Our plea has been that in the New Testament baptism is

---

89   Beasley-Murray, 'Baptism Controversy', p. 8, italics his.

inseparable from the turning to God in faith, on the basis of which God justifies, gives the Spirit, and unites to Christ.[90]

With regard to the exegesis of key texts like Romans 6.1-4 and Acts 2.38, he countered the arguments for a non-sacramental reading of them. He pointed out that the view that Romans 6 is talking about Spirit-baptism is 'an eccentric interpretation of a few earlier commentators that will not be found in any of the great contemporary expositions of *Romans*'.[91] This resort to an unnatural exegesis of Romans 6 is actually an admission that the passage is talking about baptism as the door to profound spiritual experience, not about baptism as a mere symbol. A similar response was given to A.T. Robertson's suggestion that εἰς in Acts 2.38 be translated 'because of'. Even if such a translation were possible (which he denied), it would hardly fit the context in which Peter is replying to 'conscience stricken men, convicted of their part in the murder of the Messiah and *seeking* forgiveness'. His assessment was that if Robertson were able to speak posthumously, he would admit that when he wrote his commentary on Acts 2.38, 'he must have had his tongue in his cheek and his conscience locked up'.[92]

Concerning the charge of 'magic' in his sacramentalism, he was 'amazed at the suggestion'. He had never suggested that there is power in the rite as such, only that baptism is the vehicle of confessing faith in Christ and surrendering to him as Lord. It is because of its connection to this inner attitude that it becomes an effective symbol. This idea should not have been foreign to his critics, because such symbolic acts are common in human experience. Two examples that are readily understood are the waving of a white flag which can end hostilities and a wedding ceremony in which saying 'I will' and giving a ring can unite a man and woman in marriage. Such signs are effective symbols which by their performance say, 'This here and now becomes true' (as in sacramentalism), rather than, 'This has already become true' (as in mere symbolism).[93]

Finally, Beasley-Murray dealt with the charge that he made baptism necessary for salvation and thus excluded from salvation all those not baptized as believers. His essential response was to say that his baptismal doctrine was an attempt to state 'what God has willed baptism to be', but this implies nothing about what happens when baptism is misunderstood

---

90   G.R. Beasley-Murray, 'Baptism and the Sacramental View', *Baptist Times* 11 February 1960, p. 9.

91   Beasley-Murray, 'Baptism and the Sacramental View', p. 9.

92   Beasley-Murray, 'Baptism and the Sacramental View', p. 9.

93   For an extended treatment of this kind of symbolic act, see James W. McClendon, 'Baptism as a Performative Sign', *Theology Today* 23.3 (1966), pp. 403-16.

or misapplied. He was prepared to recognize people of faith among paedobaptists and even among those who reject the use of sacraments entirely, but he insisted that this is not helpful in formulating a positive baptismal theology, for 'we get nowhere by discussing what God can do without'. In point of fact, God has given us sacraments, and 'our task is not to make the least of them but to receive in gratitude whatever God has to give through them'.[94] What the critics failed to note was that the Baptist sacramentalists never drew negative inferences about the spiritual condition of unbaptized believers from their baptismal theology. Although that has been true of some theological traditions historically, it was not true of the Baptists in question.

Conclusion

Both sides of the debate concerning *Christian Baptism* illustrate the distressing tendency of Baptists to be both theologically and historically naive. The critics of the book often naively assumed that all forms of sacramentalism are roughly equivalent to traditional Catholic teaching and thus open to all the same criticisms, but the authors of the book can also be faulted for their failure to recognize that they needed to do a preemptive response to the predictable theological criticisms. If the critics had understood the history of Baptist thought, especially the formative period of the seventeenth century, then they would have recognized that 'Baptist sacramentalism' is not an oxymoron, but the authors are equally guilty of failing to demonstrate the continuity of their perspective with their own tradition. The difficulty of discussing the sacramental question is rooted in the fact that Baptists have tended to spend their energy debating the practice of baptism while ignoring the theology of baptism, with the result that they are usually more certain of what does not happen in the sprinkling of infants than they are of what does happen in the immersion of confessing believers. There is still a lot of work to be done.

---

94   Beasley-Murray, 'Baptism and the Sacramental View', p. 10.

CHAPTER 9

The Pneumatological Key to H. Wheeler Robinson's Baptismal Sacramentalism[1]

Anthony R. Cross

The rise of the ecumenical movement in the early twentieth century meant that many principles held so dear for generations, or so it seemed, came under the theological microscope, and established practices were increasingly challenged from within and without. For Baptists associated with the Baptist Union of Great Britain (and Ireland) the issue of baptism, perhaps more than any other doctrine because of its sectarian nature, became a focus of Baptist thinking. The Baptists' leading scholar in the first half of the century, Henry Wheeler Robinson (1872–1945),[2] eloquently declared that if believer's baptism was really central and

1   This is the full version of a paper delivered to the Second International Conference on Baptist Studies held at Wake Forest University, Winston-Salem, North Carolina, July 2000, which was published as 'The Holy Spirit: The Key to the Baptismal Sacramentalism of H. Wheeler Robinson', *Baptist History and Heritage* 36.1–2 (Winter/Spring, 2001), pp. 174-89. I am grateful to the editor, Dr Merrill M. Hawkins, Jr, for permission to include this extended and updated version of the original conference paper.

2   For studies on Robinson not discussed elsewhere in this essay, see A.J. Grieve and T.H. Robinson, 'H. Wheeler Robinson', *Baptist Quarterly* 11.14–15 (July–October, 1945), pp. 373-78; 'Celebration of the Centenary of the birth of Henry Wheeler Robinson, Ninth Principal of Regent's Park College, 7th February, 1872', *Baptist Quarterly* 24.6 (April, 1972); R. Mason, 'H. Wheeler Robinson Revisited', *Baptist Quarterly* 37.5 (January, 1998), pp. 213-26; and J.T. Williams, 'The Contribution of Protestant Nonconformists to Biblical Scholarship in the Twentieth Century', in A.P.F. Sell (ed.), *Protestant Nonconformity in the Twentieth Century* (Carlisle: Paternoster, forthcoming 2002). His Festschrift was E.A. Payne (ed.), *Studies in History and Religion Presented to Dr. H. Wheeler Robinson, M.A., on his seventieth birthday* (London: Lutterworth Press, 1942). On his interpretation of scripture, see R.A. Coughenour, 'Robinson, Henry Wheeler (1872–1945)', in D.K. McKim (ed.), *Historical Handbook of Major Biblical Interpreters* (Leicester: IVP, 1998), pp. 514-18; and M.E. Polley, 'Robinson, Henry Wheeler (1872–1945)', in J.H. Hayes (ed.), *Dictionary of Biblical Interpretation, K–Z* (Nashville, TN: Abingdon Press, 1999), pp. 407-408.

fundamental enough to justify the existence of a distinct denomination to urge its claims, then Baptists should be able to show the great and permanent principles which were implied in it: personal conversion, the authority of Christ revealed in the New Testament and the doctrine of the church as the society of the converted.[3]

As the ecumenical movement was to be the major influence on the development of the Baptist theology of baptism,[4] it was to prove to be an important influence on the thought of Wheeler Robinson. His ten-year theological training only involved one year at a Baptist College (Regent's Park, London, 1890–91), while the rest of his student days were spent studying in Edinburgh (1891–95), Mansfield College, Oxford, the Congregational College (1895–98), with the final two years divided between Oxford, Marburg and Strasbourg.[5] His college days, then, brought him into constant contact with those of other traditions and this clearly had a deep and lasting effect on his attitudes towards other traditions,[6] and this is reflected in the breadth of his scholarship evinced throughout his many writings. Robinson, then, was no narrow denominationalist and was involved in local and national ecumenical work.[7] However, while he was favourably disposed towards issues of Christian unity, his early enthusiasm[8] was soon replaced by opposition to the form it was taking at the time because he believed it was based on the

---

3   *Baptist Principles* (London: Carey Kingsgate Press, 3rd edn 1938, 1960 reissue [4th edn]), pp. 16-27. This definitive edition is used throughout. It, however, first appeared, however, as 'Baptist Principles before the rise of Baptist Churches', in C.E. Shipley (ed.), *The Baptists of Yorkshire: Being the Centenary Memorial Volume of the Yorkshire Baptist Association* (London: Kingsgate Press, 1912), pp. 3-50.

4   See A.R. Cross, *Baptism and the Baptists: Theology and Practice in Twentieth-Century Britain* (Studies in Baptist History and Thought, 3; Carlisle: Paternoster, 2000) and 'Baptists and Baptism—A British Perspective', *Baptist History and Heritage* 35.1 (Winter, 2000), pp. 104-21.

5   See E.A. Payne, *Henry Wheeler Robinson: Scholar. Teacher. Principal: A Memoir* (London: Nisbet, 1946), pp. 17-37, and E. Kaye, *Mansfield College Oxford: Its Origin, History, and Significance* (Oxford: Oxford University Press, 1996), pp. 118 and 180.

6   This conclusion is supported by the fact that in later life Robinson was closely associated with the Quakers and had a keen interest in, e.g., the writings of J.H. Newman, see Payne, *Robinson*, pp. 59-60, 110-31. See also Cross, *Baptism*, pp. 49-50, especially n. 46.

7   See Payne, *Robinson*, e.g., pp. 62-63; Cross, *Baptism*, e.g., pp. 137, 148, 154-55; and B. Green, *Tomorrow's Man: A Biography of James Henry Rushbrooke* (Didcot: Baptist Historical Society, 1997), pp. 192-93.

8   Of J.H. Shakespeare's *The Churches at the Cross-Roads* (London: Williams & Norgate, 1918), he said, 'This is a book to make its readers say, "I must be in that, too"', in 'Churches at Crossroads', *Baptist Times and Freeman* 8 November 1918, p. 663.

compromising of principles, something he strongly opposed.[9] In contrast, he believed in the need for clearer thinking and greater charity,[10] and, for Baptists, this applied more to baptism than any other doctrine because baptism was the major stumbling block to the union/reunion movement being proposed at that time.

Robinson was born in mid-Victorian England in 1872 when the overwhelming majority of Baptists understood baptism to be nothing more than an ordinance: a symbol of conversion, a profession of personal faith in Christ, a witness to the gospel, an act of obedience and, in the majority of churches, a condition of membership, though the days when it was the condition for participation in communion were fast becoming a thing of the past among Baptist Union churches.[11] One of the chief factors in this Zwinglian/memorialist interpretation was the Baptists' over-reaction to the baptismal regeneration advanced by the Oxford Movement and those influenced by them.[12] If the Tractarians are viewed as adopting an extreme position in their theology of baptismal regeneration, the Baptist reaction should no less be seen as the opposite extreme: from the likes of E.B. Pusey and J.H. Newman claiming too much for baptism, many Baptists claimed too little for it. This position came under the stricture of Robinson who in 1925 commended the work of A.C. Underwood on conversion for its 'sound exegesis of the meaning of baptism in Pauline teaching, as against the "Zwinglianism" *which is too current amongst us*'.[13] This statement shows that Robinson's reading of scripture was a major factor in his departure from the traditional and tenaciously held Baptist understanding of baptism as nothing more than an ordinance, but there was also a personal experience during a serious illness in 1913 when, in his own words, 'the truths of "evangelical"

---

9   See 'The Road to Unity', *Baptist Times and Freeman* 17 March 1916, p. 164; '"Unity" and "Schism"', *Baptist Times and Freeman* 3 May 1918, p. 271; 'Expediency and Principle', *Baptist Times* 11 December 1941, p. 612. Also Payne, *Robinson*, e.g., p. 92, and Cross, *Baptism*, pp. 49-51 and 55.

10   Payne, *Robinson*, 92.

11   See Cross, *Baptism*, pp. 6-17, cf. pp. 100-102 and 414-26. For the most recent survey of this debate, see T. George, 'Controversy and Communion: The Limits of Baptist Fellowship from Bunyan to Spurgeon', in D.W. Bebbington (ed.), *The Gospel in the World: International Baptist Studies* (Studies in Baptist History and Thought, 1; Carlisle: Paternoster, 2002), pp. 38-58.

12   See M.J. Walker, *Baptists at the Table: The Theology of the Lord's Supper amongst English Baptists in the Nineteenth Century* (Didcot: Baptist Historical Society, 1992), pp. 84-120; J.H.Y. Briggs, *The English Baptists of the Nineteenth Century* (A History of the English Baptists, 3; Didcot: Baptist Historical Society, 1994), e.g., pp. 48-50, 52 and 68; Cross, *Baptism*, pp. 10 and 15.

13   'Conversion', *Baptist Times and Freeman* 8 May 1925, p. 319, italics added, reviewing Underwood's *Conversion: Christian and Non-Christian: A Comparative and Psychological Study* (London: George Allen & Unwin, 1925).

Christianity...failed to bring him personal strength.' Such strength, however, he found in 'a more "sacramental" religion' mediated through a priest and 'sacred elements'. The 'lacuna in his own conception of evangelical truth' he filled in with 'those conceptions of the Holy Spirit in which the New Testament is so rich.'[14] This theological reorientation enabled him to see that 'The Bible itself is no more than a collection of ancient documents till it becomes...a sacrament, that is, something which is a means by which the divine Spirit becomes active in the heart of reader or hearer.'[15] It is a mistake to see in Robinson's baptismal sacramentalism an innovation in Baptist thought, rather it marks the re-emergence of an interpretation which was widely held in the seventeenth century, but which lessened in the succeeding two centuries, only to be reintroduced largely through the advocacy of Robinson's many writings on it and related subjects.[16]

The consequences of rejecting the sacramental nature of baptism, he believed, were great: 'if water-baptism is not a means of grace, why keep it up?'[17] What is more, 'If baptism were a mere form, which left us just as it found us, we might well ask whether a spiritual religion has any place for it.'[18] Writing during the early days of the ecumenical movement

14   This autobiographical fragment is to be found in *The Christian Experience of the Holy Spirit* (London: Nisbet, 1928), p. 4; discussed also by Payne, *Robinson*, pp. 56-57; and W.B. Glover, *Evangelical Nonconformists and Higher Criticism in the Nineteenth Century* (London: Independent Press, 1954), pp. 232-34.

15   *Experience*, p. 190. See also pp. 160-83, especially pp. 162 and 172. Robinson also explores 'sacramental mediation' in his *Redemption and Revelation in the Actuality of History* (London: Nisbet, 1942), pp. xxxii and 103-06. His theology of baptism cannot adequately be discussed without reference to the centrality of his 'sacramental' understanding of the rite. It is precisely for this reason that D.A. Garrett's contribution on 'H. Wheeler Robinson' to T. George and D.S. Dockery (eds.), *Baptist Theologians* (Nashville, TN: Broadman Press, 1990), p. 402, is to be criticized. Though Garrett's discussion of baptism is brief, the omission of even the word 'sacrament' perhaps reflects more Southern Baptist aversion to the term than the desire to fairly represent and assess Robinson's baptismal theology.

16   See S.K. Fowler, *More Than a Symbol: The British Baptist Recovery of Baptismal Sacramentalism* (Studies in Baptist History and Thought, 2; Carlisle: Paternoster, 2002); P.E. Thompson, 'A New Question in Baptist History: Seeking a Catholic Spirit Among Early Baptists', *Pro Ecclesia* 8.1 (Winter, 1999), pp. 51-72, and 'Practicing the Freedom of God: Formation in Early Baptist Life', in D.M. Hammond (ed.), *Theology and Lived Christianity* (Annual Publication of the College Theology Society, 45; Mystic, CT: Twenty-Third Publications, 2000), pp. 119-38; A.R. Cross, 'Dispelling the Myth of English Baptist Baptismal Sacramentalism', *Baptist Quarterly* 38.8 (October, 2000), pp. 367-91.

17   'The Five Points of a Baptist's Faith', *Baptist Quarterly* 11.1–2 (January/April, 1942), p. 9.

18   'The Baptism of Power', *Baptist Times and Freeman* 16 January 1920, p. 35.

when the issue of union/reunion was very much at the forefront of the English churches' agendas,[19] Robinson stated that if Baptists were to justify their own distinctive practice 'we must show it to possess the dignity of a distinctive principle, important enough to warrant a separate denominational existence. It is not enough to say to men, however true it is, "obey this command of the New Testament"; we must show that the command carries its own intrinsic authority by being *worth while*, from the highest moral and spiritual standpoints.'[20] According to Robinson:

> The Baptist stands or falls by his conception of what the Church is; his plea for believer's baptism becomes a mere archaeological idiosyncrasy, if it be not the expression of the fundamental constitution of the Church. We become members of the living body of Christ by being consciously and voluntarily baptized in the Spirit of Christ—a baptism witnessed by the evidence of moral purpose and character as the fruit of the Spirit.[21]

As believer's baptism emphasizes the necessity of conversion and forms a direct link between the spiritual authority of the New Testament and the Lord it reveals[22] and carries with it the unmistakable definition of the church, for which it is the door,[23] believer's baptism provides a constant and much-needed testimony to the spiritual basis of the church, grounded in a spiritual relationship with Christ and answerable finally only to him.

Robinson criticized much Baptist thought on baptism on the grounds that it is too negative, 'concerned with showing what New Testament baptism is not, rather than what it is'.[24] He also warned of the dangers of the Baptists' tendency towards individualism,[25] asking, 'Does not baptism

---

19   See Cross, *Baptism*, pp. 42-97.

20   'The Distinctive Baptist Principle', *Baptist Times and Freeman* 20 April 1923, p. 275, italics his. Cf. 'The Place of Baptism in Baptist Churches To-day', *Baptist Quarterly* 1.5 (January, 1923), p. 215, where he spoke of the necessity of showing the intrinsic worth of believer's baptism. These were: 'the importance of *acts* as influencing thoughts', p. 215; immersion as a 'symbolic expression of the historical truths on which our faith rests', personal union with Christ by faith—in short, baptism is an acted creed, p. 216; and the relation of the gift of the Spirit and water-baptism, pp. 216-18.

21   *The Life and Faith of the Baptists* (London: Kingsgate Press, 2nd edn, 1946), p. 73.

22   *Principles*, pp. 22-24.

23   *Principles*, p. 24. Cf. *Faith*, p. 73, where he maintained that believer's baptism is 'the only type of baptism which is properly consistent with the logic of "Separatism" and the whole conception of a separated Church of believers'.

24   'Place', p. 209.

25   'Baptists and the Bible', *Baptist Times* 24 February 1938, p. 151. Cf. Cross, *Baptism*, pp. 12-14, 184-86 and 457, and I.M. Randall, *Evangelical Experiences: A Study in the Spirituality of English Evangelicalism 1918–1939* (Studies in Evangelical

express much more than a personal act?' As Baptists stood for the truth of a regenerated church membership expressed in believer's baptism, he believed that their testimony to that would never be as effective as it ought to be until they had added to it 'a nobler Church-consciousness, and a profounder sense of the whole group, as well as the individual life, as the arena of the Spirit's activity'.[26] He suggested that Baptists needed 'an "Oxford Movement" of their own order' that would recapture this nobler church-consciousness, which would doubtless bring some changes not only in polity but also in worship.[27] The radical nature of such a statement can only be fully realized when the strength of the Baptist reaction against Tractarianism is remembered, and is evidence of how far Baptist thinking had progressed in nearly a century. Again with an implicit reference to Baptist antagonism towards the Oxford Movement, Robinson stated that the reaction to a false doctrine of divine grace in baptism had made Baptists suspicious of the genuine sacramentalism of the New Testament. The emphasis had been so much on saying '*believer's* baptism' that they had failed, or at least were then failing, to say with anything like equal emphasis 'believer's *baptism*', by which he meant the entrance of believers into a life of supernatural powers. It is personal faith which is the realm of the Spirit's activity, so the confession of that faith in believer's baptism brings a new opportunity for divine grace, precisely because it is an act of personal faith.[28]

Robinson's critique of baptismal theology, however, was not soley directed at British Baptists. As part of its response to the 1937 Faith and Order and Life and Work conferences, the Baptist World Alliance set up two commissions in preparation for the sixth Baptist World Congress to be held in Atlanta, Georgia, in 1939, the second of which was to examine 'The Baptist Contribution to Christian Unity'. The resulting report was the work of Wheeler Robinson and underscored the Baptist testimony to the necessity of personal faith as the prerequisite for baptism; that baptism is an acted creed; that Baptists are the only tradition which can maintain baptismal grace in the New Testament sense; that baptism should be made more of within Christian experience; and also criticized the inadequacy of much baptismal instruction.[29] Further, the report

History and Thought; Carlisle: Paternoster, 1999), pp. 187-88, on Baptist individualism.

26   *Life*, pp. 142-43.
27   *Life*, pp. 143-44.
28   *Life*, p. 146.
29   Cf. 'Baptism of Power', p. 36, 'We shall find as much spiritual significance in baptism as we bring spiritual capacity to it. But spiritual capacity is itself conditioned by clear teaching, and will be found in its fulness only when such clear teaching is present. If it is worth while to teach that baptism represents cleansing, it is also worth while, *in the same sense*, to teach that it represents power. Baptists have a unique opportunity of

recognized that there were truths in the possession of other churches which Baptists needed to learn and apply. In itself this was an argument for closer co-operation with other denominations, but, 'We may be permitted to doubt...whether it is an argument for organic reunion of the kind which would subordinate truths to institutions.' The report, however, made it clear that there was little inclination among world Baptists for organic reunion.[30] Robinson admitted, though, that 'we [world Baptists] need a "higher" doctrine of baptism (in the New Testament direction) if baptism is to claim and hold its place'. It is significant that such a statement follows the discussion of the relationship between baptism and the Holy Spirit. He continued, 'We must make more of baptism, not less, if it is to retain its place and function in the Christian experience, and that "more" is surely in the direction of a humble and earnest willingness to be led by the New Testament teaching, and most of all when it rebukes Baptist failure to assimilate it.'[31]

Convinced that in the prevailing ecumenical climate the Baptists' emphasis on personal conversion was one of their greatest contributions to any united church, Robinson asked, 'have we grasped the full meaning of believers' baptism in the New Testament? It expresses not only what we give to God, but what He gives to us, the gift of the Holy Spirit which he bestows on every believer.'[32] To those who believed the Baptist emphasis on baptism was exaggerated and the rite a minor one, he replied, 'The only effective answer to this criticism is to prove that believer's baptism is actually a centre round which other doctrines can be logically and naturally grouped. We have made baptism our centre...'[33] The evangelical nature of baptism was central to Robinson's understanding of it. During the twenty-two years of his principalship of Regent's Park College (1920–42), Robinson taught both Baptist and Congregational students[34] and while he admitted the higher academic standard of the latter he maintained that the Baptist candidates had the firmer grasp of evangelical principles, a difference which he ascribed to

---

teaching both, and teaching both without any real risk of being misunderstood. Some of them are teaching both in this connection, but a great many are not', italics his.

30   'Report of Commission No.2. The Baptist Contribution to Christian Unity', in J.H. Rushbrooke (ed.), *Sixth Baptist World Congress: Atlanta, Georgia, USA, July 22–28, 1939* (Atlanta: Baptist World Alliance, 1939), pp. 115-21, quotation from p. 120.

31   'Report', p. 117-18.

32   '"The Strength and Weakness of the Baptists"', *British Weekly* 27 January 1921, p. 369.

33   'The Baptist Doctrine of the Lord's Supper', *Baptist Times and Freeman* 20 May 1904, p. 389.

34   See R.E. Cooper, *From Stepney to St. Giles': The Story of Regent's Park College 1810–1960* (London: Carey Kingsgate Press, 1960), *passim*; Kaye, *Mansfield*, p. 196.

the 'one formal distinction between the two groups—the practice of believers' baptism'. In this he was not suggesting the Baptists had a greater spirituality, but it was a high claim to what he saw as the principles of the constitution of the church 'which our distinctive practice implies and emphasises', namely, the idea of a converted and sanctified church.[35] As well as safeguarding the 'Puritan doctrine of the Church', he was convinced that believers' baptism was 'an efficient safeguard to evangelical purity'.[36] The difference between the Baptists and other evangelical churches he ascribed to 'the emphasis we place on baptism'.[37]

Robinson objected to non-Baptists who viewed believer's baptism as 'a minor and negligible idiosyncrasy' and opposed those, Baptists among them, who would have sacrificed the practice of believer's baptism for the sake of church union/reunion.[38] No reunion, he believed, would prosper when built on the compromises of expediency, which he rejected when they conflicted with or replaced principle. Expediency 'should not move us to obscure the testimony made by the maintenance of believers' baptism to the true nature of the Church',[39] and Robinson's catholicity, in the sense of the universal church, is reflected in his statement that 'When we were baptized it was into the one body.'[40]

What, then, was Robinson's understanding of 'sacrament'? After referring to *sacramentum* as an oath of allegiance, he continued, 'The term "sacrament" is...often used to imply what Baptists would regard as a mechanical or material conveyance of grace; but this misuse of a useful term ought no more to discredit it than the misuse of the term "baptism" by non-Baptists make us give up that term.'[41] This led him to reject what he termed 'sacramentarianism', though he accepted and used the term 'sacramentalism'.[42] He also spoke of baptism as the pledge of the believer to a life of faith and moral regeneration[43] as well as an

---

35   'Expediency and Principle', *Baptist Times* 11 December 1941, p. 611.

36   In 'The Baptist Church', *British Weekly* 20 January 1938, p. 321.

37   'Lord's Supper', p. 389.

38   Such as the then General Secretary of the Baptist Union, J.H. Shakespeare, see Cross, *Baptism*, pp. 46-49. On Shakespeare and the ecumenical movement, see P. Shepherd, *The Making of a Modern Denomination: John Howard Shakespeare and the English Baptists 1898–1924* (Studies in Baptist History and Thought, 4; Carlisle: Paternoster, 2001), pp. 93-138, 182-85.

39   'Expediency', p. 612.

40   'Lord's Supper', p. 389.

41   *Principles*, p. 29 n..

42   *Life*, p. 145. Cf. 'The Faith of the Baptists', *Expository Times* 38.10 (July, 1927), p. 455.

43   'Faith', p. 454.

expression of the loyalty of the soul to Christ,[44] but he also defined a sacrament as 'something whose sacredness consists in the use to which it is put',[45] seeing sacraments as vehicles of a spiritual benediction on humanity, ordained by Christ as a means of union with him.[46] More precisely, a sacrament is 'something which is a means by which the divine Spirit becomes active in the heart of reader or hearer'.[47] It is this dimension of 'sacrament' as a 'means of grace' which dominates Robinson's thought, and it also enabled him to extend the scope of 'sacrament' to include the Bible and other books that reflect its light, the fellowship of believers, the sacramental communion of the church,[48] nature and history,[49] the personal experience of preachers and their sermons,[50] the influences used by the Spirit in a person's conversion,[51] and even duty,[52] when they become means of grace to others.[53] Robinson knew that the most powerful motive to many Baptists was 'the desire to obey the direct command of Christ' (Mt. 28.19) and 'to imitate His own acceptance of baptism at the hands of John' (Mk 1.9-10). But he explained his emphasis on other themes of the doctrine of baptism when he wrote, 'I do not doubt (whatever be the date of [Mt. 28.19]) that our

---

44   *Life*, p. 98.

45   'Lord's Supper', p. 389.

46   'The Sacramental Principle', *Baptist Times and Freeman* 17 March 1905, p. 200.

47   *Experience*, p. 190.

48   'The Kenosis of the Spirit', *Expository Times* 35.11 (August, 1924), p. 490.

49   'Christian Experience and the Holy Trinity', *Baptist Times and Freeman* 12 November 1915, p. 731.

50   'Vicarious Experience', *Baptist Times and Freeman* 17 December 1915, p. 819.

51   'The Conversion of St. Augustine', *Baptist Times and Freeman* 20 October 1916, p. 639, which he referred to as the 'complex factors and manifold influences that are made sacramental to a human soul by the Holy Spirit'.

52   'The Sacrament of Duty', *Baptist Times and Freeman* 17 September 1915, p. 596, written during the First World War.

53   This is not to suggest that these means are on the same level as baptism and the Lord's Supper, for they were not ordained by Christ. Robinson used both 'ordinance' and 'sacrament', see, e.g., *Life*, p. 98. In this he was in accord with (though there is no evidence that he was aware of the fact) many seventeenth-century Baptists who spoke of baptism and the Lord's Supper as both ordinances and sacraments, e.g. 'The Orthodox Creed' (1678), Article 27, in W.L. Lumpkin (ed.), *Baptist Confessions of Faith* (Valley Forge, PA: Judson Press, 2nd edn, 1969), p. 317; B. Keach, *The Child's Delight: Or Instructions for Children and Youth* (1702), p. 38; and B. Keach and W. Collins, *The Baptist Catechism: Commonly Called Keach's Catechism* (Philadelphia, 1851), p. 23. Thompson, 'Practicing the Freedom of God', pp. 126-31, has shown that seventeenth-century Baptists also understood preaching, the pastoral office and prayer as ordinances, though only baptism and the Lord's Supper were sacraments. See also Fowler, *More Than a Symbol*, pp. 10-32; and Cross, 'Dispelling the Myth', p. 371.

Lord instituted the baptism of believers, but I believe it is in accordance with His spirit to emphasize the intrinsic meaning of the rite, rather than its extrinsic aspect, as an act of formal obedience.'[54]

Baptists have always been a confessional rather than a credal people and though Baptists in the seventeenth century declared their beliefs and principles in confessions of faith over time they became wary of and reluctant to produce formal confessions.[55] While new associations/connexions in the late eighteenth and early nineteenth centuries were not against producing such articles, their content was more covenantal and the twentieth century witnessed a significant move within the denomination to see baptism not only as an 'acted parable', but as an 'acted creed'.[56] Though the origin of these phrases is unknown, the first mention seems to be a statement by Wheeler Robinson in 1904,[57] later popularized in his *Baptist Principles*: 'baptism by immersion takes the place amongst Baptists of a formal creed'.[58] He understood both sacraments as acted parables of the Lord's death, burial and resurrection, 'the cardinal verities of evangelical faith and the historical basis of Christianity'.[59] It was by these expressive acts that the believer identifies themself with Christ, professing the simplest form of confession of faith, 'Jesus is Lord' (Rom. 10.9, cf. 1 Cor. 12.3), this later being expanded into the trinitarian baptismal formula of Matthew 28.19.[60] Robinson developed this understanding of baptism:

---

54   *Life*, p. 81.

55   See W.J. McGlothlin (ed.), *Baptist Confessions of Faith* (London: Kingsgate Press, 1910), and Lumpkin (ed.), *Baptist Confessions of Faith*.

56   See Cross, *Baptism*, pp. 31-32.

57   'The Confessional Value of Baptism', *Baptist Times and Freeman* 12 February 1904, p. 121. It would appear that he came to this position through his study of the Hebrew concept of 'prophetic symbolism', as reflected, e.g., in his later 'Prophetic Symbolism', in D.C. Simpson (ed.), *Old Testament Essays* (London: Charles Griffin, 1927), pp. 14-16; *Experience*, pp. 192-95; 'The Origin and Significance of the New Testament Baptism, by H.G. Marsh', *Baptist Quarterly* 10.6 (April, 1941), p. 351; and 'Hebrew Sacrifice and Prophetic Symbolism', *Journal of Theological Studies* 43 (January–April, 1942), pp. 137-38.

58   *Principles*, p. 28.

59   Robinson believed that both the Lord's Supper and baptism, in their different ways, have an evangelistic function as they preach the cardinal facts on which an evangelical faith rests, namely, the death and the resurrection of Jesus Christ. 'More impressively than by any verbal recital of a creed, the historical basis of every Christian creed is constantly brought before a Baptist Church', *Life*, pp. 79-80. The principle which believer's baptism expresses, he also asserted, pledged Baptists to evangelism both at home and abroad, see H.W. Robinson and J.H. Rushbrooke, *Baptists in Britain* (London: Baptist Union, 1937), p. 30.

60   *Life*, pp. 77-78.

Its symbolic significance, *i.e.*, the spiritual death to self, union with Christ, and resurrection of the believer was emphasized by Paul: it expressed in vivid manner the very heart of Christian experience, as he conceived it. It is an action that speaks louder than words; by its unspoken eloquence, it commits those who are baptized to the most essential things. Yet it leaves each generation free to interpret the fundamental truths in its own way.[61]

The most important baptismal text to Baptists is Romans 6.1-11, and what Paul says there he succinctly reiterates in Colossians 2.12. The relationship between the believer in baptism and these events, however, has been differently interpreted by Baptists. Many have been content merely to state that baptism witnesses to Jesus' death, burial and resurrection, and signifies the believer's death to sin and resurrection to a new life,[62] but others, following Robinson's lead, have developed this theology further, believing that, by faith, the believer actually participates in these events.[63]

Concerned that both the objective and subjective elements of baptism should be held together, Robinson declared that the New Testament never considered these issues apart, that the baptism of which it spoke was no formal act, but a genuine experience,[64] and, in any case, the New Testament did not know of unbaptized believers. It was only later generations which separated the outer act from the inner experience and it was this development which had made possible the rise of sacramentarianism on the one hand and the entire rejection of the

---

61   *Principles*, p. 28.

62   E.g., W.T. Whitley, *Church, Ministry and Sacraments in the New Testament* (London: Kingsgate Press, 1903), pp. 161-63.

63   In *The Christian Doctrine of Man* (Edinburgh: T. & T. Clark, 3rd edn, 1926), pp. 124-25, Robinson commented that the Romans passage implied not merely a symbolic but a realistic union with Christ.

64   Robinson's work on baptism was greatly influenced by the Psychology of Religion school of thought which tended to reflect a greater emphasis on experience. E.g., *Life*, p. 74: 'Modern psychology has thrown into brilliant relief the importance of *acts* as influencing thoughts', italics his. Cf. *Experience*, p. 41: 'the spiritual energies of God...are immeasurably enhanced when psychologically or sacramentally mediated through Jesus Christ'. See also p. 196. In *Life*, pp. 76-77, he commented that 'Those who have assigned another meaning to baptism, yet agree as to the significance of conversion, sometimes become conscious of the lack of any significant expression of it in the institutions of their Church. They find that there is a real difficulty in getting one who is brought under Christian influence to register his experience through some definite and memorable act from which to make his new start. Unless this is done in some way or other the experience is apt to fade away. But where can we find a more impressive and memorable register of the birth of a new purpose than that which is provided by believers' baptism?' See also his reviews 'The Sacrament of Baptism', *The Fraternal* o.s. 13.2 (April, 1921), pp. 3-6, and 'The Psychology of Religion', *Baptist Quarterly* 2.6 (April, 1925), pp. 283-84.

sacraments on the other. The later history of baptism was, he stated, in large measure, the history of this separation. He concluded, 'It became possible to administer baptism to unintelligent recipients only through the transference of emphasis from the moral and spiritual to the sacramental side of the rite.'[65] Accordingly, the mode is not essential, only appropriate, for to equate the practice with the principle was to stultify the principle itself, which emphasizes the inner essential of faith, declaring that without it all outward ceremonies are valueless.[66] Baptists, he claimed, only value the external rite in so far as it emphasizes the spiritual change wrought in human nature by the Spirit of God in Christ, implying both a profession of faith and a change of heart.[67] Thus baptism is the 'cardinal ceremony of union with Christ, the objective aspect of what is subjectively faith'.[68] Later he outlined the triple aspect of baptism: it implies the historical events of the death, burial and resurrection of Christ, of which submersion is the suggestive symbol; it consists of a series of acts on the part of the baptized, who goes down into the water, is submerged and rises out of it; and it supplies a visible parallel to the spiritual experience of the believer which Paul called the baptism of the Holy Spirit—their death to sin and resurrection to newness of life. 'All these three aspects are implied in the single series of visible acts, and they become sacramental to the participant for whom they have this implication.' Such significance is warranted in the light of prophetic symbolism, which is more than mere 'representation'. The charge of 'sacramental' magic can be dismissed because the person is a conscious believer, the efficacy of the rite depending on their conscious and believing participation in it. Equally there is no question of 'mere symbolism', for the act is the 'partial and fragmentary, but very real accomplishment of a divine work, the work of the Holy Spirit'.[69]

Therefore, Robinson's is an ethical sacramentalism, standing apart from other interpretations of the rite because it is *'the only baptism which is strictly and primarily an ethical act on the part of the baptized'.*[70] He wrote: 'When [Jesus] came forward, He was first baptized with John's baptism, and proclaimed John's message, as though to remind us that, whatever else Christian baptism may mean, it means something profoundly moral.'[71] Again Romans 6 is a key passage for baptism

65   *Principles*, pp. 14-15.
66   *Principles*, p. 15.
67   *Principles*, pp. 7-8.
68   *Man*, p. 124.
69   *Experience*, pp. 193-94.
70   *Life*, p. 73, italics his.
71   *Principles*, p. 13. On pp.13-15, he progressed from baptism as a moral act to implying four things: cleansing from sin; association with the gift of the Spirit; its administration to believers; and experimental union with Christ.

which forms the foundation for Paul's moral exhortations.[72] Such a position led Robinson to the view that the first and foremost contribution Baptists could make to the church catholic, like that of the Hebrew prophets, was the essential and primary place of the moral within the religious. 'The moral change wrought within conversion, the personal repentance and faith which are the religious features of that conversion, the open confession which commits the life to a new purpose—these great truths are admirably and forcibly expressed in believer's baptism by immersion, and expressed as no other Church expresses them.'[73]

Robinson's sacramental theology, then, is grounded in Christian experience and in his reading of the New Testament in which he found that 'conversion is an act in which both God and man share; it belongs to two worlds at once'.[74] In 1914 he challenged Baptists as to whether they were loyal to New Testament baptism. He outlined the accepted position that New Testament baptism was an ordinance for believers only, a personal confession of faith, an act of obedience clearly symbolizing loyal devotion to Christ, but asked whether this was the whole truth and whether there was another truth complementary to it on which Baptist witness was not equally clear. Did not baptism express more than a personal act? Was it not, by virtue of being that, also the entrance into a life of supernatural energies.[75] He contrasted the baptism of Christ with that of John as a baptism with or in the Holy Spirit. To be baptized into Christ is to put on Christ, that is, to enter that realm of the Spirit under Christ's Lordship. The connection between water-baptism and Spirit-baptism is of no mechanical kind, for he rejected outright any notion of baptismal regeneration, which, he asserted, was precluded by the exceptions recorded in the Book of Acts where all who were baptized were already believers, and he insisted that the moral and spiritual conditions of personal faith became the real channel of the Spirit's highest energies. Indeed, he said, it was the very divorce of baptism from

---

72   'Place', p. 215.
73   *Life*, p. 144.
74   'Conversion', p. 319.
75   He later developed this idea in his 'Baptism of Power', p. 35, in which he acknowledged that moral cleansing is part of the significance of baptism for all but Jesus, who gives to baptism the larger meaning as a baptism of power. The question, then, he set out to ask was 'do we lay sufficient stress on the baptism of power, as we undoubtedly do on the baptism of cleansing? Do we make the ceremony of water-baptism symbolise the gift of the Spirit as clearly as we make it symbolise conversion?' He reported that when he asked a dozen or more of his Baptist ministerial students 'the very issue seemed new to all of them. Yet I humbly suggest that what I am urging is New Testament teaching, and that its fuller recognition would go far to invest believers' baptism with an importance it hardly seems to possess in the eyes of some Baptist ministers.'

personal faith which made sacramentarianism possible, and it is this
against which Baptists rightly protest. But the energy of their protest
brings its own peril, as they tend to become suspicious of any
pronounced sacramental emphasis, even the genuine sacramentalism of
the New Testament. They have so stressed the subjects of baptism that
they fail to say anything about baptism itself. In this respect, he admitted,
'we have much to learn from the sacramental Churches themselves'.
Here, then, was an opportunity for Baptists to give a forceful testimony to
the work of the Spirit on the believer. He continued:

> If any reader is afraid that this may mean a sacramentalism of the lower kind, where
> the channel of the Spirit is thought to be the material element, rather than the
> evangelical truth in the hearts of believers, let it be said distinctly that we are
> pleading for the connection of water-baptism with the Holy Spirit exactly in the
> sense in which we plead for its connection with personal faith. If the New
> Testament teaches the latter, it assuredly teaches the former, and Baptists are really
> committed to both. Let us tell that the Church is the home of supernatural powers,
> and not merely a human society, that faith is not a mere opinion, but a personal
> surrender to Him through whose Spirit these powers are to be experienced, and that
> baptism is not simply an act of faith, but 'the sign and seal' that that faith is
> answered by the Holy Spirit of God. So, and only so, will He Himself have led us
> into all the truth concerning New Testament baptism.[76]

Later, Robinson sought to answer his critics when, after quoting with
approval the view of H.A.A. Kennedy that 'In baptism (of course, adult)
something happened', he asserted that in the New Testament baptism was
a sacrament precisely because it was 'the vehicle of the Holy Spirit' and
was '*administered, as alone it ought to be, to a converted man*'. Until
Baptists fearlessly taught this, he believed they would 'never enter into
the full New Testament heritage'.[77]

Within three weeks of Robinson's 1914 article, he was attacked for his
association of the Spirit with baptism and perceived disparagement of
faith. George W. MacAlpine, a prominent Baptist layman and
businessman, questioned whether the New Testament condition for the
gift of the Spirit was baptism, or rather faith, 'of the operations of which
baptism is only symbolical'. He felt that Robinson too strongly
associated the gift of the Spirit with the act of baptism. Surely the
Cornelius episode in Acts 10 established that the gift of the Holy Spirit
was granted to faith? 'The Holy Spirit brings to the believer the new life,
the life of the Spirit; and, precisely because baptism shows forth in
symbol the rising believer to newness of life, it also symbolises the gift of

---

76   'Are Baptists Loyal to the New Testament Baptism?', *Baptist Times and
Freeman* 26 June 1914, p. 518.
77   'Conversion', p. 319, citing Kennedy, *St. Paul and the Mystery Religions*
(London: Hodder & Stoughton, 1914), p. 249.

the Holy Spirit. But we must ever keep clearly before us the fact that the moral and spiritual conditions of *personal faith* become the *real* channel of the Spirit's highest energies.'[78]

In reply, Robinson agreed with MacAlpine that faith was the essential condition of entrance into the realm of the Spirit's energies as opposed to that work of the Spirit which preceded faith. However, he reiterated that his argument was that water-baptism in the New Testament symbolized not only this faith but also the reception of supernatural power by the believer,[79] as MacAlpine had fully recognized. But further, he had argued that the present Baptist emphasis fell too exclusively on the personal act of faith and not adequately on the spiritual energies which that act of faith mediated. To the assertion that the normal condition for reception of these energies came before baptism, that is, with faith, Robinson referred to Acts 2.38: 'The manifestation of the Spirit's power (which, of course, does not exclude the preparatory work of the Spirit prior to repentance) is regarded as the sequel or close accompaniment of baptism. As men were made disciples (according to "the great Commission") before they were baptised, so, ordinarily, they were baptised before the Holy Spirit gave visible proof of His indwelling activity and power.' This he supported by Paul's statement in 1 Corinthians 12.13. Experience of the Spirit (like faith itself) was not simply an isolated event, but covered the whole Christian life.

> I am not afraid of the consequences of such loyalty to New Testament teaching, *so long as baptism is administered to believers only*. We may easily teach our candidates for baptism to expect too little; we can hardly lead them to expect too much from the Spirit of God. New Testament writers knew nothing of the distinction between the subjective (faith) and the objective (water) conditions of baptism which Baptists have felt compelled to urge, because the New Testament knows nothing of unbaptized believers, or of a water-baptism divorced from faith. The later abuse of water-baptism by its application to infants ought not to rob Baptists of the full meaning of New Testament baptism, as the expressive symbol of new powers underlying new life, as well as of the personal act of faith by which that new life is consciously entered.[80]

---

78   G.W. MacAlpine, 'Are Baptists Loyal to the New Testament Baptism?', *Baptist Times and Freeman* 17 July 1914, p. 585. The italics were MacAlpine's, the words Robinson's in his earlier article. MacAlpine was an Accrington coal-owner and ardent supporter of the Baptist Missionary Society, on whom see Cross, *Baptism*, p. 116 n. 88.

79   Cf. *Experience*, pp. 132-35, e.g., p. 134, because the Holy Spirit is Christ's continued presence the 'Sacraments are charged with a new spiritual power...' Cf. also p. 140.

80   'Are Baptists Loyal to the New Testament Baptism?', *Baptist Times and Freeman* 24 July 1914, p. 601, italics his. Robinson reiterated many of these points in '"Unto What Were Ye Baptised?"', *Baptist Times* 25 May 1934, p. 384.

Though MacAlpine replied immediately, no new ground was covered.[81] His difficulty over Robinson's very carefully worded letters and writings can be taken as representative of Baptist dis–ease over the newly articulated Baptist sacramentalism. So entrenched were the anti-Catholic and anti-sacerdotalist feelings that anything that sounded like baptismal regeneration was greeted warily and, no doubt, many times with great hostilty.

Like many Baptists who have advocated a sacramental understanding of baptism, Robinson was suspected of advancing baptismal regeneration despite his clear repudiation of it.[82] Baptist antipathy to baptismal regeneration was a particular feature of the first half of the twentieth century, though Baptists have always staunchly opposed it, maintaining that salvation is by grace through faith, not by a rite of any kind. Regeneration, they believe, is the work of the Holy Spirit, that baptism is the outward sign of this,[83] and that Paedobaptists have confused the two. Robinson contrasted the regeneration by the Holy Spirit with the theory of baptismal regeneration:

> There are two distinct ways of representing the operation of the Spirit of God in regard to baptism. We may think of the external act, and the material means, as the prescribed channel of the work of the Spirit, and then the result is what is commonly known as sacramentarianism. Or we may think of the internal conditions, the personal faith and conversion emphasized in Believer's Baptism, and see in them the true realm of the Spirit's activity... In fact, when we speak of Believer's Baptism, we mean that baptism in the Spirit of God, of which water baptism is the expression.[84]

On the new birth Baptists are unanimous: it is by the Holy Spirit not baptism that a person is born again. A distinction, therefore, is drawn by many between the baptism of the Spirit and water-baptism,[85] but

---

81   G.W. MacAlpine, 'Are Baptists Loyal to the New Testament Baptism?', *Baptist Times and Freeman* 31 July 1914, p. 616.

82   For others see Cross, *Baptism*, pp. 28-29. This was one of the accusations levelled against the contributors to A. Gilmore (ed.), *Christian Baptism: A Fresh Attempt to Understand the Rite in terms of Scripture, History, and Theology* (London: Lutterworth Press, 1959), on which see Cross, *Baptism*, pp. 228-39, and Fowler, *More Than a Symbol*, pp. 113-33, and also Fowler's essay in the present volume.

83   *Principles*, p. 24, 'the Spirit is the agent in that regeneration which is the Godward side of conversion...'

84   *Principles*, pp. 24-25.

85   E.g., Whitley, *Church, Ministry and Sacraments*, p. 51; J.D. Freeman, 'The Lambeth Appeal', *The Fraternal* o.s. 13.5 (March, 1922), pp. 6-7. This position was maintained by K. Barth, *Church Dogmatics: The Christian Life (Fragment)* (trans. G.W. Bromiley; Edinburgh: T. & T. Clark, 1969), IV/4 (Barth's views are critically examined by Fowler, *More Than a Symbol*, pp. 178-95), and more recently by J.D.G. Dunn,

Robinson tried to bring the two together, though he continued to speak of the external act as subordinate and secondary to the baptism of the Spirit.[86] Referring to 1 Corinthians 12.13 he wrote, 'water-baptism is the outward and visible sign of an inward and spiritual baptism of the Holy Spirit',[87] though elsewhere he implicitly recognized the different situations of the early church and the contemporary church, again in a discussion of 1 Corinthians 12.13:

> Here the double reference to water-baptism, as an immersion and a saturation, suggests that the ideal beginning of the Spirit-filled life is at the water-baptism of the believer, which *in those days* would follow immediately on the credible confession of faith. A believer who did not express his faith by baptism would not then have been regarded as a believer. At the baptism, oral confession of the faith was made, and this was regarded as the decisive moment.[88]

The rite of infant baptism lends itself to a mechanical and quasi-magical conception of faith and grace which Baptists have found offensive to the gospel on the grounds that it perverts the evangelical message. On the other hand, Baptists maintain that believer's baptism stresses and preserves the personal meaning of both faith and grace. Robinson proposed that Romans 6.3-5 could legitimately be regarded as a form of symbolic magic were it not for the fact that baptism is the act of a believer.[89] He developed this line of thought further when he contended that transubstantiation is the logical outcome of the theory of baptismal regeneration and that 'believer's baptism is the logical and effective safeguard against such parodies of Scriptural truth'.[90]

Further, Robinson not only linked baptism with the gift of the Holy Spirit,[91] he developed this further. He stated that the church is the creation of the Spirit of God, for it is the Spirit who is the agent of

---

Baptism in the Holy Spirit: A Re-Examination of the New Testament Teaching on the Gift of the Spirit in Relation to Pentecostalism Today (London: SCM Press, 1970), e.g. pp. 127-31, and G.D. Fee, *God's Empowering Presence: The Holy Spirit in the Letters of Paul* (Peabody, MA: Hendrickson, 1994), e.g. pp. 178-82. I criticize the views of Dunn and Fee in particular in 'Spirit- and Water-Baptism in 1 Corinthians 12.13', in S.E. Porter and A.R. Cross (eds.), *Dimensions of Baptism: Biblical and Theological Studies* (*Journal for the Study of the New Testament*, Supplement Series, 234; Sheffield: Sheffield Academic Press, forthcoming 2002).

86   E.g., 'Place', p. 212, and *Experience*, p. 198. See his careful distinction of the primacy of 'born of the Spirit' over 'born of water and the Spirit' in John 3.5-6, in 'Believers' Baptism and the Holy Spirit', *Baptist Quarterly* 9.7 (July, 1939), pp. 393-94.

87   'Place', p. 210.

88   'Believers' Baptism and the Holy Spirit', p. 392, italics added.

89   'Hebrew Sacrifice', pp. 137-38.

90   'Lord's Supper', p. 389.

91   *Principles*, pp. 13-14.

regeneration which is the Godward side of conversion. For this reason, there is no surprise that the New Testament so closely links the gift of the Spirit with believer's baptism, indeed, it makes the experience of that gift the test of the rite.[92] This, however, did not commit Robinson to any theory of baptismal regeneration. To focus on the external act and material means as the prescribed channel of the Spirit's activity would indeed result in sacramentarianism, which in common with all Baptists he repudiated.[93] But to focus on the internal conditions, the personal faith and conversion which are emphasized in believer's baptism, seeing them as the true realm of the Spirit, both guards against and prevents this. He wrote:

> The sufficient answer [to sacramentarianism] is that neither for Jesus nor for Paul nor for ourselves does the outward ceremony secure and guarentee its spiritual significance. There is no more risk in teaching that baptism signifies power than that it signifies cleansing. Both depend on certain moral and spiritual conditions, which the outward ceremony represents, articulates and thus serves. There is no risk at all for Baptists to teach the baptism of power whatever there may be for those who practise infant baptism. To require the moral and spiritual condition of conversion in those who seek baptism is to require that obedience of faith to which alone the Holy Spirit is given.[94]

Robinson recognized that in the Christian life and experience[95] Baptists have tended to elevate the spiritual to the detriment of the material. While they are willing to accept spiritual means by which God works in peoples' lives, they have been reluctant, even refused, to accept that God uses material means to effect his grace. While Robinson believed that 'any adequate theory' of the sacraments united 'the spiritual and the

---

92   Cf. *Principles*, p. 24. In 'Baptists and the Bible', p. 151, he contended that Baptists should retain the rite of baptism 'in a form that makes it a challenging test' of belief in the necessity of personal conviction.

93   Robinson meant by 'sacramentarianism' what other Baptists meant by 'sacramentalism' or 'sacerdotalism', see Cross, *Baptism*, p. 103.

94   'The Baptism of Power', *Baptist Times and Freeman* 16 January 1920, pp. 35-36.

95   W.R. Matthews, 'H. Wheeler Robinson', *Baptist Quarterly* 12.1-2 (January–April, 1946), 1946, p. 7, noted that Robinson 'based so much' on 'experience'. 'The "validity" of the religious experience might almost be said to have been the question which he was always discussing—he returns to it again and again in his books—and the burden of his contention is invariably that there is an objective element in the spiritual experience.' Robinson concluded his article on 'The Reality of the Spirit', *Baptist Times and Freeman* 17 April 1925, p. 251, with the statement that 'the thinker must stand side by side with the humblest Christian in knowing at first hand the reality of the Spirit of God in his religious experience'. On experience and the Holy Spirit, see also his 'The Validity of Christian Experience', in J. Marchant (ed.), *The Future of Christianity* (London: John Murray, 1927), pp. 26-47.

material'[96] and rejected the separation of the spiritual and material, he nevertheless emphasized that it was the former that gave meaning to the latter, because 'form can have no spiritual value apart from the attitude of the baptised to it'.[97] He believed that one of the beliefs which distinguished the New Testament era from the present was that people believed in the supernatural 'and in influences from without which could act on human nature without passing through the channels of the senses'.[98]

What prevents baptism from becoming merely a rite, to use R.E.O. White's later phrase, is that baptism is 'faith-baptism'.[99] The validity of this is seen when Robinson wrote: 'Baptism means for Baptists the intelligent act of a believer; *apart from the personal faith of the baptized person there is no validity or, indeed, meaning in the act itself.*' Retention of the original form of immersion is because it is the more impressive and intelligible form of the rite which, more than sprinkling ever could, brings out 'the faith-union of the believer with the Lord in His death and in His resurrection. No Baptist believes that an external ceremony, apart from the faith of the recipient, can ever confer grace, or that water in itself can ever be the vehicle of grace.' He then immediately went on to state that 'On the other hand, the New Testament clearly shows that the baptism of believers—the only baptism of which it speaks—was definitely and constantly associated with the gift of the Holy Spirit.'[100] This position led him to add that 'Baptists have not adequately realised that believers' baptism can itself be a sacramental "means of grace," without any risk of "ritualism" *when it is confined to believers.*'[101]

The belief that baptism is a means of grace is inseparably linked to an identification of baptism with the working of the Holy Spirit. Robinson clearly believed that it was the marginal place given to the doctrine and work of the Holy Spirit in Baptist life and theology which prevented the rediscovery of the true, sacramental nature of New Testament baptism. In 1925 he observed that 'There is increasing recognition amongst thoughtful Christians that we have unduly neglected [the doctrine of the Holy Spirit], and that it holds a central place in the Christian life of the

---

96   *Experience*, p. 82.

97   *Principles*, p. 27. Cf. p. 15.

98   'Reality of the Spirit', p. 251.

99   R.E.O. White, *The Biblical Doctrine of Initiation* (London: Hodder and Stoughton, 1960), p. 226.

100   'Baptism and the Gift of the Holy Spirit', *Baptist Times* 29 March 1928, p. 209, italics added.

101   'Baptist Church', p. 321, italics his.

New Testament.'[102] Jim Perkin rightly observed that both Baptists and Paedobaptists during this period 'did not feel happy about the doctrine of the Holy Spirit, whether in connection with baptism or not' and that this constituted 'a serious lacuna in the theology of the period'.[103] What Perkin said of the period ending in 1920, equally applies to the late 1920s and beyond, and for Baptists Robinson led the rediscovery of this dimension of baptism, ably supported by A.C. Underwood.[104] Other writers, of course, addressed this issue, but most of the references are scattered within the discussion of other themes and are usually brief, under-developed and too often vague.[105]

It might be expected that his clearest thoughts on the relation between the Spirit and baptism would be found in the relevant chapter of his major work on the Christian's experience of the Spirit, but this is not the case. Here, the sacraments are described as the acts of believers, baptism supplying a visible parallel to the spiritual experience which Paul called the baptism of the Holy Spirit—the believer's death to sin and resurrection to newness of life.[106] Since the action corresponded to the spoken word, as with the prophetic symbolism of Israel's prophets,[107] therefore, there could be no question of 'mere symbolism' in baptism (or the Lord's Supper) 'for the act is the partial and fragmentary, but very real accomplishment of a divine work, the work of the Holy Spirit'.[108]

His clearest and most widely read thoughts on the Spirit, however, are to be found in his other works, particularly his *Baptist Principles*, in which he declared that baptism is linked to the gift of the Spirit,[109] and then, when discussing the nature of the church as a spiritual society of the converted, he declared that the church is the creation of the Spirit, for he is the agent in that regeneration which is the Godward side of conversion.

---

102 'Reality of the Spirit', p. 251. In 'The River of the Spirit', *Baptist Times* 23 September 1926, p. 672, he wrote: 'When we begin to think seriously about the Holy Spirit (and large numbers of Christian people have never got so far as this)...'

103 J.R.C. Perkin, 'Baptism in Non-Conformist Theology, 1820–1920, with special reference to the Baptists' (DPhil Thesis, Oxford University, 1955), pp. 13-14. Cf. the anonymous 'A Neglected Doctrine', *Baptist Times and Freeman* 16 January 1914, p. 43.

104 See Cross, *Baptism*, p. 240.

105 See Cross, *Baptism*, pp. 108-10.

106 *Experience*, p. 194. S. Clark, 'The shout which dislodged the avalanche of the Holy Spirit', *Baptist Times* 21 October 1999, pp. 5 and 12, describes this and his *Principles* as 'a pioneer factor in awakening awareness to our need of the Holy Spirit'.

107 *Experience*, p. 193.

108 *Experience*, p. 194. Earlier, p. 125, he wrote, 'the water-baptism was also a Spirit-baptism, the New Testament equivalent to the "prophetic symbolism" of the Old Testament.'

109 *Principles*, pp. 13-14.

As the church in the New Testament is illustrated by the three metaphors of a spiritual house, God's family and a Spirit-animated body, there is little surprise that the New Testament so closely links the gift of the Spirit with believer's baptism.[110] Water-baptism is thus the expression of the baptism in the Spirit,[111] and it is this aspect, he admitted elsewhere, which Baptists had failed to emphasize.[112]

Robinson sought to clarify two connected and related, but also much neglected, dimensions of baptism: the outer and inner, and the objective and the subjective. Robinson noted that Jesus evidently did not despise the outer ceremony—otherwise he would not have come to the Jordan to be baptized by John—though his emphasis constantly fell on the inner meaning which gave meaning to the outer.[113] 'Conversion is a reality, but it is a spiritual reality, and dramatic features belong to its accidents, not to its essentials.'[114] Because it is to be administered only to believers, the manner of administration of the rite is, therefore, subordinate to the principle and Robinson was adamant that it is not baptism which is essential but the thing signified.[115] In support of this, he highlighted the ethical aspect of baptism, speaking of moral holiness and consecrated character. 'This inward and ethical emphasis stands in contrast with the externalism of the older idolatry and the later legalism.'[116] For him, the external act of baptism was always subordinate to the conversion of the individual, their baptism of the Spirit,[117] which is, nevertheless, connected to water-baptism. Elsewhere Robinson wrote: 'Baptism in the New Testament is so identified with the new experience it initiates that it is difficult to summarize its meaning without describing that experience itself.'[118] But this does not mean that the outer rite is unnecessary, for he was convinced that baptism in the New Testament sense did justice to both the inner experience and the external expression of it, 'which', he added in parenthesis, 'is always, in some form, necessary'.[119] One of Robinson's concerns, then, was to redress Baptist aversion to ceremony.

Romans 6.5 states that if the believer is united with Christ in his death, they will be united with him in his resurrection. 'For Paul', Robinson argued, baptism 'meant an experimental union with Christ in His

---

110 *Principles*, p. 24.
111 *Principles*, p. 25.
112 'Place', p. 214.
113 'Baptism of Power', p. 35: 'There is for Him a value in the outward and visible sign, for we simply cannot think of Him as participating in a perfunctory formalism.'
114 'River of the Spirit', p. 672.
115 *Principles*, p. 27.
116 *Life*, p. 19.
117 'Place', p. 212.
118 *Principles*, p. 13.
119 'Psychology of Religion', p. 284.

redeeming acts, deeper in meaning than words can express...' Citing Romans 6.4, he pressed: 'If it is asked just what the outer act of baptism contributed to these inner experiences of forgiveness, regeneration, faith and fellowship with Christ, we must reply that *the New Testament never considers them apart* in this detached manner.'[120] This union with the church is often described in terms of initiation or incorporation into Christ, hence its proper place at the beginning of the Christian life.[121] The fullest and clearest of the Apostle Paul's associations of the outer sign and seal with the inner and invisible grace was made in Romans 6.3-5, where the act of water-baptism is said to unite the believer with the dying, buried and risen Lord on the one hand, and on the other with the new obligations and new resources of a penitent and risen life in Christ. In 1 Corinthians 12.13, the visible act of water-baptism is into the name of Jesus and expresses and mediates the invisible baptism into the Holy Spirit. The context of this verse indicates that Paul was thinking of the common act of water-baptism by which alone there is entrance into the visible body of Christ, and with this he closely associated the invisible experience as the normal accompaniment.[122] This is supported from the book of Acts (especially Acts 2.38) where water-baptism and Spirit-baptism are intimately linked.[123]

The next logical step was to address the objective and the subjective, the Godward and the human aspects of the rite. Traditionally, Baptists have tended to focus on the subjective, what the believer does in baptism, omitting reference to the activity of God in and through the rite. Robinson continued to challenge fellow Baptists, arguing that if his interpretation of the New Testament was sound, 'then there is something yet to be done if Baptists are to substantiate their claim to be fully loyal to the New Testament. Baptism is there not only a necessary profession of repentance and faith; it is also a sacrament of grace...'[124]

---

120 *Principles*, pp. 14-15, italics his.

121 'Place', p. 209. In *Life*, p. 70, he remarked that believer's baptism seemed to have been an invariable accompaniment, if not definite sign, of entry into the Christian community. This is clearly the logic of closed membership churches. Robinson believed open membership was a matter of expediency rather than principle, though he saw it as less of a peril when the minister was a convinced Baptist, see *Life*, p. 101, and 'Place', pp. 213-14.

122 He also believed that '"the Lord the Spirit"' (2 Cor. 3.18) 'was inwardly experienced by the believer who had been baptized in the Spirit' (1 Cor. 12.13), 'Holy Spirit, The', *The Encyclopaedia Britannica* (London: Encyclopaedia Britannica, 14th edn, 1929), XI, p. 685.

123 'Five Points', p. 8.

124 'Believers' Baptism and the Holy Spirit', p. 395. This article, pp. 387-97, is Robinson's most detailed biblical treatment of the relationship between baptism and the Holy Spirit.

In the last chapter of his seminal *Baptist Principles*, Robinson proposed three conditions which would ensure for Baptist churches a great future, the second of which was the recovery of the New Testament emphasis on the Spirit of God.[125] It was this emphasis, more than any other single truth, which gave the New Testament its 'expansive and vital atmosphere, the sense of great things to be and do, and great powers with which to attain them'. The recovery of this would do much to meet the growingly insistent needs of the contemporary world—witnessing to 'a baptism of the Spirit which exhilarates, expands, purifies the whole personality, intellectual and emotional and volitional'.[126] He called on Baptists to set themselves open-mindedly to the study of the New Testament references to baptism, for they might be surprised to find how closely baptism is related to the gift of the Spirit. A sharp distinction exists between John's baptism expressed as a moral decision and Christ's baptism which is with or in the Spirit. This he supported with reference to John 3.5 and 1 Corinthians 12.13. For Paul, baptism was not solely descent into the waters of baptism meaning death and burial with Christ and that mystical union with him which carried with it death to sin, but also ascent into new life, defined by Paul as newness of 'Spirit' (Col. 2.12).[127] 'Thus, to be baptized into Christ is to put on Christ, i.e. to enter that realm of the Spirit over which Christ is Lord.' He dispelled any mechanical or quasi-magical connection between water- and Spirit-baptism on the basis of Cornelius and his friends' Spirit-baptism preceding their water-baptism (Acts 10) and the Ephesian disciples in Acts 19 who received the Spirit after the laying on of hands subsequent to their baptism.[128]

He identified Baptist hesitation over the place of the Spirit in baptism not in the exegesis of biblical texts, but fear, even nearly a century after the Tractarian movement, of baptismal regeneration and magical interpretations of the rite's operation and efficacy.

> But most of all, I want to urge that our peculiar denominational emphasis on believer's baptism should enable us to meet a great need of the religious life of to-day, I mean the recovery of the New Testament emphasis on the Holy Spirit. We

125 *Principles*, pp. 65-66. It is unclear as to what Robinson had in mind at this point, but there can be little doubt that twentieth-century charismatic renewal would not have met with his approval.

126 *Principles*, p. 67.

127 He developed this idea of baptism as mystical union in *Experience*, e.g., pp. 39, 59, 82, 90, 134 and 275, and 'Believers Baptism and the Holy Spirit', p. 393.

128 *Life*, pp. 144-45. In 'Baptism of Power', p. 36, he wrote: 'I do not suggest that the actual ceremony of baptism will always or necessarily coincide with a great hour of spiritual experience, as it did with our Lord... Yet I think that baptism would mean much more to the candidate if we taught him or her to see where the New Testament emphasis falls, when it speaks of being baptised in one Spirit into one body, or of being born of water and the Spirit.'

have been unconsciously afraid of teaching the relation of the gift of the Spirit and water-baptism, because so much is made of it by those who believe in baptismal regeneration and appeal to the words, 'Ye must be born of water and the Spirit.' We have thrown our emphasis on baptism as a personal and human profession of repentance and faith. It is that, and that needed to be emphasised. But the uniquely ethical character of our baptism safeguards us from the risk of misunderstanding, and leaves full room for the more evangelical sacramentalism of the New Testament. The moral and religious experience of repentance and faith becomes the channel of the Spirit, and is psychologically reinforced by the definite expression of this experience in water-baptism. If we teach men that water-baptism is of real value on the human side—if it is not, we have no right to practice it—may we not teach that it is in the same way of value on the divine, possibly a real occasion, always a powerful declaration, of that baptism of the Spirit which is the true secret of Christian sanctification?[129]

He concluded his *The Life and Faith of the Baptists*:

there is needed a new and clear teaching of the doctrine of the Holy Spirit, as against the rationalism that rejects all mystery, and the externalism which materializes mystery into manageable forms. The true emphasis is that of the New Testament—on personal faith as the human condition of divine activity, which is the truth supremely expressed in believer's baptism.[130]

                                        * * *

The person who did more than anyone else to help Baptists rediscover the sacramental understanding of baptism, certainly in twentieth-century Britain, was Wheeler Robinson[131] and the key to his sacramentalism was the person and work of the Holy Spirit. As W.R. Matthews, Dean of St Paul's Cathedral and a close friend, said in his obituary: 'The Theology of Wheeler Robinson is, first of all, a theology of the Holy Spirit.'[132]

In several ways Robinson anticipated later developments in the debate on baptism. In that he did not demur from stating that 'The single act of

---

129 'Place', pp. 216-17.

130 *Life*, p. 147.

131 Cf. A.C. Underwood, *A History of the English Baptists* (London: Kingsgate Press, 1947), pp. 268-69: 'Largely under the influence of the writings of Dr. H. Wheeler Robinson, many English Baptists have abandoned this view [a symbolic view of baptism] in favour of a sacramental interpretation of believers' baptism.' See also Cross, *Baptism, passim*; Perkin, 'Baptism', pp. 435-40; D.M. Thompson, 'Baptism, Church and Society in Britain Since 1800' (unpublished Hulsean Lectures 1983–84, 1984), p. 83; Fowler, *More Than a Symbol*, pp. 89-97; and Randall, *Experiences*, pp. 193-95.

132 Matthews, 'Robinson', p. 8.

Baptism is the rite of initiation in the Kingdom of God',[133] he anticipated the move from the discussion of baptism as such to the broader discussion of Christian initiation which began in the late 1940s–50s.[134] Ernest Payne commented that 'in this whole matter of Christian initiation the greater casualness of recent generations is being reversed', and he identified the work of Wheeler Robinson and his plea for the recovery of the New Testament emphasis on the Spirit, along with the introduction of a service of infant dedication/presentation, as being instrumental in this turnabout.[135] His discussion of conversion as 'a spiritual journey'[136] was not really taken up until the 1970–80s[137] and was developed by Baptists in several important works in the mid-1990s.[138] Robinson's recognition that conversion is both a divine and human act was taken up by Emil Brunner who spoke of 'the divine–human encounter',[139] a phrase increasingly used by Baptists and others.[140] However, Robinson's attempt to dispel Baptists' dis-ease with the material as a means of grace has largely gone unheeded, though Paul Fiddes has recently discussed the sacraments as pieces of matter which God uses as places of encounter with himself.[141]

That Robinson, supported by Underwood and others, were successful to a point, is clear from the remark made in an official Baptist Union document in 1937 when it acknowledged that as an acted creed and

---

133 'Lord's Supper', p. 389.

134 See Cross, *Baptism*, pp. 320-21, and '"One Baptism" (Ephesians 4.5): A Challenge to the Church', in S.E. Porter and A.R. Cross (eds.), *Baptism, the New Testament and the Church: Historical and Contemporary Studies in Honour of R.E.O. White* (Sheffield: Sheffield Academic Press, 1999), pp. 173-74.

135 E.A. Payne, 'Baptists and Christian Initiation', *Baptist Quarterly* 26.4 (October, 1975), p. 154.

136 'Conversion', p. 319. Cf. 'The Holiness of Believers' Children', *Baptist Times and Freeman* 20 October 1905, p. 739: 'In our determination to maintain the full significance of New Testament baptism, we may have looked too much for cataclysmic changes instead of the still, small voice, and have failed to welcome some whose conversion was as quiet and gradual as the coming of spring.'

137 E.g., *Baptism, Eucharist and Ministry* (Faith and Order Paper 111; Geneva: World Council of Churches, 1982), p. 4.

138 See P.S. Fiddes, 'Baptism and Creation', in P.S. Fiddes (ed.), *Reflections on the Water: Understanding God and the World through the Baptism of Believers* (Regent's Study Guides, 4; Oxford: Regent's Park College/Macon, GA: Smyth & Helwys, 1996), e.g., pp. 55-56, 60; and *Believing and Being Baptized: Baptism, so-called re-baptism and children in the church* (Didcot: Baptist Union of Great Britain, 1996), e.g., pp. 9-12. See Cross, *Baptism*, e.g., pp. 372-84.

139 E. Brunner, *The Divine–Human Encounter* (London: SCM Press, 1944), 2nd edn *Truth as Encounter* (London: SCM Press, 1964).

140 See Cross, *Baptism*, pp. 127-30, 346, and '"One Baptism"', p. 188.

141 Fiddes, 'Baptism and Creation', p. 47.

declaration of the gospel, baptism expressed faith in the power and grace of God in Christ to forgive, cleanse and re-create, showing forth the way of redemption by Christ's death, burial and resurrection, with which 'spiritually and mystically the believer is identified. *It testifies to the doctrine of grace and to the necessity for the complete surrender of self to God.* It is an appointed and an approved means of grace to the believing soul.'[142] They were also successful in that they paved the way for later scholars to develop a sacramental theology of baptism from a truly Baptist perspective, the foremost being George Beasley-Murray and R.E.O. White, but also Robert C. Walton, Neville Clark, and most recently Paul Fiddes and Christopher Ellis.[143] Such observations should not, however, lead Baptists into thinking that all that can be said on baptism has been said, for it is the case that while a great many British Baptists accept the use of sacramental terminology for baptism[144] this has not been accompanied by a truly sacramental theology or practice of baptism, which is still widely understood to be a personal testimony to conversion, an evangelistic opportunity which continues to be separated from conversion[145] and from entrance into church membership.

A comment, written over half a century ago by George Beasley-Murray, still holds true today for Baptists. He noted the irony of the present generation witnessing New Testament baptism being championed by paedobaptist theologians, while Baptists lapsed into a sub-theological view of the rite: 'If we are to take that opportunity, which Wheeler Robinson foresaw a generation ago would come, of leading the Body of Christ to the true view of Baptism, we shall do it only if we rise to a clearer apprehension of it than we appear to possess to-day.'[146]

---

142 *Report of the Special Committee Appointed by the Council on the Question of Union between Baptists, Congregationalists and Presbyterians* (London: Baptist Union, n.d. [1937]), p. 6, italics added.

143 On these see Cross, *Baptism, passim*, and Fowler, *More Than a Symbol, passim*.

144 Cross, *Baptism*, p. 345.

145 See Cross, '"One Baptism"', pp. 173-209, in which I argue for a return to the New Testament theology and practice of conversion-initiation. Cf. White, *Biblical Doctrine of Initiation*, 'The Recovery of the Bibical Doctrine', pp. 305-317

146 G.R. Beasley-Murray, 'The Sacraments', *The Fraternal* 70 (October, 1948), p. 5.

CHAPTER 10

'His soul-refreshing presence': The Lord's Supper in Calvinistic Baptist Thought and Experience in the 'Long' Eighteenth Century[1]

Michael A.G. Haykin

Ernest A. Payne, the doyen of English Baptist historical studies for much of the twentieth century, has maintained that from the beginning of Baptist testimony in the seventeenth century there has never been unanimity with respect to the nature of the Lord's Supper and that no one perspective can justly claim to have been the dominant tradition.[2] If Payne's statement has in view the entire history of Baptist witness in all of its breadth and depth, it may be regarded as roughly accurate. However, as soon as specific periods and eras are examined, the evidence demands that this statement be seriously qualified.

The late Michael J. Walker has shown, for instance, that when it comes to nineteenth-century English Baptist history, 'Zwinglianism emerges as the chief contender for a blanket description of Baptist attitudes to the Lord's Supper'.[3] The Swiss Reformer Huldreich Zwingli (1484–1531) regarded the bread and the wine as mainly signs of what God has accomplished through the death of Christ and the Supper therefore as chiefly a memorial. In recent discussions of Zwingli's perspective on the

1   Some of the material in this paper has already appeared in Michael A.G. Haykin, *One Heart and One Soul: John Sutcliff of Olney, His Friends and His Times* (Darlington: Evangelical Press, 1994), pp. 294-300. For permission to use this material in this format, I am grateful to Evangelical Press. By the 'long' eighteenth century, I have in view the period that stretches from the 1660s to the 1830s. For this as an accepted historical convention, see John Kent, 'Eighteenth century: an overview', in Adrian Hastings *et al.* (eds.), *The Oxford Companion to Christian Thought* (Oxford: Oxford University Press, 2000), p. 195.
2   E.A. Payne, *The Fellowship of Believers: Baptist Thought and Practice Yesterday and Today* (London: Carey Kingsgate Press, enlarged edn, 1952), p. 61.
3   M.J. Walker, *Baptists at the Table: The Theology of the Lord's Supper amongst English Baptists in the Nineteenth Century* (Didcot: Baptist Historical Society, 1992), p. 3.

Lord's Supper it is often maintained that Zwingli was not really a
Zwinglian, that is, he saw more in the Lord's Supper than simply a
memorial.[4] Be this as it may, a tradition did take its start from those
aspects of his thought that stressed primarily the memorial nature of the
Lord's Supper and that dominated Baptist thinking in the nineteenth
century.

In the previous two centuries, however, there had prevailed quite a
different view, namely, that associated with the name of John Calvin
(1509–64).[5] In Calvin's perspective on the nature of the Lord's Supper,
the bread and wine are signs and guarantees of a present reality. To the
one who eats the bread and drinks the wine with faith there is conveyed
what they symbolize, namely Christ. The channel, as it were, through
which Christ is conveyed to the believer is none other than the Holy
Spirit. The Spirit acts as a kind of link or bridge between believers and
the ascended Christ. Christ is received by believers in the Supper, 'not
because Christ inheres the elements, but because the Holy Spirit binds
believers' to him. But without faith, only the bare elements are received.[6]

'This soul-reviving cordial'[7]

Among the key texts that have to be examined for an accurate
understanding of seventeenth-century Calvinistic Baptist doctrine in
general is *The Second London Confession of Faith*. Well described as
'the most influential and important of all Baptist Confessions',[8] this
statement of faith was first issued in 1677 and then later re-issued by the

4   See Derek R. Moore-Crispin, '"The Real Absence": Ulrich Zwingli's View of the
Lord's Supper', in *Union and Communion, 1529–1979* (London: Westminster
Conference, 1979), pp. 22-34.

5   Cf. William Henry Brackney, *The Baptists* (New York: Greenwood Press, 1988),
pp. 62-63.

6   Victor A. Shepherd, *The Nature and Function of Faith in the Theology of John
Calvin* (Macon, GA: Mercer University Press, 1983), p. 220. Other helpful studies on
Calvin's theology of the Lord's Supper include B.A. Gerrish, 'The Lord's Supper in the
Reformed Confessions', *Theology Today* 13 (1966–1967), pp. 224-43; John D.
Nicholls, '"Union with Christ": John Calvin on the Lord's Supper', in *Union and
Communion*, pp. 35-54; John Yates, 'Role of the Holy Spirit in the Lord's Supper',
Churchman 105 (1991), pp. 355-56; B.A. Gerrish *Grace and Gratitude: The Eucharistic
Theology of John Calvin* (Minneapolis, MN: Fortress Press, 1993).

7   Benjamin Keach, *TROPOLOGIA: A Key to open Scripture Metaphors* (London:
William Otridge, 1778 [1681–82]), p.621. For a recent edition of this work, see
Benjamin Keach, *Preaching from the Types and Metaphors of the Bible* (Grand Rapids,
MI: Kregel Publications, 1972).

8   W.J. McGlothlin (ed.), *Baptist Confessions of Faith* (Philadelphia, PA:
American Baptist Publication Society, 1911), p. 219.

Calvinistic Baptist denomination in 1689 as a declaration of their
doctrinal position. Incorporating large portions of the Presbyterian
Westminster Confession of Faith (1646) and the Congregationalist *Savoy
Declaration* (1658), the *Second London Confession* was clearly drawn up
in such a way as to indicate that there were extensive areas of doctrinal
agreement between the Calvinistic Baptists and these other Calvinistic
bodies. The chapter in the *Confession* that deals with the Lord's Supper,
chapter 30, is an especially good example of the way in which the
Calvinistic Baptists sought to demonstrate their fundamental solidarity
with other communities in the Reformed tradition.

Following the *Westminster Confession* and the *Savoy Declaration*, the
Baptist *Confession* denounces as unbiblical the Roman Church's doctrine
of the mass, its practice of private masses, its refusal to allow any but a
priest to partake of the cup, and its dogma of transubstantiation.[9] Having
noted such errors regarding the Lord's Table, a right understanding of
this ordinance is then inculcated. 'Worthy receivers, outwardly partaking
of the visible Elements in this Ordinance, do then also inwardly by faith,
really and indeed, yet not carnally, and corporally, but spiritually receive,
and feed upon Christ crucified & all the benefits of his death: the Body
and Blood of Christ, being then not corporally, or carnally, but spiritually
present to the faith of Believers, in that Ordinance, as the Elements
themselves are to their outward senses.'[10] Close comparison of this
statement with the parallel statements in the *Westminster Confession* and
the *Savoy Declaration* reveals two main areas of difference. The two
earlier confessions use the term 'sacrament' to describe the Lord's
Supper, whereas in the *Second London Confession* this has been altered
to 'ordinance'.[11] Neither term is actually used in the New Testament, but
the term 'ordinance' appears to have been adopted to stress the divine
institution of the Lord's Supper.[12]

The second change is an omission. The omission is best seen by
displaying the relevant passages side by side with the omitted words in
italics.

---

9   *Second London Confession* 30.2-6, in McGlothlin (ed.), *Baptist Confessions*,
pp. 270-72.

10   *Second London Confession* 30.7, in McGlothlin (ed.), *Baptist Confessions*, p.
272.

11   It should be noted that both the *Westminster Confession* and the *Savoy
Declaration* do use the term 'ordinance' in later paragraphs to describe the Lord's Supper.

12   W. Morgan Patterson, 'The Lord's Supper in Baptist History', *Review and
Expositor* 66.1 (Winter, 1969), p. 26. Cf., however, Erroll Hulse's discussion of these
two terms in 'The Implications of Baptism', E. Hulse *et al.*, *Local Church Practice*
(Haywards Heath: Carey Publications, 1978), pp. 46-47.

Westminster Confession/ Savoy Declaration[13]	*Second London Confession*[14]
The body and blood of Christ being then not corporally or carnally, *in, with, or under the bread and wine; yet, as really,* but spiritually present to the faith of believers in that ordinance, as the elements themselves are to their outward senses.	The Body and Blood of Christ being then not corporally or carnally, but spiritually present to the faith of believers in that ordinance, as the elements themselves are to their outward senses.

The phrase which has been omitted in the *Second London Confession* was intended to reject the Lutheran explanation of how Christ is present in the Lord's Supper.[15] In the view of Martin Luther (1483–1546), Christ's body and blood are present 'in, with and under' the bread and the wine. Contrary to the Roman dogma of transubstantiation, the bread remains bread; yet, in some way, it also actually contains Christ's body after the prayer of consecration. Likewise the wine contains his blood after this prayer, though it remains wine. Why the *Second London Confession* omits this phrase is not at all clear. Possibly it was thought that Luther's view was not entertained by any in the Calvinistic Baptist community during the seventeenth century, and it was thus omitted so as to avoid encumbering the *Confession* with needless statements.

The differences between the three confessions, however, are minimal compared to what they have in common. All three affirm that as believers partake of the bread and the wine, Christ is 'spiritually present' to them and nourishing them. In other words, all three documents essentially maintain the perspective of John Calvin.[16] Moreover, similar remarks can be found in the writings of those who approved this confession in 1689.

---

13   *Westminster Confession of Faith* 29.7 (in S.W. Carruthers [ed.], *The Confession of Faith of the Assembly of Divines at Westminster* [Glasgow: Free Presbyterian Publications, 1978], pp. 22-23); *Savoy Declaration* 30.7 (*The Savoy Declaration of Faith and Order 1658* [London: Evangelical Press, 1971], p. 41). There is one slight difference between the *Westminster Confession* and the *Savoy Declaration*. Where the former reads 'in, with, or under the bread *and* wine', the latter has 'in, with, or under the bread *or* wine', italics added.

14   *Second London Confession* 30.7, in McGlothin (ed.), *Baptist Confessions*, p. 272.

15   For the broader Puritan rejection of Luther's position, see John F.H. New, *Anglican and Puritan: The Basis of Their Opposition, 1558–1640* (Stanford, CA: Stanford University Press, 1964), p. 60.

16   Those who drafted these confessions would have understood the phrase 'spiritually present' to mean 'present by means of the Holy Spirit'. See E. Brooks Holifield, *The Covenant Sealed: The Development of Puritan Sacramental Theology in Old and New England, 1570–1720* (New Haven, CT: Yale University Press, 1974), pp. 131-32. For some remarks on the biblical basis of this perspective as it is found in the

Hercules Collins (d. 1702), pastor of Wapping Baptist Church in London, could state in his *An Orthodox Catechism* (1680), a Baptist version of the *Heidelberg Catechism*, that in the Lord's Supper we are made 'verily Partakers of his Body and Blood through the working of the Holy Ghost'.[17] From Collins' perspective, although Christ's body is in heaven, we can have communion with the risen Christ in the Supper through the Spirit.

Another who approved the *Confession* was William Kiffin (1616–1701), pastor of Devonshire Square Baptist Church, London, from the 1640s till his death, and one who held 'a unique place of honour and influence' amongst the early English Calvinistic Baptists.[18] Like Collins, Kiffin could also assert that 'the [Lord's] Supper is a Spiritual participation of the Body and Blood of Christ by Faith'.[19] Along the same lines, Benjamin Keach (1640–1704), the leading apologist for Calvinistic Baptist views in the final decade of the seventeenth century, could state that in the Lord's Supper 'there is a mystical Conveyance or Communication of all Christ's blessed Merits to our souls through Faith'.[20]

Second London Confession, see David. S. Dockery, 'The Lord's Supper in the New Testament and in Baptist Worship', *Search* 19.1 (Fall, 1988), pp. 44-45.

17   Cited by E.P. Winter, 'Calvinist and Zwinglian Views of the Lord's Supper Among the Baptists of the Seventeenth Century', *Baptist Quarterly* 15.7 (July, 1954), p. 327. On Collins and his ministry, see Ernest F. Kevan, *London's Oldest Baptist Church, Wapping 1633–Walthamstow 1933* (London: Kingsgate Press, [1933]), pp. 38-50, 64-68; Michael Haykin, 'A cloud of witnesses: 1. The life and ministry of Hercules Collins (d.1702)', *Evangelical Times* 35.2 (February, 2001), p. 21.

18   Barrie R. White, 'William Kiffin—Baptist Pioneer and Citizen of London', *Baptist History and Heritage* 2.2 (July, 1967), p. 91. Over the years, White has produced a number of sterling pieces on Kiffin's life and states in the above-mentioned article that he was preparing a biography of Kiffin ('William Kiffin', p. 91, n.1). This biography has yet to appear. Recently, B.A. Ramsbottom has written a popular and extremely readable biography of Kiffin: *Stranger Than Fiction: The Life of William Kiffin* (Harpenden: Gospel Standard Trust Publications, 1989). For a review of this book, see Michael A.G. Haykin, 'The Life of William Kiffin', *Reformation Today* 119 (January–February, 1991), pp. 23-26.

19   W. Kiffin, *A Sober Discourse of Right to Church-Communion* (London, 1681), p. 25.

20   Keach, *TROPOLOGIA*, p. 623. For Keach's importance as a Baptist apologist, see Murdina D. MacDonald, 'London Calvinistic Baptists 1689–1727: Tensions Within a Dissenting Community under Toleration' (DPhil Thesis, Regent's Park College, University of Oxford, 1982), p. 77. The major source of information about Keach comes from his son-in-law, the early Baptist historian Thomas Crosby, *The History of the English Baptists* (4 vols; London, 1738–40), IV, pp. 268-314. For more recent accounts of his life, see especially James Barry Vaughn, 'Benjamin Keach', in Timothy George and David S. Dockery (eds.), *Baptist Theologians* (Nashville, TN: Broadman Press, 1990), pp. 49-76, and David A. Copeland, *Benjamin Keach and the Development of*

The first paragraph of chapter 30 of the *Second London Confession* also has a detailed discussion of the importance of the Lord's Supper for the Christian life. There it is stated that the 'Supper of the Lord Jesus, was instituted by him, the same night wherein he was betrayed, to be observed in his Churches unto the end of the world, for the perpetual remembrance, and shewing forth the sacrifice in his death, confirmation of the faith of believers in all the benefits therof, their spiritual nourishment, and growth in him; and to be a bond and pledge of their communion with him, and with each other'.[21] In this enumeration of the reasons for the Lord's Table, the *Second London Confession* follows closely both the *Westminster Confession* and the *Savoy Declaration*. Christ instituted the Lord's Supper for five reasons according to this paragraph. The Supper serves as a vivid reminder of and witness to the sacrificial death of Christ. Then, participation in the Lord's Supper enables believers to more firmly grasp all that Christ has done for them through his death on the cross. In this way the Lord's Supper is a means of spiritual nourishment and growth. Fourth, the Lord's Supper serves as a time when believers can re-commit themselves to Christ. Finally, the Lord's Supper affirms the indissoluble union that exists, on the one hand, between Christ and believers, and, on the other, between individual believers.

One cannot come away from reading these paragraphs on the Lord's Supper without the conviction that those who issued this *Confession* were deeply conscious of the vital importance of the Lord's Supper for the Christian life. It should also be noted that, in this hearty appreciation of the Lord's Supper, these early Calvinistic Baptists stood squarely in the mainstream of Puritan thought. The Puritans generally regarded the Supper as a vehicle that the Spirit employed as an efficacious means of grace for the believer, and thus they opposed the Zwinglian perspective on the Lord's Supper.[22] For the Puritans and for the seventeenth-century Calvinistic Baptists the Lord's Supper was indeed, in the words of Benjamin Keach, a 'Soul-reviving Cordial'.[23]

Baptist Traditions in Seventeenth-Century England (Lewiston/Queenston/Lampeter: Edwin Mellen Press, 2001). For a brief sketch of his life, see R.L. Greaves, 'Keach (or Keeche), Benjamin', in R.L. Greaves and Robert Zaller (eds.), *Biographical Dictionary of British Radicals in the Seventeenth Century* (3 vols; Brighton: Harvester Press, 1982–84), II, pp. 150-51.

21   McGlothlin (ed.), *Baptist Confessions*, p. 270.

22   For the Puritan view of the Lord's Table, see Geoffrey F. Nuttall, *The Holy Spirit in Puritan Faith and Experience* (Oxford: Basil Blackwell, 2nd edn, 1947), pp. 90-101; New, *Anglican and Puritan*, pp. 59-76; Holifield, *Covenant Sealed*, pp. 109-38; Hywel W. Roberts, '"The Cup of Blessing": Puritan and Separatist Sacramental Discourses', in *Union and Communion*, pp. 55-71.

23   Keach, *TROPOLOGIA*, p. 621.

'His soul-refreshing presence'[24]

A random sampling of eighteenth-century Calvinistic Baptist reflections on the Lord's Supper reveals strong evidence that the perspective on the nature of the Lord's Supper that we have already noted in the seventeenth century continued to prevail for much of the following century. Consider, for instance, the views of William Mitchel (1662–1705). Between 1688 and 1705, Mitchel evangelized many of the towns and villages throughout east Lancashire and the West Riding of Yorkshire with unremitting ardour from his base at Bacup in the Rossendale Valley. In so doing, he laid the foundations for a significant number of future Baptist churches. After his death, his co-worker and cousin, David Crosley (1669–1744), published Mitchel's *Jachin & Boaz* (1707), in which the latter set forth a summary of his doctrinal convictions.[25] Strongly Calvinistic, the treatise exercised considerable influence over the life and thinking of early Lancashire and Yorkshire Baptist congregations.

Now, in the section dealing with the Lord's Table, Mitchel declares that, in the Lord's Supper, Christ's 'Death and Blood is shewed forth; and the worthy receivers are, not after a corporal and carnal manner, but by the Spirit and Faith, made Partakers of his Body and Blood, with all his Benefits, to their spiritual Nourishment and Growth in Grace'.[26] Mitchel goes on to explicitly repudiate the Roman Catholic doctrine of the Mass, and aver, in the exact words of the *Second London Confession*, that the Supper is 'only a Memorial of that one Offering up of himself,

---

24   Anne Dutton, *Thoughts on the Lord's Supper, Relating to the Nature, Subjects, and right Partaking of this Solemn Ordinance* (London, 1748), p. 33. For a good overview of the high regard in which the Lord's Supper was viewed by late seventeenth- and early eighteenth-century Dissenters, see Margaret Spufford, 'The importance of the Lord's Supper to dissenters' in Margaret Spufford (ed.), *The World of Rural Dissenters, 1520–1725* (Cambridge: Cambridge University Press, 1995), pp. 86-102. See also Karen Smith, 'The Covenant Life of Some Eighteenth-Century Calvinistic Baptists in Hampshire and Wiltshire', in William H. Brackney, Paul S. Fiddes and John H.Y. Briggs (eds.), *Pilgrim Pathways: Essays in Baptist History in Honour of B.R. White* (Macon, GA: Mercer University Press, 1999), pp. 178-82.

25   For further details about Mitchel, see W.E. Blomfield, 'Yorkshire Baptist Churches in the 17th and 18th Centuries', in C.E. Shipley (ed.), *The Baptists of Yorkshire: Being the Centenary Memorial Volume of the Yorkshire Baptist Association* (London/Bradford: Kingsgate Press/Wm. Byles & Sons, 1912), pp. 73-88; Ian Sellers (ed.), *Our Heritage: The Baptists of Yorkshire, Lancashire and Cheshire* (Leeds: Yorkshire Baptist Association/Lancashire and Cheshire Baptist Association, 1987), pp. 10-11; B.A. Ramsbottom, *The Puritan Samson: The Life of David Crosley 1669–1744* (Harpenden: Gospel Standard Trust Publications, 1991).

26   'William Mitchill's "Jachin & Boaz"—1707', *Transactions of the Baptist Historical Society* 3 (1912–1913), p. 161.

by himself, upon the Cross, once for all'.[27] Mitchel was thus quite happy
to talk about the celebration of the Lord's Supper in memorialist terms,
but his earlier statement shows that he was unwilling to regard it solely as
an act of remembrance. Following Calvin and his Baptist forebears, he
asserts that the Lord's Supper is definitely a means of spiritual
nourishment and that at the Table believers, by the Spirit, do meet with
Christ.

Another Calvinistic perspective on the Supper is found in *Thoughts on
the Lord's Supper, Relating to the Nature, Subjects, and right Partaking
of this Solemn Ordinance* (1748) by Anne Dutton (1692–1765). A High
Calvinist and prolific author, Dutton corresponded with many of the
leading evangelical figures of the eighteenth century—Philip Doddridge
(1702–51), Howel Harris (1714–73), George Whitefield (1714–70), John
Wesley (1703–91)—encouraging them, giving them advice, and
sometimes chiding them. On one occasion Whitefield confessed that 'her
conversation is as weighty as her letters'. And Harris once wrote to her
that he was convinced that 'our Lord has entrusted you with a Talent of
writing for him'.[28]

Dutton devotes the first section of her sixty-page treatise on the Lord's
Supper to outlining its nature. In this section Dutton argues that the
Supper is, among other things, a 'communication'. 'As our Lord is
spiritually present in his own ordinance', she writes, 'so he therein and
thereby doth actually communicate, or give himself, his body broken,
and his blood shed, with all the benefits of his death, to the worthy
receivers'.[29] Here Dutton is affirming that Christ is indeed present at the
celebration of his Supper and makes it a means of grace for those who
partake of it with faith. As she states later on in this treatise: in the Lord's
Supper 'the King is pleas'd to sit with us, at his Table'.[30] In fact, so
highly does she prize this means of grace that she can state, with what
other Calvinistic Baptists of her era might describe as some exaggeration,
that the celebration of the Lord's Supper 'admits' believers 'into the

---

27   'William Mitchill's "Jachin & Boaz"—1707', p. 161. For a brief discussion of
Mitchel's views, see Winter, 'Calvinist and Zwinglian Views of the Lord's Supper', p.
327.
28   Cited Stephen J. Stein, 'A Note on Anne Dutton, Eighteenth-Century
Evangelical', *Church History* 44 (1975), pp. 488-89. Stein's article is the best recent
study of Dutton. For two other earlier studies which fail to do her justice, see J.C.
Whitebrook, 'The Life and Works of Mrs. Ann Dutton', *Transactions of the Baptist
Historical Society* 7 (1921), pp. 129-46; H. Wheeler Robinson, *The Life and Faith of the
Baptists* (London: The Kingsgate Press, 1946), pp. 50-56.
29   Dutton, *Thoughts on the Lord's Supper*, pp. 3-4.
30   Dutton, *Thoughts on the Lord's Supper*, p. 21.

nearest Approach to his glorious Self, that we can make in an Ordinance-Way on the Earth, on this Side the Presence of his Glory in Heaven'.[31]

The diary of Isaac Staveley, a young clerk and a member of Eagle Street Baptist Church, London, during the latter years of the pastorate of Andrew Gifford (1700–84), provides a third witness to this perspective on the nature of the Lord's Supper. Written daily from 24 February 1771 to 22 September of that year, the diary opens a window upon 'the interests, way of life, thoughts and activities which we may suppose to have applied to a considerable number of Baptists during the later part of the 18th century'.[32] The centre of Staveley's life was the Baptist fellowship to which he belonged and his chief delight the sermons of Gifford and visiting ministers, of which he wrote extensive summaries in his diary. Participation in the Lord's Supper was also an important event for Staveley. After the evening sermon on 3 March, the young clerk recorded that he and his fellow Baptists 'came around the table of our dear dying Lord to feast on the sacrifice of his offered body, show his death afresh, to claim and recognise our interest therein, to feast on the sacrifice of his offered body as happy members of the same family of faith and love'.[33]

Staveley probably was not aware of the fact that the phrase 'to feast on the sacrifice of his offered body', which he uses twice in this short extract, had its roots in the soil of Calvin's theology of the Lord's Supper. In his *magnum opus*, *The Institutes of the Christian Religion*, the Genevan Reformer had written that the Lord's Supper confirms 'for us the fact that the Lord's body was once for all so sacrificed for us that we may now feed upon it, and by feeding feel in ourselves the working of that unique sacrifice'.[34] Such language, both that of Staveley and of Calvin, is foreign to a mindset that regards the Lord's Table merely as a memorial.

Eighteenth-century Baptist hymnology is also a good guide to Calvinistic Baptist eucharistic piety. Some of the richest texts that display this piety can be found in *Hymns In Commemoration Of the Sufferings Of Our Blessed Saviour Jesus Christ, Compos'd For the Celebration of his Holy Supper* by Joseph Stennett I (1663–1713), the pastor of a Calvinistic Seventh-Day Baptist Church that met in Pinners' Hall,

---

31   Dutton, *Thoughts on the Lord's Supper*, p. 25.

32   L.G. Champion, 'Baptist Church Life in London, 1771', *Baptist Quarterly* 18.7 (July, 1960), p. 300.

33   Champion, 'Baptist Church Life in London, 1771', pp. 301-302.

34   J. Calvin, *Institutes of the Christian Religion* 4.17.1, in John T. McNeill (ed.), *Calvin: Institutes of the Christian Religion* (trans. Ford Lewis Battles; Philadelphia, PA: Westminster Press, 1960), II, p. 1361. I am indebted for this reference to Walker, *Baptists at the Table*, p. 9.

London.[35] Stennett can describe the church's celebration at the Table as a 'perpetual memorial' of Christ's death, a death that is to be commemorated.[36] And the bread and wine he calls 'proper Symbols' and 'Figures'.[37] Yet, Stennett can also say of these symbols:

> Thy Flesh is Meat indeed,
> Thy Blood the richest wine;
> How blest are they who often feed
> On this Repast of thine![38]

And he can urge his fellow believers:

> Sing *Hallelujah* to our King,
> Who nobly entertains
> His Friends with Bread of Life, and Wine
> That flow'd from all his Veins.
>
> His Body pierc'd with numerous Wounds,
> Did as a Victim bleed;
> That we might drink his sacred Blood,
> And on his Flesh might feed.[39]

Stennett does make it clear that the feeding involved at the Table is one of faith,[40] but this is realistic language utterly foreign to the later Zwinglian perspective.

Finally, two hymns of Benjamin Beddome (1717–95), pastor of the Baptist cause in Bourton-on-the-Water, Gloucestershire, for over fifty years, can be cited as evidence for what is clearly the most prevalent belief about the nature of the Lord's Supper among eighteenth-century

---

35   On Stennett, see Bryan W. Ball, *The Seventh-day Men: Sabbatarians and Sabbatarianism in England and Wales, 1600–1800* (Oxford: Clarendon Press, 1994), pp. 120-25; B.A. Ramsbottom, 'The Stennetts', in Michael A.G. Haykin (ed.), *British Particular Baptists, 1638–1910* (3 vols; Springfield, MO: Particular Baptist Press, 1998–2000), I, pp. 136-38.

36   J. Stennett, *Hymns In Commemoration Of the Sufferings Of Our Blessed Saviour Jesus Christ, Compos'd For the Celebration of his Holy Supper* (London: N. Cliff and D. Jackson, 1713), pp. iii, 4.

37   Stennett, *Hymns*, pp. 29 and 20.

38   Stennett, *Hymns*, p. 35.

39   Stennett, *Hymns*, p. 23.

40   Thus, in one of his hymns he can state (Stennett, *Hymns*, p. 19):
      'Here may our Faith still on Thee feed
      The only Food Divine;
      To Faith thy Flesh is Meat indeed,
      Thy Blood the Noblest wine.'

Baptists. Beddome was a prolific hymn-writer and many of his hymns were still in use at the beginning of the twentieth century.[41] Although Beddome wrote only a few hymns that specifically dealt with the subject of the Lord's Supper, they are fairly explicit as to his view of its nature. In one he prays,

> Oh for a glimmering sight
> Of my expiring Lord!
> Sure pledge of what yon worlds of light
> Will to the saints afford.

> ...May I behold him in the wine,
> And see him in the bread.[42]

In another, the invitation is given:

> Come then, my soul, partake,
> The banquet is divine:
> His body is the choicest food,
> His blood the richest wine.

> Ye hungry starving poor
> Join in the sweet repast;
> View Jesus in these symbols given,
> And his salvation taste.[43]

Beddome did not hold to a Roman Catholic or Lutheran view of the 'real presence'. The bread and the wine, he asserted, are 'symbols'. Nevertheless, he did expect the Lord's Supper to be a place where the 'sweet repast' of salvation is savoured and Christ himself seen. The 'realism' of the language in the first of these two stanzas especially bespeaks the conviction that Christ is present in the ordinance.

---

41   On Beddome and his ministry, see Thomas Brooks, *Pictures of the Past: The History of the Baptist Church, Bourton-on-the-Water* (London: Judd & Glass, 1861), pp. 21-66; William Boswell Lowther, 'Benjamin Beddome', *The Dictionary of National Biography* (London: Oxford University Press, 1963–64 [1885–86]), II, pp. 97-98; W.R. Stevenson and John Julian, 'Beddome, Benjamin', in John Julian (ed.), *A Dictionary of Hymnology* (London: John Murray, 1908), pp. 121-24; Michael A.G. Haykin, 'Benjamin Beddome (1717–1795)', in Haykin (ed.), *British Particular Baptists*, I, pp. 167-82. One recent hymnal, *Grace Hymns*, contains five of his hymns: *Grace Hymns* (London: Grace Publications Trust, 1975), nos. 288, 351, 470, 496 and 514.

42   *Hymns adapted to Public Worship, or Family Devotion* (London, 1818), no. 672.

43   *Hymns adapted to Public Worship*, no. 669.

A 'memorial of the absent Saviour'[44]

The view that the Lord's Supper is primarily or merely a memorial only began to become widespread in Calvinistic Baptist circles during the last quarter of the eighteenth century. Abraham Booth (1734–1806), the influential London Baptist leader, stated in 1778 that the Lord's Supper was designed to be 'a memorial of God's love to us and of Immanuel's death for us'.[45] Twenty or so years later, the Yorkshire Baptist leader John Fawcett (1740–1817), declared in the minor spiritual classic, *Christ Precious to those that Believe* (1799), that the

> Lord's Table...is wisely and graciously designed to revive in our minds the remembrance of him who gave his life a ransom for our souls. This institution is happily contrived to represent, in a lively and striking manner, the love, the sufferings, and the death of our blessed Redeemer, together with the benefits which we derive from them. When we unite in this solemnity, all the springs of pious affection should be let loose, while we contemplate the dying agonies of the Prince of Peace. We should feel the sweet meltings of godly sorrow, and the warmest exertions of gratitude, love and joy.[46]

A most striking acceptance of the Zwinglian perspective on the Lord's Supper is found in a tract written by John Sutcliff (1752–1814), the pastor of the Baptist church in Olney, Buckinghamshire, a close friend of William Carey (1761–1834) and one of the founders of the Baptist Missionary Society. Sutcliff also played a central part in bringing revival to the Calvinistic Baptists, far too many of whose churches were largely stagnant and somewhat moribund in the mid to late eighteenth century.[47]

Entitled *The Ordinance of the Lord's Supper considered* and written in 1803 as a circular letter for the Baptist churches belonging to the Northamptonshire Association, this text abounds in memorialist language and the Calvinist tradition hardly makes a showing. Sutcliff took for his guiding verse throughout this letter the statement of Christ in Luke 22.19: 'This do in remembrance of me'. Seen through the lens of this text, the Lord's Supper 'is a standing memorial of Christ. When you see the table spread and are about to partake of the bread and wine, think you hear Christ saying, "Remember me." Remember who he is... Again:

---

44   John Sutcliff, *On Obedience to Positive Institutions* (Circular Letter of the Northamptonshire Association, 1808), p. 6.

45   Cited by Payne, *Fellowship of Believers*, p. 65.

46   J. Fawcett, *Christ Precious to Those that Believe* (Minneapolis, MN: Klock & Klock Christian Publishers, 4th edn, 1979 [1839]), pp. 230-31.

47   For a study of Sutcliff's life and ministry, see Haykin, *One Heart and One Soul: John Sutcliff of Olney*.

Remember what he has done... Once more: Remember where he is, and what he is doing'.[48]

The fact that Christ instructed us to remember him, Sutcliff continued, clearly 'implies his absence'. Moreover, if a friend, who has gone away, left us with a small present prior to his departure and asked us to 'keep it as a memorial of his friendship', then, even if the present has 'little intrinsic worth, we set a high value on it, for his sake'. Gazing upon this present aids in the 'recollection of our absent friend'. So it is with the ordinance of the Lord's Supper. It is designed 'to draw our attention to, and assist our meditations upon an unseen Jesus'.[49]

This emphasis upon Christ's absence, and thus upon the Supper as a place primarily for mediation and remembrance, dominates Sutcliff's thinking about the Lord's Table. In a catechism that he had written and first published in 1783, the Lord's Supper is said to be 'a solemn eating of bread, and drinking of wine, in commemoration of the death of Christ'.[50] And in a later circular letter that he drew up in 1808, *On obedience to Positive Institutions*, he unequivocally stated that baptism and the Lord's Supper are 'memorials of the absent Saviour'. In baptism we behold Jesus dying for our offences, and rising again for our justification' and in the Supper 'we see his body broken, and his blood shed for the remission of sins'.[51]

Towards the end of *The Ordinance of the Lord's Supper considered* Sutcliff also emphasized that remembrance of what Christ has done for the believer should lead him or her to a renewed commitment to the Saviour.

> To him who gave his life a ransom, it becomes you to devote your lives. Bought with a price, remember you are not your own. Resolve therefore in the strength of divine grace, to glorify God in your body and in your spirit, which are God's. Each time you approach this sacred ordinance consecrate yourselves anew to the service, honour and glory of the blessed Jesus.[52]

The Lord's Table is thus a place of reconsecration.

Finally, Sutcliff stresses that participation in the Supper is a matter of obedience to the command of Christ; it is an open avowal of one's 'subjection to him as a Sovereign'. As such he warned his readers: 'Never treat the positive institutions of the Redeemer as matters of

---

48   J. Sutcliff, *The Ordinance of the Lord's Supper considered* (Circular Letter of the Northamptonshire Association; Dunstable, 1803), pp. 2 and 3.

49   Sutcliff, *Ordinance of the Lord's Supper*, pp. 3-4.

50   J. Sutcliff, *The First Principles of the Oracles of God* (rev. by Joseph Belcher; Whitchurch, Shropshire, 1820), p. 14.

51   Sutcliff, *Obedience to Positive Institutions*, p. 6.

52   Sutcliff, *Ordinance of the Lord's Supper*, p. 7.

indifferency'.[53] But, as Michael Walker has cogently shown with respect to the memorialist position in the later decades of the nineteenth century, such a position was generally accompanied by some degree of ambivalence with regard to the importance of the Table for the believer's Christian experience. Thus, although Sutcliff sought to guard against indifference about the Supper, his perspective on the nature of the Table would, in time, help to foster such an attitude.

For only two brief moments does an inkling of the Calvinistic perspective on the Supper shine through in this strongly memorialist interpretation of the Table. Near the beginning of the tract, it is stated that Christ 'still often visits in a spiritual manner his saints in attending divine ordinances'.[54] This statement reveals an awareness that the Supper is more than simply a memorial, but it remains undeveloped.

Then, in a section of the tract which deals with those who, for no apparent reason, occasionally absented themselves from the celebration of the Supper, Sutcliff asks a pointed question: 'Is not this the way to grieve the holy Spirit by which "you are sealed unto the day of redemption"? That Spirit whose delight it is on one hand, to glorify Jesus; and on the other, to see him glorified by you'.[55] It may be the case that here Sutcliff simply has in view the fact that failure to be present at the Table constitutes an act of disobedience, and it is for this reason alone that the Spirit is grieved. On the other hand, does this question betray a belief that the Supper is a means by which the Spirit provides God's people with spiritual nourishment? An earlier statement that Sutcliff had made in a sermon entitled *Jealousy for the Lord of Hosts illustrated* (1791) does seem to indicate that Sutcliff had not totally ruled out as inadmissible a Calvinistic view of the Lord's Supper. Speaking of the Spirit as 'the grand promise of the New Testament', he affirmed that his 'influences are the soul, the great animating soul of all religion. These withheld, divine ordinances are empty cisterns and spiritual graces are withering flowers'.[56] Without the Spirit the ordinances of baptism and the Lord's Supper are devoid of any spiritual value for those who receive them. With him present, though, they become vehicles of blessing. Apart from these spare hints of the richer, Calvinistic view of the Lord's Table, however, Sutcliff's tract on the Supper marks a definite setting aside of this view in favour of the leaner memorialist perspective. And it presaged

---

53   Sutcliff, *Ordinance of the Lord's Supper*, p. 9.
54   Sutcliff, *Ordinance of the Lord's Supper*, p.2.
55   Sutcliff, *Ordinance of the Lord's Supper*, p.6. See also Sutcliff, *Obedience to Positive Institutions*, pp. 8-9.
56   J. Sutcliff, *Jealousy for the Lord of Hosts illustrated* (London: W. Button, 1791), p. 12.

what would come to be the majority view among British Baptists in the nineteenth century.[57]

Walker has argued that nineteenth-century British Baptists became enamoured of the memorialist position from the 1830s onwards in reaction to a revival of English Roman Catholicism and the emergence of Tractarianism in the Church of England, a movement that was open to Roman Catholic theology and piety.[58] When Sutcliff wrote his letter on the Lord's Table, however, neither of these events was even on the horizon. Why then did he embrace the memorialist position? Payne has suggested that eighteenth-century rationalism with its 'suspicion of the mysterious and inexplicable' may have been a major factor in the advance of memorialist views among the Calvinistic Baptists.[59] It is indeed fascinating to observe that Joseph Priestly (1733–1804), one of the leading opponents of the mystery of the Trinity in this era, can speak of the Lord's Supper in terms identical to those of Sutcliff. The Supper, he maintained, was instituted by Christ 'in commemoration of his death'. It is intended to serve as 'a memorial' of Christ's death and as a means whereby Christians make a public declaration of their allegiance.[60]

Shaping Sutcliff's view of the Supper, however, was a major shift in British Baptist ecclesiology that was underway during the final decades of the eighteenth century.[61] This shift involved nothing less than the transformation of the Calvinistic Baptist denomination in the British Isles from an inward-looking, insular body primarily concerned with the preservation of its ecclesial experience and heritage into a body of churches that was outward-looking with hands outstretched to evangelical believers in other denominations and vitally concerned about the advance of Christ's kingdom throughout the earth. Earlier Calvinistic Baptist authors like Benjamin Keach had sought to orient their ecclesiology by

57   It is interesting to note that the two earliest articles on the Lord's Supper in the denominational paper of the Calvinistic Baptists, *The Baptist Magazine*, which began in 1809, are from a fully memorialist point of view. See T.W., 'On The Lord's Supper', *Baptist Magazine* 2 (1810), pp. 504-506; T[homas] G[riffin], 'On The Lord's Supper', *Baptist Magazine* 3 (1811), pp.361-68.

58   Walker, *Baptists at the Table*, pp. 84-120.

59   Payne, *Fellowship of Believers*, pp. 64-65. For a similar argument, see also Susan J. White, 'Christian Worship since the Reformation', in Paul F. Bradshaw and Lawrence A. Hoffman (eds.), *The Making of Jewish and Christian Worship* (Notre Dame: University of Notre Dame Press, 1991), pp. 194-95.

60   J. Priestley, *Institutes of Natural and Revealed Religion* (1772–1774), in J.T. Rutt (ed.), *The Theological and Miscellaneous Works of Joseph Priestley* (25 vols; London, 1817-31), II, pp.336-37.

61   On this shift, see Michael A.G. Haykin, 'The Baptist Identity: A View From the Eighteenth Century', *Evangelical Quarterly* 67 (1995), pp. 137-52. The material in this paragraph and the next one is taken from this article. For permission to use this material, I am grateful to the editor of this journal, I. Howard Marshall.

means of those marks traditionally identified by sixteenth- and seventeenth-century Reformed theology as vital for a genuine church of Christ. From the vantage-point of this theological tradition, a true church can be said to exist where God's Word is faithfully preached, the sacraments of baptism and the Lord's Supper are administered, and biblical discipline is exercised. Thus, Keach, in what is the earliest Calvinistic Baptist book primarily devoted to issues of ecclesial polity, *The Glory of a True Church and its Discipline display'd* (1697), maintained that a church of Christ is composed of 'Converted Persons', it is a community where 'the Word of God and Sacraments are duly administered, according to Christ's Institution', and it has 'regular and orderly Discipline'.[62]

While Sutcliff did not disagree with this way of reflecting on the identity of the church, it was the proclamation of the Word of God, in particular evangelistic preaching, which dominated his conception of the church's nature. For it was such preaching of the Word that enabled the kingdom of God to move forward and to occupy the realms of darkness and convert them into strongholds of light. This perspective is clearly seen in the reasons that Sutcliff delineates for the existence of local churches. In an address that Sutcliff gave in 1802 at the ordination of Thomas Morgan (1776–1857) to the pastoral oversight of Cannon Street Baptist Church, Birmingham, he specifically mentioned three: 'the honor of Christ, the advancement of his cause, and their [i.e. the members of the church] own profit'.[63] By 'the advancement of [Christ's] cause' Sutcliff has in mind uninhibited evangelism at home and abroad. Again, in *Qualifications for Church Fellowship*, a circular letter that Sutcliff drew up in 1800 for the Northamptonshire Association, he maintained that local churches have been designed for two principal reasons: the upbuilding of believers and 'the promotion of the cause of Christ at large'.[64] A statement of one of Sutcliff's closest friends, Andrew Fuller (1754–1815), encapsulates well the Olney Baptist's thinking in this regard: 'The *true* churches of Jesus Christ travail in birth for the salvation of men. They are the armies of the Lamb, the grand object of whose existence is to extend the Redeemer's kingdom'.[65]

---

62   B. Keach, *The Glory of a True Church, And its Discipline display'd* (London, 1697), pp. 6, iii.

63   J. Sutcliff, 'Introductory Discourse', in John Sutcliff, John Ryland and Andrew Fuller, *The Difficulties of the Christian ministry, and the Means of surmounting them; with the Obedience of Churches to their Pastors explained and enforced* (Birmingham, 1802), p. 3.

64   J. Sutcliff, *Qualifications for Church fellowship* (Clipstone, 1800), p. 3.

65   A. Fuller, *The Promise of the Spirit, the Grand Encouragement in Promoting the Gospel* (1810), in Andrew Gunton Fuller (ed.), *The Complete Works of the Rev. Andrew*

Such an evangelistic force tended to downplay the importance of the Lord's Supper, an ordinance that was expressly designed for believers and, in the minds of increasing numbers of Baptists in the nineteenth century, an aspect of the Christian life that played little part in the evangelization of the lost. In the words of W.R. Ward: 'to the devotees of the Missionary Church, bent on the business of conversion, ordinances which did not convert (as by the end of the eighteenth century they did not) were a matter of diminishing interest'.[66] The memorialist view of the nature of the Lord's Supper was well suited to the growing ambivalence regarding its importance.

Sutcliff had been privileged to have played a central role in the transformation referred to above, in which the Calvinistic Baptists moved from being a largely static denomination preoccupied with the preservation of its ecclesial heritage to one that was passionately involved in the missionary advance of Christ's kingdom throughout the earth. It was a movement in which much was gained, but also something lost. For Sutcliff's own theology of the Lord's Supper was indeed a poor alternative to the rich perspective of his seventeenth- and eighteenth-century Baptist forebears, who had come to the Table believing that there Christ would meet them and give them something deeply satisfying and precious.

Fuller (rev. by Joseph Belcher; 3 vols; Harrisonburg, VA: Sprinkle Publications, 1988 [1845]), III, p. 359, italics added.

66   W.R. Ward, 'The Evangelical Revival in Eighteenth-Century Britain', in Sheridan Gilley and W.J. Shiels (eds.), *A History of Religion in Britain: Practice and Belief from Pre-Roman Times to the Present* (Oxford: Basil Blackwell, 1994), p. 271. Nevertheless, it is fascinating to note that while this change in viewpoint about the nature of the Lord's Supper was taking place among the Calvinistic Baptists, many of their evangelical counterparts in the Church of England still held to a robust eucharistic spirituality. See Christopher J. Cocksworth, *Evangelical Eucharistic Thought in the Church of England* (Cambridge: Cambridge University Press, 1993), pp. 72-78.

CHAPTER 11

'To Feed Upon by Faith':
Nourishment from the Lord's Table

Curtis W. Freeman

In the bread of heaven discourse, Jesus declares: 'Those who eat my flesh and drink my blood have eternal life' (Jn 6.54). Although the sacramental allusion is unavoidable, the theological interpretations have proven intractable. Nevertheless, it is hard to miss the apparent linkage between salvation and communion with Christ as displayed in the Lord's Supper.[1] The Free Church tradition has been ever suspicious of sacramental theories that disconnect the operations of grace from personal faith.[2] This suspicion seems warranted by a close reading of the

---

1   R.E. Brown, *The Gospel According to John The Gospel According to John* (2 vols; Garden City, NJ: Doubleday, 1966), I, pp. 284-94, and *New Testament Essays* (Garden City: Doubleday, 1968), pp. 108-27, displays the eucharistic shape of Jn 6.51-58 which, he contends, is consistent with the rest of the discourse in the chapter and thus represents true Johannine thought. Brown's account makes implausible Bultmann's theory that a later redactor added these verses to correct the chapter and render it more acceptable to the Church. Cf. R. Bultmann, *The Gospel of John: A Commentary* (Philadelphia, PA: Westminster Press, 1971), pp. 218-37. Brown further suggests that it is not implausible to conceive that Jn 6.51-58 was spoken by Jesus in Capernaum. M.C. de Boer, *Johannine Perspectives on the Death of Jesus* (Kampen: Kok Pharos, 1996), pp. 226-28, following M.J.J. Menken, argues that Jn 6.51-58 is christological rather than eucharistic. Therefore, to eat Jesus' flesh and drink his blood means 'to believe in him as the one who dies for the life of the world'.

2   The term 'Free Church' does not enjoy a standard definition that may be simply assumed. I use the term to denote a wide array of Christian groups that share affinity, and in some cases continuity, with the Left Wing of the Protestant Reformation and that stand distinct from the broad Catholic and magisterial Protestant traditions. As I define it, the Free Church tradition possesses at least five traits that may be understood negatively and positively: 1. freedom of the church (non-hierarchical order/congregational polity); 2. freedom of worship (non-prescribed liturgy/spiritual worship); 3. freedom of confession (non-binding confession/gathered community); 4. freedom of conscience (non-coercive authority/soul liberty); and 5. freedom of religion (non-established religion/separation of church and state). Miroslav Volf, *After Our Likeness: The Church as the Image of the Trinity* (Grand Rapids, MI: Eerdmans, 1998),

passage as Jesus announces that faith is also a condition of eternal life (Jn 6.47).[3] Free Churches have not always been as conscientious about resisting the temptation to reduce these sacramental references to the experience of unmediated spiritual communion with Christ. They have, however, perceived that unchecked spiritualism ultimately eviscerates the Supper of its vitality and leaves little room for the visible working of God in history. Free Churches have thus often found themselves caught between the unhappy extremes of empty formalism and unceremonious spiritualism.

In the difficult years before the Act of Toleration in 1689, the General Baptists of England confessed that as Israel 'had the manna to nourish them in the wilderness to Canaan; so have we the sacraments, to nourish us in the church, and in our wilderness-condition'.[4] The Baptists understood that their survival in the spiritual desert depended on something other than a sacramentalist view that observed formal ritual but overlooked the necessity of personal faith and a spiritualist perspective that emphasized the importance of piety but neglected the practice of the Supper. For the General Baptists, the living Christ was true spiritual food to be received by faith, but this heavenly manna was to be gathered at God's Table. Thomas Grantham, one of their most important theological voices, maintained that at the Lord's Supper there is a real offer of the

---

pp. 9-25, exhibits the theological coherence of a Free Church ecclesiology within ecumenical dialogue. The notion that the Free Church is a distinct tradition owes much to F. Littell, who popularized it in his book *The Free Church* (Boston, MA: Starr King Press, 1957), pp. 1-2. Although dated, G. Westin, *The Free Church Through the Ages* (trans. V.A. Olson; Nashville, TN: Broadman Press, 1958), provides the best historical account of the Free Church. E.A. Payne attests to the Free Church in England in *Free Churchmen, Unrepentant and Repentant and Other Papers* (London: Carey Kingsgate Press, 1965); and S.A. Newman, *A Free Church Perspective* (Wake Forest, NC: Stevens Book Press, 1986), gives a helpful account from the context of the American South. Although he prefers the term 'Believers Church', Donald Durnbaugh's treatment is consistent with what is said above about the Free Church in *The Believers' Church* (Scottdale, PA: Herald Press, 1968), pp. 4-8.

3   Of course for those who with Brown read Jn 6.54 as sacramental, this statement is also understood eucharistically, just as those who with Menken interpret the previous passage as christologial take Jn 6.47 to be the same.

4   W. L. Lumpkin (ed.), *Baptist Confessions of Faith* (Valley Forge, PA: Judson Press, rev. edn, 1969), pp. 311-12.

flesh and blood of Christ 'to feed upon by faith'.[5] Grantham's wise leadership provided Baptists with a theological alternative to the external and objective sacramentalism exemplified in Catholicism and the internal and subjective spiritualism that they encountered among the Quakers. Grantham's 'spiritual sacramentarianism' combined practice and piety, objective and subjective, external and internal. Existential faith and orderly practice were both regarded as indispensable conditions for the reception of grace.

For Baptists now as then, sacramentalism is rarely a live option, in spite of the quite remarkable developments in Catholic eucharistic theology in the twentieth century.[6] Spiritualism, on the other hand, remains an ever-present challenge, especially in North American Free Churches which are haunted by the spirit of Ralph Waldo Emerson (1803–82), who resigned as minister when he was unsuccessful in getting his congregation to displace the observance of the Lord's Supper with a more pleasing mode of remembrance.[7] Emerson revered Jesus but refused to administer the Supper because it was not meaningful and he found it distasteful. Baptist spiritualists today are probably closer to their American forebear, John Leland (1754–1841), who explained that he had 'no complaint against communing with bread and wine'. Rather his reasons for refusing to administer the Supper were more utilitarian. He had seen many brought to faith through preaching, praying, singing, and baptizing but had known 'no instance that God evidently blessed the observance of

---

5   T. Grantham, *Christianismus Primitivus: Or, The Ancient Christian Religion* (London: Francis Smith, 1678), II.7.IV, p. 88.

6   E.g., H. de Lubac, *Corpus Mysticum: L'Eucharistie et l'Église Au Moyen Age* (Paris: Aubier, 1948), pp. 162-88, calls attention to the migration of terminology whereby language describing the eucharist as the mystical body was gradually applied to the Church. The result is that by the twelfth century the eucharist was understood as the true body (*corpus verum*) while the Church became known as the mystical body (*corpus mysticum*). See also S.K. Wood, *Spiritual Exegesis and the Church in the Theology of Henri De Lubac* (Grand Rapids, MI: Eerdmans, 1998), pp. 63-70; and H.U. von Balthasar, *The Theology of Henri de Lubac* (San Francisco, CA: Ignatius Press, 1991), pp. 36-37. The displacement of the eucharist from the social aspects of ecclesiology paved the way for individualistic eucharistic piety among Catholics in much the same way that the disjunction of the visible and invisible Church in Protestantism made possible the movement to private experiential religion. De Lubac's attention to the 'real' presence located in the Church and the 'spiritual' presence in the eucharist suggests new possibilities and contours for sacramental discussions between Catholics and Baptists. Interestingly de Lubac's work was not mentioned in the bilateral Catholic–Baptist discussions on grace. See W.E. Reiser, 'Roman Catholic Understanding of the Eucharist', *Southwestern Journal of Theology* 28.2 (Spring, 1986), pp. 85-89.

7   R.W. Emerson, 'The Lord's Supper', in *The Complete Writings of Ralph Waldo Emerson* (2 vols; New York: Wm. H. Wise and Company, 1929), II, pp. 1104-1105.

[communion] for the conversion of sinners'.[8] A minority of the congregation regarded his views as heretical, coming perilously close to the Quakers who nullified all external ordinances. After an unsuccessful attempt to remove him as pastor, the disgruntled group appealed for disciplinary action to the Shaftsbury Association who resolved 'to hold fellowship with no man or church, embracing or countenancing such sentiments'.[9]

Although there was enough residual sacramentarianism in early nineteenth-century New England among Unitarians and Baptists to steer through the swirling romantic and pragmatic currents, the same cannot be said for Free Churches today. The problem as with Leland perhaps stems more from neglect than contempt. Yet no matter the motive, the Lord's Supper has become an empty relic as the spirituality of unmediated and individualistic piety reigns supreme in American religion.[10] The Supper consequently suffers from an infrequent and enfeebled practice. As a result many Christians are spiritually starved. How can Free Churches reclaim a healthy sacramental faith and practice so that Christians receive spiritual nourishment from the Lord's Table, yet do so from the standpoint of personal faith? In what follows I will describe four trajectories that move us from the current state of affairs to a renewal of a higher and holier understanding of the Supper.

From Private Devotion to Common Prayer

For many Baptists, the Lord's Supper is a matter of individual piety. Although it is something shared with other Christians, the ordinance is widely regarded as a private experience of remembrance and a personal matter of obedience.[11] Baptist observance of the Supper, which was rooted in the rich soil of an earlier more communal life, gradually became democratized.[12] As personal autonomy became for many the

---

8   J. Leland, 'Letter to the Shaftsbury Association', in L.F. Green (ed.), *The Writings of the Late Elder John Leland* (New York: G.W. Wood; reprint edn, New York: Arno Press, 1969), pp. 59-60.

9   S. Wright, *History of the Shaftsbury Association, From 1800–1829* (New York: Macmillan, 1951), pp. 151-52; and Green (ed.), *Writings of the Late Elder John Leland*, p. 62.

10   R.N. Bellah, R. Madsen, W.M. Sullivan, A. Swidler and S. Tipton, *Habits of the Heart* (Berkeley, CA: University of California Press, updated edn, 1996), pp. 142-63.

11   J. Wayland, 'Lord's Supper, Administration', in *Encyclopedia of Southern Baptists* (2 vols; Nashville, TN: Broadman Press, 1958), II, pp. 794.

12   For the story of the democratization of American Christianity and Baptists in particular, see N.O. Hatch, *The Democratization of American Religion* (New Haven, CT: Yale University Press, 1989).

pre-eminent value to be preserved and served, the American ideal of the competent individual displaced the Baptist sense of the gathered community.[13] It goes too far to suggest, as Robert Bellah has, that Baptists are the source of this culture of autonomous individualism, although they have often embraced it as their own.[14] It is probably fair to say that if American Christianity became democratized in the nineteenth century by populist individualism, no denomination embodied this shift any more than did the Baptists.[15]

There is perhaps no better representative figure or harbinger of the Baptist future in America than the great prophet of religious individualism, John Leland. Whether he was opposing state supported churches, mission societies, slavery, hierarchical religion, or the Lord's Supper, the source of his protest was the conviction that nothing should come between God and the soul. Leland maintained the conviction of 'the inalienable right that each individual has, of worshipping his God according to the dictates of his conscience, without being prohibited, directed, or controlled therein by human law'.[16] As J. Bradley Creed concludes, Leland defended to the end 'an unvarnished, undiluted, individualism'.[17]

Insofar as it concerned individualism, Leland and the Baptists reflected the spirit of their age. Robert Handy nicely summarizes five factors that led to the Baptist embrace of 'the gospel of individualism' in America: 1.

---

13   B.A. Shain, *The Myth of American Individualism* (Princeton, NJ: Princeton University Press, 1994), displays how the communal and republican vision of the American founders was gradually replaced by the expressivist voices of individualism through a fundamental mis-reading of history, but more importantly he shows how mistaken revisionists invented the myth of individualism as the original ethos of America. R.C. Walton, *The Gathered Community* (London: Carey Press, 1946), pp. 110-17, agues that among English Baptists the decline of communal life and the rise of individualism was more a result of the disintegrating economic pressure of the Industrial Revolution. Both American and English Baptists were deeply influenced by the cultural forces of individualism.

14   R. Bellah, 'Is There a Common American Culture?', *Journal of the American Academy of Religion* 66.3 (Fall, 1998), p. 620. For my critique of Bellah, see C. Freeman, 'A New Perspective on Baptist Identity', *Perspectives in Religious Studies* 26.1 (Spring, 1999), pp. 60-65.

15   W. Hudson, 'Shifting Patterns of Church Order in the Twentieth Century', in W.S. Hudson (ed.), *Baptist Concepts of the Church* (Philadelphia, PA: Judson Press, 1959), p. 215, notes that this highly individualistic and democratized account of Baptist identity 'was derived from the general culture of the nineteenth century rather than from any serious study of the Bible'.

16   J. Leland, 'A Blow at the Root', in Greene (ed.), *Writings of the Late Elder John Leland*, p. 239.

17   J.B. Creed, 'John Leland, American Prophet of Religious Individualism' (PhD thesis, Southwestern Baptist Theological Seminary, 1986), p. 203.

Puritan experientialism, 2. Enlightenment individualism, 3. Romantic expressivism, 4. frontier independence, and 5. liberal economics.[18] This anthropological turn virtually identified the gospel of Christ with the gospel of individualism and eroded the earlier Baptist concerns about the gathered community and associational connectionalism. Carlyle Marney seems to have in mind this sort of stripped down version of Baptist individualism when he observed:

> We talked so long about the 'competency of the individual to deal with God' that we turned it into a stupid folk-lie: 'every tub should set on its own bottom'. This produced a mis-reading of the universal priesthood that virtually destroyed the notion of Church and fellowship.[19]

If individualism is the sickness of Baptist life, what is the antidote? The answer lies in part in the healing grace that comes by recovering a sense of the Lord's Supper as an act of common prayer.

In his magnificent study, *The Eucharistic Memorial*, Max Thurian examines the imagery of remembrance, which is connected to the Lord's Supper in two of the accounts (Lk. 22.19 and 1 Cor. 11.24-25).[20] What does it mean to observe the Supper as a memorial? The Greek word *anamnesis*, the Hebrew term *zakhar*, and their cognates in both Testaments do not suggest a mere subjective recollection. Rather they indicate an objective act 'to memorialize'. More specifically, Thurian identifies these words as part of the rich liturgical language of Israel and the Church that recalls God's past redemption as historically paradigmatic, God's present deliverance as sacramentally signified, and God's coming salvation as eschatologically anticipated. The association of these liturgical words (i.e., *anamnesis, zakhar*) in the biblical narrative displays that the Passover, the feast of unleavened bread, acts of charity, the lives of saints, and pre-eminently the Lord's Supper perform the enacted prayers of God's people. As remembering signs, they place before God the covenant promises and saving acts of the Exodus and the Cross and Resurrection. As common prayers, they invoke God's coming to complete the work of salvation already begun.

---

18   R.T. Handy, Foreword to W.S. Hudson, *Baptists in Transition: Individualism and Christian Responsibility* (Valley Forge, PA: Judson Press, 1979), pp. 9-13. See also C. Freeman, 'Can Baptist Theology Be Revisioned?', *Perspectives in Religious Studies* 24.3 (Fall, 1997), pp. 273-302, and 'E.Y. Mullins and the Siren Songs of Modernity', *Review and Expositor* 96.4 (Winter, 1999) pp. 23-42, on how individualism came to be identified as the Baptist orthodoxy.

19   C. Marney, 'Hail and Farewell!', being The Dickson Lectures at Myers Park Baptist Church, Charlotte, North Carolina, published as *Beyond Our Time and Place* (Charlotte, NC: Myers Park Baptist Church, 1974), p. 38.

20   M. Thurian, *The Eucharistic Memorial*, in *Ecumenical Studies in Worship*, nos. 7-8 (trans. J.G. Davies; 2 vols; Richmond, VA: John Knox Press, 1960-61).

Thurian summarizes: 'For Christians "to remember" or "to make remembrance" is the equivalent of "to pray", and, for God, it is the equivalent of "to hear, to grant, to show mercy".'[21] The *anamnesis* of the Supper understood in continuity with Old Testament covenant language does not call merely for God to bring to mind what has been promised but rather to act decisively so as to complete the work of salvation already begun by bringing in the kingdom through the *parousia*, thus affirming the eschatological horizon of the Supper as a covenant meal (1 Cor. 11.26).[22] The Lord's Supper, then, is not merely a matter of subjective recollection or private devotion. It is a liturgical action of common prayer that recalls as a memorial before the Father the unique sacrifice of the Son and invokes God's abiding and eschatological presence through the Spirit.

From Obligatory Ordinance to Life-Giving Practice

In the seventeenth century, Baptists used a variety of almost interchangeable terms to describe the Lord's Supper, frequently invoking the language of sacrament.[23] But the range of words narrowed during the years of rapid growth for Baptists in America as a result of eighteenth and nineteenth-century revivals. Growing gradually less comfortable with sacramental language that attempted to say something about God's activity in the Supper, they began to speak of it more as an 'act of obedience'.[24] Language that describes the Lord's Supper as an ordinance consequently became more dominant. Typical of the new theology were the Separate Baptists of North Carolina who declared that 'baptism and the Lord's Supper are ordinances of the Lord...to be continued by his church until his second coming'.[25]

There is nothing inherently incorrect about the nomenclature of 'ordinance' as commonly used by Baptists and other Christians.[26] Jesus Christ did institute the Supper to be performed regularly as a memorial

---

21   Thurian, *The Eucharistic Memorial*, II, p. 33.
22   J. Jeremias, *The Eucharistic Words of Jesus* (New York: Charles Scribners, 1966), pp. 249-55. See also G. Wainwright, *Eucharist and Eschatology* (New York: Oxford University Press, 1981), pp. 64-68.
23   Lumpkin (ed.), *Baptist Confessions of Faith*, pp. 311-13, 317 and 321. British and some American Baptists have continued to describe the Supper as a sacrament.
24   Lumpkin (ed.), *Baptist Confessions of Faith*, p. 396.
25   Lumpkin (ed.), *Baptist Confessions of Faith*, p. 358.
26   Although the most widely regarded Baptist confession of the seventeenth century, *The Second London Confession* (1677), does not exclude other more sacramental terminology about the Supper, it employs the language of ordinance. Lumpkin (ed.), *Baptist Confessions of Faith*, p. 290.

until his return. It is important, then, to understand the Supper in terms of Christian obedience and discipleship. One obvious advantage of describing the Lord's Supper as an ordinance was that it gave Baptists the greatest rhetorical traction to oppose what they considered to be the 'erroneous views' of 'transubstantiation' and 'consubstantiation'.[27] Baptist views did not agree with any position that affirmed a physical presence in the Lord's Supper, whether Catholic or Protestant. For this reason, following the well-worn paths of the Reformation debates on the sacraments rarely shed any light. This inherited theology of the elements pushed Baptists to say little about God's activity in the Supper, and so frequently stopped with the Lord's command. The Supper thus came to be viewed as a matter of personal and communal piety.

A deeper problem is that the term 'ordinance' carries a certain sense of arbitrariness—of something to be done simply because it has been commanded—often leading to blind obedience and legalism. The withering of an earlier and more vital sacramental theology in Baptist life is explicable given that the word 'ordinance' has all but fallen out of conventional discourse. The conspicuous exceptions are the specialized meanings in legal discourse and military jargon: 'In accordance with city ordinance 165B you are hereby directed to appear in municipal court' or 'The aircraft discharged its ordnance on the enemy target.' Neither of these connotations, however, commends the continued use of the language of ordinance in theology or liturgy. Is there an alternative to the stalemated language of the theology and liturgy of the elements?

Earlier generations of Christians in the Free Church tradition had another way of speaking about the Lord's Supper. In 1651 a group of English General Baptists issued a statement that they called *The Faith and Practise of Thirty Congregations* in which they declared that the Lord's Supper as a 'practise is left upon record as a memorial of [Christ's] suffering'.[28] Free Church folk found the language of practice congenial to their understanding of living according to the primitive and apostolic pattern. Early Baptists clearly saw themselves as a mean between formalist ritualism (Anglo–Catholicism) and formless pietism (Quakers and other expressions of spiritualism), but it was the latter that was the greatest temptation. Thomas Grantham rightly worried that

Where the form [i.e., practice] of Godliness is neglected, Religion will in a little time either vanish, or become an unknown conceit, every man being at liberty to follow (what he supposes to be) the motions of the Spirit of God, in which there is so great a probability of being mistaken as in nothing more; for Man's ignorance

---

27   E.g., A.H. Strong, *Systematic Theology* (3 vols; Philadelphia, PA: Judson Press, 1907–09), III, pp. 965-69.
28   Lumpkin (ed.), *Baptist Confessions of Faith*, p. 183.

Baptist Sacramentalism

being very great, and Satan very subtile, and the way of the Lord neglected, Men ly open to every fancy which pleaseth best.[29]

For Baptists like Grantham, the church is spiritually fed and renewed through gospel practices. Focusing on the theology of practice attends more closely to Christ's ordinance which was not 'Remember me' but rather '*Do this* in remembrance of me.'

Retrieving this language of practice from the storehouse of tradition is timely given the contemporary interest in practice for Christian theology.[30] In the widely acclaimed book *Practicing Our Faith*, Dorothy Bass describes practices as 'those shared activities that address fundamental human needs and that, woven together, form a way of life', or as she later states, 'a life-giving way of life'.[31] Alasdair MacIntyre offers a more precise definition:

> By a 'practice' I am going to mean any coherent and complex form of socially established cooperative human activity through which goods internal to that form of activity are realized in the course of trying to achieve those standards of excellence which are appropriate to, and partially definitive of, that form of activity, with the results that human powers to achieve excellence, and human conceptions of the ends and goods involved, are systematically extended.[32]

MacIntyre's definition qualifies the more compacted statement of Bass. First, to be understood as practices, shared activities must be complex, socially established, and cooperative. Second, addressing fundamental human need should be understood in terms of the standards of excellence that are evaluated in terms of goods that are internal to the practice. Third, the life-giving way of life suggests the advance of these shared conceptions of what is good. In the case of the Lord's Supper, the practice is commended to the church, not individual Christians, for performance. Moreover, the Supper is to be observed in service of a good that is internal to the practice (i.e., remembering Jesus), not for any utilitarian reasons (e.g., Leland's conversion of sinners). Finally, as a gospel practice the Lord's Supper advances the Christian life by offering a real way of knowing the abiding presence of Jesus Christ and nourishing the faith of believers.

Whereas theological discussions seeking a consensus ecclesial orthodoxy with regard to the relation of Christ's presence and the

---

29   Grantham, *Christianismus Primitivus*, II.I.1, p. 2.
30   E.g., M. Volf and D.C. Bass (eds.), *Practicing Theology* (Grand Rapids, MI: Eerdmans, 2002).
31   D.C. Bass (ed.), *Practicing Our Faith* (San Francisco, CA: Josey-Bass Publishers, 1997), pp. xi and 2.
32   A. MacIntyre, *After Virtue* (Notre Dame, IN: University of Notre Dame Press, 1981), p. 175.

elements of communion have fallen along predictable lines, theological conversations about eucharistic practice that aim toward ecumenical orthopraxy offer new signs of hope. These gestures toward a common understanding of Christian practice should not be taken as attempts to smother diversity of liturgical expression but rather are to be received as efforts to display for those who gather in his name what Jesus commended with his words 'Do this'.[33]

One such example is a constructive proposal by the Joint Liturgical Group in Great Britain entitled *Initiation and Eucharist*. The study suggests that the practice of the Supper at minimum conform to the fourfold action set forth in the biblical pattern: That Christ 'took...blessed (or gave thanks)...broke...gave'.[34] As an alternative I propose a threefold action. The first is *paradosis* that proclaims the gospel story of God's salvation beginning with Israel and its covenant, continuing through Jesus and his way, and culminating in the cross and resurrection. Here the move is to construe the actions of breaking bread within the drama of redemption so as to understand them as a performative practice. The second is *anamnesis* that recalls the words of institution either from one of the Gospels or Paul. Because Free Church worship tends to be more at home with the words of the Pauline account and sometimes from one the Synoptic Gospels but rarely in the Gospel of John, care should be taken to embrace the language of all three sources in liturgical *anamnesis*. The final feature is *paraclesis* (traditionally called *epiclesis*) invoking the presence of the Holy Spirit to unite in mystery this practice with the sacrifice of Christ so God's people may by faith receive nourishment from the Table. Remembering Jesus in the Supper is more than an obligatory ordinance. It is, by the power of the Holy Spirit, a life-giving practice.

From Real Absence to Real Presence

When it comes to the question of the God's omnipresence, Free Church faith and practice affirms that God can be present anywhere—almost anywhere, that is, except on the communion table. What is the basis of this curious doctrine of 'real absence'?[35] Several heterodox factors

---

off

33   See for instance E. Newman, 'The Lord's Supper', in the present volume.

34   N. Clark and R.C.D. Jasper (eds.), *Initiation and Eucharist* (London: SPCK, 1972), p. 24.

35   C.W. Dugmore, *The Mass and the English Reformers* (London: Macmillan, 1958), p. 160, attributes the doctrine of real absence to Zwingli. I will show in the next section that this reading of Zwingli is mistaken. Of course the doctrine of real absence is more common in populist rhetoric than in careful theology. For example, Baptist theologian W.T. Conner, *Christian Doctrine* (Nashville, TN: Broadman Press, 1937), p.

inform it. One is a deep-rooted tradition of *suspicious anti-magicalism* based on a medieval stereotype of the sacraments as automatic media of grace coupled with a *rigid tropism* inherited from the Radical Reformation that posits an absolute ontological barrier between the sign (e.g., bread and wine) and the signified (e.g., body and blood). A second is a *latent Gnosticism* that sharply distinguishes between spiritual and material and is thus skeptical of identifying the divine presence with anything in the physical (or biological) world often accompanied by an *incipient Marcionism* that separates the spheres of creation and redemption. A third source is a *persistent Donatism* that assumes effective grace depends entirely on the faithfulness of the administrative agent and a *individualistic spiritualism* that tends to reduce all things sacramental to merely outward signs of inward experience. More than anything, however, the Free Church reticence about the real presence in communion has to do with the default theological categories in the received tradition that rejected the transubstantiation teaching of Catholicism and the consubstantiation doctrine of Lutheranism and tended toward a memorial view that became associated with the Zwinglian tradition.

Yet not all within the Free Church tradition have held to a memorial understanding of the Supper. The early nineteenth century English Baptist, Robert Hall, railed against the inadequate consideration of the Lord's Table as 'a mere commemoration' and contended that the Supper is 'a spiritual participation of the blood...and body of the crucified Saviour...'[36] Hall continued that those who receive communion 'are actual partakers by faith of the body and blood of the Redeemer offered upon the Cross'.[37]

Hall was not alone in rejecting mere memorialism in quest of a more sacramental theology. None other than Charles Haddon Spurgeon joined his voice to the growing Free Church sacramental chorus:

It is the actual, though spiritual, coming of Christ which we so much desire. The Romish church says much about the real presence; meaning thereby, the corporeal presence of the Lord Jesus. The priest who celebrates mass tells us that he believes in the real presence, but we reply, 'Nay, you believe in knowing Christ after the flesh, and in that sense the only real presence is in heaven; but *we firmly believe in the real presence of Christ which is spiritual, and yet certain.*' By spiritual we do not mean unreal; in fact, the spiritual takes the lead in real-ness to spiritual men. *I*

287, explains that the symbolic view of the Lord's Supper 'does not deny the spiritual omnipresence of Christ, but it does deny that Christ is present in the bread and wine of the Supper any more than he is present in any other material substance'.

36   R. Hall, *Terms of Communion*, I.III, in O. Gregory (ed.), *The Works of Robert Hall* (6 vols; London: Henry G. Bohn, 1851-53), III, p. 45.

37   Hall, *Terms of Communion*, II.1, in *Works*, III, p. 62.

believe in the true and real presence of Jesus with His people: such presence has been real to my spirit. Lord Jesus, Thou Thyself hast visited me. As surely as the Lord Jesus came really as to His flesh to Bethlehem and Calvary, so surely does He come really by His Spirit to His people in the hours of their communion with Him. We are as conscious of that presence as of our own existence.[38]

While clearly rejecting a stereotypical understanding of physical presence, Spurgeon nevertheless affirmed the real presence of Christ in communion with language closer to Calvin than to Zwingli. By all accounts Spurgeon avoided any attempt to reduce Christ's presence to a mere commemoration. It is a real presence, albeit a spiritual one, that Spurgeon avowed.

In the seventeenth century, Thomas Grantham attempted to strike a balance between formalism and spiritualism. With other General Baptists of the seventeenth century he was more concerned about the spiritualism that left no room for God's acts in history or in the continuing incarnation of sacramental practice. Not only did the Quakers refuse to observe the Lord's Supper, they went so far as to deny that the blood of Christ was ever seen with human eyes. On the basis of Luke 24, Grantham argued that Christ was (and continues to be) known in the breaking of bread. Yet he was limited by a residual anti-Catholic prejudice and the fixed doctrinal categories of the seventeenth century. These left him with relatively little sacramental latitude and few theological resources to account for God's presence.[39]

What may be the most significant resources in the Free Church tradition lie in a time before the collective theological views on communion had hardened. John Rempel suggests that in the sixteenth century, before an unyielding memorial view became entrenched, there was greater freedom when it came to reflection on the sacraments. Rempel contends that the most notable and creative sacramental theologian of the Radical Reformers was Pilgram Marpeck, a leader among South German Anabaptists. His was not a theology of individual inwardness but of the gathered community. He did not offer a theology of the elements but a theology of the practices (or ceremonies). Rempel explains that the goal of Marpeck's theology of the sacraments 'was to create an apology for ceremonies as external works which were of one being with the inward reality they represented'.[40] Rempel further states that 'Marpeck was convinced that, unless the spiritual impulse were

38   C.H. Spurgeon, 'Mysterious Visits', in *Till He Come* (London: Passmore & Alabaster, 1894), p. 17, emphasis mine.

39   Grantham, *Christianismus Primitivus*, II.7.III.3, pp. 86-87.

40   J.D. Rempel, *The Lord's Supper in Anabaptism* (Scottdale, PA: Herald Press, 1993), p. 97.

balanced by the sacramental one, the gospel would be reduced to a biblical, ahistorical, nonchurchly, individualized piety.'[41]

Marpeck's sacramental reflection was deeply christological. He considered the ceremony of the Lord's Supper to be an extension of the incarnation 'that must remain...until the end of the world'.[42] Just as the inner spiritual reality of Christ is revealed in the outer material form of his humanity, so the same spiritual reality is revealed in the outward ceremony of bread and wine.[43] The result is an understanding of the Lord's Supper as a means of conveying the nourishing spiritual food of grace. Marpeck's sacramental theology was also richly trinitarian. In the Supper the Father works internally through the Spirit, and the Son acts externally through his humanity.[44] The efficacy of the ceremony thus depends on the simultaneous interaction of all three persons of the Trinity: Father, Son, and Spirit. Likewise only a trinitarian theology can adequately account for Christ's presence in the Supper. Regarding his physical presence, Christ is in heaven. Regarding his spiritual presence, he is on earth with the fellowship of the Holy Spirit who gather in his name and partake of the bread and wine in faith and love.[45] More such theological reflection is needed to facilitate a move from a theology of real absence to a theology of real presence.

From Mere Symbols to Powerful Signs

In characterizing Baptist views on the Lord's Supper, John Wayland states that 'some consider the elements mere symbols'.[46] One preacher is said to have regularly admonished his congregation upon observing the Supper: 'Now, remember that this doesn't mean anything. These are just symbols.' It is not an overstatement to say that a 'sub-Zwinglian' theology of the Lord's Supper has become entrenched as a *de facto* orthodoxy among Free Churches. British Baptist Robert Walton sounds the high note of those that would resist the theology of mere symbolism:

---

41   J.D. Rempel, 'Toward an Anabaptist Theology of the Lord's Supper', in Dale R. Stoffer (ed.), *The Lord's Supper: Believers Church Perspectives* (Scottdale, PA: Herald Press, 1997), p. 244.

42   P. Marpeck, *A Clear Refutation*, II, in William Klassen and Walter Klaassen (eds), *The Writings of Pilgram Marpeck* (Scottdale, PA: Herald Press, 1987), p. 47.

43   P. Marpeck, *A Clear and Useful Instruction*, in Klassen and Klaassen (eds), *Writings*, pp. 78-79.

44   P. Marpeck, *The Admonition of 1542*, in Klassen and Klaassen (eds), *Writings*, p. 195.

45   Marpeck, *Admonition of 1542*, pp. 288-91.

46   Wayland, 'Lord's Supper', II, p. 794.

> The Lord's Supper is also a means of grace and the Real Presence of Christ is manifested therein. To interpret the Supper as a memorial feast and no more is to reduce it to a method of auto-suggestion. Sacraments are not only symbols: they are also instruments. They tell the truth and convey the grace. They speak, but they speak with power.[47]

To be sure, Baptists affirm that the bread and wine of the Supper have symbolic significance, but as W.T. Conner noted, many Baptists do not believe that these symbols 'contain or convey [Christ's] spiritual presence'. Instead, he continued, 'they only...picture it so that it may be real to the mind and thus strengthen faith'.[48] Conner's younger colleague Franklin Segler, however, argued that such 'mere symbolism' is inadequate to convey the depth of meaning and significance of the Lord's Supper. Indeed, Segler asserted, 'None of the historic views— Roman Catholic, Lutheran, Calvinistic, Zwinglian—adequately delineates the dynamic, revelational aspects of baptism and the Lord's Supper as acts of worship.'[49] Clearly the *consensus fidelium* among Baptists and other Free Churches pertains more to what the Supper is *not* than to what it positively signifies. Therein lies the problem. Can Free Churches move from a theology of mere symbols to a rich and robust sense of powerful signs?

A shift in this direction requires a reassessment of Zwingli in context.[50] Misinterpretations of Zwingli as the champion of 'mere memorialism' have become standard. He is widely regarded by Catholic, Reformed and Free Church theologians to be a defender of all who observe the Supper with the understanding that the bread and wine are but reminders of salvation already achieved. According to the conventional account of Zwingli, the Supper enshrines no mystery; Christ is not really present; and the elements convey no grace. Ernest Payne quotes H. Wheeler Robinson's astute observation that 'there was a recognition of a mystical union with Christ in Zwingli's teaching which did not find full expression in his controversies'.[51]

Those within the Free Church tradition seeking to retrieve theological resources for a more powerful understanding of symbolism in the Lord's

---

47   Walton, *Gathered Community*, p. 170.

48   Conner, *Christian Doctrine*, p. 287.

49   F.M. Segler, *Christian Worship* (Nashville, TN: Broadman Press, 1967), pp. 138-39.

50   I allude here to my colleague David Steinmetz's careful treatments of Luther and Calvin. D.C. Steinmetz, *Luther in Context* (Bloomington, IN: Indiana University Press, 1986), and *Calvin in Context* (New York: Oxford University Press, 1995).

51   E.A. Payne, *The Fellowship of Believers: Baptist Thought and Practice Yesterday and Today* (London: Carey Kingsgate Press, enlarged edn, 1952), p. 60, citing H.W. Robinson, *The Life and Faith of the Baptists* (London: Methuen, 1927), p. 118 n. 1.

Supper may be surprised by what they find in a closer reading of
Zwingli.[52] H. Wayne Pipkin has concisely summarized the development
of Zwingli's sacramental theology.[53] In his early writings (1523), Zwingli
criticizes the abuses of the Mass, referring to the eucharist as 'a memorial
of the sacrifice', but not a sacrifice. The 'remembrance' which Zwingli
mentions is no mere intellectual exercise, but it is a reception by faith of
God's gift. Moreover, the posture of the 'memorial' is not merely
looking back, but rather of bringing the past into the present. Zwingli at
no point in these works denied the presence of Christ in the eucharist.[54]

During the period of the institutionalization of the reform (1524–25),
Zwingli developed a symbolic understanding of the Supper in dialogue
with radicals on one extreme pressing for changes along the lines of
Karlstadt and Catholics on the other end wanting to hold the line against
any changes. In April 1525 he began to interpret the eucharist as a
Passover meal. It is, he reasoned, the divinity of Christ, not the bodily
presence in the Lord's Supper, that saves. Faith then is required for the
spiritual meal, which is not merely the physical eating of the elements, but
is not unrelated to the Supper either. Those who receive the Lord's
Supper signify their membership in the church.[55]

In the polemical period (1526–29), Zwingli was concerned that Luther
was opening the door to a return to Catholicism. It is important to note
that even in these writings Zwingli did not exclude the presence of Christ
in the Supper, but preferred to speak of God's omnipresence through the
Spirit.[56]

In the final two years of his ministry (1530–31), Zwingli emerged as a
reformed–catholic theologian in which the bread and wine are
transformed, not in substance but in significance. He asserted: 'I do not
believe it is the Supper unless Christ is there.' Pipkin explains that what is
present is not the physical body of Christ, which is in heaven, but the
spiritual body of Christ made near by faith.[57]

There are as well creative contemporary theological reflections on the
sacraments from the standpoint of the Free Church that merit serious
attention. One is the work of British Baptist Paul Fiddes, who considers
sacramental acts within recent theological conversations about the Trinity.
Whereas an earlier generation of British Baptist theologians, following

52   Huldrych Zwingli, *Writings* (2 vols; trans. E.J. Furcha and H.W. Pipkin;
Allison Park, CA: Pickwick Publications, 1984).
53   I have not attempted to give a close reading of Zwingli's text but rather have
reported Pipkin's research in H.W. Pipkin, *Zwingli: The Positive Value of His
Eucharistic Writings* (Leeds: Yorkshire Baptist Association, 1986).
54   Pipkin, *Zwingli*, pp. 10-11.
55   Pipkin, *Zwingli*, pp. 11-16.
56   Pipkin, *Zwingli*, pp. 16-19.
57   Pipkin, *Zwingli*, pp. 19-22.

Neville Clark, proposed that Free Churches think about the sacraments as 'energised elements',[58] Fiddes moves beyond wondering whether or how ordinary substances can become divinely energized. He urges readers to think in more dynamic terms of movement and relationship. So conceived, the sacraments become 'doors into the dance of *perichoresis* in God'.[59] Fiddes borrows language from Paul Tillich's theory of symbols that open up new reality and participate in the reality to which they point.[60] Yet Fiddes seeks to push past Tillich's notion of symbol, which is static, and suggests a more dynamic interplay wherein the whole of each sacramental action (or practice?) enables participation in the life of the triune God.[61]

A second recent Free Church theology of the sacraments that deserves careful attention is James McClendon's systematic project. McClendon's account of the sacraments extends his earlier work that appropriated J.L. Austin's speech-act theory to display and justify religious convictions.[62] In his treatment of doctrinal theology, McClendon reflects on the sacramental practices of baptism, preaching and the Lord's Supper as 'remembering signs' that the church enacts as repeatable monuments of faith and through which God acts so as to make them effectual like God originally acted in the great historic signs of salvation.[63] The sacramental practices are not only symbols. They are signs of salvation that look backward and forward, declaring 'the present presence of Christ with his people'.[64] As signs, these practices are not merely symbolic—they are performative. The Lord's Supper conceived as a speech-act signifies forgiveness, solidarity, thanksgiving and the future.[65] McClendon's fresh reappraisal of the sacraments displays the conviction that the Lord is present and active both in the performance of these remembering signs and with the community that performs them.[66]

---

58   N. Clark, *An Approach to the Theology of the Sacraments* (Studies in Biblical Theology, 17; London: SCM Press, 1956), p. 75.

59   P.S. Fiddes, *Participating in God: A Pastoral Doctrine of the Trinity* (Louisville, KY: Westminster John Knox, 2000), p. 281.

60   P. Tillich, *Dynamics of Faith* (New York: Harper and Row, 1957), p. 42.

61   Fiddes, *Participating in God*, p. 282.

62   J.W. McClendon, Jr. and J.M. Smith, *Convictions* (Valley Forge, PA: Trinity Press, 1994); reprint of *Understanding Religious Convictions* (Notre Dame, IN: University of Notre Dame Press, 1975).

63   J.W. McClendon, Jr., *Systematic Theology: 2. Doctrine* (Nashville, TN: Abingdon Press, 1994), p.382.

64   McClendon, *Doctrine*, p. 386.

65   McClendon, *Doctrine*, p. 401.

66   C. Freeman, M. Broadway, B. Harvey, J. McClendon, E. Newman, P. Thompson, 'Re-Envisioning Baptist Identity', *Perspectives in Religious Studies* 24.3 (Fall, 1997), pp. 303-10. This appears as an appendix to C. Freeeman, 'Can Baptist Theology be Revisioned?'

A sub-Zwinglian orthodoxy will not satisfy the soul's hunger. Yet there is a way from a low view of the Lord's Supper as private devotion, obligatory ordinance, real absence and mere symbol to a rich communion worship of common prayer, life-giving practice, real presence and powerful signs. All God's people are invited to be nourished at the Lord's Table where is spread a spiritual meal of divine grace to feed upon by faith. Come and dine!

CHAPTER 12

The Lord's Supper: Might Baptists Accept a Theory of Real Presence?

Elizabeth Newman

This essay will address two concerns. The first has to do with how Baptists understand themselves as Church. The second has to do with how all Christians might understand the real presence of the Lord's Supper in a way that unites them together as the body of Christ in our day. These are both, of course, large topics and this essay only aims to put forth for consideration a few theological points, but ones I hope move us closer to living faithfully as the body of Christ for the world.

Reconsidering the Lord's Supper in our Current Context

Why revisit this topic? Or why try to breach the differences in understanding the Lord's Supper that have for so long separated Protestants and Catholics? Volumes have been written from various perspectives about the Lord's Supper; and much helpful historical and liturgical ground has been covered. Yet it still remains the case that *in practice* Christians are not united at the Lord's Table. As Gerhard Lohfink rightly reminds us, the differences that divide the Church and 'the condition of Christianity at the present time is nothing like a colorful field in which wheat is growing and poppies and cornflowers are blooming; it is rather like a broken mirror that distorts the image of Christ'. Lohfink adds that one of 'the deepest wounds' of the Church is its disunity.[1] Certainly one of the signs of this disunity is the inability of Christians to worship fully together around the table. Such disunity is a 'counter-mark' of the Church; it is a sign of what the Church is not or should not be. We should remember, of course, that unity is not the same as uniformity. As the Trinity itself indicates, unity is not mere sameness.

---

1   G. Lohfink, *Does God Need the Church? Toward a Theology of the People of God* (Collegeville, MN: Liturgical Press, 1999), p. 298.

Difference is crucial for the unity of mutual love that is the Trinity. So too the Church needs, or we could even say requires, difference in order to manifest the kind of unity displayed in the Godhead: a unity of mutual love, a unity of different 'persons'. But to fail to seek unity—to be satisfied with only difference ('different churches believe and worship in different ways')—is to accept as normal a deep wound on the body of Christ.

Secondly, and perhaps as important as the unity of the Church, the Lord's Supper, faithfully practiced, enables the Church more truthfully to understand the world and its contemporary cultural situation. In the current North American culture, 'religion' has increasingly come to mean something an *individual* believes, something that pertains to one's *private* life, or even more, something that deals only with the '*spiritual*' realm. As William Cavanaugh puts it: 'The modern construction of religion interiorizes it, and makes religion only a motivating force on bodily political and economic practices. The modern Church thus splits the body from the soul and purchases freedom of religion by handing the body over to the State.'[2] When 'religion' is so interiorized, the Church, in the final analysis, becomes unnecessary for salvation.[3]

Contemporary Baptists have at times accepted this ideology. Baptists along the theological spectrum often accord priority to the interpreting individual. While conservatives emphasize the importance of a 'literal' reading of scripture and those more theologically moderate a wider range of various interpretations, both groups give priority to the *individual* over the *community*. For those who support an inerrantist reading of scripture, it is as if the individual stands 'naked' before the word of God, which is self-interpreting. The Church herself does not interpret or produce God's word in the lives of her members, such as in the formation of saints. Rather the individual before the static and literal word takes priority over the Church. While other Baptists might not share this inerrantist interpretation, they nonetheless share the belief that discipleship begins with faith, which is understood as a *private* matter between God and the

---

2   W.T. Cavanaugh, '"A Fire Strong Enough to Consume the House:" The Wars of Religion and the Rise of the State,' *Modern Theology* 11.4 (October, 1995), p. 415.

3   Cavanaugh, '"A Fire Strong Enough to Consume the House:"', p. 405, argues that when the Church is only understood to govern the 'interior souls' of its members, the bodies of its members are quite easily handed over to secular authorities. Christians then give their loyalty to the unity of the State, 'to which the unity of religion must give way'. In discussing the political influence of Thomas Hobbes, Cavanaugh notes that Hobbes made two crucial and deadly moves: 'to make individuals adhere to the sovereign instead of to one another, and to deny the international character of the Church', p.415. Under the influence of this ideology, Christians have been trained to be willing to kill other members of Christ's own body in the name of their country, or in the name of democracy or freedom.

individual. This individualized faith then gives birth to the Church.[4] One of the key purposes of the Church, so understood, is to protect the freedom of the individual who has a right and responsibility to private interpretation of scripture.[5]

I contend that the Lord's Supper, rightly understood, forms a people who can resist both a claustrophobic and privatized understanding of 'religion' and a domesticated understanding of the Church. By resisting this interiorizing of 'religion', the faithful practice of the Lord's Supper can make the marks of the Church (one, holy, catholic and apostolic) more visible. Those working in ecumenical dialogue remind us that 'the Church as a "mystery" is required to strive to become more "catholic" and "reformed" in the sense of always moving to reclaim its...reality, and to overcome any contradictory attitude to the Christian Gospel'. [6] As this statement indicates, reforms which enable the Church to become more truly herself will because of that fact also enable the Church to

---

4   Walter Shurden, 'The Baptist Identity and the Baptist *Manifesto*', *Perspectives in Religious Studies* 25.4 (Winter, 1998), p. 331. Shurden, p. 324, emphasizes in his essay that 'Baptist life historically affirms the theme of "the individual in community"'. The Church is a 'valid hermeneutical "core value" for understanding the Baptist identity as long as one does not ignore the role of the individual', p. 325. Elsewhere Shurden notes that 'what gives dynamism to the life of a Baptist church is the deep and devoted personal faith that *individuals bring* to the corporate body of believers... A personal faith born in the privacy of the human heart is of the essence of both Baptist and Protestant life', p. 329, my emphasis. While Shurden does stress the importance of 'community', he nonetheless gives *precedence* to the private faith of the individual. While I do not wish to deny the importance of personal faith, I do take issue with priority given to the individual over the community. At a philosophical level, we can say, as does W.H. Poteat, *A Philosophical Daybook: Post-Critical Investigations* (Columbia, MO: University of Missouri, 1990), p. 90, that we learn the grammar of 'I' and 'you' together. 'Individuation and socialization are not two different processes, but two faces of the same process. As we do not, strictly, could not, learn the meaning of *I* without, in the same instant, learning the meaning of not-*I*, of *you, they, we*; so our individuation can only proceed simultaneously with our socialization. They emerge together—as the pronouns *I* and *you* and our power to use them emerge...' Stated theologically, individuals do not gain faith and then bring this to the life of the Church. Rather through the community called Church, we learn in the self-same moment what it means to have 'personal faith' *and* to be members of Christ's body.

5   Such an understanding of Church mirrors, in many ways, the modern understanding of the nation-state. That is, just as the citizen has rights which are ultimately legislated and controlled by the nation-state, so also the Church is primarily understood as that which protects and defends the 'rights' of its members: the right to freedom of conscience, the right to worship as one pleases, the right to believe what one wants. Even though Baptists strongly support the separation of church and state, the concept of Church in many instances echoes the ideology of the nation-state.

6   J. Gros, FSC, E. McManus and A. Riggs, *Introduction to Ecumenism* (New York: Paulist Press, 1998), p. 245.

become more truly catholic. In this spirit, then, I wish to give an account of the Lord's Supper that is both catholic and reformed, one not contradictory to the Christian gospel. This sounds like a grand claim or goal, but I do not intend it to be such. I only wish to suggest an account of the Lord's Supper that might allow Baptists (and perhaps some others) to embrace a more sacramental understanding of this practice, and thus, I would also say, a more catholic understanding.

What do I mean by catholic at this point? Etymologically speaking, catholic means 'toward wholeness' and, as is well known, we can also interpret 'catholic' to mean 'universal'. A more sacramental understanding of the Lord's Supper would bring Baptists closer to the Church universal, in the sense that Catholic, Orthodox and many Protestants (for example, United Methodists, Episcopalians, Lutherans) regard this practice as a sacrament. Yet the fact that 'everybody believes this' is not in itself a sufficient reason to accept it. Baptists have a rich heritage of often going against what the majority believes, and at times, rightly so. I think we ought, however, at least consider that 'what is properly required for the unity of the whole of Christ's Church must by that very fact be God's will for his Church'.[7] We hasten to ask whether understanding the Lord's Supper as a sacrament is *properly* required for the unity of the whole Church. Certainly, for Baptists and other Reformers what is 'proper' must be consistent with the Christian gospel. Consistency with the gospel and the building of unity in the Church would both be powerful reasons that Baptists might move in the direction I am indicating. We may also ask, however, in light of Roman Catholic belief and practice, is transubstantiation (the belief that the substance of bread and wine become the body and blood of Christ while the accidents remain the same) as a theory of real presence *fully catholic*, since only the Roman Catholic Church has embraced this position? Might there be a 'reformed' way to understand the Lord's Supper as sacrament that is at the same time catholic and consistent with God's word?

Protestant Concerns

Before moving to an alternative understanding of the Lord's Supper and real presence, let us review the typical modern Baptist understanding of the Lord's Supper as a *memorial*. In terms of practice, this has meant that during the Lord's Supper, the participants remember the words of Jesus, and recall his gathering with the disciples. Worshippers break bread in remembrance of Christ's broken body and drink the cup in

---

7   As quoted from the 1986 Nairobi Report of the World Methodist Council and the Roman Catholic Church, in Gros, McManus, and Riggs, *Introduction*, p. 205.

remembrance of Christ's shed blood. The bread and wine remain symbolic (a 'mere symbol'). The primary meaning of the practice remains located in the individual believer, as he or she recalls the words of Jesus. Hence the words of the hymn, 'In Remembrance': 'Don't look above, look in your hearts, yes, in your hearts for God.'[8] Baptist worship re-enacts this individualized focus as participants remained seated in their pews during the Lord's Supper and, even more, eat bread already separated and drink from individual cups. As a symbol and a memorial, the practice of the Lord's Supper stands at one remove from the actual reality it represents. So understood, the Lord's Supper is often only as 'real' as one can believe it to be.[9]

What theological concerns have generated this particular understanding of the Lord's Supper as mere symbol? We can begin with the testimony of Christians who in fact gave their lives for this understanding. In his essay on Radical Reformation spirituality, Timothy George recounts the final words of some Anabaptist martyrs, many of whom were cross-examined about their eucharistic theology. In one such case, when West Friesland, an Anabaptist, was asked, 'What do you hold concerning the sacrament?', he famously replied, 'I know nothing of your baked God.'[10] In another case, a widow, who was eventually strangled to death, was asked on the morning of her execution about the sacramental efficacy of the Supper. She replied, 'What God would you give me? One that is perishable and is sold for a farthing?' She also told a priest who had celebrated Mass that he had crucified God anew.[11] We see clearly reflected in these words the conviction, shared by many Protestants, that

8   As quoted by P.E. Thompson, 'Re-envisioning Baptist Identity: Historical, Theological, and Liturgical Analysis', *Perspectives in Religious Studies* 27.3 (Fall, 2000), p. 295, who notes that this is the first communion hymn in the 1991 Southern Baptist hymnal.

9   S. Ozment more broadly situates this particular theological understanding in the teaching of Scotus and Ockham. Under their influence 'traditional religious institutions ceased to be the essential link in a great hierarchical chain of being. Their uniqueness lay rather in the contingent divine act; from an infinite number of theoretical possibilities God had chosen them to be the instruments of his will in time. For those who subscribed to such a point of view *the things of religion were only as real as one could believe them to be*'. Quoted in D.N. Power, *The Sacrifice We Offer: The Tridentine Dogma and Its Reinterpretation* (New York: Crossroad, 1987), p. 35, emphasis mine.

10   Quoted in T. George, 'The Spirituality of the Radical Reformation', in Jill Raitt (ed.) *Christian Spirituality: High Middle Ages and Reformation* (New York: Crossroad, 1989), p. 348.

11   George, 'Spirituality', p. 348, importantly notes that the minimalist theology of these Anabaptists did not translate into a casual observance of the Lord's Supper. Instead, they saw it as a 'vivid reenactment of Jesus' last meal and an anticipation of the eschatological messianic banquet', p. 348. George notes that although the Lord's Supper was interpreted as a memorial it 'was not without soteriological implications'.

the sacrifice of Jesus occurred only *once*. Centuries later John Wesley, among others, would vehemently condemn those who believed Jesus' sacrifice was repeated.[12] From this perspective, the bread and wine cannot *really* be the body and blood of Christ because Christ gave his body once for all, a key theological rationale given by those who rejected the doctrine of real presence.

Additionally many Reformers reacted against what they took to be a 'magical' understanding of the sacraments or of God's grace. The Christian could do certain things (or pay a certain amount of money) and 'automatically' or 'mechanically' receive God's grace. Such a mentality, as Luther clearly saw, easily underwrote the conviction that believers could *earn* God's grace.[13] This understanding easily led to a form of Pelagianism, that is, the belief that humans had the power to effect or control their own salvation. We could even say that these Reformers saw early on a problem with a common view of the Church still with us today, that is the market exchange model of the Church in which you earn or pay for certain services to meet your needs.[14]

---

12   Article XX, from the United Methodist *Articles of Religion* which John Wesley adapted from the Church of England, states: 'The offering of Christ, once made, is that perfect redemption, propitiation, and satisfaction for all the sins of the whole world, both original and actual; and there is none other satisfaction for sin but that alone. Wherefore the sacrifice of masses, in the which it is commonly said that the priest doth offer Christ for the quick and the dead, to have remission of pain or guilt, is a blasphemous fable and dangerous deceit', in *The Book of Discipline* (Nashville, TN: United Methodist Publishing House, 1988), p. 66. The early Baptists also clearly rejected transubstantiation and the sacrifice of the Mass while affirming real presence in a manner found in other Reformed bodies. See W.L. Lumpkin (ed.), *Baptist Confessions of Faith* (Valley Forge, PA: Judson Press, rev. edn, 1969), pp. 291-93, and 321-22.

13   This concern, that grace could be automatically earned, also shaped Protestant reaction to the theology of sacraments efficacious *ex opere operato*. In this the objective efficacy of the sacrament, not independent of the faith of the recipient or the presider, is stressed. *Ex opere operato* sacramentalism does entail the conviction that participants must place no obstacle. For further discussion, see Power, *Sacrifice*, pp. 27-49 and 56-58.

14   Power, *Sacrifice*, pp. 37-38, recounts the interesting example of Damoiselle Guillemette Coquillant, a wealthy woman of the sixteenth century who made the following provisions in her will: On the day of death, she ordered the celebration of thirty low masses. For her burial day, she wanted three more masses, and for the Sunday following her death, she requested three solemn masses and thirty low masses. A year later, she asked for a daily low mass and on her anniversary, one high and thirty low requiem masses. Power notes further that this, and other wills, rather than giving us a 'picture of the people dominated by the clergy', give us instead 'an impression of clergy at the beck and call of the people' and laid open the way for turning the mass and other religious services into *business* transactions.

In summary, at least two key concerns have underwritten an emphasis on the symbolic nature of the Lord's Supper: the conviction that Jesus' sacrifice on the cross occurred once and for all; and a suspicion of the sacraments as underwriting a Pelagian soteriology and a mechanical understanding of God's grace. These are, of course, legitimate theological concerns and thus call for a fuller and deeper account of firstly, the relation between the Lord's Supper and sacrifice and, secondly, a way of understanding God's grace specific to the Lord's Supper, but one that is not 'automatic' or 'magical' in its reception.

While acknowledging the legitimacy of these concerns, we need also to be aware of some of the weaknesses to which this position exposed its practitioners. As *symbol* became emphasized over against *reality*, the practice itself atrophied. Thus many Baptists and other communions came to celebrate the Lord's Supper only a few times each year.[15] More significantly, a kind of 'divorce' occurred in Baptist theology between creation and salvation, with the effect of moving salvation more and more inward and associating it almost entirely with the inner self or soul. Hence the idea that God was in Christ reconciling the *whole world*, or all of creation, to God's own self often faded into the background. Philip Thompson describes how over the past two centuries 'Baptists have devalued physical creation vis-a-vis the spiritual as the means by, through, and in which God works.'[16] As an example, Thompson refers to Elias Johnson who claimed that the Holy Spirit relates to the individual rather than the church, and believed that is was 'unfitting' to speak of the Holy Spirit operating through physical matter.[17] This 'scorning of creation', as Thompson names it, and the corresponding elevation of the spiritual, drove de-sacramentalization in Baptist life. It also quite naturally had the effect of de-emphasizing the necessity of the church. As Thompson puts it: 'Since God was no longer thought to work through the physical, the physical gathering of Christians was bound to lose place in Baptist thought.'[18]

The location of salvation in the individual, the emphasis of the Lord's Supper as symbolic rather than real and the elevation of the spiritual over the physical are convictions that reinforce each another. That is, if the Lord's Supper is only a symbol, then there is a sense in which God is not *really* present at the table; it is as if an empty chair were placed at the table to symbolize Jesus' original presence with his disciples. Jesus is spiritually present and communes with one's spirit, but not one's body or the gathered body of Christ.

---

15   See B. Harvey, 'The Eucharistic Idiom of the Gospel', *Pro Ecclesia* 9.3 (Summer, 2000), pp. 297-99.

16   Thompson, 'Re-envisioning', p. 296.

17   Thompson, 'Re-envisioning', p. 96.

18   Thompson, 'Re-envisioning', pp. 296-97.

While we can acknowledge as legitimate some of the theological concerns motivating our Protestant forebears, we can also see some of the theological inadequacies in this understanding of the Lord's Supper. To relate to Jesus as a Spirit who communes with our inner spiritual selves is more gnostic than it is Christian. Such gnosticism is especially apparent in the conviction that creation and therefore the church are not *necessary* for salvation. The ancient Gnostics, we can recall, had a *dark view* of creation, saw our place in terms of limitation, and sought 'to remove from God (or from the God beyond God) the stigma of Creation'.[19]

Baptists do indeed have other vital practices enabling them to avoid such gnosticism. They would *not* be inclined to say, for example, that the preaching of the word or the singing of hymns are 'just symbolic' or mere symbols. Why is this? There is the realization that when the word is rightly preached, and when the community gathers to sing hymns, God is really present in the spoken and heard word. Baptists in America often cite the biblical promise that 'where two or three are gathered together in my name, there am I in the midst of them' (Mt. 18.20). This emphasis on the reality of the spoken and heard word, on preaching as an event, provides some space for Baptists and others to move beyond the real versus symbol dichotomy that has so haunted our understanding of the Lord's Supper.

Literal versus Figurative: Real versus Symbol

There is an analogy between the Baptist battle over the Bible, as the literal word of God, and the debate over the eucharist as real or symbol. The comparison rests primarily in a particular understanding of literal or real. A 'literal' interpretation of scripture rests on a particular understanding of truth. Namely, truth is that which corresponds to an already present reality. For example, the creation stories are thought to record the exact way that the world came to be in terms of time, order and objective facts. If this is not the case, then, so this position maintains, the word of God must not be true.

Analogously, the bread and wine in communion are thought to be either the real body and blood of Jesus or, if not, then 'just a symbol'. Typically, Catholic teaching has invoked the theory of transubstantiation to show that the substance of the bread and wine really changes, even though the appearance or accidents of the bread and wine remain the same. To respond to transubstantiation that communion or the Lord's

---

19   P.J. Lee, *Against the Protestant Gnostics* (New York: Oxford University Press, 1987), p. 9.

Supper is 'just a symbol', parallels the response often given to the word of God as literally true, that is, this is 'just a story' or 'just a myth'.

What are we to make of this analogy? In both cases, a particular understanding of 'real' or 'literal' is invoked, one that positions the real over against the merely symbolic or accidental. In both cases, too, I would say that the meanings of 'real' or 'true' are narrowly circumscribed. For those who read the Bible literally, 'true' is that which is factually true, where facts are understood to be empirical and scientific judgments about reality. For communion, the 'real' is identified exclusively with the substance or essence of the thing, while the accidents are seen as superfluous to reality. As one definition puts it: 'Transubstantiation differs from every other substantial conversion in this, that only the substance is converted into another—the accidents remaining the same—just as would be the case if wood were miraculously converted into iron, the substance of the iron remaining hidden under the external appearance of the wood.'[20] Because of this over-identification of the presence of Christ with the substance of bread and wine, Protestant reformers at times associated transubstantiation with a sort of magical view, as it focuses attention on the change of an invisible essence.[21]

While I would agree that the Catholic doctrine of transubstantiation has set up 'a mighty bulwark around the dogma of the Real Presence',[22] I believe we also need to ask if there might be a more adequate way today to talk about 'real presence', one that is not so bound by an Aristotelian metaphysics? Is there an alternative way to conceive of reality that moves beyond the real/symbol or literal/figurative dichotomy? Even more, are there alternative resources, derived from the Bible itself that might give us another understanding of reality? In responding to these questions, it is helpful to remember that while real presence is a dogma in the Catholic Church, transubstantiation is not, a conviction that provides a tremendous ecumenical opening.[23]

---

20   'The Real Presence of Christ in the Eucharist', in *The Catholic Encyclopedia* (http://www.newadvent.org/cathen/O5573a.htm#1).

21   As is well known, the incantation 'hocus pocus' originally came from *Hoc est corpus meum*, 'This is my body.'

22   'The Real Presence'.

23   Transubstantiation as a belief *de fide* is usually traced back to the Fourth Lateran Council. G. Macy, 'The Dogma of Transubstantiation in the Middle Ages', *Journal of Ecclesiastical History* 45.1 (January, 1994), pp. 11-41, points out, however, that thirteenth-century theologians did not understand this council as defining transubstantiation, 'nor did they feel compelled to condemn other possible theories that explained the real presence'. Macy suggests that theologians at the time of the Fourth Lateran Council 'fell roughly into three camps with regard to the eucharistic change'. Some believed the bread and wine remained present with the body and blood; others that the body and blood alone remained while the substance of the bread and wine were

Philosopher William H. Poteat points us in a helpful direction in re-
evaluating the real/symbol dichotomy in his 'post-critical' philosophical
and theological reflections which he begins:

> When (how) does the distinction between direct and figurative language arise? Does
> not this very question about the force of different forms of discourse presuppose
> that the only (principal) function of language is the making of assertions? Or can
> we issue commands, offer prayers, utter blessings, solemnize marriages
> *figuratively*... But what would the *figurative* solemnization of a marriage be? And
> could this not occur even with all the felicities (Austin) provided? Would we say,
> 'Well, all of the participants didn't mean what they said and did *literally*.' Or is it
> rather that they *really, fully, unequivocally* meant what they said and did, only
> differently?[24]

Poteat goes on to note that 'our ingenuous and acritical confidence' in
the integrity of the world we live in is 'in jeopardy to the supposition that
only that is *really* real which is the *terminus ad quem*, quite narrowly
construed, of a name-relation theory of meaning'.[25] At this point, Poteat
is challenging a particular limited understanding of 'reality', one formed
by a name-relation theory of meaning in which the meaning of a word
derives from the object for which it stands.[26] Inasmuch as
transubstantiation locates 'reality' in the essence of an object, 'the
substance of the bread and wine departs in order to make room for the
Body and Blood of Christ',[27] it relies upon a name-relation theory of
meaning. In its more truncated interpretation, as David Power notes,
transubstantiation can lead to an objectified understanding of grace,
where grace becomes a commodity and 'even God is fitted into an order

---

'annihilated'; and a third group believed that the substance of the bread and wine was
changed into the substance of the body and blood at the words of consecration. Macy
labels these positions 'coexistence', 'substitution' and 'transmutation', respectively.
While transubstantiation came to be equated with 'transmutation', Macy argues that in
medieval times transubstantiation was used to mean any of the three positions mentioned
above. Macy relies upon and analyzes the work of H. Jorissen, *Die Entfaltung der
Transsubstantiationslehre bis zum Beginn der Hochscholastik* (Münster:
Aschendorffsche Verlagsbuchhandlung, 1965), and J. McCue, 'The doctrine of
transubstantiation from Berengar through the Council of Trent', *Harvard Theological
Review* 61.3 (July, 1968), pp. 385-430.
  24   Poteat, *Philosophical Daybook*, p. 7.
  25   Poteat, *Philosophical Daybook*, p. 8.
  26   Elsewhere Poteat argues that our modern conception of reality owes a
tremendous experiential dept to the *written* word, as opposed to the *spoken* word.
Following theorists such as Walter Ong, Poteat notes how the spoken word is dynamic,
contextual and communal in a way that the written word seems not to be, at an
experiential level. Writing easily leads us to identify the meaning of a word with a static
object.
  27   'The Real Presence of Christ'.

of production'.[28] Nicholas Lash further describes how this essentialist understanding of the body of Christ affected medieval practice: 'It can hardly be denied that what the church was doing (and she teaches as much by what she does as by what she says) in the late medieval period was calculated to give the impression that the mass was something "done" by the celebrant and "watched" by the church at large.'[29]

Like Poteat, H.A. Nielsen provides philosophical discussion of the limits of this essentialist understanding of reality which identifies the real with the essence of a thing in his essay 'A Meeting of Minds on Water'. Nielsen refers to Wittgenstein's observation that when school children are taught that water *consists* of hydrogen and oxygen, and that anyone who doesn't understand this is stupid, 'the most important questions are concealed'. We could say in a similar fashion that when the 'real presence' is equated only with the substance of bread and wine, then the more important questions about the reality of Christ's body are concealed. Nielsen argues that water understood as two parts hydrogen and one part oxygen is an *abstraction* in which 'the ways of its own that water possesses do not figure very centrally'. While we can certainly acknowledge that the scientific account of water is helpful for certain purposes, when taken as the essence of water, it restricts and limits our understanding. As Nielsen notes: 'Here someone might say, "But don't you see, in science we try to get at *water itself*?" No, I don't see. What on earth do you mean by "water itself"? When is it *not* itself? What keeps us from seeing that water in existence has as many manifestations as a symphony orchestra has sounds?'[30]

Poteat likewise suggests that name-relation theory of meaning *abstracts* reality from our 'mindbodily existence'.[31] The real is taken to be that which is *'objective'*, regardless of our *personal* status. Poteat notes, however, that the question 'is this real'? is 'not the question—or not often the question—"Does this have any standing in the (real?) world"? but "What kind of standing does it have?" "If we take X to be our paradigm for the real, is *this* real?"'[32] The paradigm for the real that has all too often shaped the debates about the real/symbol understanding of

---

28   D.N. Power, 'Sacrament: Event Eventing', in M. Downey and R. Fragomeni (eds), *A Promise of Presence* (Washington DC: Pastoral Press, 1992), p. 280.

29   N. Lash, *His Presence in the World: A Study of Eucharistic Worship and Theology* (Dayton, OH: Pflaum, 1968), p. 128.

30   H.A. Nielsen, 'A Meeting of Minds on Water', in Richard H. Bell (ed.), *The Grammar of the Heart* (San Francisco, CA: Harper & Row, 1988), pp. 77-78.

31   Poteat uses the phrase 'mindbody' to indicate the intimate and necessary unity of our 'minds' and our 'bodies'.

32   Poteat, *Philosophical Daybook*, p. 13.

the Lord's Supper has been one that has abstracted us from our 'mindbody' existence.[33]

The shift Poteat desires to make is from a disincarnate view of reality to a 'mindbody' or incarnate understanding of real. Thus, 'real' is not primarily that which matches an object, but rather that which flows from the way we rely upon and inhabit the world. From this perspective, scientific or mathematical speech is no more direct or truth-bearing than other forms of speech, but rather a way of communicating a different kind of reality. Two plus two equals four and the solemnization of a marriage are both direct, unequivocal and real. Poteat, who was influenced by Wittgenstein, would agree with Wittgenstein's claim that the meaning of a word derives from its use. While this might be taken as supporting a kind of relativism, Wittgenstein rather intended to point to the 'form of life' that makes our speech possible. Thus he refers time and again to language that is not 'on holiday' but that which arises from the 'rough ground' of our daily and communal lives.

If we interpret Poteat and Wittgenstein theologically, we could say that both of them share an *incarnate* understanding of language and of the 'real'. Certainly, a truly biblical understanding of reality would flow from a sense and acknowledgement of our human and incarnate status in the world. Thus, a biblical understanding of reality (and language) *opposes* the Enlightenment myth that embraces a vision of our status as godlike in relation to the subject of our knowledge. In addition to an incarnate understanding of reality, I would say that both Poteat and Wittgenstein share a 'Hebraic' worldview inasmuch as they rely upon the conviction that speech creates or brings into being the world in which we dwell. This can be called 'Hebraic' because it flows from and is shaped by an understanding of the speech-creating powers of Yahweh. In the Old Testament, God speaks and the world comes into being. And it is God's faithfulness to his own words that sustains the reality that he calls forth. For example, God's covenant with Abraham remains or is 'stabilized' by God's faithfulness to his own words. This understanding of the intimate connection between our words or our deeds so informed the Hebraic way of life that, as is well known, the Hebrew word for 'word,' *dabhar*, can mean both word and deed. For the ancient Hebrew, the opposite of word/deed could not be a mere word (or mere symbol as that which opposes the real). As Thorleif Boman notes, 'An Israelite

---

33   While Aquinas' understanding of transubstantiation is beyond the scope of this paper, I think we can occasionally see traces of an abstract, unmediated understanding of reality in Aquinas' thought. As D.N. Power, *The Eucharistic Mystery* (New York: Crossroad, 1992), pp. 208-40, notes, a Dionysian negation shapes in part his understanding of the eucharist and contemplation, inasmuch as his analysis rests on a 'need to rise above the senses and the direct perceptions of reason in order to commune with God'.

would not therefore be able to burst out contemptuously like Hamlet, "Words, words, words!" for "word" is in itself not only sound and breath but a *reality*.' For the Hebrews, what opposed *dabhar* was not mere word, but 'a counterfeit word, an empty word, or a lying word which did not possess the inner strength and truth for accomplishment or accomplished something evil'.[34] For the Hebraic world, then, words are deeds and an unfaithful word is an unfaithful or counterfeit deed, both of which usher in certain realities.

To summarize, a theological understanding of language and speech, one reflected in the Baptist understanding of the preached word, needs to be grounded in a sense of our incarnate (rather than abstract) status in the world as God's creatures. Even more, as creatures in God's image, we could say that our words, like God's, are deeds. They create the worlds in which we dwell just as God's Word (Logos) created and continues to create the world (as Goethe interpreted it, 'in the beginning was the deed'). What then is the relation, we might ask, between our words/deeds and God's? Since God's words/deeds are prior, our own words/deeds remain in the position of response, a fact exemplified throughout the Bible. For example, God invites Abraham to say 'yes' to the covenant and a *new reality* comes into being; or God waits for Mary to say 'yes' to his invitation to bear God's Son, the beginning of a *new creation*. In these and other stories, a certain world is brought into being through the mutual and faithful words of the participants.

The Real Presence of Christ at the Table

It is this biblical understanding of our words as deeds that, I believe, provides a helpful way beyond the real versus mere symbol impasse of understanding the Lord's Supper. Such an understanding provides 'space' to perceive of Christ as really present when the community gathers to celebrate the Lord's Supper, but in a way that does not abstractly locate that reality in the substance of the bread and wine.[35] To

---

34   T. Boman, *Hebrew Thought Compared with Greek* (Philadelphia, PA: Westminster, 1960), p. 66, emphasis mine. I incorporate Boman's insight but develop it in a somewhat different direction in E. Newman, 'Rethinking the Eucharist: Towards a Unity of Word and Deed', *Ecumenical Review* 45.4 (October, 1993), pp. 454-62.

35   The Catholic Church, too, it is important to note, objects to this 'localizing' of Christ's presence. As Lash, *His Presence*, pp. 149-50, notes: 'If we conceive of the presence of Christ in the consecrated bread and wine as a "local" presence, we tear the heart out of sacramental theology. The teaching authority in the Church has always reacted sharply against the idea that Christ is locally present, but it can hardly be denied that many Catholics, not helped by the sort of distorted popular theology to which I referred earlier, do conceive of his presence in this way. The story of the child who, after

elaborate, we might turn to the celebration of a marriage. At a marriage ceremony when the minister says, 'I pronounce you husband and wife', the status of the individuals change. That they are no longer single but are now married means that the words were in fact deeds that brought about a new reality. So also we can say that the words 'this is my body' and 'this is my blood', pronounced in the communal context of the celebration of the Lord's Supper, are deeds, bringing about a new reality.

How might we describe this new reality that is ushered into being? Orthodox theologian Alexander Schmemann begins his own reflections on the eucharist with Feuerbach's maxim, 'Man is what he eats.'[36] While materialist philosopher Feuerbach most certainly meant something different, Schmemann uses this saying to challenge the opposition between the spiritual and the material. We could apply it as well to the dichotomy between 'the real' and 'symbol'. For our purposes, we could state Feuerbach's maxim a bit differently: 'We are what *we receive*', or 'we become what we receive'. What is it we receive into our very being that forms us to become who we are? Worship, oriented around the word and table, is structured so that we receive, through the power of the Holy Spirit, God's word and deed, manifest most fully in the person of Christ. In receiving this gift, that is, Christ, the Church herself becomes Christ's own body for the world. The new reality that is brought into being and extended is the body of Christ, as those gathered around word and table are incorporated into Christ's body. Thus, the *real presence* of God is manifest in the gathered community as it becomes the body of Christ for the world. This occurs through our faithful response to the real presence of God in word and table. Paul Lehmann notes that 'just as there is no Messiah without his people, so there is no real presence of Jesus in history without or apart from the true people of God which as the work of the Holy Spirit is always at the same time a spiritual and visible reality'.[37] The Church, in other words, is that which mediates Christ for the world. But this can only happen because God mediates himself through the life, death and resurrection of Christ. And Christ mediates and gives himself to the gathered community through water, word and table. In the words of the hymn, the Church is Christ's '*new creation* by water and by word'. We could add 'by bread and wine'.

This is not to deny, of course, the sinfulness of the Church. To say that the Church is the 'body of Christ' does not mean that it can be equated

---

making her first communion, refused an ice-cream because she "did not want to make Jesus' head cold" is only a bizarre illustration of a wide-spread malaise.' The difficulty, as I see it, with the theory of transubstantiation is that it does tend to form the 'lay faithful' in such a way that they perceive of Christ's presence as localized.

36   A. Schmemann, *For the Life of the World* (New York: St Vladimir's Seminary, 1963), p. 11.

37   Quoted in Lee, *Protestant Gnostics*, p. 160.

with Christ. As Lohfink notes, 'It can never equal his word, his life, his purity, his absolute surrender, and his complete unity with the will of the Father in this world. It is not only the Church of the saints, but always the Church of sinners as well. And yet it is *the real and physical presence of Christ* in history.'[38]

Such an understanding of the Church and the Lord's Supper, which relies upon God's words/deeds and upon God's own reliance upon creation to make known his desires for the Church and the world, stands in opposition to a Gnosticism which sees creation and the Church as unnecessary for salvation. As noted above, for the Gnostic, salvation has to do with the individual and his or her internal spiritual life. Hence, Gnostic salvation relies upon a certain kind of gnosis which *bypasses* creation.[39] For the Gnostic, knowledge of God, a 'cognitive apprehension of the divine', requires a 'turning away from this world'.[40] For the early Christian Gnostic, 'the world and history were *merely symbols* referring to an inner process'.[41] We noted above that such an understanding seems indeed to have shaped modern Baptist conceptions of the Lord's Supper, as it is often interpreted as a mere symbol of a meaning generated by the believing subject.

Lee notes, however, that orthodox Christianity stands in stark contrast to a world-denying and solitary Gnostic view of salvation. Above all, both the Old and New Testaments describe salvation as resting finally in the mighty acts of God in history, in, we could say, God's *words* and *deeds* in space and time. Furthermore, scripture testifies to the fact that what a 'person can know about God is not self-discoverable. It can be learned only through the community because only through the community has He revealed Himself.'[42] As Lohfink emphasizes, God needs a concrete people to make known his desires for the world. 'The reign of God requires a space in which to exercise its sovereignty; it needs a people.'[43]

The shift from Gnosticism to Christianity means that the meaning of the Lord's Supper is not simply located in the internal spiritual life of the individual. Rather as a communal celebration, the Lord's Supper draws its 'meaning', or better stated, is part of the economy of salvation because of God's superabundant gift to creation *through* creation. Hence, we cannot separate creation and redemption as God acts in

---

38   Lohfink, *Does God Need the Church?*, p. 259, emphasis mine.

39   Lee, *Protestant Gnostics*, p. 19, notes of St Irenaeus' argument with ancient Gnosticism, 'The central purpose of Irenaeus's polemical theology was to understand clearly the relationship between creation and redemption so that the gnostic wedge between the God of Israel and the Savior Christ could be once and for all removed.'

40   Lee, *Protestant Gnostics*, p. 23.

41   Lee, *Protestant Gnostics*, p. 20.

42   Lee, *Protestant Gnostics*, p. 30.

43   Lohfink, *Does God Need the Church?*, p. 133.

creation to effect redemption, a fact most fully revealed in the incarnation. To say that we cannot separate creation and redemption means that God needs the Church, a created people, to 'body forth' his new creation, the body of Christ.

We can, at this point, revisit the Protestant concern over the Lord's Supper and its relation to the sacrifice of Christ. As we noted, this concern centered on the fact that understanding the real presence of Christ in the Lord's Supper would indicate that Christ himself was being re-sacrificed. Catholic teaching has upheld that in celebrating the Lord's Supper we are drawn into communion with Christ himself, especially Christ in his passion. This does not mean, however, that Christ's own sacrifice is repeated; it is indeed complete and unique, made once and for all. At the same time, however, it is ever present in the sense that the *efficacy* of Christ's sacrifice continues today. This sacrifice, as others have noted, is not one made to appease an angry God, but is better understood as a sacrifice of love. As we receive Christ's love and sacrifice, his body and blood—a sacrifice made once but available to all today—we are receiving and being drawn into communion with God. 'The cup of blessing', wrote St Paul, 'which we bless, is it not a communion with the blood of Christ? The bread which we break, is it not a communion in the body of Christ? Because there is one bread, we who are many are one body, for we all partake of the one bread' (1 Cor. 10.16-17). One of the reasons we can, in fact, call the Lord's Supper a sacrament is because it is not an empty sign but a *living, effective sign*. In receiving Christ's own sacrifice of love, his forgiveness, we enter into communion with Christ and the body of Christ, the Church.

We can also respond, at this point, to the Protestant concern that a doctrine of real presence leads to an understanding of grace as 'mechanical'. While this is an easy interpretation to latch on to, it nonetheless is one that obscures the 'hospitality' of God, who desires not a mechanical response but our true friendship.[44] As suggested above, the

---

44 Aquinas, *Summa Theologiae*, III, Question 75, Article 1, himself situates his understanding of the 'real presence' of Christ in the eucharist within God's desire for our friendship. 'Secondly, this belongs to Christ's love, out of which for our salvation He assumed a true body of our nature. And because it is the special feature of friendship to live together with friends, as the Philosopher says (Ethic. ix), He promises us His bodily presence as a reward, saying (Mt. 24:28): "Where the body is, there shall the eagles be gathered together." Yet meanwhile in our pilgrimage He does not deprive us of His bodily presence; but unites us with Himself in this sacrament through the truth of His body and blood. Hence (John 6:57) he says: "He that eateth My flesh, and drinketh My blood, abideth in Me, and I in him." Hence this sacrament is the sign of supreme charity, and the uplifter of our hope, from such familiar union of Christ with us.' My thanks to Joseph Incandela for drawing this to my attention. I would also like to thank Kevin McDonnell and Keith Egan for pointing me in helpful directions on this topic.

'real presence' of God in the Lord's Supper requires our *own* presence and participation. At the same time, I would want to emphasize that our own subjective feelings or how much we 'mean' our particular response on a given day is irrelevant. To return to our marriage analogy, the particular feelings of the bride, groom or minister on their wedding day are beside the point as to whether or not, in the speaking of the words in the context of the ceremony, the couple actually becomes married. If we understand that our words are deeds, we can see that the real presence of Christ in the celebration of the Lord's Supper is not 'automatic' or 'magical', but rather relies upon our Hebraic and biblical heritage: that a word/deed spoken in response to God ushers in a new reality.

As in the word so also at the table, Christ is really present, offering us his very self: 'This is my Body. This is my Blood.' This is the gift of God, always available, continually offered, because God desires that through this offering we become one with God and with each other, and so become the real presence of Christ for the world.

CHAPTER 13

The Sacramental Nature of Ordination: An Attempt to Re-engage a Catholic Understanding and Practice

John E. Colwell

Some time ago I was asked by a ministerial student at the college where I teach to preach at his ordination—except that he insisted on referring to it as a 'commissioning' service since he did not believe in ordination. Being a contrary individual I accepted the invitation but insisted that I would use the occasion to preach on the meaning of ordination. To my astonishment, he agreed.

One of the many privileges consequent on being a tutor at a Baptist college is that often I have been asked to preach at services of ordination. Almost always an Area Superintendent has been present to lead the act of ordination itself, though usually I have been invited to participate in the praying and in the laying on of hands. But principally I have been asked to preach and have accepted this as an opportunity to reaffirm the nature of that ministry to which the candidate is called and for which they are being ordained. This privilege, however, is not without its complications: time and again one is confronted with instances of confusion and contention; not infrequently those participating in the service, including Area Superintendents and candidates, hold markedly differing views of what is occurring and even of whether such a service really is necessary or appropriate. Only rarely, I suspect, is there a lively expectation that something actually happens when a candidate is ordained.

This degree of confusion and contention, of course, is hardly surprising. In a context where the majority of Baptist ordinands have pursued a church-based pattern of training, a pattern of training where they already have been leading worship, preaching, presiding at Communion, where they may even have been acting effectively as sole pastor of a local church, what is the significance of ordination? What, if anything, is expected to occur here?

But the confusion goes deeper than consequences of more recent patterns of ministerial training: since the Reformation the notion of the priesthood of all believers has been appropriated (or maybe misappropriated) amongst several radical expressions of the Church to oppose every form of clericalism and to foster an 'anybody can' approach to ministry. In the course of the last thirty or forty years this vocationally egalitarian culture has been reinforced through the charismatic movement and its emphasis on the Church as Christ's body—an emphasis which surprisingly issues too often, not in a recognition of the appropriateness of certain gifts to certain persons within the Christian community, but rather in resistance to the formal and structured and in encouragement to all to seek virtually every form of gift.[1] In most baptistic churches today, or at least in those positively influenced by the charismatic and restorationist movements, ordained ministry, if it is acknowledged at all, is identified with respect to the leadership of the congregation. The leading of public worship, the ministry of the Word, the presidency at the Communion table, while perhaps not the prerogative of all, are certainly not perceived as restricted to the ordained.

However, as I have already intimated, these more recent emphases on the spontaneous ought not to be over-stated: a mere cursory knowledge of Anabaptist and Baptist roots identifies markedly differing understandings of the nature of ministry and of the nature and significance of ordination.[2] In preparing this paper I had intended to interact with one or two significant thinkers from our Baptist beginnings with respect to the nature of ordained ministry: I was hard pressed to identify suitable candidates and the subtitle of this paper is a consequence of this frustration. For instance, while John Smyth's *Principles and Inferences* list the offices of ministry within the Church, and do so in sacramental fashion, these are merely stated rather than discussed or

---

1   So for instance *Viewpoint: The Ministry Today* (Glasgow: Baptist Union of Scotland, undated), p. i: 'Those within the Charismatic Renewal Movement are re-emphasising the giftedness of every believer for some form of christian ministry and would question the "one-man ministry" concept... Ministry, it is claimed, is the ministry of the *whole* Church not the special office of the few, and the lay/clerical distinction is an ultimate denial of the priesthood of all believers.'

2   Hence, in a very general analysis of early Baptist history, M.S. Helm, 'Improving Our Gifts: Ordination in Baptist Perspective', *American Baptist Quarterly* 14.3 (September, 1995), p. 193, comments that '[s]ome Baptist churches shunned any ordination ceremony as such completely. The invitation to serve a congregation as its pastor and the acceptance of that call constituted the only "ordination" that was needed. Other Baptist churches, strongly aware of the biblical practice of laying on hands to set people apart for special service, did use such a ceremony, but went to some length to stress that this event was only a confirmation and recognition of the gifts of God and the church's invitation to exercise them—carefully denying that the office itself had authority of its own or that any sacramental power was granted by the ritual'.

defined.[3] Indeed, the same is true of his more lengthy account in *The Differences of the Churches*: objections are countered but little is elaborated or explained. Smyth assumes his orders to be clear in scripture and therefore without need of defending.[4]

The temptation for any radical group (if not its *raison d'être*) is to define itself in distinction to the catholic tradition of the Church, as if nothing positive could be learnt from the past, as if it were the first generation to engage with scripture.[5] In so many respects our Baptist forbears (in distinction to so much of the Anabaptist tradition) showed some resistance to this common fault, drawing influence from the Magisterial Reformers and the wider Puritan movement if not always so explicitly from the older tradition. As Barrie White notes, the Particular Baptist Confession of 1677 was a modification of the Savoy Declaration of 1658 which was itself a modification of the Westminster Confession of 1646.[6] Nonetheless it is difficult not to conclude that with respect to the nature of ministry and ordination there has been sparse engagement with a sacramental tradition, little systematic thought, and a marked lack of consensus.[7]

---

3   John Smyth, *Principles and Inferences*, in W.T. Whitley (ed.), *The Works of John Smyth* (2 vols; Cambridge: Cambridge University Press, 1915), I, pp. 258-61.

4   John Smyth, *The Differences of the Churches*, in *Works*, I, pp. 307-20.

5   Thus, speaking of the 'largely negative context within which early Baptists developed their view', C. Penrose St. Amant, 'Sources of Baptist Views on Ordination', *Baptist History and Heritage* 23.3 (July, 1988), p. 13, opines that '[o]rdination is not a sacrament, ordination is not an ordinance, ordination does not link the one ordained in unbroken historical succession to the apostles and Christ, ordination does not confer new authority in the church upon the one ordained, ordination does not create a priesthood, ordination does not confer a gift but is recognition by the church of a gift already given, and ordination confers no "indelible character" on the one ordained.' Similarly, with reference to Southern Baptists in the USA, Philip E. Thompson, 'A New Question in Baptist History: Seeking a Catholic Spirit among Early Baptists' in *Pro Ecclesia* 8.1 (Winter, 1999), p. 52, contends 'that they suffer from an under developed catholic mind...'. Thompson proceeds to argue for a discernible concern for the catholic creeds and for the ministry amongst early General Baptists, but his focus is really quite narrow (on the work of Thomas Grantham and General Baptist 'Orthodox Creed' of 1679), and even within this focus his conclusions are less than fully convincing. On the other hand, Barrington R. White's booklet, *Authority: A Baptist View* (London: Baptist Publications, 1976), on a Baptist view of authority reads as a sustained refutation of any simplistic dismissal of tradition.

6   See also B.R. White's comment, *Authority*, p. 5, that '[t]here have often been those who have believed themselves to be faithful Roman Catholics who yet have pitted their consciences against their church and, on the other hand, there have been those who have believed themselves to be good Baptists who have treasured not only their own denominational traditions but also the traditions of the universal church'.

7   For an overview of this lack of consensus see John F.V. Nicholson, *The Ministry: A Baptist View* (London: Baptist Publications, 1976), pp. 7-17.

In essence (and at risk of oversimplification) the sources for these tensions can be traced negatively to the desire to be distanced from any form of sacerdotalism, and positively to a commitment to give priority to the local. Illustrative of the former is the observation of Barrington White that, in the Particular Baptist London Confession of 1644, 'the position accorded to the ministry was measurably less significant than it had been among the Separatists... [i]n 1596 no sacraments were to be administered until ministers had been appointed, in 1644 any "preaching disciple" could baptise and the administration of the Lord's Supper was not even mentioned'.[8] Similarly John Briggs records Andrew Fuller as believing 'the practice of ordination to be wise rather than essential' and that a similar view emerges in the correspondence of the *Baptist Magazine* of 1828.[9] In consequence of the latter and positive priority of the local we find a strong tendency to view ordination as specific to the pastoral care of a local congregation—with the possibility of a fresh act of ordination should a pastor move to another congregation[10]—combined with differing attitudes concerning the appropriateness of 'ministers' or 'messengers' from other congregations participating in such acts of ordination.[11] Thus again, Barrington White comments with regards to the early General Baptists that officers of the church (i.e., elders and deacons) 'must be elected by "that church and congregation whereof they are members" and have no authority outside it'.[12]

---

8   B.R. White, *The English Baptists of the Seventeenth Century* (A History of English Baptists, 1; London: Baptist Historical Society, 1983) p. 62. For an outline of the 1679 Confession, with its more clearly defined notion of ordained ministry amongst General Baptists and particularly of the role of 'the Messenger for that district' in ordination, see pp. 118-20.

9   'Eschewing anything that smacked of Catholicism, the argument was that commissioning came with the church's call, not through any subsequent ceremony. Occasional omission of a service of setting apart was a helpful demonstration that such services were far from essential', 'A Country Minister', 'On Ordinations' [Letter to the Editor of the *Baptist Magazine*], *Baptist Magazine* 20 (April, 1828), pp. 151-52, cited in J.H.Y. Briggs, *The English Baptists of the Nineteenth Century* (A History of English Baptists, 3; London: Baptist Historical Society, 1994), p. 87.

10   Helm, 'Improving Our Gifts', p. 194: 'A basic commonality across Baptist groups was that "ordination" was for a single church and for the duration of one's service in that church. It was limited geographically and temporally.' Thus also G. Hugh Wamble, 'Baptist Ordination Practices to 1845', *Baptist History and Heritage* 23.3 (July, 1988), p. 19, notes that Andrew Fuller was 'ordained' in the Soham church and was 'ordained' again at Kettering.

11   White, *English Baptists of the Seventeenth Century*, p. 50: 'It seems to have been customary, though not invariably so, for elders to share in the ordination of officers (both elders and deacons) in other sister congregations.'

12   White, *English Baptists of the Seventeenth Century*, p. 27. Similarly Helm, 'Improving Our Gifts', p. 191, notes that 'The key element in the Baptist approach to the

At various points in his account of *The English Baptists of the Eighteenth Century* Raymond Brown records the concerns of both General and Particular Baptists for an educated ministry and for the adequate financial support of that ministry. He records nothing specifically, however, concerning the recognition of such a ministry or of a separation through ordination to a ministry of Word and Sacrament.[13] Similarly John Briggs observes that '[a]longside accounts of formal ordinations in the later 1830s there appear simple notices that "a pastor had commenced upon his labours" in a given location' and that 'Spurgeon himself deliberately rejected ordination and his example was nationally very influential'.[14] Briggs also notes the reluctance of the Baptist Union Council in 1930 to affirm a separated ministry of Word and Sacrament as 'essential to the existence of a true Christian Church'.[15]

The primary purpose of this paper is to argue for a sacramental understanding of the act of ordination—a discussion which necessarily will engage with complementary definitions of the sacramental and with consideration of a possible differentiation between the sacramental and the sacraments. This central discussion will then be followed by a series of subordinate and consequential theses: that ordination is a mediation of 'grace'; that ordination, thus understood, need not imply any absolute restriction of ministry to the ordained; that ordination is specific to a ministry of Word and Sacrament (that is to say that this—rather than 'leadership'—is the specific nature of Christian ministry, and that ordination is appropriate to this calling rather than to any other); that ordination is inclusive of the work of chaplaincy and academy; that ordination implies a 'way of being'; and finally that ordination is 'indelible'. Since I consider these subordinate theses to be consequences of a sacramental understanding of ordination I do not expect them to be in the least persuasive to those who cannot accept my central argument. Indeed, I recognise that this central argument, far from being persuasive, is sure to alienate some of my readers (if the title of this collection has not already achieved this). I would plead, however, that we move beyond anxieties about offending Protestant shibboleths in order to engage in an urgent discussion concerning the nature of Christian ministry since—and with this observation this paper will conclude—if the Church in Britain is in grave crisis it may to some measure be an outcome of a crisis in our understanding of Christian ministry.

---

ministry was the same key element in Baptist views of the church generally: the idea that the best way for Christ to be head of the Church was for scripture to be interpreted by a congregation of gathered believers!'

13   Raymond Brown, *The English Baptists of the Eighteenth Century* (A History of English Baptists, 2; London: Baptist Historical Society, 1986).
14   Briggs, *English Baptists of the Nineteenth Century*, p. 88.
15   Briggs, *English Baptists of the Nineteenth Century*, p. 70.

In the course of a quite excellent discussion of the doctrine of revelation, Colin Gunton comments that, while propositional statements may not themselves be revelation, 'they may in a derivative sense be revelatory'.[16] I would venture that this distinction is helpful and has interesting parallels. To argue for a sacramental understanding of ordination would seem immediately to revisit the ancient debate concerning the number of the sacraments and this is a diversion I wish to avoid (at least in this present context). The number of the sacraments inevitably is an outcome of the manner in which they are defined and it is this definition that is the more important (not to say more interesting) question. If sacraments are identified exclusively as 'gospel sacraments', or restricted to explicit dominical ordinances, then it is difficult to argue that ordination should be included in their number. But this is to identify sacraments by means of a perceived outcome or an authoritative origin rather than simply by the recognition of an underlying dynamic. As I hope to demonstrate, this restrictive classification was not the primary manner in which the catholic tradition identified the sacramental. Now it may be appropriate to identify a sacrament as deriving its status as such from an explicit dominical ordinance, but to recognise an event more broadly as sacramental is simply to acknowledge a sacramental dynamic without prejudice to any explicit dominical institution. Ordination, therefore, may not be a sacrament (if a sacrament is to be defined in this restrictive and categorical manner), but ordination may yet be sacramental if it is nonetheless an instance of a particular dynamic. And if ordination is sacramental in this latter sense, it is so in a manner not derivative from the 'gospel sacraments' or 'ordinances', but rather derivative from the sacramental dynamic that would seem to characterise every action of God within the world—that the presence and promises of God are mediated under signs of that presence and of those promises.

For Augustine a sacrament is simply a sign that pertains to divine things,[17] a sign which itself resembles the thing signified,[18] a 'kind of visible word'.[19] While Augustine's understanding of the sacraments is hardly systematically developed and is scattered throughout his writings,

---

16   C.E. Gunton, *A Brief Theology of Revelation* (Edinburgh: T. & T. Clark, 1995), p. 105.

17   Augustine, *Letter to Marcellinus* 7, Letter 138, in Philip Schaff (ed.), *A Select Library of the Nicene and Post-Nicene Fathers of the Christian Church* (Grand Rapids, MI: Eerdmans, 1994 [1886]), 1st series, vol. I.

18   Augustine, *Letter to Boniface* 9, Letter 98, in Schaff (ed.), *Nicene and Post-Nicene Fathers*, 1st series, vol. I.

19   Augustine, *Homilies on the Gospel of John*, Tractate 80.3, in Philip Schaff (ed.), *A Select Library of the Nicene and Post-Nicene Fathers of the Christian Church* (Grand Rapids, MI: Eerdmans, 1991 [1888]), 1st series, vol. VII: 'The word is added to the element, and there results the Sacrament, as if itself also a kind of visible word'.

this more general definition enabled him to apply the term sacrament far more widely even than the later Roman tradition. From a Baptist perspective, surely the laying on of hands at ordination could be considered as a 'visible word', as an act which in some way resembles that which it signifies. Here perhaps in an initial manner it is possible for us to speak of ordination as sacramental, even if we do not classify the act as itself a sacrament. However, the more crucial issue to be established is whether ordination is a sign 'pertaining to divine things' (*sacrum res signum*): is ordination sacramental in this dynamic and effectual sense?

On the one hand, Thomas Aquinas explicitly concurs with Augustine that 'every sign of a sacred thing is a sacrament'.[20] However, reflecting the general medieval view, Thomas infers from Augustine that a sacrament is no empty sign, it causes grace: 'the sacraments of the New Law not only signify, but also cause grace'.[21] But once again, this classic and most common definition of a sacrament as a 'means of grace' falls short of identifying a sacrament categorically as a dominical ordinance; it rather identifies a dynamic—a sacrament is that through which grace is mediated.

This use of the term 'grace', of course, was not without its own inherent problems. In correspondence with the Western tendency to depersonalise the Spirit, grace came increasingly to be conceived, not as an attitude of God or an outcome of his action, but as a something, as an entity at our disposal *ex opere operato*, and therefore as an entity capable of manipulation. Qualify the freedom of God, depersonalise the Spirit, objectify grace, and *mysterium* quickly gives way to *magice*, the sacramental gives way to the sacerdotal.

It deserves to be recognised more widely that Thomas avoided this danger. Though he tends to use the term 'grace' where it may have been more appropriate to refer specifically to a work or gift of the Spirit, he nonetheless continues to affirm that God alone is the efficient or principal cause of grace through a sacrament; a sacrament is the instrumental means of grace, but neither the sacrament nor any human minister can be the agent or efficient cause of grace; the agent or efficient cause of grace in a sacrament can only be God himself.[22] The

---

20   Thomas Aquinas, *Summa Theologica* (trans. Fathers of the English Dominican Province; 5 vols; Westminster, MD: Christian Classics, 1981), III.60.2.

21   Thomas, *Summa Theologica*, III.62.1: 'Augustine says...that the baptismal water *touches the body and cleanses the heart*. But the heart is not cleansed save through grace. Therefore it causes grace: and for like reason so do the other sacraments of the Church.'

22   Thomas, *Summa Theologica*, III.62.1: 'the instrumental cause works not by the power of its form, but only by the motion whereby it is moved by the principal agent: so that the effect is not likened to the instrument but to the principal agent...it is thus that

significance of Thomas' qualification at this point cannot be overstated: simply put, it preserves the freedom of God within the sacraments; it affirms the sacramental while avoiding the sacerdotal; a sacrament can be celebrated in the confident expectation of faith but never in the presumption that grace (or God's action in that sacrament) can be manipulated.

I am increasingly impressed by the similarities, rather than dissimilarities, between Thomas Aquinas and John Calvin at this point. Certainly Calvin speaks explicitly of the action of the Spirit in the sacraments and avoids any objectification of grace. Certainly Calvin reinforces a rejection of any manipulative or sacerdotal understanding by his emphasis on the divine promise. But Calvin (like Thomas) views the sacraments as means through which God accomplishes something. This is explicit in his discussion of the action of the Spirit in the sacraments:

the sacraments properly fulfill their office only when the Spirit, that inward teacher, comes to them, by whose power alone hearts are penetrated and affections moved and our souls opened for the sacraments to enter in. If the Spirit be lacking, the sacraments can accomplish nothing more in our minds than the splendor of the sun shining upon blind eyes, or a voice sounding in deaf ears. Therefore, I make such a division between Spirit and sacraments that the power to act rests with the former, and the ministry alone is left to the latter—a ministry empty and trifling, apart from the action of the Spirit, but charged with great effect when the Spirit works within and manifests his power.[23]

Earlier, at the commencement of his discussion of the sacraments, recognising the brevity and consequent obscurity of Augustine's definition of a sacrament as a 'visible sign of a sacred thing', Calvin offers the following definition:

It seems to me that a simple and proper definition would be to say that it is an outward sign by which the Lord seals on our consciences the promises of his good will toward us in order to sustain the weakness of our faith; and we in turn attest our piety toward him in the presence of the Lord and of his angels and before men. Here is another briefer definition: one may call it a testimony of divine grace toward us, confirmed by an outward sign, with mutual attestation of our piety toward him.[24]

---

the sacraments of the New Law cause grace: for they are instituted by God to be employed for the purpose of conferring grace.' Cf. 64 1-2.

23   John Calvin, *Institutes of the Christian Religion* (ed. J.T. McNeill; trans. F.L. Battles; 2 vols; Philadelphia: Westminster Press, 1960), IV.xiv.9. Clearly a comparison can be drawn here with the Eastern Orthodox practice of ἐπίκλησις, the calling down of the Spirit upon the elements at the Eucharist.

24   Calvin, *Institutes*, IV.xiv.1.

A sacrament for Calvin then is both a promise we make in the light of a prior promise of God and also an event in which God, by his Spirit, seals and confirms that prior promise to us; it is a sign or token of the covenant but, through the presence and action of the Spirit when received in faith, it is no empty sign. Calvin's primary definition therefore, like that of Augustine and Thomas, defines a sacrament in terms of a dynamic, albeit a dynamic specifically related to God's covenant promises. Such a definition, as Calvin himself acknowledges, is both general and broad; it 'embraces generally all those signs which God has ever enjoined upon men to render them more certain and confident of the truth of his promises'.[25] Subsequently Calvin focuses his discussion on the 'ordinary' (*ordinaria*) sacraments of the Church,[26] ceremonies which specifically are 'testimonies of grace and salvation from the Lord'.[27] He follows this distinction with a lengthy discussion of Baptism[28] and the Lord's Supper[29] supported immediately by an extended refutation of the Roman Mass[30] which concludes with an explicit limitation of the sacraments to the two previously discussed.[31] In the course of discussion, therefore, Calvin moves from a general and dynamic definition of sacraments to a more specific definition synonymous with explicit dominical ordinance. The next chapter of the *Institutes* consists of a denunciation of the five remaining sacraments as recognised by the Roman communion,[32] including a censure of the supposed sacrament of holy orders.[33] However, in the course of this final refutation Calvin surprisingly concedes that the laying on of hands, in the context of true ordination, is itself a sacrament:

> There remains the laying on of hands. As I concede that it is a sacrament in true and lawful ordinations, so I deny that it has place in this farce, where they neither obey Christ's command nor consider the end to which the promise should lead us. If they

---

25   Calvin, *Institutes*, IV.xiv.18.
26   John Calvin, *Institutes*, IV.xiv.19: 'Verum praesentis instituti est, de his Sacramentis peculiariter disserere quae Dominus ordinaria esse voluit in sua Ecclesia.' Battles' translation of *ordinaria* as 'ordinary' is both lame and misleading at this point; surely 'ordered' or 'regular' would be more appropriate.
27   Calvin, *Institutes*, IV.xiv.19.
28   Calvin, *Institutes*, IV.xv-xvi.
29   Calvin, *Institutes*, IV.xvii.
30   Calvin, *Institutes*. IV.xviii.
31   Calvin, *Institutes*. IV.xviii.19: 'Apart from these two, no other sacrament has been instituted by God, so the church of believers ought to recognize no other; for erecting and establishing new sacraments is not a matter of human choice.'
32   Calvin, *Institutes*, IV.xix.
33   Calvin, *Institutes*, IV.xix.22-35.

do not wish the sign to be denied them, they must apply it to the reality, to which it was appointed.[34]

Earlier in this final book of the *Institutes*, Calvin writes of the laying on of hands in the 'rite of ordination' which 'will be no empty sign if it is restored to its own true origin'.[35] One could conclude simply that Calvin is contradicting himself, affirming ordination as a sacrament at one point and denying its sacramental status at another. It is more reasonable, surely, to conclude that, while in a strict sense he limits the sacraments of the Church to explicit dominical ordinances, he nonetheless holds ordination to be a sacrament in the more general and dynamic sense of the term—or, to accord with the terminology I am suggesting in this paper, ordination may not be a sacrament but it is sacramental.

As I have argued elsewhere (in the course of a discussion of Karl Barth's changing understanding of Baptism), the one element I would wish to add to Calvin's description of this sacramental dynamic is Barth's insight with regard to Baptism: that as the seal of a divine promise or the sign of a divine act (which Barth eventually came to dispute), this is a responsive human act of prayer.[36] That the element of human act (or outward sign) in any sacramental rite is both a prayer and a promise I find illuminating: to consider the sacrifices and rites of the Old Testament, along with the ecclesial sacraments of the New Testament, as enacted forms of prayer in the light of divine promises identifies the specifically responsive and trustful character of the human element in such rites. But, unlike Barth, I do not believe that such rites can be reduced to these human elements: if the sacraments are prayers in the light of prior divine promises then such prayers are offered in the confident expectation that those promises will be fulfilled; if the sacraments are human promises in the light of divine promises then those human promises are dependent upon those divine promises being

---

34   Calvin, *Institutes*, IV.xix.31: 'Superest impositio manuum, quam ut in veris legitimisque ordinationibus Sacramentum esse concedo, ita nego locum habere in hac fabula, ubi nec Christi mandato obtemperant, nec finem respiciunt quo nos ducere debet promissio. Signum si non negari sibi volunt, ad rem ipsam, cui dedicatum est, accommodent oportet.' Compare the parallel passage in the 1545 edition of the *Institutes, Institutio Christianae Religionis (1559)* in *Johannis Calvin Opera Selecta* (eds. P. Barth and W. Niesel; vols. 3–5; Munich: Chr Kaiser, 1928–36), V, p. 465, n. 35: 'laquelle ie confesse bien povoir estre nommée Sacrement, quand on en useroit comme il faut, en faisant une vraye promotion des Ministres legitimes. Mais ie nie qu'elle ait lieu en ceste farce qu'ilz iouent en ordonnant leurs Prestres. Car ilz n'ont nul commandement'.

35   Calvin, *Institutes*, IV.iii.16.

36   John E. Colwell, 'Baptism, Conscience and the Resurrection: A Reappraisal of 1 Peter 3.21', in S.E. Porter and A.R. Cross (eds.), *Baptism, the New Testament and the Church: Historical and Contemporary Studies in Honour of R.E.O. White* (JSNTSup, 171; Sheffield: Sheffield Academic Press, 1999), pp. 210-227.

fulfilled if the human promises are not to remain empty. To affirm the action of the Spirit in any sacramental event is not to undermine or qualify the human element in that event, but rather to establish it; a human prayer and promise is only *truly* human here inasmuch as it is dependent upon an act that is truly divine.[37] That which distinguishes these specific human prayers and promises as sacramental is precisely that they are enacted in response to specific divine promise and in expectation of specific divine action. By referring to the sacramental, therefore, I am referring to any outward sign through which the Holy Spirit confirms and effects a promise of God in correspondence with our prayers and our promises: this dynamic is true of the dominical ordinances of Baptism and the Eucharist, properly called sacraments, but it is also true more generally of other signs, and specifically—and this is the point of this paper—I maintain it to be true of ordination.

The church that commended me for Christian ministry was quite exemplary in its support throughout my training. One woman in particular prayed for me regularly throughout my college course and through the early years of pastoral ministry until the day of her death. A few weeks before my ordination she asked to meet with me. She was clearly deeply troubled and told me that she would not be able to attend my ordination; she did not believe in human ordination; she believed in the 'ordination of the nail-pierced hands'. I am an expert at identifying the intelligent riposte several hours after the event: I wish that I had then had the presence of mind to reply that I too believed in the 'ordination of the nail-pierced hands', but could it not be possible (not to say usual) that the Saviour uses our human hands to represent his hands.

The theological issue underlying this rather quaintly expressed conversation is the recognition (or otherwise) of the mediate manner of God's action within creation. Every action of the Father in and through the Son is mediated by the Spirit; every action of the Son towards the Father is similarly mediated. And it would seem that *almost* every action of God within creation (I do not wish to limit the freedom of God here) is an action of the Spirit mediated through human instrumentality. The Spirit of God parts the Red Sea, but he does so as Moses raises his staff. God provides water for the people of Israel in the desert, but he does so as Moses strikes the rock. God maintains his covenant of grace with Israel, but he does so through the sacrificial system that is his gift to his

---

37   Compare Karl Barth, *Church Dogmatics* IV.4 (trans. and eds. G.W. Bromiley and T.F. Torrance; Edinburgh: T. & T. Clark, 1969). It is this relatedness of the *truly* human to the truly divine that Karl Barth seems to abandon in this final *Fragment* of his *Dogmatics* with disastrous and inherently dualistic consequences. For a fuller account of this argument see my 'Baptism, Conscience and the Resurrection'; see also the ch. 8 of my book *Living the Christian Story: The Distinctiveness of Christian Ethics* (Edinburgh: T. & T. Clark, 2001).

people for this purpose. By his Spirit, God anoints David as king and as shepherd of his people, but he does so through Samuel and through an anointing with oil. Every miracle of Jesus is precisely that, a miracle *of Jesus*; a work of the Father by the Spirit through the Son in his true humanity. Overwhelmingly God works mediately rather than immediately within the world; he works by his Spirit through human instrumentality.

The implicit 'romanticism' of the conversation recorded previously is typical of one stream of popular Evangelicalism that gives priority to the supposedly immediate and tends to be dismissive of the mediate as merely human, 'fleshly', formal, institutional. It is an instance of that same disease that inflicted the 'spirituals' and 'fanatics' that Calvin repudiated for confusing their feelings with the inspiration of the Spirit by belittling the Word and the sacraments.[38] And note how quickly pseudo-sacraments (not to mention pseudo-words) come to take the place of the sacraments that we belittle: belittle Baptism and we promote the 'sacrament' of public response in a meeting or of decision cards; belittle the Eucharist and we promote the 'sacrament' of ministry times, of being prayed with and having some supposedly immediate experience. Too easily we give primary emphasis to a personal experience of conversion (which like any other feeling might be fleeting) rather than to the covenantal promise of God represented in the sacrament of Baptism. Too easily we give primary emphasis to feelings of assurance rather than to the covenantal promise of God in the Eucharist. And too easily we give primary emphasis to a personal testimony of 'being called' rather than to the promise and seal of God in the act of ordination.

I am not denying, of course, the reality and significance of personal conversion, assurance or calling; I am merely questioning this prioritising of the supposedly immediate. As the dilemma has often been expressed: how can I distinguish between the claim that an angel spoke to me in a dream and the phenomenon of dreaming that an angel spoke to me? How can a religious feeling be anything other than fleeting? I write as one who has struggled with recurrent depression throughout my adult life: my feelings are always fleeting. Of course I believe that God spoke to me by his Spirit and called me into Christian ministry, but on the many occasions when I have doubted this feeling of 'calledness' I have remembered that this call was affirmed by the local church of which I was a member, was affirmed by the Ministerial Recognition Committee, was affirmed by the college in which I was trained, was affirmed by the church that first called me to be its pastor, and finally—and herein lies

38   Calvin, *Institutes*, I.ix.

the point at issue—was confirmed and sealed somewhere between 6.30 pm and 8.00 pm on 30 June 1974 when I was ordained.[39]

It is possible that someone might object that, notwithstanding these tests and confirmations, it is the sense of personal call that remains primary and decisive. I can only respond by considering such an objection simplistic and naïve. To begin with, personal calls themselves are overwhelmingly mediate rather than immediate: only rarely does anyone hear a voice or see a light (Acts 9.1-6); generally such a personal call is received through a sermon, a conversation, an incident that portends of personal significance—and my reading of this significance might be mistaken; I might be self-deceived. But more fundamentally, the call to Christian ministry is inherently ecclesial; Jesus does not by-pass his Church; he mediates his call through his Church. No one should take this responsibility upon themselves (Heb. 5.4). The process of testing and confirming a personal sense of call, then, is intrinsic to that call itself; precisely through the testing and confirming process the call itself is uttered and effected. And only at the conclusion of that testing process, in the act of ordination, is the call that previously was personally intimated now declared authoritatively; in the act of ordination the Church through its appropriate representatives declares this call conclusively and does so in the name of Christ—and that which is done on earth has been done in heaven (Mt. 18.18).[40]

---

39   At one point Calvin, *Institutes*, IV.xiv.3, notes that 'a sacrament is never without a preceding promise but is joined to it as a sort of appendix, with the purpose of confirming and sealing the promise itself, and of making it more evident to us and in a sense ratifying it.' While affirming a sacrament as the seal and confirmation of a preceding promise, I would deem the term 'appendix' to be inadequate and unhelpful. The notion of appendix implies a supplementary and extraneous addition whereas a sacrament is a vital representation of the promise itself.

40   It is this divine element in ordination that seemingly is denied by John Smyth, 'Lettre written to Mr. Ric. Bernard (1607)', in Whitley (ed.),*Works*, II, p. 510, in the following extract: 'For election is the verie essence & forme of the minister: for in election powre to administer is given to the officer elect: For when the Church cho(o)seth the minister doth not the Church in effect say: we give thee A. B, powre to administer the word, seales of the covenant, & censures in the behalf of the whole Church? & the minister Elect doth then actually possesse & assume that powre delegated vnto him by the Church: so when the Church cho(o)seth her Deacons doth she not in effect speake thus: we give you, C.D.E.F. powre to collect, & distribute the Churches Treasury, & to minister for the body & mebers of the Church in other general services, helpful to the body & outward part: this is evident enough if you wil not be blind wilfully: For as in matter of mariage, this is the very forme of mariage: I take the for my wife, & I take the for my husband: So in the matter of office this is the very forme therof: we take the for our Pastor: I take you for my flock: & so forth of the rest: now ordination is nothing but the publishing of the officers election with prayer made for him & admonition given to him to be faithful...' Later, p. 513, Smyth argues that, since the church has power to

It is for this reason that the Church, in the act of ordination, ought to be represented as broadly as possible. Tragically, in days of continuing division, no-one is in a position to represent the Church catholic in its wholeness or fullness: only before God does it exist whole and undivided. In such a context there can only be authority to ordain on behalf of a distinct communion or denomination—but even such a restricted act is nevertheless done in the name of Christ and thereby, albeit provisionally, on behalf of the whole Church. Ordination properly can never be sectarian. That which does not acknowledge the Church catholic, and itself as a part of the Church catholic, has no authority to ordain.

I am arguing, therefore, that ordination is not merely an outward and supplementary expression of an inward call: it is rather the definitive uttering and effecting of that call and its consequent authority and responsibility. It is an action of the Holy Spirit in and through an action on behalf of the Church and in the name of Christ. It is a mediation of grace (understood as an action of the Spirit). It is sacramental.

All this necessarily raises the question of the validity or otherwise of ministerial acts prior to ordination or by those not seeking ordination. What of the preaching, nurturing and presidency at Communion by those preparing for ordination? What of 'lay' preaching? What of 'lay' presidency?

In responding to this question I believe we need to recognise a further significance of defining the sacramental in terms of promise and prayer in the light of a promise of God, as a mediation of the work of the Spirit rather than a determining of that work, as a means of grace rather than an effecting of grace. To conceive of the human action in any sacramental rite as itself effecting a work of the Spirit *ex opere operato* is to imply that the Holy Spirit is subject to human manipulation, is effectively to imprison the Spirit within the human action. No sacrament is God's prison. God has promised to act here, but the fulfilment of that promise is to be sought humbly and prayerfully; it is not to be presumed upon as if the Holy Spirit had been reduced to an automaton. God has promised to act here, but he is free to act elsewhere. God has promised the gift of his Spirit through the sacrament of Baptism (Acts 2.38-39), but he remains free to give that Spirit prior to that rite (Acts 10.44). Jesus has promised that we will meet with him and be nourished by him through the bread and wine of the Eucharist (Jn 6.53-58), but he remains free to meet with us and to nourish us elsewhere and otherwise. We have the promise

---

make itself a Church, it certainly has of itself the power to make ministers. Smyth understands ordination as the election of the pastor by the congregation and likens this with marriage; election by the church itself bestows power to minister within the church; that is to say, though prayer is said within the act, the power in question is a delegated and human power; there is nothing sacramental here or, for that matter, in marriage.

sacramentally, we do not have the promise elsewhere, but God is not imprisoned by his promise.

In the act of ordination, therefore, we humbly and prayerfully appropriate the promise that God will speak through, act through, and mediate his presence through the one being ordained. But God is not restricted by this promise or this act. He remains free to speak and act through others. However, the reference here is to God's freedom, not ours; the recognition of this freedom of God is no sanction for spiritual anarchy or ministerial independence. Without devaluing the significance of ordination it may be appropriate for the Church to grant some form of limited licence to those preparing for ordination or to recognise some form of 'lay' or locally restricted ministry. But here too the authority to preach or to preside at Communion should be acknowledged as mediated through the Church; there should be no place for individual autonomy or presumption in this respect. God generally works in a mediate manner.

This entire discussion is dependent, of course, upon a complementary discussion of the nature and validity of Christian ministry as a ministry of Word and Sacrament. My friend and colleague Steve Holmes is contributing a chapter to this collection on this issue and I affirm everything I confidently anticipate he will write in this context. I have no desire to infringe on his theme beyond the acknowledgement that overwhelmingly the Church catholic has recognised that, while Jesus calls all to love him and to follow him, he does not call all to feed his sheep (Jn 21.15-19); has recognised that the ascended Christ gives pastors and teachers for the equipping and maturing of his Church (Eph. 4.7-16); has consequently ordained some to this ministry in Christ's name through prayer and through the laying on of hands (2 Tim. 1.6). This feeding of Christ's people, this ministry of Word and Sacrament, I take— again in line with the overwhelming tradition of the Church catholic—to be the nature of Christian ministry.[41] It may be appropriate for some ordained ministers to act as leaders of local congregations. It may be appropriate for some ordained ministers to utilise counselling skills. It may be appropriate for some ordained ministers (in true servant spirit) to stack chairs or to sweep floors. But none of this is either the focus or the essence of ordained ministry. Ordination is specific to the ministry of the Word and Sacrament, to the proclaiming of the 'unsearchable riches of Christ' (Eph. 3.8), to the tending of God's flock (1 Pet. 5.2).

Neither is this to deny a doctrine of the priesthood of all believers— though certainly it is to repudiate the common misappropriation of this

---

41   This is clearly contrary to Paul Beasley-Murray's contention, 'The Ministry of All and the Leadership of Some: A Baptist perspective', in P. Beasley-Murray (ed.), *Anyone for Ordination?* (Tunbridge Wells: Marc, 1993), p. 161, that '[l]eadership is the distinguishing mark of the ordained'. Beasley-Murray, pp. 167-68, specifically maintains that ordination is *not* to a ministry of Word and Sacrament.

doctrine. Luther's concern was to affirm the whole of life as vocational—as response to a call of God—and so to claim every aspect of life as appropriate in God's service. It was not Luther's aim to undermine the significance of ordained ministry. It certainly was not Luther's concern to endorse the obscene individualism of the 'my ministry' brigade. His purpose was not to sanction the priesthood of 'each' in an individualistic and autonomous sense, but rather to affirm the priesthood of all in a participatory sense: all believers participate in the single and ultimate priesthood of Christ.[42] And, in this sense, all believers are ordained through Baptism into this single ministry of Christ. Or, to put the matter another way, the service of 'ordination' appropriate to this priesthood of all believers is Christian Baptism, there is no supplementary rite of ordination to this priesthood of all, the distinct rite of ordination is specific to a ministry of Word and Sacrament.

This point perhaps needs to be laboured since there are those who apparently would accept the appropriateness of a service of ordination (though probably not in the sacramental sense I have been advocating) but would wish to apply it more widely, ordaining deacons (in the Baptist sense of the term), Sunday School teachers, pastoral assistants, *et al*. It is true that, since all reality is continually sustained by God, any word whatsoever about any reality is implicitly theological, but we then need another word meaning what 'theology' meant before we broadened its definition. It is true that worship includes the whole of life, but similarly we then need another word meaning what 'worship' meant before we broadened its definition. Overwhelmingly the Church catholic has used the term 'ordination' to speak specifically of a separation to this ministry of Word and Sacrament. To broaden the term is disingenuous (and is usually a mask for not believing in the appropriateness of ordination in the first place). To affirm ordination as specific to this ministry of Word and Sacrament is not to belittle other forms of ministry or service within the Church as insignificant. To affirm ordination as specific to this ministry of Word and Sacrament is not necessarily to imply some form of clerical elitism—this may too often have been an outcome of an emphasis on ordained ministry, but the misappropriation or distortion of a practice is never by itself sufficient grounds for the abandonment of a practice. By all means let there be 'commissioning' services for other valid ministries within the Church, by all means let such ministries receive due honour, but ordination is specific to this particular calling and this particular responsibility.

---

42   For an able and thorough exposure of this confusion, see Thomas F. Torrance, *Royal Priesthood: A Theology of Ordained Ministry* (Edinburgh: T. & T. Clark, 2nd edn, 1993).

But to affirm ordination as specific to this ministry of Word and Sacrament is not to limit this ministry to the pastoral charge of a local church. It is in this respect that current practice within the Baptist Union of Great Britain appears incoherent. On the one hand, those who move into chaplaincy work (be it hospital, industrial or military) together with those who become theological educators generally continue to be included within the accredited list of ministers. On the other hand, the call to ministry within a local church is perceived as the final (and exclusively final) confirmation of call and the prerequisite for ordination and inclusion within the accredited list.[43] The work of chaplaincy and the academy either are valid expressions of the ministry of Word and Sacrament or they are not. It is not hard at present to find examples of artificiality as means of circumventing these rules. Neither is it hard to find examples of extreme discouragement or of those seeking ordination within other denominations because their specific calling (a calling capable of confirmation within the local church, by a Ministerial Recognition Committee, and through a process of training) is a calling precisely to the work of chaplaincy or the academy. I recognise that appropriate pastoral experience is usually a prerequisite for the work of chaplaincy (in any form), but ought we not to recognise and accept that this is an appropriate goal and calling for ministry and that those perceiving and proving their call in this form will inevitably view ministry within the local church as a means to this end? I recognise that ordination is not necessary to the work of the academy, but I do affirm the work of the academy to be an appropriate outworking of ordained ministry. For too long the theological academy has been subservient to the delusory modernist assumption of non-confessional neutrality: the reaffirmation of an appropriate ecclesial context for the theological academy is well overdue. Without prejudice to the appropriateness of religious studies (the study of the phenomena of religious belief and practice), the study of theology properly cannot be pursued in detachment, it is necessarily participatory, it is doxological.

Also underlying this entire discussion is the assumption that ordained ministry, thus described and defined, is not merely functional. It is not merely that I have been called to do or to perform; I have been separated to this ministry; I have been separated to be this; this now is the manner and focus of my life (Acts 13.1-3). Within the parameters discussed previously, others may minister the Word, but those ordained have been separated to this ministry of the Word. Similarly others may celebrate the sacraments, but again those ordained have been separated to this

---

43   For an account of the development of accreditation within Baptist churches of Great Britain, see Douglas C. Sparkes, *An Accredited Ministry* (Didcot: Baptist Historical Society, 1996).

celebration. Consequently Paul Fiddes, in his recent discussion of the pastoral implications of an understanding of the Trinity, can speak of a pastor as 'a living sacrament, *embodying* the accepting and healing love of God'.[44] As with every other Christian believer, I have been called to love Jesus and to follow him, but I have also been called to feed his sheep; this now is the irreducible and inescapable focus of my life.[45]

And it is inescapable. I cannot 'uncall' myself. I cannot 'unordain' myself. I can disown my ordination, I can deny my ordination, I can betray my ordination, I can live in unfaithfulness to my ordination, I can besmirch and tarnish my ordination, but I cannot undo my ordination. That which was done on earth has been done in heaven (Mt. 18.18); that which was done in ordination is, in this sense, indelible: I can be censured, I can be banned, but I cannot be unordained.[46] Now the indelibility of ordination need not necessarily imply a corresponding indelibility of accreditation, but surely it has implications regarding the circumstances under which accreditation might be withdrawn. Without prejudice to the indelibility of ordination, accreditation ought to be withdrawn, or at least suspended, in cases of gross moral failure or gross theological error, but it is hard to conceive of any other circumstance where accreditation could be withdrawn for valid theological reasons. An ordained minister may not be in a so-called qualifying occupation, but the basis of their accreditation remains unchanged (unless such occupation itself is perceived as that basis—as distinct from the call effected in ordination). If ordination implies a way of being, rather than merely a function, then only that which qualifies such a way of being is sufficient grounds for censure; mere suspension of function is insufficient ground for such censure.

I am, I trust, acutely conscious of the dangers of clericalism lurking beneath every argument and assertion of this paper. I suspect, however, that the threat of a resurgent and elitist clericalism is the least of the perils confronting the contemporary Church in a context of rampant individualism and suspicion of every form of authority. I also note that in days when clericalism was a far greater threat there was also a far greater clarity concerning the nature and focus of Christian ministry. I am

---

44   Paul S. Fiddes, *Participating in God: A Pastoral Doctrine of the Trinity* (London: Darton Longman and Todd, 2000), p. 296.

45   Fiddes, *Participating in God*, p. 294: 'the vocation to Christian ministry is a call to a *way of being*, not just the exercise of skills or the carrying out of a set of functions.'

46   Once again this is in explicit conflict with Paul Beasley-Murray who argues, 'Ministry of All and the Leadership of Some', p. 166, that '[i]f ordination is primarily functional, and has more to do with role than with status, then it is possible for that function to be given up. Ordination cannot therefore be indelible, in the sense that it is for life.'

persuaded that the problems of the contemporary Church are complex and certainly am not suggesting that they can be reduced to a single issue or resolved by any simplistic strategy or isolated element of renewal. I do, however, note that the crisis for the Church in Britain (and it really is a most serious crisis) has deepened in parallel to a crisis concerning the nature and function of Christian ministry.[47] The rise of an 'anyone can' culture has been accompanied by a shift of focus from a ministry of Word and Sacrament towards an understanding of ministry in terms of leadership and counselling. If a generation is abandoning the Church in droves (and it is), could it not partly be because the Church has been forgetful of what, through its ministry, it is called to deliver? There is no shortage today of impressive programmes, but there is an acute shortage of presence and profundity. Could it not be that a renewed focus on a ministry of Word and Sacrament constitutes at least a partial antidote to the ultimately vacuous spirituality that has come to characterise so much of the contemporary Church?

---

47   So Douglas Sparkes, *An Accredited Ministry*, p. 4, begins his account of the development of accredited ministry with the following assumption: '[e]very part of the Christian church that has a separated ministry knows that the health of the church is, in large part, dependent upon the effectiveness of its ministers.'

CHAPTER 14

Towards a Baptist Theology of Ordained Ministry

Stephen R. Holmes

Introduction and Definitions

There is considerable confusion, or so it seems to me, about what Baptist[1] Christians believe about ordination.[2] The presence of an ordained ministry is universal (or at least near-universal) amongst us, and what our pastors do day by day is not greatly different from the activity of pastors of other traditions. Ecclesiologically, however, our account of what the Church[3] is and how it is properly grounded is rather different from most other Christian denominations, and so we need either a different defence and explanation of why we ordain certain people, and of why some tasks are seen as properly their responsibility, or to critique the concept of ordination from our particular perspective. Within British Baptist life at least, the latter appears to be an increasingly popular option, often with a justification claimed from an Anabaptist tradition.[4] In contrast to this current fashion, it is my conviction that an ordained ministry is a proper

---

1   By 'Baptist' here I mean to refer to those churches in membership of unions which are affiliated to the Baptist World Alliance, and any other churches which share similar principles and practices. I am, however, writing as a minister accredited by the Baptist Union of Great Britain, a context which no doubt shapes my perception of what 'Baptists in general' believe and do.

2   Some helpful witness to the various forms this confusion has taken in British Baptist life may be found in Nigel G. Wright, 'Inclusive Representation: Towards a Doctrine of Christian Ministry' *Baptist Quarterly* 39.4 (October, 2001) pp. 159-74.

3   I am adopting the practice of using 'Church' to refer to the universal church (usually as a theological concept), and 'church' to refer to a particular local fellowship.

4   It seems to me that such a claimed justification ignores the diversity of both the original Anabaptist movement, and those currently active Christian traditions that are descended from it. At least one recent Mennonite treatment of the subject not only supports the idea of an ordained ministry, but is even prepared to use the image of incarnation in discussing it. See Wright, 'Inclusive Representation', p. 173.

part of the heritage of the Church, and that ecumenically we must be able to explain why it exists in the particular form it does from a specifically Baptist ecclesiology. This paper is the beginning of an attempt to do that.

Our ecclesiology is congregational, so the primary instantiation of the *ecclesia* is not a universal or national body, or even a diocese, but the local covenanted congregation. Each local church has the liberty, and the responsibility, to discern God's will; this is properly done in church meeting, relying on Christ's promise to be present when we gather in his name. Already some implications for ordained ministry,[5] assuming that such a thing properly exists, are obvious: the primary location of ministry is the local fellowship of believers; the discerning and confirming of a 'call' to this ministry is properly done by such local fellowships; and this is properly done in church meeting. Can we, however, find resources within a Baptist account of ecclesiology to account for the apparently 'permanent' nature of ordination, what the wider tradition has witnessed to in its doctrine of the *character indelebilis* (permanent character), or for the practice of gathering tasks of liturgical (and sacramental) presidency, pastoral care, and preaching, together in this one role, or for the practice of ordination itself?[6]

Before I attempt to address these questions, some definitions of terms used are necessary. The following three are affirmed ecumenically, and offer both some important distinctions and a useful starting-point:

charism 'denotes the gifts bestowed by the Holy Spirit on any member of the body of Christ for the building up of the community and the fulfilment of its calling'.

ministry 'in its broadest sense denotes the service to which the whole people of God is called, whether as individuals, as a local community, or as the universal Church. Ministry or ministries can also denote the particular institutional forms which this service may take.'

---

5   I will define 'ordained ministry' later in the paper, and will sometimes use 'ministry' as a short-hand for the phrase—to conflate the two is theologically indefensible from a Baptist perspective, of course, but the briefer term is extremely useful stylistically, and in context the meaning will, I trust, be clear.

6   It seems to me that much writing on ministry assumes too much, for instance that the (admittedly near-universal) linkage of pastoral care, liturgical presidency, and proclamation is given. Whilst we must believe that the Spirit is guiding the Church into all truth, and so take seriously the witness of the ecumenical tradition, no theology which has learnt from the Reformation—particularly, perhaps, its radical and Anabaptist wing—can simply assume that universal Church practice is theologically sanctioned. For a clear exposition of the range of questions that need to be asked, see A.T. Hanson and R.P.C. Hanson *The Identity of the Church: A Guide to Recognising the Contemporary Church* (London: SCM Press, 1987), p. 144; for an attempt to describe how this relative authority can be ascribed to the tradition, see my *Theology by Example: On the Theory and Practice of Historical Theology* (Carlisle: Paternoster, forthcoming 2002).

ordained ministry 'refers to persons who have received a charism and whom the church appoints for service by ordination through the invocation of the Spirit and the laying on of hands'.[7]

Three Contexts for Ordained Ministry

Ministry, in every possible sense, describes some form of human service offered to God. As soon as this statement is made, there is surely only one conceivable starting point for a theological account of ministry: the perfect service to God offered by the man from Nazareth. The first and fundamental context of any Christian ministry is the ministry of Christ, the ministry given to him by the Father. Whatever roles may be ascribed to our ordained ministers—leadership, authority, teaching, priesthood— are all roles first held by Christ, and so we must take our pattern from him. The defining characteristic of Christ's earthly ministry was service: he came not to be served but to serve (Mt. 20.28 and par.; the word used is *diakonos*); in Jn 13.4-17 he is described as a slave (*doulos*). The content of Christ's ministry included teaching, preaching, healing and deliverance. The central act of Christ's ministry was his priestly self-offering.

A traditional heuristic device divides his ministry into the threefold office of prophet, priest and king;[8] these are the three lasting orders of human ministry discernible in the life of the people of God in the Old Testament, and so this heuristic can be theologically grounded, although the order is reversed: if the ministry of the prophets, priests and kings who God called to serve his people had any validity, then it can only be the validity gained by some form of participation in the ministry of Christ. The particular form of participation here is a prefiguring. Given this, it must be theologically legitimate to use this scheme to describe and illuminate the content of Christ's ministry.[9]

---

7   *Baptism, Eucharist and Ministry* (Faith and Order Paper, 111; Geneva: World Council of Churches, 1982) (hereafter *BEM*), Ministry II.7.a)-c), p. 21. Notice particularly how these various definitions manage to capture the diversity of Baptist concerns, at least as they are represented by Wright, 'Inclusive Representation', pp. 159-63.

8   This may be found, for instance, in Thomas Aquinas, *Summa Theologiae* (London: Blackfriars, 1963–76), IIIa q.22 art. 1 (reply obj. 3); or John Calvin, *Institutes of the Christian Religion* (trans and eds J.T. McNeill and F.L. Battles; 2 vols; London: SCM Press, 1960 [1559]), II.xv.1.

9   Assuming, of course, that there is no aspect of Christ's ministry that is not prefigured in the Old Testament. There is not room to defend this assumption here, but I think it is defensible.

As prophet Christ is the fulfilment of the Old Testament prophetic ministry; he is the Word of God that came to the prophets in all its creative power. The classical prophetic formula, usually rendered in English versions 'The Word of the LORD came to me' is literally in Hebrew 'The Word of LORD *happened* to me'.[10] Thus translated, the formula emphasises what should already be clear from the scriptures: God's word is creative; it will not return to him without accomplishing his will (Isa. 55.11; see also Pss 33.6-9; 107.20, and many similar passages). When God speaks, things happen: worlds come into being, or people are born anew. Christ is this Word, and in his ministry the eschatological event that the prophets had spoken about happens. He does not return to the Father until the will of the Father is accomplished, despite the anguish the doing of the Father's will costs him. As prophet Christ is the Word of God who comes with transforming power.

As priest Christ fulfils the Old Testament priestly ministry. This ministry is presented in the scriptures as centred on sacrifice, but it is noteworthy that there is little or no account as to how or why the performance of cultic ordinances is acceptable to God. As Gerhard von Rad observes of the great catalogue of sacrificial commands at the beginning of Leviticus, 'It was obviously entirely outwith P's intention to suggest to the worshipper any specific understanding of the sacrifices. The Code's concern was that where sacrifices are offered, the ritual traditions should be strictly observed.'[11] Whatever explanations for this might be offered from the study of the history of religions, or anthropological sciences, within the internal logic of the scriptures the reason is clear: there is nothing in the offering of sacrifice, or any of the detailed regulations that surround it in the levitical code, that has any power or virtue to reach God or make him well-disposed. Instead, it is the fact that God commanded sacrifices to be observed in a particular way, and promised to find them acceptable when they were so observed, that makes them efficacious. At the very heart of the priestly cultus is an awareness that only obedience to the Word of God can find favour with God; as von Rad again says, 'it was Israel's belief that Jahweh's turning towards her in salvation was not exhausted in historical deeds and in the gracious guidance of individual lives, but that in the sacrificial cult too he had ordained an instrument which opened up to her a continuous

---

10   The formula, or something closely related, occurs 123 times in the Old Testament (so Gerhard von Rad, *Theology of the Old Testament* [trans D.M.G. Stalker; 2 vols; Edinburgh: Oliver & Boyd, 1962 and 1965], II, p. 87). According to von Rad, p. 87 n. 15, Mowinckel offered 'the word of Jahweh became active reality...'; von Rad himself, p. 87, states 'it represents the apperception of the divine word as event, a unique happening in history...which sets the person concerned in a new historical situation.'

11   G. von Rad, *Theology*, I, p. 260.

relationship with him'.[12] The scriptures witness to a constant danger that this would be forgotten in the life of the nation, and so prophetic denunciations of reliance on empty ritual (e.g., Amos 4–5), and ringing declarations that God has no need of sacrifice (e.g., Ps. 50), regularly call the people back to this fundamental understanding. Christ fulfils and defines this priestly and sacrificial ministry as he offers himself in obedience to the Word of God which he himself is.[13]

As priest Christ also fulfils the mediatory role of the Aaronic priesthood. He is the one who can, in obedience to the proclaimed Word of God, enter into the presence of God and make atonement for sin. As Hebrews makes clear, however, unlike the Aaronic priesthood he does not need to do this again and again, but offers his one, complete and perfect sacrifice and oblation for the sins of the whole world, and then takes his seat at the right hand of God until the day we shall be admitted to God's presence.[14] Thus the Jewish man Jesus Christ, the incarnate Word of God, is the one mediator between God and humanity.

As king Christ reigns over his people and fulfils the Old Testament kingly role, which is a role of service. The great vision of Old Testament kingship was that Israel's kings would not be like the kings of the nations around: the covenant established the LORD as Israel's king, modelled as it was on the suzerainty treaties of the kingdoms around.[15] Given this, there is a strand within Israel's history that sees monarchy as a rejection

---

12　G. von Rad, *Theology*, I, p. 260.

13　Thus understood, the picture, painted so effectively by Hebrews, of Christ as the end of the sacrificial cult, is entirely consonant with the biblical understanding of that cult, and Paul's identification of a desire to be circumcised with a failure to believe in Christ is both necessary and straightforward.

14　Although the spatial images of the second coming of Jesus to earth in scripture must be taken with full seriousness, whatever may happen geographically, theologically it is the creation that moves from its present, alienated, location to full fellowship with God. The world will become the Holy of Holies, and so there will be no temple in the new Jerusalem (Rev. 21.22), because there will be no barrier left between God and his creation. Unless the temple could exist without an outside, there is no spatial location it could properly occupy in the Holy City. (For the theological geography that lies behind these comments, see Douglas Farrow, *Ascension and Ecclesia: On the Significance of the Doctrine of the Ascension for Ecclesiology and Christian Cosmology* [Edinburgh: T. & T. Clark, 1999].)

15　On which see, for example, Dennis J. McCarthy, *Treaty and Covenant* (Analecta Biblica, 21a; Rome: Biblical Institute Press, 1978), or Klaus Baltzer, *The Covenant Formulary: In Old Testament, Jewish and Early Christian Writings* (trans D.E. Green; Oxford: Blackwell, 1971), pp. 1-93. For some criticism of this conclusion, see Ernest W. Nicholson, *God and His People: Covenant and Theology in the Old Testament* (Oxford: Clarendon Press, 1986), pp. 56-82.

of God's covenant.[16] The solution to this would seem to be a vision of kingship as a role within the cult, enabling and enacting the theocratic rule of God. It is this vision of kingship that Jesus fulfils. Christ is king over the Church in that he loved her and gave himself up for her (Eph. 5.25); his kingly ministry is defined as he washes the feet of his people.

This, then, is the first context for a theological understanding of ministry. All human participation in the work of God, all human service of God, is summed up in the ministry of Jesus Christ. If we are to make theological space for any other ministry, such as the service offered by prophets, priests and kings amongst the people of Israel, it will only be by linking it to this prior and basic ministry. The scriptures offer us a way to do this for the ministry of the Church, however: in Acts 1.1 Luke speaks of his gospel being about 'all that Jesus began to do and teach', implying that Acts will be about what Jesus continues to do and to teach. The text that follows, however, focuses on the outworking of Pentecost, the coming of the Spirit. The second context for ministry, then, is pneumatological, and may be summed up very briefly: the Church participates in the ministry of Christ through the Spirit. Luke's picture of the work of the Spirit being the continuing work of Jesus must be held on to: to fail so to do would be a failure to be appropriately Trinitarian, since *opera trinitatis ad extra sunt indivisa* (the external works of the Trinity are undivided) as the great patristic slogan has it.[17] God's work is not divided and we may not pretend that the mission of the Spirit is a different

---

16   1 Sam. 8.4-22 is the obvious textual evidence. For some analysis, see for example, Tomoo Ishida, *The Royal Dynasties in Ancient Israel: A Study on the Formation and Development of Royal-Dynastic Ideology* (Berlin: Walter de Gruyter, 1977), pp. 26-117. Lyle Eslinger's attempt, *Kingship of God in Crisis: A Close Reading of I Samuel 1–12* (Sheffield: JSOT Press, 1985) p. 267, to rebut this conclusion finally relies on an assertion that 'the narrator's voice is the ultimate authority in the narrative world which he creates, and...the narrator's voice contradicts and overrules Yahweh's... Within the context of the voice-structure of the whole narrative, therefore, Yahweh may voice anti-monarchic sentiments in v. 8, but his views, because they are subordinate to the narrator's, are to be regarded as expressions of personal opinion', but this seems a difficult reading.

17   The various current debates about the precise way in which this slogan should be applied do not affect my point here materially; all orthodox trinitarian theology confesses that the three persons share 'one essence, one divinity, one power, one will, one energy, one beginning, one authority, one dominion, one sovereignty, made known in three perfect subsisitences and adored with one adoration' (the quotation is from John of Damascus, *Exposition of the Orthodox Faith* 1.8, in W. Sanday (ed.), *A Select Library of Nicene and Post-Nicene Fathers of the Christian Church* (trans. S.D.F. Salmond; Grand Rapids, MI: Eerdmans, 1997 [1898]), 2nd series, IX, p. 6; the point may be found throughout the patristic tradition), and this is all that is needed. For the record, I am inclined to agree with Colin Gunton's distinctions, as made in *The Promise of Trinitarian Theology* (Edinburgh: T. & T. Clark, 2nd edn, 1997), p. 4.

mission to that of the Son. T.F. Torrance identifies three ways in which the Spirit works to complete the work of Christ, to create the Church:[18]

—The Spirit creates out of the world a body which is to be the body of Christ. This body is to be both the place where the redemption won by Christ is realised and the place where the continuing ministry of Christ in proclaiming the good news is to occur.
—The body reaches out through the Spirit to fulfilment, intensively as it grows in the fullness of Christ, but also extensively as it reaches out to the ends of the earth and the end of the age. 'It is at once a teleological and an eschatological movement of fulfilment.'[19]
—The Spirit brings this movement to pass through word and sacrament. The witness of the body to the death and resurrection of Christ is *kerygma*, that which is preached, and those who hear the preaching receive both initiation and maintenance in the body through the bath, the loaf and the cup.

We thus find a third context for ministry, an ecclesiological context. The ministry of the Church as the body of Christ is clearly a participation in Christ's ministry, and bears the same marks. Service, the central mark of Christ's work, is enjoined upon the Church in Matthew 25.31-46; the use of the *charismata* for mutual benefit is clearly an element of *diakonia*, and regularly commanded by Paul. The Church is to be the place where the Word of God continues to be preached and heard. Priestly language is used both of the community (1 Pet. 2.5) and of individuals (Rom. 12.1), and the intercession demanded of the Church is a mediatory act. This ministry, in the pattern of the ministry of Christ is clearly a responsibility of the whole Church, and of every particular member of the Church.

The nature of this participation requires careful definition, however: the Church cannot have a 'separate' ministry to that of Christ as there is simply no more work to be done. In Christ, the Word of God has come in the decisive, full and final revelation; in Christ atonement for sin has been made once and for all; in Christ, in this homeless Jewish artisan, the universe has met its true king, and there is room for no other. The Church continues to speak God's Word, and so serves as prophet; it continues to hold the world before God in prayer, and so serves as a 'kingdom of priests'; it continues to give itself in love and service for the world, and its members will sit on thrones judging the tribes of Israel and the angels, and so serve as kings; but in all of this there is no sense of completing Christ's ministry, but of participating in the working out of an act that is already eschatologically complete. Neither has the Church

18   T.F. Torrance, *Royal Priesthood* (Edinburgh: T. & T. Clark, 2nd edn, 1993).
19   Torrance, *Royal Priesthood*, p. 24.

'taken over' aspects of Christ's ministry; this would deny the resurrection and ascension, and separate the ministry of the Spirit from that of the Son. So we must say that through the Spirit Christ continues his unique ministry in and through the Church.

We may, then, define the context of any understanding of ministry (of whatever variety) in the Church by asserting that the Church participates through the Spirit in the ministry of Christ, which was given him by the Father. This ministry of the Church is primarily a corporate ministry of the whole Body.

One Crucial Contention

This brings me to the crucial contention of this paper: everything I have to say stands or falls on this. It is simply the assertion that this ministry of the Church is precisely that—the ministry of 'the Church'. It is not the ministry of individuals in the Church, nor even the ministry of every individual within the Church, but a corporate ministry of the whole Church which is indivisible. The point might be made clearer by reflection on a shift in language in Baptist church life: where once we talked of 'the priesthood of all believers', now we talk of 'every-member ministry'. The move from 'priesthood' to 'ministry' may conceal something interesting, but my concern is with the move from 'all' to 'every', which implies a shift from a corporate understanding of service to an account based on a collection of individuals each with their own gifting and ministry. The former, corporate, understanding seems to me to be more defensible biblically and theologically, and to cohere better with classical Baptist principles.

Biblically, there is much data to support this contention. It is a commonplace that the New Testament will not use the word *hagioi*, 'saints', in the singular: Christian believers exist together or not at all, and so, necessarily, Christian believers minister together or not at all. Even the *locus classicus* used in discussions of 'every member ministry', 1 Corinthians 12, demands such a corporate understanding: whilst the gifts may be various, their source is one (vv. 4-11), and their purpose is one, the good of the whole (v. 7). The image of the body stresses the point: particular believers are hands, ears, eyes and feet, all of which belong together, indeed, need to be connected to each other to survive (vv. 14-23). Just so, it is simply a statement of fact that the good of one member is the good of all, and the suffering of one member damages all (v. 26). Again, it is obvious on this reading why 1 Corinthians 12 is followed by 1 Corinthians 13: love is what holds the members together, and so without love, whatever gifts a person may have been given, he is no more than a hand or eye seeking to exist outside the body; merely grotesque and doomed.

1 Corinthians 12 also at least implies the key theological resource for arguing this contention: the doctrine of the Trinity (the parallelism of vv. 4-6 is, it seems to me, most naturally read as a Trinitarian formula). Much recent Free Church ecclesiology has used Trinitarian doctrine as a model for picturing relationships within the Church. Miroslav Volf, for instance, argues that '[t]he future of the church in God's new creation is the mutual personal indwelling of the triune God and of his glorified people... Such participation in the communion of the triune God, however, is not only an object of hope for the church, but also its present experience.'[20] On this basis, he argues that the structures of the Church, which are defined by and derived from the charismatic gifts that the Spirit gives, give rise to institutions which 'correspond' to the relational life of the Trinity.[21] Paul Fiddes, in his recent book on the practical implications of believing in the Trinity, makes some very similar points.[22]

If the relationship, and ministry, of believers in church fellowship is to be modelled on the relationships and working of the triune God, we simply cannot talk about 'individual ministries' or 'my gifts', as so much recent Baptist writing, under the influence of charismatic renewal, has. Certainly we are all called to serve, and the Spirit of course gives the gifts that enable this, and if this had been forgotten by earlier generations of Baptist believers, then they were failing to be true to their own heritage, but the service of members of the body is not separable into pieces, and the gifts are given to the Church for the Church. The work of the triune Lord is not divisible into separate 'bits', so that perhaps the Father creates and the Son redeems—that would be a version of the ancient heresy of modalism—rather God, who is Father, Son and Holy Spirit acts, and *opera trinitatis ad extra sunt indivisa*. Distinctions may be made, as when St Basil suggests that each divine work is initiated by the Father, operated by the Son and perfected by the Spirit,[23] but it is one work and not three, and proper distinctions may never become improper divisions.

Just so, the ministry of the Church must be understood, if this model has any validity, as a corporate ministry. No person in the church has a ministry of preaching, or care, or healing; rather the church has all these

---

20   Miroslav Volf, *After Our Likeness: The Church as the Image of the Trinity* (Grand Rapids, MI: Eerdmans, 1998) pp. 128-29.

21   Volf, *After Our Likeness*, pp. 191-257. The particular language of institutions 'corresponding' to the triune relations is found on p. 235.

22   Paul S. Fiddes, *Participating in God: A Pastoral Doctrine of the Trinity* (London: Darton, Longman and Todd, 2000), see especially pp. 82-89.

23   Basil of Caesarea, *On the Spirit* 16.37, in P. Schaff and H. Wace (eds), *A Select Library of Nicene and Post-Nicene Fathers of the Christian Church* (trans. B. Jackson; Grand Rapids, MI: Eerdmans, 1996 [1894]), 2nd series, VIII, p. 23.

ministries, although it works them in different ways through particular individuals. Ministry is corporate, not distributed; this is a necessary derivation from Trinitarian dogma, and whilst there may and should be distinct activities within the corporate ministry of the church, the ministry must not be divided so that, again, proper distinctions become improper divisions.

Turning to traditional Baptist principles, the practice of church meeting which, properly understood, demonstrates so much of what Baptists believe the Church to be, would also imply that the ministry of the church is not a collection of individual ministries, but an irreducibly corporate ministry. In church meeting, hearing from God is the task and calling of all. There are not particular individuals, whether appointed leaders or those with 'gifts of discernment', who may abrogate this task to themselves; rather, the mind of Christ is known by the whole church gathered.

The various gifts that the Spirit is pleased to give to the church are necessary here, whether it be wisdom, prayer, discernment, knowledge or administration, and these gifts will of course be exercised by individual believers. In one sense it may even be not incorrect to say that they are given to individual believers, as particular people will often contribute in similar ways time after time. To think that the work of the Spirit in individual believers is at the heart of what is going on here, however, is to mistake badly what church meeting is about. All that is given is not an end in itself, but the means to a further end, the mind of Christ being known by the gathered body of Christ in a particular congregation. If great wisdom and greater discernment are variously in operation, and if even prophecy is brought, but the meeting breaks up with no common mind, the church has failed in its calling and the Spirit's gifts have failed in their purpose—all that has happened has been empty words, clanging gongs, sounding cymbals. In this case, no member of the church can pretend that she has exercised 'her' gifts faithfully; she, like every other member present, has failed. It is thus more correct theologically to say that the various gifts of the Spirit are given to the church, since it is the church's calling which they serve. The work of church meeting, like all the ministry of the people of God, is a corporate work, which cannot be divided up into individual tasks.

Ordained Ministry in the Church

Given all this, we are now in a position to explore the ministry of the Church. By the Spirit the Church participates in the prophetic ministry of Christ in her proclamation of the *kerygma*, the Word of God that continues to go forth with transformative, re-creative, effect. By the Spirit the Church participates in the priestly ministry of Christ by participating in his final and complete priestly offering by faith through sacrament, and by living under the reality of his redeeming sacrifice. By the Spirit the Church participates in the kingly ministry of Christ by giving herself in love and service for the world. This is the ministry of the Church.

In carrying out this ministry the Church has an ordained leadership, that is, leaders who have 'received a charism and whom the church appoints for service by ordination through the invocation of the Spirit and the laying on of hands' (the definition quoted above, from *BEM*). This been a more-or-less universal practice within the Church through history; is it, however, biblical?

Here we must make a crucial distinction between an *ordered* ministry and an *ordained* ministry. It is a common assertion that we find no basis for ordained ministry in the New Testament; this is simply not true: we find no ordered ministry, no organised ministry, but there is an abundance of evidence for ordained ministry, within the definition that I am using. Saul and Barnabas were ordained to the work of mission (Acts 13.1-3); Timothy was ordained (2 Tim.1.6); and so on. What there is no evidence for in the New Testament is any Church-wide order of ministry into which individuals were ordained. Rather, the Church as a whole has a ministry, and individuals are occasionally set apart for individual tasks within that ministry. These may be itinerant ministries (apostles, evangelists, prophets[24]) or local leadership ministries (overseers ['bishops'], elders ['presbyters'], deacons, exorcists[25]). The forms of leadership are varied (at least seven different words are used in the New Testament[26]), but leadership appears to have been always present, from the very earliest New Testament documents (1 Thess. 5.12). The question that remains, then, is how this ordained leadership, clearly present in and demanded by the New Testament documents, relates to the ministry of the Church.

---

24   Itinerant apostles and prophets appear to have been a part of the Church's ministry in the sub-apostolic period, see *Didache* 11–13, in G.P. Goold (ed.), *The Apostolic Fathers I* (trans K. Lake; Loeb Classical Library, 24; Cambridge, MA: Harvard University Press, 1912), pp. 325-29.

25   Cornelius, Bishop of Rome 251–53, mentions in a letter recorded by Eusebius of Caesarea, *Ecclesiastical History* 6.43.11, in H.J. Lawlor (ed.), *Eusebius: The Ecclesiastical History* (trans. J.E.L. Oulton; Loeb Classical Library, 265; Cambridge, MA: Harvard University Press, 1932), II, p. 119, that he had 'forty-six presbyters, seven deacons, seven sub-deacons, forty-two acolytes, fifty-two exorcists, readers and door-keepers...'.

26   For a survey of the texts, and a reconstruction of apostolic church life which I find broadly convincing, see R. Alastair Campbell, *The Elders: Seniority within Earliest Christianity* (Edinburgh: T. & T. Clark, 1994), especially pp. 120-26 and 151-72.

The Meaning of Ordination

The next strand of argument is an attempt to define the nature of
ordained leadership: in particular, is ordination ontological or functional,
a new 'way of being' or a new 'way of doing'? I want to argue for the
former, on three grounds.

First, Baptist practice suggests that this is what we believe. In a British
context at least, an ordained minister who gives up performing all the
functions of that task may be removed from the accredited list,[27] but is
not in any sense 'unordained', as is demonstrated by the fact that the
ordination will not be repeated should the minister ever return to pastoral
oversight. If this practice is at all coherent, then there must be something
conferred in ordination that is more than a set of functions to be
performed.

Second, recent Baptist and Methodist reports have suggested that it is
impossible to define the nature of ordained ministry functionally[28]—the
question simply does not admit of an answer from this direction. This
might be a failure of discernment or imagination on the part of the report
writers, of course. If, however, we read these reports with an appropriate
charity, we must assume that they are right (at least until we have good
reason to think otherwise); in this case we might assume that it is not
possible to define ministry on a merely functional understanding, and
that there must be something more involved.

Third, and most importantly, we may return to the theological
arguments above. There is a proper order of precedence within the triune
relations. Whether we choose to read that ordering as a result of
relationships of origin, or in another way,[29] it is clear that, the
subordination to the Father displayed by Jesus in the Gospels is not
merely a result of his self-humiliation in the incarnation, but a reflection
of the inner-Trinitarian relationships. In the Trinity we can see freely
offered and freely accepted authority, within an utter unity of love. If the
Church is to in some sense image forth or mirror the life of the Trinity, it
too will offer and accept authority within its fellowship. This is real
authority, not something that can be reduced to a function of leadership,

---

27   Although they should not be: accreditation should surely, theologically, be an
expression of good standing amongst the churches. Gross ethical failure may be a reason
to remove accreditation, but a change of function should not, unless the move away from
pastoral oversight is seen as in some way a failure to be true to the original calling.

28   Baptist Union Doctrine and Worship Commission Report, *Ministry and
Ordination Amongst Baptists* (n.d.), see esp. p. 3; Methodist Faith and Order Committee
Report, *The Methodist Diaconal Order* (1994), see esp. para. 10.5.

29   For some account of what is at stake in this question, see Alan J. Torrance,
Persons in Communion: Trinitarian Description and Human Participation (Edinburgh: T.
& T. Clark, 1996).

as the doctrine of perichoresis will not allow us to assign any function to the Father that is not shared by the Son and the Spirit. Thus the authority of the Father must be a part of his particular personal hypostatic existence, and so something that is in some sense ontological.

In what sense might this authority be ontological? Many proposals within recent Trinitarian theology have followed John Zizioulas's lead in identifying Trinitarian ontology with the inner-triune relationships.[30] To speak of an ontological authority, then, is to recognise that within the life of the triune God, the authority of the Father is an intrinsic part of the shape of the eternal relationships of love. This way of understanding the issue perhaps offers a way forward in attempting to find the proper analogy for this Trinitarian dogma in the life of the Church. The act of ordination so re-orders the relationships within the body of Christ that the one ordained stands in relationships of authority to other members of the body.

The biblical and universal practice of ordination, then, confers a proper authority which is not merely a result of a function performed by the one ordained, but intrinsic to their personal existence—in ordination, people are, by an act of the Spirit in response to prayer, set apart to exercise authority within the Church. Ordination thus confers a way of being oriented towards leading the Church in the accomplishing of the ministry sketched above. There is a need, however, to say more than this. In particular, the twin traditional functions of ordained leaders (preaching and liturgical presidency) are not yet brought within this doctrinal account, and should be, if it is to be a successful doctrine of ministry.

Alongside the doctrine of perichoresis in Trinitarian dogma is its necessary complement: the doctrine of appropriation. Although all acts of the Trinity are undivided, it is still possible to 'appropriate' certain acts to certain persons, recognising a primacy of role within the undivided act. Thus, the creed will speak of creation under belief in God the Father, redemption under belief in God the Son, and sanctification and final consummation under belief in God the Spirit. Each named act is an undivided act of the Trinity, to be sure, but in each case there is also a proper appropriating to a particular person. In the same way, we might argue that certain functions of the Church are appropriately performed by the particular people in the Church, thus giving the necessary biblical content to the language of 'personal' or 'individual' *charismata* ('*to each one* is given the manifestation of the Spirit for the common good...', 1 Cor. 12.7), without compromising the fact that the ministry of the Church is undivided. It would then be possible to locate certain tasks

---

30   John D. Zizioulas, *Being as Communion: Studies in Personhood and the Church* (Crestwood, NY: St Vladimir's Seminary Press, 1985). Zizioulas discovers this position within the work of the Cappadocian Fathers, of course.

as appropriate to the ordained leadership of the Church, and preaching and liturgical presidency might fit here.

The doctrine of appropriation does not remove any act from being an act of the Trinity, and so these functions do not cease to be part of the ministry of the Church just because they are being performed by an ordained minister. Rather, the undivided ministry of the Church, without ceasing to be a corporate act, finds a particular focus in one of the members of the Church. It is as inappropriate to speak of the minister as 'representing' the Church as it is to speak of the Father as representing the Trinity in creation or the Son as representing the Trinity in redemption; equally, it is as proper to link liturgical presidency with ordained ministry as it is to link the act of redemption with the Word who became flesh.

What tasks within the corporate ministry of the Church are particularly appropriate to the ordained ministry? It may be that there is a need to recover an ancient wisdom here, with different orders of ministry (the diaconate, the presbyters, the episcopate, catechists, apostles, exorcists, and so on) accepting different tasks.[31] Nonetheless, perhaps certain things may be said. If it is the case that leadership (the exercise of authority to enable the Church to perform its fundamental ministry) is central to the role of this ordained ministry, then certain other things follow from that. For Baptists, authority in the Church is found in the mind of Christ as revealed in scripture. The exercise of authority, then, must be intimately connected with the faithful exposition of scripture, with speaking forth the Word of God to the Church in the ministry of edification, and to the world, in making known the gospel of the kingdom of God. Thus both preaching the good news and teaching 'the whole counsel of God' are properly appropriated to the ordained ministry within the undivided ministry of the Church.

The task of the Church in speaking forth the Word of God is not exhausted in proclamation, however: the Word is also spoken to God, in praise and petition. This is perhaps most fully the case when, in obedience to God's Word, bread is broken and wine is shared, and when those who have been called by the gospel of Christ are made members of the body of Christ through the waters of baptism. If it is appropriate to link the speaking of the Word to ordination, then, the exercise of liturgical presidency, of shaping the worship of the church and celebrating the sacraments, is also a proper part of the role of the ordained ministry.

---

31   The recent decision by the Baptist Union of Great Britain to include youth specialists and evangelists on the list of accredited ministers could be interpreted as an attempt to return to a form of such patristic practice.

(The precise implication of the language of 'appropriation' here can remain a matter for debate. It would be possible to develop the Trinitarian analogy above in a way that suggested that, whilst preaching and liturgical presidency are intimately connected to the ordained ministry of the Church, they nonetheless remain within the corporate ministry of the Church, and so may properly be performed by any member of the body. This would offer a theological legitimisation for present Baptist practice. On the other hand, the analogy with appropriation might be thought to lead to an account whereby the role of the ordained minister is central, and so no other should preach or celebrate the sacrament, whilst insisting that this role is not separable from the ministry of the Church, and so the gathered faithful have their own proper but subordinate part to play in the celebration of the liturgy. This would lead to an account similar to that advanced by the Second Vatican Council, for instance, where there is a particular 'priesthood of the laity' that cannot replace, but equally must supplement, the role of the priest in the celebration of mass.[32])

This account also places clear theological limits on the role of the ordained ministry: if ordained ministry is a part of the ministry of the Church, which is in turn a participation through the Holy Spirit in the ministry that Christ received from the Father, then both the Triune God and the Church have authority over the ordained ministry. Thus we can find a theological legitimisation for the apparently rather convoluted Baptist practice whereby the church delegates its authority over its members to be exercised by the ordained minister, but retains authority over that minister in his or her exercise of the delegated authority. In saying this, however, I would immediately want to stress that there is an authority independent of the church conferred by ordination. This stems from the fact that the minister is responsible to both God and the Church and not to the Church alone. The Trinitarian image of the Church, or the body of Christ image, both suggest that there is some authority which, although received through the community, may oppose the community in the name of Christ.[33] Thus, ordained ministry carries the possibility of

32   *Lumen Gentium* 2.10, which speaks of 'the common priesthood of the faithful' who 'join in the offering of the Eucharist by virtue of their royal priesthood' (translation from Walter M. Abbott, SJ [ed.], *The Documents of Vatican II* [Piscataway, NJ: America Press, 1966], p. 27).

33   This account of balancing authorities is further complicated by the recognition that the mind of Christ is properly known in church meeting, by the gathered people of God. Nonetheless, church meeting is not akin to a Quaker meeting, seeking some inner light: it is a place where the scriptures are to be interpreted for the edification and guidance of the community. It may, then, become clear that in a particular instance a gathered church is wilfully refusing to hear the voice of Christ, and at this point every

a prophetic function. This authority, received from God directly, rather than through the Church, is how I would wish to understand the *character indelebilis*. This authority, in common with every authority attached to ordained ministry, is authority to serve the Church, authority to seek the furtherance of the Church's ministry, not authority to rule. This understanding of authority is forced upon us by a context of ministry which has already been identified: any authority attached to ministry can only ever be exercised in the way that Christ chose to exercise his authority, in *diakonia*, as a *doulos*.

Concluding Remarks

There are, of course, many remaining issues around the ministry of the Church which there is not space to touch on in this paper, but I hope the argument as it stands is reasonably complete. Christ's Church has a ministry, both in the sense of a task to perform, and a group of people called of God and commissioned in solemn prayer by the Church, in obedience to God's call, to a particular role within this task. I do not for a moment suppose that ordained ministry is of the *esse* of the Church, in the sense that prevailing confusion in this area could separate gathered believers from the body of Christ. That it is of the *bene esse* of the Church, that in his wisdom God has been pleased to order his Church in this way and not another, seems to me to be luminously clear, and something that Baptist Christians, in Britain at least, need urgently to recover.

---

faithful member, but particularly the ordained minister, has prophetic authority (and, indeed, responsibility) to rebuke and call for repentance and reformation.

CHAPTER 15

Towards a Sacramental Understanding of Preaching

Brian Haymes

'But how are they to call on one in whom they have not believed?
And how are they to believe in one of whom they have never heard?
And how are they to hear without someone to proclaim him?
And how are they to proclaim him unless they are sent?'
Romans 10.14-15[1]

It may come as a surprise to find an essay on preaching, even in the form of a brief note, in a volume given over to an exploration of Baptist sacramentalism. It is readily acknowledged that many Baptists are wary of sacramental language, some deliberately declining to use it because it expresses theological concepts for which they claim to find little biblical evidence and which may even compromise the doctrine of justification by grace through faith alone. Among some British Baptists there has been a caution about the concept of sacrament originating to some extent in a reaction against the sacramentalism of the Oxford Movement. Sacramentalism was taken to be the belief that the act of receiving a sacrament was, in itself, efficacious. However, historians have argued that such a negative response to the sacraments has not been and is not universal among Baptists.[2]

---

1   All biblical quotations are from the New Revised Standard Version (Cambridge: Cambridge University Press).

2   Philip E. Thompson, 'A New Question in Baptist History: Seeking A Catholic Spirit Among Early Baptists', *Pro Ecclesia* 8.1 (Winter, 1999), pp. 66-68, and 'Practicing the Freedom of God: Formation in Early Baptist Life', in David M. Hammond (ed.), *Theology and Lived Christianity* (Annual Publication of the College Theology Society, 45; Mystic, CT: Twenty-Third Publications, 2000), pp. 126-31; Anthony R. Cross, 'Dispelling the Myth of English Baptist Baptismal Sacramentalism', *Baptist Quarterly* 38.8 (October, 2000), pp. 367-91; Stanley K. Fowler, *More Than a Symbol: The British Baptist Recovery of Baptismal Sacramentalism* (Studies in Baptist History and Thought, 2; Carlisle: Paternoster, 2002); and Stanley Grenz's essay in the present volume.

My concern in this essay is to reflect on sacramental and non-sacramental theologies and their consequences for preaching. Positively in this essay I shall argue that a theology that is sacramental produces a strong theology of preaching related to the world in which we live, and a history in which God is at work, while, negatively, a non-sacramental theology diminishes preaching both in understanding, practice and effect. The distinction between them focuses on the understanding of grace.

A sacramental theology has three necessarily inter-related elements. As my argument develops it will become apparent that these cannot properly be separated and the attempt to do so here is only made for the sake of analysis.

First, such a theology affirms the doctrine of creation, the original and continuing work of God. Matter is what God makes in love. It is the very 'stuff' of creation.[3] The material universe is called and held in being by God to God's own purposes and it is in the context of creation, of time and history, that God reveals God's providential ways. The creative Word God speaks is both the formation of creation and the hope of its redemption. The only God known in the Christian story is the God who loves and uses matter. It is in history that humankind has come to know God's purpose, our need, and the divine response. Sacramental theology affirms the doctrine of creation and the work of God in history. Moreover, and crucially, such a theology, while asserting the importance of the Fall, understands that the image of God is marred but not destroyed by this disaster. Thus, although we might speak of original sin we must also acknowledge an original righteousness that is marred but not utterly destroyed in humankind and the rest of creation. Theologies that overlook or deny any serious place to matter as being significant in itself, or for redemption, are inadequate.

Second, God uses the world of matter to mediate divine grace. In history God acts out God's mighty works, involving wind and fire, monarchs and military, priests and prophets. Most significantly of all, God becomes incarnate. The Word that was in the beginning by whom all things were made becomes flesh and dwells among us (Jn 1.1-18). It is the fundamental Christian claim that in the flesh and blood figure of history, Jesus Christ, 'God's address to humanity and humanity's response to God the Father are ultimately actualised.'[4] These actions in history are all of them, including the incarnation of the Son of God,

---

3   See Paul S. Fiddes, 'Baptism and Creation', in Paul S. Fiddes (ed.), *Reflections on the Water: Understanding God and the World through the Baptism of Believers* (Regent's Study Guides, 4; Oxford: Regent's Park College, Oxford, 1996), pp. 47-67

4   Christoph Schwöbel, 'The Preacher's Art: Preaching Theologically', in Colin Gunton (ed.), *Theology Through Preaching* (Edinburgh: T. & T. Clark, 2001), p. 2

expressions of God's gracious self. There are no a-historical or a-material expressions of grace in the biblical witness.

Third, the activity of God, in grace and judgement, is always addressed to human need born of the love of God. Thus God is always about the work of creation and redemption, seeking lost humankind with saving and transforming grace. It is by God's own work, the activity of Holy Spirit, who makes connections possible, opening our eyes and minds to the divine mercy and grace. In particular, in the history Christians recount, there are two God-ordained meeting places. 'It is no new thought, but it cannot be too often before our eyes, that the grace offered in baptism, as in the Eucharist, is no impersonal influence, injected through material substance, but *the gracious action of God himself.*'[5] God has promised to be with God's people always but particularly in the pool and at the table. These are moments when the story of God is told, a story in which we find, by the gracious work of the Holy Spirit, that we have a special part. A conversation is held and we are partners. God's gracious blessing is known by us in our own history as the Spirit continues to take of the things of Christ and show them to us. These actions, symbolic but not 'mere symbols', convey the divine will, love and grace to God's people. It is then no surprise to learn that some Christians, while stressing the dominical injunctions to baptism and remembrance at table, should also recognize other moments in our personal stories in which the grace of our saving God is known. Thus, without suggesting for a moment that these are of similar nature and significance to baptism and Eucharist, many would say that marriage has a sacramental character as in the flesh the grace of God is known. So also, for some, ordination has meant more than the choice of the people, or their own decision, but God meeting in blessing the one whom God has called to a life of ministry focused on Word and Sacraments. Or take the reading of scripture. Has not the print on paper, the material things of creation, the creation shared by the Son of God, become by the Holy Spirit the means by which we receive God's blessing?[6]

The way we speak of these things may reveal a difference of some significance. Is it more appropriate to speak of God being gracious, acting graciously in creation, redemption and sanctification? Or is grace a characteristic of God, an attribute he sometimes employs? Does God's grace relate only to certain specific acts of salvation, focused in Jesus Christ? Or is Jesus Christ the incarnation of the God who is always gracious, such that we can speak of nature being graced?

---

5   George R. Beasley-Murray, *Baptism in the New Testament* (London: Macmillan, 1962), p. 265

6   I have never understood the phrase used by some readers of the Bible in worship when they ask that God should add his blessing the reading of his Word. Is not the Word read and heard a blessing?

In any sacramental theology, Word and Sacraments belong together. Sacraments without the Word, without the story proclaimed, run the risk of becoming 'magical', unworldly and spiritualized. Word without Sacrament, without the grounding of the story in the flesh and blood world we share in the purposes of God, runs the risk of being rational and spiritualized, of being turned back from the world in which our redemption has been wrought. How shall they hear without a preacher indeed? And how shall they know and experience the active grace of God without it being mediated in a universe in which God uses matter to bless, heal and save? What I am arguing is that Christian preaching implies, as do the sacraments, a trinitarian understanding of God, Creator, Saviour, Sanctifier.

Our experience of God is trinitarian and sacramental. Baptists have always recognized the importance of the existence of the Church and the possibility of our personal experience of God. We have called for personal decision, for trust in Jesus Christ as Lord and Saviour and many have spoken of the experience of being 'born again'. However, we do not simply have experience. It is always experience of something. In this sense, all experience is conceptually loaded and context dependent.[7] Thus Christian experience is shaped by the story of the God revealed in Jesus Christ by the activity of the Holy Spirit. The story is told and by the work of God lives are touched, turned and healed. And often the context of all this is Christian worship, Word and Sacrament, the Church of Jesus Christ.

It is a conviction held by many Baptists that, by the Spirit, God meets us in the preaching of God's word. Many, in fact, would agree with the affirmation of P.T. Forsyth on the crucial nature of preaching with regard to the gospel, that with preaching the gospel prolongs and declares itself and so Christianity stands or falls by preaching.[8] In some places the minister is straightforwardly called the Preacher. The call to preach is an honoured one in the recognition that the message needs messengers as Paul affirms rhetorically in Romans 10.15. Descriptions of worship among early dissenters indicated the emphasis they placed on preaching.[9]

This conviction about the importance of preaching used to be reflected in our architecture as, in the old meeting houses, the central pulpit stood high, with its large Bible. Below and central was the table with cup and plate. The very stones and wood carried their own message about the nature of God and the calling of God's people. So God uses such matter

7   See the discussion of these issues in my *The Concept of the Knowledge of God* (London: Macmillan, 1986), pp. 44-46, where I draw upon the argument of Karl Popper.

8   P.T. Forsyth, *Positive Preaching and the Modern Mind* (London: Independent Press, 1905), p. 3

9   See the excerpt in A. Bradstock and C. Rowland (eds.), *Radical Christian Writings: A Reader* (London: Blackwell, 2002), pp. 105-106.

upon which human minds and hands have worked. There is no doubt but that with every building a statement is made and a theological message conveyed. As such, these 'sermons in stone' may be good or bad, appropriate to God or otherwise. Working in London, one could not help but be struck by the way in which, immediately upon the terrorist attacks in America on 11 September 2001, people sought 'sacred space' and those churches which were open soon found people coming to pray and to reflect. The buildings were being used while symbolically they were speaking.

What does preaching involve? First, it involves matter in several forms. There is the need for a human being, woman or man, capable of speech. 'Preaching will never die because a witness to the precise personal center of reality—God—is most effective when we receive it through a medium that expresses the fullness and wonder of what personality is, and that is accomplished more completely by speech than by the written word.'[10] They shall not hear without a preacher. It is often argued that the work of God in the sacraments is not dependent on the spiritual quality of the minister. However that may be, in the case of preaching, while it is not beyond God to use the poorest of human material, the preacher does matter. Paul argued that they can only preach if they are sent. There has been an emphasis among many Baptists that those called should further submit themselves to careful preparation, of study and prayer, that their usefulness to God might be increased. The 'recognition' of preachers is no light matter for the church to consider. As H.H. Farmer once put it: 'God may indeed use the foolishness of preaching, but we are under obligation to see that it is not more foolish than it need be.'[11]

The preacher further needs a Bible, the collection of canonical writings received as print on paper. There may be many descriptions of the relationship of text to sermon but that there is a relationship is not to be doubted. Bernard Lord Manning's definition of preaching makes the point: 'a manifestation of the Incarnate Word, *from the Written Word,* by the spoken word.'[12]

And the preacher needs hearers. As such, a sermon is always an event between flesh and blood persons, an event in space and time. It is by this work that the Church is built up. Indeed, Baptists have held that the proclamation of the Word in the community of believers is a priority. Charles Rice argues that there is a danger that detached television evangelists may, precisely because of the discarnate relationship to the hearers, distort both preaching and the gospel. 'Any notion of

---

10   Thomas H. Troeger, *Imagining a Sermon* (Nashville, TN: Abingdon Press, 1990), p. 69

11   H.H. Farmer, *The Servant of the Word* (London: Nisbet, 1960), p. 31.

12   Quoted by W.E. Sangster, *The Craft of the Sermon* (London: Epworth Press, 1954) p. 4, italics mine

evangelism that does not take the visible body seriously will not only pervert preaching, but will in the long run, weaken its own witness. In this sense, the typical religious orator appearing on the media frustrates the proper work of evangelism, which is to bring people into flesh-and-blood connection with Christ's Church.'[13] Preaching involves preacher, Bible and hearers, all expressions at one level of God's created matter. The usual context then for preaching is the liturgical assembly, the God-gathered church.

Second, preaching involves God's use of this matter and moment. By the voice and the ear, through the printed word read and heard, God makes God's own approach to humankind. Preaching is God's continuing work with the preacher as God's partner. It is important, of course, to recognize the distinction between divine and human words. Speaking of the prophets, Christoph Schwöbel asserts: 'Only by distinguishing their words from God's word, by pointing away from themselves as the source of the message to God, can it become clear that God employs their human word as a means of relating to people.'[14] Nonetheless, preaching has a necessary incarnational aspect. God uses humankind to embody and proclaim the gospel but there remains a gap that denies any absolute one-to-one identification between human and divine words. 'The incarnational approach has a concern for the objective reality of the content of revelation, but it differs from fundamentalism because it recognises that all truths are mediated through historical and sociological relativities.'[15]

Then third, developing God's use of matter, preaching involves God's promise to meet with God's people. The Word God speaks will not return to God void but will accomplish God's purpose (Isa. 55.10-11). Behind this assertion lies a biblical doctrine of God's Word which is inseparable from God's action. God said, 'Let there be light', and there was light (Gen. 1.3). God's Word is God's deed. Utterance, event and act are all fundamentally related.[16] It is the work of the Spirit to take of the things of Christ and show them to us. In this sense, all effective preaching is charismatic and trinitarian.

---

13   Charles L. Rice, *The Embodied Word: Preaching as Art and Liturgy* (Minneapolis, MN: Fortress Press, 1991), p. 36

14   C. Schwöbel, 'Introduction: The Preacher's Art: Preaching Theologically', in Colin Gunton (ed.), *Theology Through Preaching* (Edinburgh: T. & T. Clark, 2001), p. 3

15   Duncan Macpherson, 'God so loved the World', in Gregory Heille, OP (ed.), *Theology of Preaching: Essays on Vision and Mission in the Pulpit* (London: Melisende, 2001), p. 25

16   See the discussion by G. Henton Davies, 'Concepts of the Word of God in the Old Testament', in L.G. Champion (ed.), *The Communication of the Christian Faith* (Bristol: Bristol Baptist College, 1964), pp. 1-16.

But it is God who effects the encounter with the hearers that is the work of preaching. This is the case both with the calling of the preacher and also with God speaking through the human words the Word of life. This is not to say that every sermon is a hearing of the Word. It may be no more than the enduring of the preacher's utterance from the pulpit. The charism of preaching is not in the particular gift of the preacher but in the activity of God by which the hearers know themselves addressed by God. Because it is the work of God then we must acknowledge the freedom of the Spirit to act as and when God wills. Just as Baptists reject any *ex opere operato* understanding of the acts of baptism and the Lord's Supper, so they might also reject any identification with the act of preaching with the hearing of God's Word. If the Word is heard then it is the work of the Spirit. There can be no divorce here between natural and supernatural gifts. Any charisma is a divine event or action which relates to the human gifts employed. So, in preaching, the Spirit may chose to act, the preacher and hearer being the means by which God chooses to act graciously.[17]

One of Thomas Helwys' criticisms of the Church of England was the way in which it was assumed that bishops were the only proper interpreters of the texts of scripture. He saw this as an attempted imposition on the activity of the Spirit. He asked how the Word of God was made effectual to salvation and argued that 'the Spirit of God makes the reading, but especially the preaching of the Word and effectual means of convincing and converting sinners, and of building them up in holiness and comfort, through faith unto salvation'.[18] Philip Thompson also argues from the history of Baptists that, 'In the context of the Church the proclamation of the Word was still seen as the primary means by which God effectually called and then built up the elect. "It seems plain", explained John Gill, "that the ministry of the Word is the vehicle in which the Spirit of God conveys himself and his grace into the hearts of men". This proclamation was a call to the ordinances, to the means and blessings of grace which would strengthen faith.'[19] One might argue, as is done for example by David Buttrick, that just as the preacher is not a reporter but a witness, so the task of preaching is the Spirit's work of *anamnesis*.[20] Or as John P. Burgess has suggested, if a sacrament is an

---

17   See the discussion on the nature of charismata by Paul S. Fiddes, *Charismatic Renewal: A Baptist View* (London: Baptist Publications, 1980), pp. 9-13.

18   W.L. Lumpkin (ed.), *Baptist Confessions of Faith* (Chicago: Judson Press 1959), p. 39.

19   P.E. Thompson, 'Toward Baptist Ecclesiology in Pneumatological Perspective' (PhD Thesis, Emory University, 1995), p.128. The quotation of John Gill is from *A Body of Divinity* (Grand Rapids, MI: Baker Book House, 1951 [1770]), p. 534.

20   See further Daniel Francis, CSsR, 'The Pulpit is a Mountain', in Gregory Heille, OP (ed.), *Theology of Preaching* (London: Melisende, 2002), pp. 81-90.

outward sign of an invisible grace, might preaching be an audible sound of an inaudible word of grace, with the capacity to move, inspire and claim us.[21]

Hence the purpose of preaching is not fundamentally the giving of information. It is a different, yet related, task to that of teaching. It is not an act of memorialism, the recalling a history alone. It is a work of God effecting a divine encounter, a meeting. A theology which takes creation seriously and expects God to use such 'natural means' implies a sacramental theology.

So, argues, H.H. Farmer: 'preaching is telling me something. But it is not merely *telling* me something. It is God actively probing me, challenging my will, calling on me for decision, offering me His succour, through the only medium which the nature of His purpose permits Him to us, the medium of personal relationship.'[22] Thus a sermon is not a lecture. It is an event. It happens when there is attention given by preacher and hearer to scripture, tradition, and the present. The preaching 'moment' is God's gracious presence in our midst, enabling the preacher to speak and the congregation to hear.

Just as the sacraments are divine gifts in which God is active, given to build up the life and faith of the people of God, so they need the preaching of the Word, calling people not the least to the ordinances. More than that, preaching might well be called both 'naming grace' in human experience, as well as the proclamation of God's Word.[23] Such preaching, as the sharing of the Word, the encountering of divine grace in the midst of life, is also the work of the Spirit, the work of God. Hence preaching is both a divine and human activity and God continues the divine conversation in and through worship, not least at those God given meeting places in order that we might discover the presence of the gracious God potentially in all of life.

---

21   John P. Burgess, 'Scripture as Sacramental Word: Rediscovering Scripture's Compelling Power', *Interpretation* 52.4 (October, 1998), pp. 380-91.

22   Farmer, *Servant of the Word*, pp. 27-28.

23   See the fascinating discussion by Mary Catherine Hilkert, *Naming Grace: Preaching and the Sacramental Imagination* (New York: Continuum, 1997).

Index

Studies in Baptist History and Thought

(All title uniform with this volume)
(Volumes in this series are not always published in sequence.)

David Bebbington and Anthony R. Cross (eds)
Global Baptist History
(SBHT vol. 14)
This book brings together studies from the Second International Conference on Baptist Studies which explore different facets of Baptist life and work especially during the twentieth century.
2005 / ISBN 1-84227-214-4

David Bebbington (ed.)
The Gospel in the World
International Baptist Studies
(SBHT vol. 1)
This volume of essays from the First International Conference on Baptist Studies deals with a range of subjects spanning Britain, North America, Europe, Asia and the Antipodes. Topics include studies on religious tolerance, the communion controversy and the development of the international Baptist community, and concludes with two important essays on the future of Baptist life that pay special attention to the United States.
2002 / ISBN 1-84227-118-0 / xiv + 362pp

Anthony R. Cross
Baptism and the Baptists
Theology and Practice in Twentieth-Century Britain
(SBHT vol. 3)
At a time of renewed interest in baptism, *Baptism and the Baptists* is a detailed study of twentieth-century baptismal theology and practice and the factors which have influenced its development.
2000 / ISBN 0-85364-959-6 / xx + 530pp

Anthony R. Cross and Philip E. Thompson (eds)
Baptist Myths
(SBHT vol. 11)
This collection of essays examines some of the 'myths' in Baptist history and theology: these include the idea of development in Baptist thought, studies in the church, baptismal sacramentalism, community, spirituality, soul competency, women, Baptist bishops, creeds and the Bible, and overseas missions.
2004 / ISBN 1-84227-122-9

Anthony R. Cross and Philip E. Thompson (eds)
Baptist Sacramentalism
(SBHT vol. 5)
This collection of essays includes historical and theological studies in the sacraments from a Baptist perspective. Subjects explored include the physical side of being spiritual, baptism, the Lord's supper, the church, ordination, preaching, worship, religious liberty and the issue of disestablishment.
2003 / ISBN 1-84227-119-9 / xvi + 278pp

Paul S. Fiddes
Tracks and Traces
Baptist Identity in Church and Theology
(SBHT vol. 13)
This is a comprehensive, yet unusual, book on the faith and life of Baptist Christians. It explores the understanding of the church, ministry, sacraments and mission from a thoroughly theological perspective. In a series of interlinked essays, the author relates Baptist identity consistently to a theology of covenant and to participation in the triune communion of God.
2003 / ISBN 1-84227-120-2 / xvi + 304pp

Stanley K. Fowler
More Than a Symbol
The British Baptist Recovery of Baptismal Sacramentalism
(SBHT vol. 2)
Fowler surveys the entire scope of British Baptist literature from the seventeenth-century pioneers onwards. He shows that in the twentieth century leading British Baptist pastors and theologians recovered an understanding of baptism that connected experience with soteriology and that in doing so they were recovering what many of their forebears had taught.
2002 / ISBN 1-84227-052-4 / xvi + 276pp

Michael A.G. Haykin (ed.)
Fuller as an Apologist
(SBHT vol. 6)
One of the greatest Baptist theologians of the eighteenth and early nineteenth centuries, Andrew Fuller has not had justice done to him. There is little doubt that Fuller's theology lay behind the revitalization of the Baptists in the late eighteenth century and the first few decades of the nineteenth. This collection of essays fills a much needed gap by examining a major area of Fuller's thought, his work as an apologist.
2004 / ISBN 1-84227-171-7 / approx 300pp

Michael A.G. Haykin
Studies in Calvinistic Baptist Spirituality
(SBHT vol. 15)
In a day when spirituality is in vogue and Christian communities are looking for guidance in this whole area, there is wisdom in looking to the past to find untapped wells. The Calvinistic Baptists, heirs of the rich ecclesial experience in the Puritan era of the seventeenth century, but, by the end of the eighteenth century, also passionately engaged in the catholicity of the Evangelical Revivals, are such a well. This collection of essays, covering such things as the Lord's Supper, friendship and hymnody, seeks to draw out the spiritual riches of this community for reflection and imitation in the present day.
2005 / ISBN 1-84227-149-0

Brian Haymes, Anthony R. Cross and Ruth Gouldbourne
On Being the Church
Revisioning Baptist Identity
(SBHT vol. 21)
The aim of the book is to re-examine Baptist theology and practice in the light of the contemporary biblical, theological, ecumenical and missiological context drawing on historical and contemporary writings and issues. It is not a study in denominationalism but rather seeks to revision historical insights from the believers' church tradition for the sake of Baptists and other Christians in the context of the modern–postmodern context.
2005 / ISBN 1-84227-121-0

Ken R. Manley
From Woolloomooloo to 'Eternity'
A History of Baptists in Australia
(SBHT vol. 16)
From their beginnings in Australia in 1831 with the first baptisms in Woolloomooloo Bay in 1832, this pioneering study describes the quest of Baptists in the different colonies (states) to discover their identity as Australians and Baptists. Although institutional developments are analyzed and the roles of significant individuals traced, the major focus is on the social and theological dimensions of the Baptist movement.
2005 / ISBN 1-84227-194-6

Ken R. Manley
'Redeeming Love Proclaim'
John Rippon and the Baptists
(SBHT vol. 12)
A leading exponent of the new moderate Calvinism which brought new life to many Baptists, John Rippon (1751–1836) helped unite the Baptists at this significant time. His many writings expressed the denomination's growing maturity and mutual awareness of Baptists in Britain and America, and exerted a long-lasting influence on Baptist worship and devotion. In his various activities, Rippon helped conserve the heritage of Old Dissent and promoted the evangelicalism of the New Dissent.
2004 / ISBN 1-84227-193-8 / xviii + 340pp

Peter J. Morden
Offering Christ to the World
Andrew Fuller and the Revival of Eighteenth Century Particular Baptist Life
(SBHT vol. 8)
Andrew Fuller (1754–1815) was one of the foremost English Baptist ministers of his day. His career as an Evangelical Baptist pastor, theologian, apologist and missionary statesman coincided with the profound revitalization of the Particular Baptist denomination to which he belonged. This study examines the key aspects of the life and thought of this hugely significant figure, and gives insights into the revival in which he played such a central part.
2003 / ISBN 1-84227-141-5 / xx + 202pp

Peter Naylor
Calvinism, Communion and the Baptists
A Study of English Calvinistic Baptists from the Late 1600s to the Early 1800s
(SBHT vol. 7)
Dr Naylor argues that the traditional link between 'high Calvinism' and 'restricted communion' is in need of revision. He examines Baptist communion controversies from the late 1600s to the early 1800s and also the theologies of John Gill and Andrew Fuller.
2003 / ISBN 1-84227-142-3 / xx + 266pp

Ian M. Randall, Toivo Pilli and Anthony R. Cross (eds)
Baptist Identities
International Studies from the Seventeenth to the Twentieth Centuries
(SBHT vol. 19)
These papers represent the contributions of scholars from various parts of the world as they consider the factors that have contributed to Baptist distinctiveness in different countries and at different times. The volume includes specific case studies as well as broader examinations of Baptist life in a particular country or region. Together they represent an outstanding resource for understanding Baptist identities.
2004 / ISBN 1-84227-215-2

James M. Renihan
Edification and Beauty
The Practical Ecclesiology of the English Particular Baptists, 1675–1705
(SBHT vol. 17)
Edification and Beauty describes the practices of the Particular Baptist churches at the end of the seventeenth century in terms of three concentric circles: at the centre is the ecclesiological material in the Second London Confession, which is then fleshed out in the various published writings of the men associated with these churches, and, finally, expressed in the church books of the era.
2004 / ISBN 1-84227-251-9

Frank Rinaldi
'The Tribe of Dan'
A Study of the New Connexion of General Baptists 1770–1891
(SBHT vol. 10)
'The Tribe of Dan' is a thematic study which explores the theology, organizational structure, evangelistic strategy, ministry and leadership of the New Connexion of General Baptists as it experienced the process of institutionalization in the transition from a revival movement to an established denomination.
2005 / ISBN 1-84227-143-1

Peter Shepherd
The Making of a Modern Denomination
John Howard Shakespeare and the English Baptists 1898–1924
(SBHT vol. 4)
John Howard Shakespeare introduced revolutionary change to the Baptist denomination. The Baptist Union was transformed into a strong central institution and Baptist ministers were brought under its control. Further, Shakespeare's pursuit of church unity reveals him as one of the pioneering ecumenists of the twentieth century.
2001 / ISBN 1-84227-046-X / xviii + 220pp

Brian Talbot
The Search for a Common Identity
The Origins of the Baptist Union of Scotland 1800–1870
(SBHT vol. 9)
In the period 1800 to 1827 there were three streams of Baptists in Scotland: Scotch, Haldaneite and 'English' Baptist. A strong commitment to home evangelization brought these three bodies closer together, leading to a merger of their home missionary societies in 1827. However, the first three attempts to form a union of churches failed, but by the 1860s a common understanding of their corporate identity was attained leading to the establishment of the Baptist Union of Scotland.
2003 / ISBN 1-84227-123-7 / xviii + 402pp

Philip E. Thompson
The Freedom of God
Towards Baptist Theology in Pneumatological Perspective
(SBHT vol. 20)
This study contends that the range of theological commitments of the early Baptists are best understood in relation to their distinctive emphasis on the freedom of God. Thompson traces how this was recast anthropocentrically, leading to an emphasis upon human freedom from the nineteenth century onwards. He seeks to recover the dynamism of the early vision via a pneumatologically oriented ecclesiology defining the church in terms of the memory of God.
2005 / ISBN 1-84227-125-3

Linda Wilson
Marianne
A Plain Working Woman
(SBHT vol. 18)

Marianne Farningham, of College Street Baptist Chapel, Northampton, was a household name in evangelical circles in the later nineteenth century. For over fifty years she produced comment, poetry, biography and fiction for the popular Christian press. This investigation uses her writings to explore the beliefs and behaviour of evangelical Nonconformists, including Baptists, during these years.

2004 / ISBN 1-84227-124-5

Other Paternoster Press titles
relating to Baptist history and thought

Paul Beasley-Murray
Fearless for Truth
A Personal Portrait of the Life of George Beasley-Murray

Without a doubt George Beasley-Murray was one of the greatest Baptists of the twentieth century. A long-standing Principal of Spurgeon's College, he wrote more than twenty books and made significant contributions in the study of areas as diverse as baptism and eschatology, as well as writing highly respected commentaries on the Book of Revelation and John's Gospel.

2002 / ISBN 1-84227-134-2 / xii + 244pp

David Bebbington
Holiness in Nineteenth-Century England

David Bebbington stresses the relationship of movements of spirituality to changes in the cultural setting, especially the legacies of the Enlightenment and Romanticism. He shows that these broad shifts in ideological mood had a profound effect on the ways in which piety was conceptualized and practised. Holiness was intimately bound up with the spirit of the age.

2000 / ISBN 0-85364-981-2 / viii + 98pp

Christopher J. Clement
Religious Radicalism in England 1535–1565
(Rutherford Studies in Historical Theology)
In this valuable study Christopher Clement draws our attention to a varied assemblage of people who sought Christian faithfulness in the underworld of mid-Tudor England. Sympathetically and yet critically he assess their place in the history of English Protestantism, and by attentive listening he gives them a voice.

1997 / ISBN 0-946068-44-5 / xxii + 426pp

Anthony R. Cross (ed.)
Ecumenism and History
Studies in Honour of John H.Y. Briggs
This collection of essays examines the inter-relationships between the two fields in which Professor Briggs has contributed so much: history – particularly Baptist and Nonconformist – and the ecumenical movement. With contributions from colleagues and former research students from Britain, Europe and North America, *Ecumenism and History* provides wide-ranging studies in important aspects of Christian history, theology and ecumenical studies.

2002 / ISBN 1-84227-135-0 / xx + 362pp

Keith E. Eitel
Paradigm Wars
The Southern Baptist International Mission Board Faces the Third Millennium
(Regnum Studies in Mission)
The International Mission Board of the Southern Baptist Convention is the largest denominational mission agency in North America. This volume chronicles the historic and contemporary forces that led to the IMB's recent extensive reorganization, providing the most comprehensive case study to date of a historic mission agency restructuring to continue its mission purpose into the twenty-first century more effectively.

2000 / ISBN 1-870345-12-6 / x + 140pp

Mark Hopkins
Nonconformity's Romantic Generation
Evangelical and Liberal Theologies in Victorian England
(Studies in Evangelical History and Thought)
This is a study of the theological development of key leaders of the Baptist and Congregational denominations at their period of greatest influence, including C.H. Spurgeon and R.W. Dale, and of the controversies in which those among them who embraced and rejected the liberal transformation of their evangelical heritage opposed each other.
2004 / ISBN 1-84227-150-4 / approx 290pp

Galen K. Johnson
Prisoner of Conscience
John Bunyan on Self, Community and Christian Faith
(Studies in Evangelical History and Thought)
This is an interdisciplinary study of John Bunyan's understanding of conscience across his autobiographical, theological and fictional writings, investigating whether conscience always deserves fidelity, and how Bunyan's view of conscience affects his relationship both to modern Western individualism and historic Christianity.
2003 / ISBN 1-84227- 223-3 / xvi + 236pp

R.T. Kendall
Calvin and English Calvinism to 1649
(Studies in Evangelical History and Thought)
The author's thesis is that those who formed the Westminster Confession of Faith, which is regarded as Calvinism, in fact departed from John Calvin on two points: (1) the extent of the atonement and (2) the ground of assurance of salvation.
1997 / ISBN 0-85364-827-1 / xii + 264pp

Donald M. Lewis
Lighten Their Darkness
The Evangelical Mission to Working-Class London, 1828–1860
This is a comprehensive and compelling study of the Church and the complexities of nineteenth-century London. Challenging our understanding of the culture in working London at this time, Lewis presents a well-structured and illustrated work that contributes substantially to the study of evangelicalism and mission in nineteenth-century Britain.
2001 / ISBN 1-84227-074-5 / xviii + 372pp

Stanley E. Porter and Anthony R. Cross (eds)
Semper Reformandum
Studies in Honour of Clark H. Pinnock
Clark Pinnock has clearly been one of the most important evangelical theologians of the last forty years in North America. Always provocative, especially in the wide range of opinions he has held and considered, Pinnock, himself a Baptist, has recently retired after twenty-five years of teaching at McMaster Divinity College. His colleagues and associates honour him in this volume by responding to his important theological work which has dealt with the essential topics of evangelical theology. These include Christian apologetics, biblical inspiration, the Holy Spirit and, perhaps most importantly in recent years, openness theology.
2003 / ISBN 1-84227-206-3 / xiv + 414pp

Meic Pearse
The Great Restoration
The Religious Radicals of the 16th and 17th Centuries
Pearse charts the rise and progress of continental Anabaptism – both evangelical and heretical – through the sixteenth century. He then follows the story of those English people who became impatient with Puritanism and separated – first from the Church of England and then from one another – to form the antecedents of later Congregationalists, Baptists and Quakers.
1998 / ISBN 0-85364-800-X / xii + 320pp

Charles Price and Ian M. Randall
Transforming Keswick
Transforming Keswick is a thorough, readable and detailed history of the Convention. It will be of interest to those who know and love Keswick, those who are only just discovering it, and serious scholars eager to learn more about the history of God's dealings with his people.
2000 / ISBN 1-85078-350-0 / 288pp

Ian M. Randall
Educating Evangelicalism
The Origins, Development and Impact of London Bible College
London Bible College has been at the centre of theological education in Britain for over fifty years. Through its staff and former students it has had a significant influence on post-war evangelical life and has in turn been shaped by evangelical currents. This book is the story of LBC's sometimes difficult progress through the changing tides of evangelical opinion and support to its current position as a touchstone for the finest in distinctly evangelical scholarship.
2000 / ISBN 0-85364-873-5 / xx + 320pp

Ian M. Randall
One Body in Christ
The History and Significance of the Evangelical Alliance
In 1846 the Evangelical Alliance was founded with the aim of bringing together evangelicals for common action. This book uses material not previously utilized to examine the history and significance of the Evangelical Alliance, a movement which has remained a powerful force for unity. At a time when evangelicals are growing world-wide, this book offers insights into the past which are relevant to contemporary issues.

2001 / ISBN 1-84227-089-3 / xii + 394pp

Ian M. Randall
Evangelical Experiences
A Study in the Spirituality of English Evangelicalism 1918–1939
(Studies in Evangelical History and Thought)
This book makes a detailed historical examination of evangelical spirituality between the First and Second World Wars. It shows how patterns of devotion led to tensions and divisions. In a wide-ranging study, Anglican, Wesleyan, Reformed and Pentecostal–charismatic spiritualities are analysed.

1999 / ISBN 0-85364-919-7 / xii + 310pp

Ian M. Randall
Spirituality and Social Change
The Contribution of F.B. Meyer (1847–1929)
(Studies in Evangelical History and Thought)
F.B. Meyer was one of the most prominent Free Church ministers of his day. He had a number of successful local church ministries in which he gave priority to work as an evangelist, an emphasis which owed much to the decisive influence of the American revivalist D.L. Moody. Meyer's theology was essentially devotional in character and he was also able to relate to different doctrinal perspectives within evangelicalism.

2003 / ISBN 1-84227-195-4 / xx + 184pp

Geoffrey Robson
Dark Satanic Mills?
Religion and Irreligion in Birmingham and the Black Country
(Studies in Evangelical History and Thought)
This book analyses and interprets the nature and extent of popular Christian belief and practice in Birmingham and the Black Country during the first half of the nineteenth century, with particular reference to the impact of cholera epidemics and evangelism on church extension programmes.

2002 / ISBN 1-84227-102-4 / xiv + 294pp

Alan P.F. Sell and Anthony R. Cross (eds)
Protestant Nonconformity in the Twentieth Century
In this collection of essays scholars representative of a number of Nonconformist traditions reflect thematically on Nonconformists life and witness during the twentieth century. Among the subjects reviewed are biblical studies, theology, worship, evangelism and spirituality, and ecumenism. Over and above its immediate interest, this collection provides a marker to future scholars and others wishing to know how some of their forebears assessed Nonconformity's contribution to a variety of fields during the century leading up to Christianity's third millennium.
2003 / ISBN 1-84227-221-7 / x + 398pp

Martin Sutherland
Peace, Toleration and Decay
The Ecclesiology of Later Stuart Dissent
(Studies in Evangelical History and Thought)
This study re-examines a neglected strand of Nonconformist thought and proposes a new understanding of later Stuart Dissent. The distinct characteristics of the movement are freshly defined and Dissent is situated in historical continuity between Puritanism and early Evangelicalism. The book provides a scholarly reinterpretation of an important group in a crucial period of English history. The themes which emerge inform the wider study of English ecclesiology and·practical theory under the Tudors and Stuarts.
2003 / ISBN 1-84227-103-2 / xxii + 216pp

Linda Wilson
Constrained by Zeal
Female Spirituality amongst Nonconformists 1825–1875
(Studies in Evangelical History and Thought)
Dr Wilson investigates the neglected area of Nonconformist female spirituality. Against the background of separate spheres she analyses the experience of women from four denominations, and argues that the churches provided a 'third sphere' in which they could find opportunities for participation.
2000 / ISBN 0-85364-972-3 / xvi + 294pp

Haddon Willmer
Evangelicalism 1785–1835: An Essay (1962) and Reflections (2004)
Awarded the Hulsean Prize in the University of Cambridge in 1962, this interpretation of a classic period of English Evangelicalism, by a young church historian, is now supplemented by reflections on Evangelicalism from the vantage point of a retired Professor of Theology. Haddon Wilmer was Professor of Theology, University of Leeds, UK.
2005 / ISBN 1-84227-219-5 / 80,000 words

Nigel G. Wright
Disavowing Constantine
Mission, Church and the Social Order in the Theologies of John Howard
Yoder and Jürgen Moltmann
(Paternoster Biblical and Theological Monographs)
This book is a timely restatement of a radical theology of church and state
in the Anabaptist and Baptist tradition. Dr Wright constructs his argument
in dialogue and debate with Yoder and Moltmann, major contributors to a
free church perspective.
2000 / ISBN 0-85364-978-2 /xvi + 252pp

Nigel G. Wright
New Baptists, New Agenda
New Baptists, New Agenda is a timely contribution to the growing debate
about the health, shape and future of the Baptists. It considers the steady
changes that have taken place among Baptists in the last decade – changes
of mood, style, practice and structure – and encourages us to align these
current movements and questions with God's upward and future call. He
contends that the true church has yet to come: the church that currently
exists is an anticipation of the joyful gathering of all who have been called
by the Spirit through Christ to the Father.
2002 / ISBN 1-84227-157-1 / x + 162pp

The Paternoster Press
PO Box 300,
Carlisle,
Cumbria CA3 0QS,
United Kingdom
Web: www.paternoster-publishing.com

April 2004